Vital Statistics
on American Politics

Vital Statistics on American Politics 2009–2010

Harold W. Stanley
Southern Methodist University

Richard G. Niemi
University of Rochester

CQ PRESS

A Division of SAGE
Washington, D.C.

CQ Press
2300 N Street, NW, Suite 800
Washington, DC 20037

Phone: 202-729-1900; toll-free, 1-866-4CQ-PRESS (1-866-427-7737)

Web: www.cqpress.com

Cover design: Mike Grove, MG Design
Composition: C&M Digitals (P) Ltd.

♾ The paper used in this publication exceeds the requirements of the American
National Standard for Information Sciences—Permanence of Paper for Printed
Library Materials, ANSI Z39.48-1992.

Printed and bound in the United States of America

13   12   11   10   09   1   2   3   4   5

ISBN: 978-1-60426-994-9
ISSN: 1534-4762

Contents

Tables and Figures

Acknowledgments

As we prepare each new edition of this book, we are reminded of the considerable debt we owe the people who have helped us in the past. These individuals, and the organizations to which they belong, are thanked in previous acknowledgments. For this edition, Christine Carberry and Jennifer McLernon again did a fine job of updating and proofreading many of the tables and figures. We could not have completed the work without their assistance.

In this edition, we have made considerable use of material from the Pew Research Center. For nearly two decades now, this organization, under its various initiatives, has been conducting quality research and reporting it in ways that are informative and easy to understand, while adhering to the kind of technical standards academics appreciate. We are happy to acknowledge our reliance on Pew's wide-ranging research capabilities (*www.pewtrusts.org*).

Help with specific tables or figures was provided by Lawrence Baum, Walter Dean Burnham, Rhodes Cook, Richard Curtin, Sheldon Goldman, Kimberly Hallock, Stanley Henshaw, Scott Keeter, Martha Joynt Kumar, Michael Malbin, Ann Marshall, Michael McDonald, Barbara Palmer, Dennis Simon, John Swain, and Daniel Trisi.

We are especially grateful to the many, often anonymous government officials who helped us out with this and all previous editions. They have almost always been courteous, helpful, and prompt in providing us with information, books, Web site assistance, and so on. They clearly belie negative stereotypes of government bureaucrats.

And we again wish to thank all of the colleagues who have given us useful suggestions—whether by pointing out errors or by suggesting improvements in the content and format of individual tables or groups of tables.

CQ Press has been helpful as always, and Andrea Cunningham ably oversaw the development of this new edition. Sabra Bissette Ledent did another outstanding job of copyediting. Finally, Anne Stewart deftly handled production chores under tight deadlines.

Introduction

- **Accuracy of Published Data**
- **Obtaining Additional Material**

In creating this volume of basic statistical information on American government and politics, our goal has always been to provide broad coverage that spans, whenever possible, a lengthy time perspective. The text, along with the Guide to References for Political Statistics, on pages 402–419, can serve as a fundamental reference book for those who wish to stay informed about numerous aspects of American politics.

This volume covers a wide range of topics as we seek to offer readers the numbers that count in American politics. In addition to standard subjects such as elections, Congress, the presidency, and the judiciary, this book provides information on the media; campaign finances; foreign, social, and economic policy; and a variety of issues related to state and local government. Coverage is not limited to "hard" data such as votes cast and offices won; rankings of public officials' reputations, content analyses of media coverage, and public opinion data on policy issues are also included. The information ranges from simple lists to compilations of outcomes based on implicit analytical concerns. A historical perspective is maintained throughout; depending on the available data, the longest possible time periods are covered, even with public opinion data. The sources of material range from the findable to the fugitive: reference volumes, government publications, political science journals, monographs, the Internet, and press releases, among others. Indeed, the time span is sometimes so great, and the amount of information so large, that we report data for a limited number of years in the present volume, noting that additional data can be found in previous editions of *Vital Statistics on American Politics*.

The quantity and quality of statistical information have grown enormously in recent years, and this trend is unlikely to peak anytime soon. In fact, the Internet makes data overload just a click away. But statistics have a bad image. Even the numerically innocent can retort that "there're lies, damn lies, and statistics" and that "figures don't lie but liars can figure." However, anyone seeking to understand politics—past, present, or future—would be ill-advised to take refuge in such skepticism. Increasingly, both public debates and political analyses contain points couched in or accompanied by statistics. Democracy turns in part on the ability of an informed public to follow such debates and analyses. Now more than ever, understanding politics requires an ability to comprehend numerical data and the assumptions behind them.

Although data are more essential and more readily available, the potential users of data are all too often lacking interpretive skills. Unless one knows how to read them, tables and figures can be less than useful; rather, they can be intimidating, incomprehensible, and boring. Yet properly understood, tables and figures can be a resource of considerable value and, surprisingly to many students, even intelligible and interesting.

This volume will not teach statistical methods, but it will foster a greater familiarity with the appropriate cautions about reading too much or too little into tables and figures. This introduction, the chapter introductions, and the Guide to References are all intended to enhance readers' understanding of how to make better use of data displayed in tables and figures. More specifically, they are designed to help readers extract the maximum amount of information from tables and figures, understand the level of accuracy and kinds of inaccuracies in displays of data as well as the various sources used, and find additional information, including the up-to-date information that must be found in serial publications rather than books.

Some readers, particularly students who are accustomed to working with numbers as they appear in textbooks, are sometimes frustrated, perhaps even mystified, when confronted with whole tables of numbers—not to mention a whole book of tables and figures. An important point of departure for these readers is to realize that this book is based principally on simple numerical data, not on the results of complicated statistical manipulations. The fanciest statistics presented are averages or medians. Regression coefficients, chi-squares, and the like can be revealing and useful, and, in fact, increasingly political science has become so methodologically sophisticated that many journal articles are opaque to those without the ability to cope with advanced statistics. This book, however, fills a more fundamental need for a single volume encompassing a broad range of data about American politics, and, as such, it should be useful to the methodologically skilled and unskilled alike.

The figures and tables are easy to read. Many are merely lists, but useful lists. They are often lengthy because they cover as many as two hundred years. Long historical stretches mean change, and that creates some complexities, such as when the names of the dominant parties change so that going back in time introduces unfamiliar labels (Figure 1-3). Notes to the tables and figures contain the necessary explanations as well as important qualifications and details; they must be read to understand the table or figure content. Following conventional practice, large numbers are sometimes expressed in units of thousands, millions, or billions to enhance readability. Although this practice, too, can lead to minor problems for readers unaccustomed to reading tabular material, with a bit of practice readers should be able to overcome any such difficulties. In general, a little care and caution in reading and interpreting numbers are all that is required.

Accuracy of Published Data

Errors in Data

The material selected for this volume is intended to be the most accurate, up-to-date information possible from the most reputable sources available. But anyone who has used statistical information realizes that it is almost never completely error-free. This is inevitably true here as well. Consider, for example, Tables 11-4 and 11-5. Both are taken from the same government publication, a hundred pages apart. The figures reported for total federal budget outlays, which appear in both tables, typically match. For example, the $590.9 billion total outlay for 1980 noted in Table 11-4 matches exactly the 1980 outlay shown in Table 11-5. Similarly, the total outlays for the other years match perfectly. Yet inexplicably the figures for national defense never quite match, differing by as little as $.4 billion and as much as $5.9 billion.

Why do such discrepancies and other kinds of errors (or what appear to be errors) occur? The answer varies.

Rounding. Sometimes what appears to be an error is simply a matter of rounding. For example, 20.2 plus 20.4 equals 41 if one adds and then rounds, but equals 40 if one rounds and then adds. This explains why the sum of the numbers in certain columns in Table 10-4 does not quite match the total. A similar sort of "error" occurs when percentages sum to 99.8 or 100.2 rather than to 100 plus or minus 0.1 percent.

Exact Date of Data Collection. Accurate interpretation of data depends on knowing the precise date of collection and the period covered. Sometimes the period of collection and any implication for interpretation are obvious. For example, the unemployment rate "at the end of the year" may differ if the phrase means the average of the November and December figures rather than the December figure alone. The time factor can be more subtle—for example, if a U.S. senator-elect dies and someone from the other party is appointed to fill the seat, the number of Democrats and Republicans elected will differ slightly from the number of Democrats and Republicans that actually take office a few months later. Even seemingly similar time spans sometimes conceal important differences. For example, dollar amounts for given years are likely to differ if the researcher is using calendar years rather than fiscal years.

The date of data collection is important from another perspective as well. Data are often updated, and researchers need to know whether they are dealing with the "original" or the "revised" figures. Sometimes data providers make it clear that initial figures are subject to change (such as when the government reports preliminary economic statistics), and they will label revised statistics as such. But not always. We have found numerous instances in which data have been revised—and not only for the most recent period. It is always a good idea to check the latest publication of a time series to see if there have been changes to previously reported information.

Handling of "Minor" Categories.   "Minor" categories may be uncounted, ignored, or dropped for analytical reasons. Often, for example, votes are given only for the candidates of the two major parties. The small number of votes for the Socialist, Libertarian, and Prohibition candidates, not to mention the stray ballots cast for Mickey Mouse or "none of the above," are unreported or lumped together under "other." Thus a vote may be correctly reported as 42.7 percent (of the total vote) and just as correctly reported as 42.9 percent (of the two-party vote). Occasionally, minor categories create more complicated problems. For example, in New York State the same candidate may be nominated by two parties, such as the Democratic Party and the Liberal Party. The percentage of Democratic votes then differs from the percentage of votes received by the Democratic candidate.

A similar problem occurs in the reporting of survey data. In any large survey, in response to almost every question a small number of respondents give "oddball" responses, refuse to answer, or say that they do not know. Depending on how these responses are handled—often, but not always, they are eliminated before any further percentaging is done—simple distributions of responses can vary up to a few percentage points or more. "Don't know" responses are especially problematic. It is sometimes important to know how many individuals are uncertain of their response, so we include them in many of our tables (such as Table 3-12 and Tables 3-14 through 3-18). Tabulations of the same items with these responses removed will differ by varying, unknown amounts.

Changes in Measurement Techniques.   Changes in the way measurements are made can produce different figures and can lead to time series that are not fully comparable. Although the two categories sometimes meld together, we might distinguish between (1) changes in operationalization and (2) changes in conceptualization.

A change in *operationalization* occurs when the underlying idea remains the same but there is a change in the precise way in which the measurement is carried out. A classic example occurs in survey research, in trying to measure concepts such as "political efficacy" and "political trust" or even concepts such as "support for gun control." Researchers at different times may define the concept in the same way but believe that they can "improve" on previous measures by changing the specific questions used to determine a person's efficacy, trust, or support. A consequence of doing so may be that we cannot measure change in public opinion because the new results are not truly comparable with those of earlier polls. Sometimes such changes are forced on reluctant researchers. For example, the "market basket" of items in the Consumer Price Index (Table 11-2) has changed over time. Fountain pens or carbon paper might have been reasonable items to include in the 1950s, but not in the 2000s; technological progress means some items could hardly have been included until recently.

A change in *conceptualization* occurs when researchers develop a new understanding of what is meant by some idea. A good example comes from the Current Population Survey (CPS), in which the U.S. Department of Labor tries to determine the status of "discouraged workers"—defined for many years as persons who are not employed and who want a job, but who are not looking for work because of perceived job market factors. Also, for many years the measure of discouraged workers was based on the relatively subjective notion of "desire for work," whereas a newer definition relies on more objective measures of recent efforts to search for a job. This altered conceptualization of what it means to be looking for work was one of many changes made in the CPS during the early 1990s. (These changes are described in the September 1993 issue *Monthly Labor Review.*)

Inability to Carry out Exact Measurements.   Sometimes problems arise not because the underlying concept is unclear, but simply because researchers are unable to complete the measurements called for. Consider, for example, the decennial census—the effort to measure the total population of the United States. The concept is clear enough—count every individual living in the United States at a specific time (now designated as April 1 of each census year). However, in fact it is impossible to carry out such a measurement with absolute precision on such a vast population. Homeless persons, for example, are exceedingly difficult to count, and then there are always those individuals who for one reason or another do not want to be identified and make an effort *not* to be counted.

A more vexing example is the effort to estimate voter turnout. Some of the problems are questions of conceptualization. For example, in calculating "presidential" turnout (Table 1-1), does one want to include individuals who go to the polls but do not in fact cast a ballot for president? There is also the question of how well researchers can obtain the count they seek. If they define the basis for the calculation (the "denominator") as all those eligible to vote, numerous problems arise, such as determining the number of felons or ex-felons in the voting-age population who are ineligible. For this reason, even simple-sounding numbers are estimated variously.[1]

Ad Hoc Problems.   All sorts of small discrepancies can occur, with ad hoc explanations for each one. One fairly well-known example is counting presidents. Barack Obama is usually said to be the forty-fourth president, but he is only the forty-third person to hold the office. Grover Cleveland is counted twice because his two terms were separated by four years. So, is the correct number forty-three or forty-four? It depends on precisely what one means. A less obvious problem occurs in counting Supreme Court nominations that failed. In 1987 Douglas Ginsburg was publicly announced as President Ronald Reagan's choice, but his name was withdrawn before it was formally submitted to the Senate. Technically, was he nominated? This kind of subtlety is exacerbated when dealing with events of the distant past. It would be easy, for example, to think that the multiple listings of certain nominees to the Supreme Court by President John Tyler are an egregious typographical error. In fact, these multiple nominations occurred (all unsuccessfully) in a fight between the president and Congress (Table 7-4).

Solutions to Errors in Data

Awareness that data may contain inaccuracies is no reason to ignore the data; nor is it an excuse to ignore the possible inaccuracies. Consideration of some "solutions" to data errors helps to illustrate this point. The solutions, like the problems just described, are suggestive rather than exhaustive.

Sometimes errors are relatively obvious and can be easily corrected. One example is misprints. One might encounter references to the 535 members of the House of Representatives when obviously the whole Congress is meant. Checking with alternative or more authoritative sources when mistakes are suspected can help to remedy such problems.

Outlandish or illogical numbers should also be checked. A classic example of finding and explaining nonsensical results is the case of two researchers who were not willing to believe data from the 1950 census showing "a surprising number of widowed fourteen-year-old boys and, equally surprising, a decrease in the number of widowed teenage males at older ages."[2] They wrote a "detective story" about how they traced the problem to systematic errors in the way certain data were entered into the census records.

Another method—one that should always be used—is to check footnotes and accompanying text for exceptions and special comments. Recognize that the problem may not really be error, but misreading. Consider the table on U.S. casualties in the Vietnam War (Table 9-5). For 1973–1993, the bottom row shows there were no U.S. military forces in Vietnam but 1,118 battle deaths—surely an anomaly. The note reveals, however, that there were troops in Vietnam for nearly a month at the beginning of this period—the zero indicates the force count as of December 31, 1973, and U.S. forces were withdrawn on January 27, 1973. In addition, forces dying of wounds incurred earlier or those who were missing and later classified as deceased are also considered battle deaths.

Another solution is what is formally called *sensitivity analysis*. When values are inexact or differ across sources, a researcher should ask how sensitive the conclusion is to the precise values used. If the true values differ by some specified amount from the reported values, would the conclusion change? If not, the researcher can be more confident about the conclusion. Similarly, if sources differ, consider the actual values from several sources. If the conclusion to be drawn does not vary with the different values, the discrepancies are only a minor problem. For example, almost any conclusion about national defense expenditures would be the same whether 1995 expenditures were $272.1 billion (Table 11-4) or $273.6 billion (Table 11-5), even though the difference represents what in other contexts would be an astonishing $1.5 billion.

For the researcher examining over-time data, one way to avoid possible errors is to be sure the data are truly comparable. For one thing, check for indications that the data were revised or updated. Preliminary reports sometimes are not directly comparable with initial reports. In addition, check that the data were collected uniformly or know what the differences are over time and their probable effects. Occasionally, guesses about probable error can be confirmed by formal tests. An excellent example is a study in which both old and new survey questions were asked. Differences that had previously been attributed to changes in the electorate over time were shown to be methodological artifacts.[3]

Sometimes when changes occur, one can develop new estimates, or incorporate ones that are supplied, for an entire existing time series. For example, in the mid-1990s the Bureau of Economic Analysis undertook a comprehensive revision of the National Income and Product Accounts (NIPA), and in doing so it published new estimates of the gross domestic product back to 1929, which, in turn, affected many other calculations. Along the same lines, in 2004 the General Social Survey, used as a basis for some tables about public opinion in Chapter 3, changed its sample design. This change required the use of sample weights for that and earlier years, resulting in slight changes in previously reported figures. While frustrating in that the older series might have to be replaced entirely by the new numbers, the new data provide a comparable time series for the entire period. Of course, in such situations researchers also must ask themselves which figures should be used. The original calculations are arguably better if a researcher is asking questions that depend on how people viewed the world at the time the original data were collected.

All data, perhaps especially data over time, should be examined for "outliers." If a series of values, say the percentages of votes for the Republican candidate in a given district, are 52, 56, 49, 85, and 50, the accuracy of the 85 percent must be checked. Is the 85 a transposition of 58? If 85 is the correct number, what is the reason for it? Was the candidate essentially unopposed that year? What conclusion should be drawn if the 85 were omitted?

Researchers should always think carefully about what information is really wanted. There are instances in which it is necessary to decide which of two or three sets of equally valid data are most appropriate to answer a given question. We noted, for example, that one might wish to employ only the two-party vote or the vote for all parties, include survey respondents who answer "don't know" or eliminate them, or use contemporary data rather than re-estimates made years later.

Finally, after taking all reasonable steps to ensure the data are as good as can be obtained and that they address the question at hand, the researcher should indicate known errors. It is better to point out that there is some question about certain figures than to pretend that they are perfect. If a loftier reason does not come to mind, being straightforward about inaccuracies at least prevents readers from lobbing them back, implying the researcher was too ignorant to notice the problems.

Obtaining Additional Material

This book provides essential figures and tables, but the coverage is far from exhaustive. Many readers may want data with a slightly different twist or of another sort altogether. The Guide to References for Political Statistics in this volume should help to orient readers who seek information beyond that contained here. The sources given for the tables and figures in this book should also be considered in such searches. They will especially alert readers to the many electronic sources now available.

Data on current events can be found in newspapers, weekly news magazines, *CQ Weekly,* and the *National Journal.* The indexes of *CQ Weekly, National Journal,* and the major newspapers are a valuable guide. Online sources such as Newspaperlinks.com or Refdesk.com provide useful links to newspapers on the Web, as does Newslink.org, which also covers magazines as well as radio and television stations. Subscription services such as LexisNexis, Newsbank, and ProQuest Historical Newspapers provide additional coverage, not only of current events but also of historical and legal materials. Many of these are now available on the Web or as electronic databases available at research libraries.

Reference librarians should never be overlooked in the quest for information. Librarians for government document collections are also invaluable resources. Interlibrary loans can help to secure less readily available volumes, although principal reference works and current material seldom circulate in this fashion.

For some material, one may need to contact organizations that compile or disseminate the data. Various directories (most now online as well as in hard copy) are available—of party organizations, interest groups, associations, research institutions, and state agencies. At the federal level, CQ Press's *Washington Information Directory* is a valuable guide to potential sources. The

Council of State Governments, with its *CSG State Directories* of administrative and elected officials, provides a similar service at the state level.

Data and texts are now often available in electronic form. Numerous commercial vendors offer online data services, and government agencies have moved many publications onto the Web, some of them exclusively so. Although such a change makes information widely available, it also means that consumers of information must be computer literate. Fortunately, producers are providing more user-friendly sites at the same time that consumers are becoming more sophisticated.

Archives of electronic data also constitute a valuable source of information and were the source of several tables and figures for this volume. The Inter-university Consortium for Political and Social Research (ICPSR) at the University of Michigan has the largest collection of digital social science data. A guide to its resources is available at *www.icpsr.umich.edu,* and some of its data are made available there for observation and analysis online. Most major research universities are members of the consortium. Anyone wishing to learn how to obtain data should contact the official university representatives of ICPSR. Other large data repositories exist in other countries (see *www.iassistdata.org*).

Because of the tremendous growth of sites on the Web, the appearance and disappearance of useful sites, and the availability of powerful search engines, it would be pointless (as well as impossible) to try to develop anything like a comprehensive list. Nevertheless, the Guide to References lists sites that may be of special interest in searching for political statistics. As noted, we also recommend using the sources we cite in the tables and figures as a starting point for gathering additional information.

These hints are merely suggestions for those who wish to go beyond this volume to track down particular pieces of information. We hope readers will find the extensive coverage in this obviously not exhaustive volume to be convenient and valuable.

Notes

1. On this matter, see the lengthy but informative discussions in the following, along with the work cited in the notes and sources for Table 1-1: Walter Dean Burnham, "Triumphs and Travails in the Study of American Voting Participation Rates, 1788–2006," *Journal of the Historical Society* 7 (2007): 505–519; Curtis Gans, *Voter Turnout in the United States, 1798–2008* (Washington, D.C.: CQ Press, 2010).
2. Ansley J. Coale and Frederick F. Stephan, "The Case of the Indians and the Teen-Age Widows," *Journal of the American Statistical Association* 57 (1962): 338.
3. John L. Sullivan, James E. Piereson, and George E. Marcus, "Ideological Constraint in the Mass Public: A Methodological Critique and Some New Findings," *American Journal of Political Science* 22 (1978): 233–249.

1

Elections and Political Parties

- **Turnout**
- **Political Parties**
- **Election Results (president, Congress, and state)**
- **Minority Elected Officials**
- **Presidential Nominations**
- **Districting**
- **Voting Rights**
- **Term Limits**
- **Voting Equipment**

Elections and campaigns provide an abundance of numbers. Indeed, if asked for examples of political statistics, most people would think first of election results. Not only are there a great many electoral statistics, but they extend back to the early years of the country. Here, for example, data are provided on voter turnout (Figures 1-1 and 1-2 and Tables 1-1 and 1-2) and on presidential (Table 1-7) and congressional (Table 1-10) election results going back to 1788. Results abound as well because of the federal system in the United States and because of the nature of the U.S. party system. Thus the most recent results for elections to the governorships and to the state legislatures (Table 1-6) are provided, as well as information on presidential primaries and caucuses (Tables 1-23 through 1-26).

In part because there are so many results, some form of summarization is needed. Typically, such summaries are in partisan terms, such as in the contrast between a party's share of the vote won and the share of House seats gained (Table 1-12). Wins by the major parties are presented in a variety of ways, but sometimes such results need to be broken down further. Reporting results by region (Table 1-4 and Figure 1-4) or by state (Tables 1-3, 1-5, and 1-9) is frequently informative. In addition, historians and political scientists often report election results by so-called party systems separated by periods of "realignment"—that is, fundamental shifts in support for parties and the coalitions supporting them. Scholars most often claim that such realignments occurred

1

in the 1850s, 1890s, between 1928 and 1932, and probably in the 1960s.[1] This way of defining party systems is freely employed in the reporting for this analysis (Tables 1-4, 1-8, and 1-11).

There is particular interest in the current period. The available data document recent trends in campaigns and elections: the decline in presidential voter turnout between 1960 and 1996 and the recent upsurge (Table 1-1 and Figure 1-1), the electoral advantages of incumbency (Table 1-19), the frequently lengthened quests for the presidential nominations (Figure 1-5), the greater emphasis on primaries (Tables 1-23 and 1-24), and, in Chapter 2, the growing contributions from political action committees (Table 2-14) and the expense of political campaigns (Tables 2-3 through 2-5).

Besides the arsenal of statistics reporting and summarizing election results by party, other characteristics of the individuals elected to office are of interest. Information is included on the election of African Americans, Hispanics, and women (Tables 1-21 and 1-22) and on their districts (Table 1-20). Political scientists and others also find it useful to consider the frequency of "divided government" between the presidency and Congress (Table 1-13), to tabulate numbers of House districts in which the votes for president and Congress go to different parties (Table 1-14), to determine individual and partisan turnover rates for members of Congress (Tables 1-15, 1-16, 1-18, and 1-19), and to document the regular pattern of losses by the president's party at midterm elections—disrupted, incidentally, in 1998 and 2002 (Table 1-17).

Auxiliary information is often useful in interpreting these election results. One helpful item is a list of political parties that have competed in elections at various times in U.S. history (Figure 1-3). The location and size of presidential nominating conventions (Table 1-27) are also provided, as well as information on the types of delegates who have attended them (Table 1-28). Relevant to the election of minorities is information on legislative districts (Table 1-29) and application of the Voting Rights Act (Table 1-30). Of recent interest is information on which states have passed term limits, the length of the limits they have imposed, the representatives in Congress who have pledged to limit their terms voluntarily, and the numbers of state representatives who have been "termed out" of office (Tables 1-31 through 1-33). In light of the experience in Florida during the 2000 presidential election and in the state's Sarasota County during the 2006 congressional election, a previously utilitarian table on types of voting equipment used throughout the country has taken on new meaning (Table 1-34).

Despite the large quantity of data in this chapter, there are gaps that reflect the limits on what is known about campaigns, elections, and parties. The lack of survey data on realignments before the 1930s, for example, is troublesome because it robs researchers of helpful historical comparisons. Also, not as much data are readily available on state and local elections as on federal elections. Nevertheless, in the area of campaigns and elections, more than anywhere, there is almost an embarrassment of riches.

Note

1. John Aldrich and Richard G. Niemi, "The Sixth American Party System: Electoral Change, 1952–1992," in *Broken Contract? Changing Relationships Between Americans and Their Government,* ed. Stephen Craig (Boulder, Colo.: Westview Press, 1996).

Table 1-1   Voter Turnout Rates, United States, South, and Non-South, 1789–2008 (percent)

	Presidential elections[a]				Nonpresidential elections[b]		
Year	United States	Non-South	South[c]	Year	United States	Non-South	South[c]
1789	11.6	11.1	14.3	1790	19.7	19.2	23.3
1792	6.2	5.8	14.4	1794	23.0	22.9	23.5
1796	19.9	19.5	24.9	1798	34.7	33.4	38.0
1800	32.2	40.5	28.7	1802	38.6	36.8	41.0
1804	23.7	27.9	13.1	1806	36.5	35.2	40.2
1808	34.9	42.8	19.1	1810	42.1	40.7	46.8
1812	38.2	43.9	18.9	1814	45.5	45.4	46.0
1816	16.8	20.7	8.1	1818	37.1	33.9	45.8
1820	10.5	12.6	5.2	1822	41.4	38.9	48.0
1824	26.7	26.6	27.2	1826	47.0	45.5	52.1
1828	57.6	62.0	42.5	1830	54.2	55.3	50.6
1832	56.5	64.0	30.1	1834	63.0	63.7	60.7
1836	56.5	58.5	49.2	1838	70.2	72.0	63.7
1840	80.3	81.6	75.4	1842	62.4	63.5	58.3
1844	79.2	80.5	74.2	1846	60.6	62.2	55.2
1848	72.7	74.0	68.0	1850	60.5	61.0	58.5
1852	69.8	72.5	59.3	1854	66.1	65.0	70.0
1856	80.0	81.9	72.2	1858	69.6	71.7	61.5
1860	82.9	84.4	76.7	1862	64.9	64.9	—
1864	77.0	77.0	—	1866	71.2	71.8	51.2[d]
1868	80.9	82.8	71.6	1870	67.0	67.1	66.7
1872	72.5	74.2	67.2	1874	65.0	65.5	63.2
1876	83.4	86.0	75.1	1878	65.1	70.5	48.4
1880	81.2	86.4	65.2	1882	64.2	68.1	51.5
1884	79.1	83.7	64.3	1886	63.9	70.6	42.0
1888	80.9	86.1	64.0	1890	64.6	70.4	44.7
1892	76.2	81.2	59.4	1894	67.5	73.5	47.2
1896	79.9	86.4	57.7	1898	60.1	68.0	33.6
1900	73.9	82.9	43.5	1902	55.7	65.2	23.8
1904	65.8	76.8	29.0	1906	51.4	61.1	18.6
1908	65.9	76.4	30.8	1910	51.8	61.0	20.6
1912	59.0	67.5	27.9	1914	50.1	58.5	18.6
1916	61.7	69.1	31.6	1918	39.9	45.8	14.8
1920	49.3	57.4	21.8	1922	35.7	42.7	11.8
1924	49.0	57.7	19.0	1926	33.0	40.0	8.5
1928	57.1	66.8	23.6	1930	36.9	44.0	12.2
1932	57.3	66.7	24.5	1934	44.7	53.9	13.1
1936	61.4	72.0	25.0	1938	46.9	57.3	11.3
1940	62.9	73.6	26.5	1942	34.1	42.0	7.2
1944	56.2	65.6	24.5	1946	38.8	47.2	10.4
1948	52.2	59.1	23.7	1950	43.6	51.9	13.6
1952	62.3	70.0	38.9	1954	43.5	51.2	17.2
1956	60.2	67.2	37.4	1958	45.0	53.6	16.1
1960	63.8	70.1	40.2	1962	47.7	54.1	24.0
1964	62.8	67.4	45.6	1966	48.7	52.9	33.1
1968	62.5	64.4	51.4	1970	47.3	50.9	34.7

Table 1-1 *(Continued)*

	Presidential elections[a]				Nonpresidential elections[b]		
Year	United States	Non-South	South[c]	Year	United States	Non-South	South[c]
1972	56.2	59.6	44.8	1974	39.1	43.1	26.1
1976	54.8	57.1	47.6	1978[e]	39.0	41.8	30.0
1980	54.2	56.4	47.6	1982[e]	42.1	44.7	31.0
1984	55.2	57.2	49.7	1986	38.1	39.3	34.7
1988	52.8	54.7	47.3	1990	38.4	39.5	35.2
1992	58.1	59.9	53.0	1994	41.1	42.8	36.5
1996	51.7	53.1	47.7	1998	38.1	40.1	32.8
2000	54.2	55.9	50.1	2002	39.5	40.5	37.1
2004	60.1	61.6	56.5	2006	40.3	42.8	34.6
2008	61.7	62.5	59.7				

Note:"—" indicates not available. In presidential election years, these turnout figures represent, insofar as possible, the percentage of the eligible electorate that cast votes in presidential elections. In nonpresidential election years through 1946, the figures are the percentage voting in elections for the U.S. House of Representatives. Since 1948, they are the "vote for highest office"—that is, the largest number of votes for a statewide office (U.S. senator or governor) or, if lacking a statewide office, the sum of the votes for the U.S. House of Representatives. In recent years, the problem of estimating turnout for the House has been complicated by the fact that Arkansas, Florida, Louisiana, and Oklahoma do not tally votes when races are uncontested. The definition of *eligibility* has varied considerably over the years, depending on age, race, gender, felony convictions, and citizenship status. Some states during some periods allowed noncitizens to vote, but this practice has not been permitted nationwide since 1924. Estimating the eligible electorate is especially difficult for the nineteenth century. For details, see Walter Dean Burnham, "The Turnout Problem," in *Elections American Style,* ed. A. James Reichley (Washington, D.C.: Brookings, 1987). From 1924 through 1946, the base is what is known as the citizen voting-age population. From 1948 through 2008, the base is the citizen-eligible population, which begins with the voting-age population but removes noncitizens and ineligible felons and adds in overseas eligible voters. Turnout based on the voter-eligible population is higher than that based on the voting-age population. For 2000–2008, the figures for voters living abroad are apportioned between the South and the non-South based on a 2008 estimate, state by state, of the number of citizens living abroad. For the methodology, see George Mason University (*http://elections.gmu.edu/voter_turnout.htm*) and Michael P. McDonald and Samuel L. Popkin, "The Myth of the Vanishing Voter," *American Political Science Review* 95 (2001): 963–974. Note that the 2000–present numbers will become "final" only once the 2000–2010 intercensal adjustments are released sometime in 2012. It should also be noted that the number of people actually going to the polls is slightly higher than these percentages indicate; some voters do not vote for a given office such as president or U.S. representative, and a small number of ballots are spoiled.

[a] Before 1828, only a limited number of states held popular votes for president. Numbers shown reflect turnout in those states.
[b] Before 1880, one or more states held elections for the U.S. House of Representatives in the year following the presidential election year. Before the Civil War, this practice was quite common, especially in the South and New England. Thus, for example, "1840" should be read as "1840/41."
[c] The eleven states of the Confederacy.
[d] Tennessee only.
[e] Because of Louisiana's second ballot system, Louisiana is excluded from the numerator and denominator for 1978 and 1982.

Source: 1789–1946: Walter Dean Burnham, personal communication; 1948–2008: Michael P. McDonald, George Mason University (*http://elections.gmu.edu/voter_turnout.htm*) and personal communication.

Figure 1-1 Voter Turnout Rates, Presidential and Midterm Elections, 1789–2008

Percent

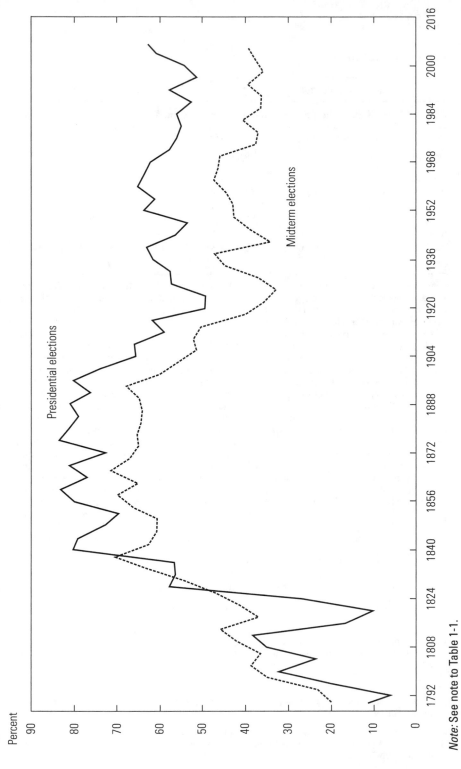

Note: See note to Table 1-1.

Source: Table 1-1, this volume.

Figure 1-2 Voter Turnout Rates, Presidential Elections, South and Non-South, 1789–2008

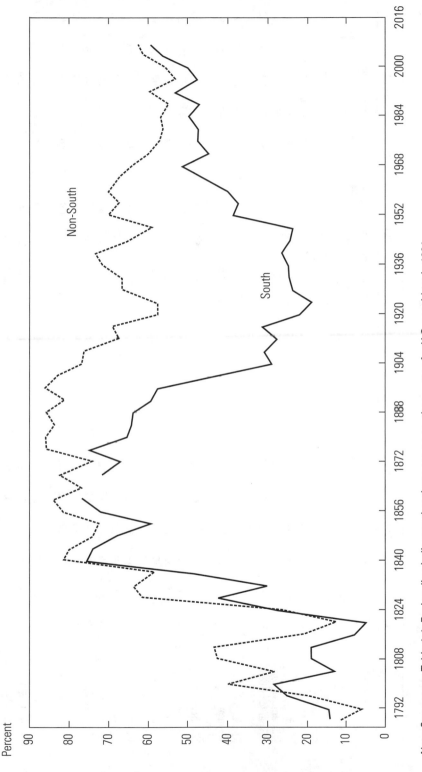

Note: See note to Table 1-1. Broken line indicates that there are no southern votes for U.S. president in 1864.

Source: Table 1-1, this volume.

Table 1-2 Voting-Age Population Registered and Voting, Cross Sections, 1990–2008 (percent)

| | Percentage reporting they registered | | | | | | | | | | Percentage reporting they voted | | | | | | | | | |
| | Presidential election years | | | | | Congressional election years | | | | | Presidential election years | | | | | Congressional election years | | | | |
	1992	1996	2000	2004	2008	1990	1994	1998	2002	2006	1992	1996	2000	2004	2008	1990	1994	1998	2002	2006
Race/ethnicity																				
White[a]	70	68	66	68	67	64	65	64	63	64	64	56	56	60	60	47	47	43	44	46
Black[a]	64	64	64	64	66	59	58	60	59	57	54	51	54	56	61	39	37	40	40	39
Hispanic origin[b]	35	36	35	34	38	32	31	34	33	32	29	27	28	28	32	21	20	20	19	19
Hispanic citizen[b]	59	59	57	58	59	52	53	55	53	54	48	44	45	47	50	34	34	33	30	32
Sex																				
Men	67	64	62	64	63	61	61	61	59	60	60	53	53	56	56	45	45	41	41	42
Women	69	67	66	68	67	63	64	64	63	63	62	56	56	60	60	45	45	42	43	45
Region[c]																				
Northeast	67	65	64	65	64	61	61	61	61	60	61	54	55	59	57	45	45	41	41	43
Midwest	75	72	70	73	71	68	69	68	66	68	67	59	61	65	63	49	49	47	47	51
South	67	66	65	65	66	61	61	63	62	62	59	52	54	56	58	42	41	39	42	40
West	64	61	57	60	59	58	58	56	54	55	59	52	50	54	55	45	46	42	39	42
Age																				
18–20 years	48	46	41	51	49	35	37	32	33	37	38	31	28	41	41	18	17	14	15	17
21–24 years	55	51	49	52	56	43	46	45	42	45	46	33	35	42	47	22	22	19	19	22
25–34 years	61	57	55	56	57	52	52	52	50	50	53	43	44	47	48	34	32	28	27	28
35–44 years	69	67	64	64	61	66	63	62	60	59	64	55	55	57	55	48	46	41	40	40
45–64 years	75	74	71	73	70	71	71	71	69	70	70	64	64	67	65	56	56	54	53	54
65 years and older	78	77	76	77	75	80	76	75	76	75	70	67	68	69	68	66	61	60	61	60
Employment																				
Employed	70	67	65	67	66	63	63	63	62	63	64	55	56	60	60	45	45	41	42	44
Unemployed	54	53	46	56	57	45	46	48	48	48	46	37	35	46	49	28	28	28	27	28
Not in labor force	67	65	64	64	63	63	62	62	61	61	59	54	55	56	56	47	45	44	44	44

Education (years)																			
8 or less	44	41	36	33	30	44	40	40	32	30	35	30	27	24	23	28	23	24	19	17
1–3 of high school	50	48	46	45	43	48	45	43	42	39	41	34	34	34	34	31	27	25	23	22
4 of high school	65	62	60	60	59	60	59	59	57	55	58	49	49	50	51	42	40	37	37	36
1–3 of college	75	73	70	74	72	69	68	68	67	68	69	61	60	66	65	50	49	46	46	47
4 or more of college	85	80	77	78	77	77	76	75	74	74	81	73	72	74	73	63	63	57	58	60
Total	68	66	64	66	65	62	62	62	61	62	61	54	55	58	58	45	45	42	42	44

Note: Data for earlier years can be found in previous editions of *Vital Statistics on American Politics*.

[a] In 2002 and after, whites are individuals identifying with that race alone; blacks are individuals identifying with that race alone.
[b] Persons of Hispanic origin may be of any race.
[c] For composition of regions, see Table A-1, this volume.

Sources: Calculated by the editors from U.S. Census Bureau, "Current Population Reports, Voting and Registration in the Election of November 1990," series P-20, no. 453, 1–2, 4, 13–14, 17; "November 1992," no. 466, v–vii, 1, 5; "Voter Turnout in November 1994 Election," press release, June 8, 1995; "November 1996," no. 504; "November 1998," no. 523; "November 2000," no. 542; "November 2002," no. 552; "November 2004," no. 556; "November 2006"; "November 2008" (*www.census.gov*).

Figure 1-3 American Political Parties Since 1789

1789		Federalist			
1792					
1796	Democratic-Republican				
1800				**——** Major parties	
1804				**– – –** Third parties	
1808					
1812					
1816					
1820					
1824					
1828		National Republican			
1832	Democratic		Anti-Mason		
1836		Whig			
1840					
1844		Liberty	Free Soil		
1848					
1852	Republican		Whig-American		
1856					
1860		Constitutional Union		Southern Democratic	
1864					
1868			Liberal Republican		
1872					
1876			Greenback		
1880				Prohibition	
1884		Union Labor			
1888			Populist		
1892		National Democratic			
1896					
1900				Prohibition	
1904			(Bull Moose)	Socialist	
1908			Progressive		
1912					
1916		(La Follette)	Farmer Labor		
1920		Progressive			
1924					
1928		(Lemke)		Socialist	
1932		Union			
1936				States' Rights	
1940				Democratic	
1944		Progressive			
1948					
1952					
1956					
1960		American			
1964		Independent		American	
1968				Independent	
1972					
1976		Libertarian			
1980					
1984					
1988					
1992		Reform			
1996		Green			
2000					
2004					
2008					

Note: In 1824 and later, the chart indicates the years in which the presidential candidate of a political party received 1.0 percent or more of the popular vote. Minor parties are not included if the minor-party candidate is also the candidate of one of the two major parties (as happened in 1896 when the Populists endorsed William Jennings Bryan, the Democratic candidate). Party candidates sometimes run under different designations in different states (in 1968 George C. Wallace ran for president under at least ten party labels). In such cases, the vote totals for the candidate were aggregated under a single party designation. Sometimes candidates run under no party label as H. Ross Perot did in 1992. (In 1996 Perot ran under the Reform Party label.)

Sources: 1789–1820: U.S. Bureau of the Census, *Historical Statistics of the United States, Colonial Times to 1970* (Washington, D.C.: Government Printing Office, 1975); 1824–2000: *Congressional Quarterly's Guide to U.S. Elections,* 4th ed. (Washington, D.C.: CQ Press, 2001), 225–232, 644–699; 2004–2008: Table 1-9, this volume, and previous editions of *Vital Statistics on American Politics.*

Table 1-3 Party Competition: Presidency, by State, 1992–2008

		Number of times Democratic presidential candidate carried the state			
0	1	2	3	4	5
Alabama (9)	Arizona (10)	Arkansas (6)	Nevada (5)	Iowa (7)	California (55)
Alaska (3)	Georgia (15)	Colorado (9)	Ohio (20)	New Hampshire (4)	Connecticut (7)
Idaho (4)	Indiana (11)	Florida (27)		New Mexico (5)	Delaware (3)
Kansas (6)	Montana (3)	Kentucky (8)			District of Columbia (3)
Mississippi (6)	North Carolina (15)	Louisiana (9)			Hawaii (4)
Nebraska (5)	Virginia (13)	Missouri (11)			Illinois (21)
North Dakota (3)		Tennessee (11)			Maine (4)
Oklahoma (7)		West Virginia (5)			Maryland (10)
South Carolina (8)					Massachusetts (12)
South Dakota (3)					Michigan (17)
Texas (34)					Minnesota (10)
Utah (5)					New Jersey (15)
Wyoming (3)					New York (31)
					Oregon (7)
					Pennsylvania (21)
					Rhode Island (4)
					Vermont (3)
					Washington (11)
					Wisconsin (10)

Total electoral votes:

0	1	2	3	4	5
96	67	86	25	16	248

Note: Numbers of electoral votes for 2008 are shown in parentheses. For similar data on other time periods, see previous editions of *Vital Statistics on American Politics.*

Sources: Congressional Quarterly's Guide to U.S. Elections, 5th ed. (Washington, D.C.: CQ Press, 2005), 801–804; Table 1-9, this volume; and previous editions of *Vital Statistics on American Politics.*

11

Table 1-4   Party Competition, by Region, 1860–2008 (percent)

Region/office	1860–1895	1896–1931	1932–1965	1966–2008
New England				
President	85.2	85.5	53.7	40.9
Governor	74.3	85.5	63.1	51.8
U.S. representative	86.8	82.8	60.6	29.6
U.S. senator	[a]	83.3	65.1	45.1
Middle Atlantic				
President	38.9	88.9	47.2	38.6
Governor	34.9	66.7	51.4	45.5
U.S. representative	59.3	68.9	52.9	41.5
U.S. senator	[a]	76.9	57.7	45.6
Midwest				
President	77.8	84.4	44.4	58.2
Governor	78.8	78.9	46.9	66.1
U.S. representative	61.1	74.5	57.8	50.2
U.S. senator	[a]	83.3	50.8	35.1
Plains				
President	88.9	77.8	57.4	80.3
Governor	94.4	71.3	70.4	54.7
U.S. representative	88.6	84.2	76.4	59.4
U.S. senator	[a]	83.9	79.7	48.8[b]
South				
President	18.4	6.1	15.8	76.0
Governor	21.2	4.2	0.0	50.0
U.S. representative	25.0	7.5	7.2	40.8
U.S. senator	[a]	0.0	1.5	60.5
Border South				
President	8.6	56.8	22.2	58.2
Governor	22.2	38.6	16.7	31.5
U.S. representative	19.4	36.5	18.7	36.7
U.S. senator	[a]	42.4	23.4	45.3
Rocky Mountain				
President	73.3	57.8	35.2	85.2
Governor	58.3	51.1	38.5	50.0
U.S. representative	70.0	67.6	30.3	61.7
U.S. senator	[a]	32.4	20.6	62.6
Pacific Coast				
President	75.0	75.0	37.5	50.9
Governor	47.4	70.8	59.4	41.8
U.S. representative	64.4	85.6	49.0	38.9
U.S. senator	[a]	73.7	44.4	41.9

Note: Table entries are the percentages of all elections won by Republicans. For composition of regions, see Table A-3, this volume.

[a] Direct election of U.S. senators began after passage of the Seventeenth Amendment in 1913.

[b] Reflects the win of the November 2008 Senate election in Minnesota by Democrat Al Franken. Incumbent Norm Coleman apparently lost the election by 225 votes, filed suit challenging the final tally, and conceded June 30, 2009, after an adverse Minnesota State Supreme Court decision.

Sources: Congressional Quarterly's Guide to U.S. Elections, 3rd ed. (Washington, D.C.: Congressional Quarterly, 1994), 1344; *Congressional Quarterly Weekly Report (CQ Weekly)* (1996), 3192, 3226, 3238, 3242; (1998), 3002, 3004, 3010–3011; (2000), 2671, 2704–2706; (2002), 3289–3297; (2004), 2653–2660; (2006), 3068–3078, 3132, 3186, 3238, 3381; (2008), 3019, 3043–3052, 3056, 3102, 3153, 3206, 3293, 3374; National Governors Association (*www.nga.org*); Table 1-9, this volume.

Table 1-5   Party Competition in the States, 1992–2008

Percentage of Democratic wins[a]				
0–20	21–40	41–60	61–80	81–100
Alaska	Indiana	Colorado	Alabama	Arkansas
Arizona	Michigan	Georgia	California	Hawaii
Florida	Montana	Iowa	Connecticut	Maine
Idaho	Nebraska[b]	Minnesota	Delaware	Maryland
Kansas	New Hampshire	Missouri	Illinois	Massachusetts
North Dakota	Pennsylvania	Nevada	Kentucky	New Mexico
Ohio	South Carolina	New Jersey	Louisiana	North
South Dakota	Texas	New York	Mississippi	Carolina
Utah	Virginia	Oregon	Oklahoma	Rhode Island
Wyoming		Wisconsin	Tennessee	West Virginia
			Vermont	
			Washington	

Note: For similar data on other time periods, see previous editions of *Vital Statistics on American Politics.*

[a] The governorship, control of the lower chamber, and control of the upper chamber are figured separately—that is, if in a given year the Democrats won the governorship and control of one chamber, they had 66.7 percent of the wins.

[b] Results are for the governorship only because the legislature is nonpartisan.

Sources: Calculated by the editors. When legislators up for election: Council of State Governments, *The Book of the States, 1992–93* (Lexington, Ky.: Council of State Governments, 1992), 269–272; *1996–97*, 153–156; *2004,* 269–270; *2006,* 270–271, *2008,* 305–306; National Conference of State Legislatures, "Legislative Seats to be Elected 2006" and "2008 Legislative Seats to be Elected" (*www.ncsl.org*); governors, 1992–2002: Richard Scammon and Rhodes Cook, eds., *America Votes 25, 2001–2002: A Handbook of Contemporary American Election Statistics* (Washington, D.C.: CQ Press, 2003); governors and legislators, 2003–2004: National Conference of State Legislatures, "State Vote 2003" and "State Vote 2004" (*www.ncsl.org*); National Governors Association, "Governors' Political Affiliations and Terms of Office, 2005" (*www.nga.org*); governors and legislators, 2005–2006: National Conference of State Legislatures, "State Political Control Unchanged after Off-Year Elections" and "2006 Post-Election Partisan Composition of State Legislatures" (*www.ncsl.org*); National Governors Association, "2005 Governors' Election Results" and "2006 Governors' Election Results" (*www.nga.org*); governors and legislators, 2007–2008: National Conference of State Legislatures, "2007 Election Wrap-Up" and "2008–09 (Post-Election) Partisan Composition of State Legislatures" *(www.ncsl.org)*; National Governors Association, "2007 Gubernatorial Election Results" and "2008 Gubernatorial Election Results" (*www.nga.org*); legislators, 1991–1992: Council of State Governments, *The Book of the States, 1990–91* (Lexington, Ky.: Council of State Governments, 1990), 123; *1992–93,* 141; *Congressional Quarterly's Politics in America 1994* (Washington, D.C.: CQ Press, 1993); legislators, 1993–1994: National Conference of State Legislatures, "Partisan Composition of State Legislatures," press release, November 15, 1994; legislators, 1995–1996: Council of State Governments, *The Book of the States, 1996–97* (Lexington, Ky.: Council of State Governments, 1996), 68–69; *Congressional Quarterly's Politics in America 1998* (Washington, D.C.: CQ Press, 1997); legislators, 1997–1998: National Conference of State Legislatures, "Partisan Composition of State Legislatures" (*www.ncsl.org*); legislators, 1999–2000: National Conference of State Legislatures, "State Vote 1999" (*www.ncsl .org*); legislators, 2001–2002: National Conference of State Legislatures, "State Vote 2001" and "State Vote 2002" (*www.ncsl.org*); National Conference of State Legislatures, "2000 Pre-Election Partisan Composition of State Legislatures" and "2000 Post-Election Partisan Composition of State Legislatures" (*www.ncsl.org*).

Table 1-6 Partisan Division of Governors and State Legislatures, 2009

| | Governor | | | Legislature | | | | | |
| | | | | Upper house | | | Lower house | | |
State	Name	Party	Next up for election	Democrats	Republicans	Seats up in 2010	Democrats	Republicans	Seats up in 2010
Alabama	Bob Riley	R	2010	19[a]	13	35	62	43	105
Alaska	Sarah Palin	R	2010	10[b]	10	10	18	22	40
Arizona	Jan Brewer	R[c]	2010	12	18	30	25	35	60
Arkansas	Mike Beebe	D[b]	2010	27	8	17	71[d]	28	100
California	Arnold Schwarzenegger	R	2010	26	14	20	51	29	80
Colorado	Bill Ritter Jr.	D[b]	2010	21	14	18	38	27	65
Connecticut	M. Jodi Rell	R	2010	24	12	36	114	37	151
Delaware	Jack Markell	D	2012	16	5	0[e]	24[b]	17	0[e]
Florida	Charlie Crist	R	2010	14	26	20	44	76	120
Georgia	Sonny Perdue	R	2010	22	34	56	75	105	180
Hawaii	Linda Lingle	R	2010	23	2	13	45	6	51
Idaho	C. L. "Butch" Otter	R	2010	7	28	35	18	52	70
Illinois	Pat Quinn	D	2010	37	22	20	70	48	118
Indiana	Mitch Daniels	R	2012	17	33	25	52	48	100
Iowa	Chet Culver	D	2010	32	18	25	56	44	100
Kansas	Kathleen Sebelius	D	2010	9	31	0[f]	48	77	125
Kentucky	Steven L. Beshear	D[b]	2011	15	22[d]	19	65	35	100
Louisiana	Bobby Jindal	R[b]	2011	22[g]	15	0[h]	52[i]	50	0[h]
Maine	John Baldacci	D	2010	20	15	35	96[d]	54	151
Maryland	Martin O'Malley	D[b]	2010	33	14	47	104[d]	36	141
Massachusetts	Deval Patrick	D[b]	2010	35	5	40	143[d]	16	160
Michigan	Jennifer M. Granholm	D	2010	17	21	38	67	43	110
Minnesota	Tim Pawlenty	R	2010	46	21	67	87	47	134
Mississippi	Haley Barbour	R	2011	27	25	0[j]	74	48	0[j]
Missouri	Jay Nixon	D[b]	2012	11	23	17	74	89	163

State	Governor	Party	Year						
Montana	Brian Schweitzer	D	2012	23	27[b]	25	50[b]	50	100
Nebraska	Dave Heineman	R	2010	k	k	k	k	k	k
Nevada	Jim Gibbons	R	2010	12[b]	9	11	28	14	42
New Hampshire	John Lynch	D	2010	14	10	24	225	175	400
New Jersey	Jon Corzine	D	2009	23	17	0[l]	48	32	0[l]
New Mexico	Bill Richardson	D	2010	27	15	0[m]	45	25	70
New York	David Paterson	D[n]	2010	33[b]	29	62	109	41	150
North Carolina	Beverly Perdue	D	2012	30	20	50	68	52	120
North Dakota	John Hoeven	R	2012	21	26	24	36	58	47
Ohio	Ted Strickland	D[b]	2010	12	21	17	53[b]	46	99
Oklahoma	Brad Henry	D	2010	22	26[b]	24	40	61	101
Oregon	Theodore R. Kulongoski	D	2010	18	12	15	36	24	60
Pennsylvania	Edward G. Rendell	D	2010	20	29[o]	25	104	99	203
Rhode Island	Donald L. Carcieri	R	2010	33[d]	4	38	69	6	75
South Carolina	Mark Sanford	R	2010	19	27	0[p]	53	71	124
South Dakota	Michael Rounds	R	2010	14	20[d]	35	24	46	70
Tennessee	Phil Bredesen	D	2010	14	19	17	49	50[b]	99
Texas	Rick Perry	R	2010	12	19	16	74	76	150
Utah	Jon Huntsman Jr.	R	2012	8	21	15	22	53	75
Vermont	Jim Douglas	R	2010	23	7	30	95[q]	48	150
Virginia	Tim Kaine	D	2009	21[b]	19	0[r]	45	53[r]	0[s]
Washington	Christine Gregoire	D	2012	31	18	24	64	34	98
West Virginia	Joe Manchin III	D	2012	28	6	17	79	21	100
Wisconsin	James E. Doyle	D	2010	18	15	17	52[b,d]	46	99
Wyoming	Dave Freudenthal	D	2010	7	23	15	18	41[o]	60
Total		D 28, R 22		1,025	888	1,124[t]	3,059	2,334	4,916[t]

Note: Governors as of February 13, 2009; legislatures as of February 16, 2009. Legislative divisions reflect seated members; some vacancies exist. Data for earlier years can be found in previous editions of *Vital Statistics on American Politics.*

[a] Plus three vacancies.

[b] Change in party control from previous election.

[c] The change in party control in Arizona from Democratic to Republican governor is not due to election; rather, Secretary of State Jan Brewer (R) succeeded Gov. Janet Napolitano (D) when the latter resigned in January 2009 to accept a position in the Obama administration.

(Table continues)

Table 1-6 *(Continued)*

d Plus one independent.

e Eleven upper-house seats and forty-one lower-house seats up for election in 2012.

f Forty upper-house seats up for election in 2012.

g Plus two vacancies.

h Thirty-nine upper-house seats and 105 lower-house seats up for election in 2011.

i Plus three independents.

j Fifty-two upper-house seats and 122 lower-house seats up for election in 2011.

k Nebraska's forty-nine-member state legislature is nonpartisan and unicameral; twenty-four seats are up for election in 2010.

l Eighty lower-house seats up for election in 2009; forty upper-house seats and eighty lower-house seats up for election in 2011.

m Forty-two upper-house seats up for election in 2012.

n Lt. Gov. David Paterson (D) became governor when Eliot Spitzer (D) resigned from office in March 2008. Party control of the governor's office had last changed when Spitzer succeeded Republican George Pataki after the 2006 election.

o Plus one vacancy.

p Forty-six upper-house seats up for election in 2012.

q Plus seven independents.

r Plus two independents.

s One hundred lower-house seats up for election in 2009; forty upper-house seats and one hundred lower-house seats up for election in 2011.

t Totals do not include the twenty-four seats in the unicameral, nonpartisan Nebraska legislature up for election in 2010.

Sources: Governors, name and party: National Governors Association (*www.nga.org*); state legislative partisan composition: National Conference of State Legislatures (*www.ncsl.org*); next up for election, governors and state legislatures: Council of State Governments, *The Book of the States*, vol. 40 (Lexington, Ky.: Council of State Governments, 2008), 303–306, and National Conference of State Legislatures (*www.ncsl.org*); change in party control, governors and state legislatures: calculated by the editors from these sources and previous editions of *Vital Statistics on American Politics*.

Table 1-7 Popular and Electoral Votes for President, 1789–2008

Year	Number of states	Candidates	Electoral vote (number and percent)	Popular vote (number and percent)
1789[a]	10[b]	*(Federalist)* George Washington	*(Federalist)* 69 — 100%	
1792[a]	15	George Washington	132 — 98%	
1796[a]	16	*(Federalist)* John Adams	*(Federalist)* 71 — 51%	
		(Democratic-Republican) Thomas Jefferson	*(Democratic-Republican)* 68 — 49%	
1800[a]	16	John Adams	65 — 47%	
		Thomas Jefferson	73 — 53%	
1804	17	Charles C. Pinckney	14 — 8%	
		Rufus King		
		Thomas Jefferson	162 — 92%	
		George Clinton		
1808	17	Charles C. Pinckney	47 — 27%	
		Rufus King		
		James Madison	122 — 69%	
		George Clinton		
1812	18	George Clinton	89 — 41%	
		Jared Ingersoll		
		James Madison	128 — 59%	
		Elbridge Gerry		
1816	19	Rufus King	34 — 15%	
		John Eager Howard		
		James Monroe	183 — 83%	
		Daniel D. Tompkins		
1820	24	*(Independent Democratic-Republican)* John Q. Adams	*(Independent Democratic-Republican)* 1 — 0%	
		Richard Stockton		
		(Democratic-Republican) James Monroe	*(Democratic-Republican)* 231 — 98%	
		Daniel D. Tompkins		

(Table continues)

17

Table 1-7 (Continued)

Year	Number of states	Candidates	Electoral vote (number and percent)	Popular vote (number and percent)
1824[c]	24	Andrew Jackson / Nathan Sanford (Democratic-Republican)	99 38%	
		John Q. Adams / John C. Calhoun (National-Republican)	84 32%	
1828	24	Andrew Jackson / John C. Calhoun (Democratic-Republican)	178 68%	642,553 56.0%
		John Q. Adams / Richard Rush (National-Republican)	83 32%	500,897 43.6%
1832	24	Andrew Jackson / Martin Van Buren (Democratic)	219 76%	701,780 54.2%
		Henry Clay / John Sergeant (Whig)	49 17%	484,205 37.4%
1836	26	Martin Van Buren / Richard M. Johnson (Democratic)	170 58%	764,176 50.8%
		William Henry Harrison / Francis Granger (Whig)	73[d] 25%	550,816 36.6%
1840	26	Martin Van Buren / Richard M. Johnson (Democratic)	60 20%	1,128,854 46.8%
		William Henry Harrison / John Tyler (Whig)	234 80%	1,275,390 52.9%
1844	26	James K. Polk / George M. Dallas (Democratic)	170 62%	1,339,494 49.5%
		Henry Clay / Theodore Frelinghuysen (Whig)	105 38%	1,300,004 48.1%
1848	30	Lewis Cass / William O. Butler (Democratic)	127 44%	1,223,460 42.5%
		Zachary Taylor / Millard Fillmore (Whig)	163 56%	1,361,393 47.3%
1852	31	Franklin Pierce / William R. King (Democratic)	254 86%	1,607,510 50.8%
		Winfield Scott / William A. Graham (Whig)	42 14%	1,386,942 43.9%
1856	31	James Buchanan / John C. Breckinridge (Democratic)	174 59%	1,836,072 45.3%
		John C. Fremont / William L. Dayton (Republican)	114 39%	1,342,345 33.1%
1860	33	Stephen A. Douglas / Herschel V. Johnson (Democratic)	12 4%	1,380,202 29.5%
		Abraham Lincoln / Hannibal Hamlin (Republican)	180 59%	1,865,908 39.8%

Year	No.	Candidate (1)	Candidate (2)	EV (1)	%	EV (2)	%	Popular vote (1)	%	Popular vote (2)	%
1864	36[e]	George B. McClellan	Abraham Lincoln	21	9%	212	91%	1,809,445	44.9%	2,220,846	55.1%
		George H. Pendleton	Andrew Johnson								
1868	37[f]	Horatio Seymour	Ulysses S. Grant	80	27%	214	73%	2,708,744	47.3%	3,013,650	52.7%
		Francis P. Blair Jr.	Schuyler Colfax								
1872	37	Horace Greeley	Ulysses S. Grant	g	g	286	78%	2,835,315	43.8%	3,598,468	55.6%
		Benjamin G. Brown	Henry Wilson								
1876	38	Samuel J. Tilden	Rutherford B. Hayes	184	50%	185	50%	4,288,191	51.0%	4,033,497	48.0%
		Thomas A. Hendricks	William A. Wheeler								
1880	38	Winfield S. Hancock	James A. Garfield	155	42%	214	58%	4,445,256	48.2%	4,453,611	48.3%
		William H. English	Chester A. Arthur								
1884	38	Grover Cleveland	James G. Blaine	219	55%	182	45%	4,915,586	48.9%	4,852,916	48.2%
		Thomas A. Hendricks	John A. Logan								
1888	38	Grover Cleveland	Benjamin Harrison	168	42%	233	58%	5,539,118	48.6%	5,449,825	47.8%
		Allen G. Thurman	Levi P. Morton								
1892	44	Grover Cleveland	Benjamin Harrison	277	62%	145	33%	5,554,617	46.0%	5,186,793	43.0%
		Adlai E. Stevenson	Whitelaw Reid								
1896	45	William Jennings Bryan	William McKinley	176	39%	271	61%	6,370,897	45.8%	7,105,144	51.1%
		Arthur Sewall	Garret A. Hobart								
1900	45	William Jennings Bryan	William McKinley	155	35%	292	65%	6,357,698	45.5%	7,219,193	51.7%
		Adlai E. Stevenson	Theodore Roosevelt								
1904	45	Alton B. Parker	Theodore Roosevelt	140	29%	336	71%	5,083,501	37.6%	7,625,599	56.4%
		Henry G. Davis	Charles W. Fairbanks								
1908	46	William Jennings Bryan	William Howard Taft	162	34%	321	66%	6,406,874	43.0%	7,676,598	51.6%
		John W. Kern	James S. Sherman								
1912	48	Woodrow Wilson	William Howard Taft	435	82%	8	2%	6,294,326	41.8%	3,486,343	23.2%
		Thomas R. Marshall	James S. Sherman[h]								
1916	48	Woodrow Wilson	Charles E. Hughes	277	52%	254	48%	9,126,063	49.2%	8,547,039	46.1%
		Thomas R. Marshall	Charles W. Fairbanks								

(Table continues)

Table 1-7 *(Continued)*

Year	Number of states	Candidates	Electoral vote (number and percent)	Popular vote (number and percent)
1920	48	James M. Cox / Franklin D. Roosevelt	127 24%	9,134,074 34.2%
		Warren G. Harding / Calvin Coolidge	404 76%	16,151,916 60.3%
1924	48	John W. Davis / Charles W. Bryan	136 26%	8,386,532 28.8%
		Calvin Coolidge / Charles G. Dawes	382 72%	15,724,310 54.0%
1928	48	Alfred E. Smith / Joseph T. Robinson	87 16%	15,004,336 40.8%
		Herbert C. Hoover / Charles Curtis	444 84%	21,432,823 58.2%
1932	48	Franklin D. Roosevelt / John Nance Garner	472 89%	22,818,740 57.4%
		Herbert C. Hoover / Charles Curtis	59 11%	15,760,425 39.6%
1936	48	Franklin D. Roosevelt / John Nance Garner	523 98%	27,750,866 60.8%
		Alfred M. Landon / Frank Knox	8 2%	16,679,683 36.5%
1940	48	Franklin D. Roosevelt / Henry A. Wallace	449 85%	27,343,218 54.7%
		Wendell L. Willkie / Charles L. McNary	82 15%	22,334,940 44.8%
1944	48	Franklin D. Roosevelt / Harry S. Truman	432 81%	25,612,610 53.4%
		Thomas E. Dewey / John W. Bricker	99 19%	22,021,053 45.9%
1948	48	Harry S. Truman / Alben W. Barkley	303 57%	24,105,810 49.5%
		Thomas E. Dewey / Earl Warren	189 36%	21,970,064 45.1%
1952	48	Adlai E. Stevenson II / John J. Sparkman	89 17%	27,314,992 44.4%
		Dwight D. Eisenhower / Richard Nixon	442 83%	33,777,945 54.9%
1956	48	Adlai E. Stevenson II / Estes Kefauver	73 14%	26,022,752 42.0%
		Dwight D. Eisenhower / Richard Nixon	457 86%	35,590,472 57.4%
1960	50	John F. Kennedy / Lyndon B. Johnson	303 56%	34,226,731 49.7%
		Richard Nixon / Henry Cabot Lodge Jr.	219 41%	34,108,157 49.5%
1964	50	Lyndon B. Johnson / Hubert H. Humphrey	486 90%	43,129,566 61.1%
		Barry M. Goldwater / William E. Miller	52 10%	27,178,188 38.5%
1968	50	Hubert H. Humphrey / Edmund S. Muskie	191 36%	31,275,166 42.7%
		Richard Nixon / Spiro T. Agnew	301 56%	31,785,480 43.4%
1972	50	George S. McGovern / R. Sargent Shriver Jr.	17 3%	29,170,383 37.5%
		Richard Nixon / Spiro T. Agnew	520 97%	47,169,911 60.7%

Year	States	Democratic candidates	Electoral vote	%	Popular vote	%	Republican candidates	Electoral vote	%	Popular vote	%
1976	50	Jimmy Carter / Walter F. Mondale	297	55%	40,830,763	50.1%	Gerald R. Ford / Robert J. Dole	240	45%	39,147,793	48.0%
1980	50	Jimmy Carter / Walter F. Mondale	49	9%	35,483,883	41.0%	Ronald Reagan / George H. W. Bush	489	91%	43,904,153	50.7%
1984	50	Walter F. Mondale / Geraldine Ferraro	13	2%	37,577,185	40.6%	Ronald Reagan / George H. W. Bush	525	98%	54,455,075	58.8%
1988	50	Michael S. Dukakis / Lloyd M. Bentsen Jr.	111	21%	41,809,074	45.6%	George H. W. Bush / Dan Quayle	426	79%	48,886,097	53.4%
1992	50	Bill Clinton / Al Gore	370	69%	44,909,326	43.0%	George H. W. Bush / Dan Quayle	168	31%	39,103,882	37.4%
1996	50	Bill Clinton / Al Gore	379	70%	47,402,357	49.2%	Robert J. Dole / Jack Kemp	159	30%	39,198,755	40.7%
2000	50	Al Gore / Joseph I. Lieberman	266	49%	50,992,335	48.4%	George W. Bush / Dick Cheney	271	50%	50,455,156	47.9%
2004	50	John Kerry / John Edwards	251	47%	59,028,439	48.3%	George W. Bush / Dick Cheney	286	53%	62,040,610	50.7%
2008	50	Barack Obama / Joseph R. Biden Jr.	173	32%	59,930,608	45.7%	John McCain / Sarah Palin	365	68%	69,459,909	52.9%

Note: For details of the electoral system as well as popular and electoral votes polled by minor candidates, see first source. Popular vote returns are shown beginning in 1828 because of availability and because by that time most electors were chosen by popular vote.

[a] The elections of 1789–1800 were held under different rules, which did not include separate voting for president and vice president. Scattered electoral votes are not shown.

[b] Eleven states could have voted, but a dispute between its two chambers prevented the New York state legislature from choosing electors. North Carolina and Rhode Island had not yet ratified the Constitution.

[c] All candidates in 1824 represented factions of the Democratic-Republican Party. Figures are for the two candidates with the highest number of electoral votes. The two other candidates were William H. Crawford and Henry Clay with forty-one and thirty-seven electoral votes, respectively.

[d] Three Whig candidates ran in 1836. Their electoral votes totaled 113.

[e] Eleven southern states had seceded from the Union and did not vote; twenty-five states voted.

[f] Mississippi, Texas, and Virginia were not yet readmitted to the Union and did not vote; thirty-four states voted.

[g] The Democratic presidential nominee, Horace Greeley, died between the popular vote and the meeting of presidential electors. Democratic electors split sixty-three votes among several candidates. Congress refused to count the three Georgians who insisted on casting their votes for Greeley, and an additional fourteen electoral votes were not cast. Congress also did not count the electoral votes from Arkansas and Louisiana because of "disruptive conditions during Reconstruction."

[h] James S. Sherman died on October 12, 1912. Nicholas Murray Butler was nominated as the substitute candidate.

Sources: 1789–2004: *Congressional Quarterly's Guide to U.S. Elections*, 5th ed. (Washington, D.C.: CQ Press, 2005), 674–719, 750–759; 2008: Table 1-9, this volume.

Table 1-8 Party Winning Presidential Election, by State, 1789–2008

State	1789–1824			1828–1856			1860–1892			1896–1928			1932–1964			1968–2008		
	D	F	O	D	R	O	D	R	O	D	R	O	D	R	O	D	R	O
Alabama	2	0	0	8	0	0	6	2	0	9	0	0	7	1	1	1	9	1
Alaska	—	—	—	—	—	—	—	—	—	—	—	—	1	1	0	0	11	0
Arizona	—	—	—	—	—	—	—	—	—	2	3	0	5	4	0	1	10	0
Arkansas	—	—	—	6	0	0	6	1	0	9	0	0	9	0	0	3	7	1
California	—	—	—	2	0	0	2	7	0	1	7	1	6	3	0	5	6	0
Colorado	—	—	—	—	—	—	0	4	1	5	4	0	4	5	0	2	9	0
Connecticut	2	8	0	2	6	0	4	4	0	1	8	0	5	4	0	6	5	0
Delaware	2	8	0	2	6	0	7	1	1	1	8	0	5	4	0	6	5	0
District of Columbia[a]	—	—	—	—	—	—	—	—	—	—	—	—	1	0	0	11	0	0
Florida	—	—	—	2	1	0	4	3	1	8	1	0	6	3	0	3	8	0
Georgia	8	2	0	5	3	0	7	0	1	9	0	0	8	1	0	3	7	0
Hawaii	—	—	—	—	—	—	—	—	—	—	—	—	2	0	0	9	2	0
Idaho	—	—	—	—	—	—	—	—	1	4	5	0	6	3	0	0	11	0
Illinois	2	0	0	8	0	0	1	8	0	1	8	0	7	2	0	5	6	0
Indiana	3	0	0	6	2	0	3	6	0	1	8	0	3	6	0	1	10	0
Iowa	—	—	—	2	1	0	0	9	0	1	8	0	4	5	0	5	6	0
Kansas	—	—	—	—	—	—	0	7	1	3	6	0	3	6	0	0	11	0
Kentucky	8	1	0	2	6	0	8	0	1	6	3	0	7	2	0	3	8	0
Louisiana	4	0	0	6	2	0	5	1	1	9	0	0	6	2	1	3	7	1
Maine	2	0	0	5	3	0	0	9	1	1	8	0	1	8	0	6	5	0
Maryland	4	6	0	1	6	1	7	1	1	4	5	0	6	3	0	8	3	0
Massachusetts	3	7	0	0	8	0	0	9	0	2	7	0	7	2	0	9	2	0
Michigan	—	—	—	4	2	0	0	9	0	0	8	1	5	4	0	9	2	0
Minnesota	—	—	—	—	—	—	0	9	0	0	8	1	7	2	0	10	1	0
Mississippi	2	0	0	7	1	0	5	1	1	9	0	0	6	1	2	1	9	1
Missouri	—	—	—	8	0	0	7	2	0	4	5	0	8	1	0	3	8	0
Montana	—	—	—	—	—	—	0	1	0	4	5	0	6	3	0	1	10	0

Nebraska	—	—	—	—	—	—	0	7	0	4	5	0	3	6	0	0	11	0
Nevada	—	—	—	—	—	—	1	6	1	5	4	0	7	2	0	3	8	0
New Hampshire	4	6	0	6	2	0	0	9	0	2	7	0	4	5	0	4	7	0
New Jersey	5	5	0	3	5	0	7	2	0	1	8	0	6	3	0	5	6	0
New Mexico	—	—	—	—	—	—	—	—	—	2	3	0	7	2	0	4	7	0
New York	6	3	0	5	3	0	4	5	0	1	8	0	6	3	0	8	3	0
North Carolina	8	1	0	5	3	0	5	2	1	8	1	0	9	0	0	2	9	0
North Dakota	—	—	—	—	—	—	—	—	—	2	7	0	3	6	0	0	11	0
Ohio	6	0	0	4	4	0	0	9	0	2	7	0	5	4	0	4	7	0
Oklahoma	—	—	—	—	—	—	—	—	—	4	2	0	6	3	0	0	11	0
Oregon	—	—	—	—	—	—	1	8	0	0	8	1	5	4	0	6	5	0
Pennsylvania	8	2	0	6	2	0	0	9	0	0	8	1	5	5	0	7	4	0
Rhode Island	4	5	0	2	6	0	0	9	0	2	7	0	7	2	0	9	2	0
South Carolina	8	2	2	6	0	2	4	3	1	9	0	0	7	1	1	1	10	0
South Dakota	—	—	—	—	—	—	—	—	—	1	7	1	3	6	0	0	11	0
Tennessee	8	0	0	3	5	0	6	1	1	7	2	0	6	3	0	3	8	0
Texas	—	—	0	3	0	0	7	0	0	8	8	0	7	2	0	2	9	0
Utah	—	—	—	—	—	—	—	—	—	2	7	0	6	3	0	0	11	0
Vermont	6	3	0	7	1	0	0	9	0	0	9	0	1	8	0	5	6	0
Virginia	8	2	0	8	0	0	5	1	1	8	1	1	6	3	0	1	10	0
Washington	—	—	—	—	—	—	0	1	0	2	6	1	6	3	0	7	4	0
West Virginia	—	—	—	—	—	—	5	3	0	1	8	1	8	1	0	6	5	0
Wisconsin	—	—	—	2	1	0	1	8	0	1	7	1	5	4	0	7	4	0
Wyoming	—	—	—	—	—	—	0	1	0	3	6	0	5	4	0	0	11	0
Total[b]	113	61	0	136	79	3	118	189	15	170	244	7	274	158	5	198	358	5

Note: Table entries indicate number of times party indicated won the state. "D" indicates the Democratic-Republican Party from 1796 to 1820 and in 1828, the Jackson faction in 1824, and the Democratic Party in 1832 and later; "F" indicates the Federalists from 1792 to 1816, Independent Democratic-Republicans in 1820, and the Adams faction in 1824; "R" indicates the National Republicans in 1828 and 1832, Whigs from 1836 to 1852, and the Republican Party in 1856 and later. The "O" column refers to other (third party) parties. Southern Democrats in 1860 are counted as Democratic. "—" indicates that the state was not yet admitted to the Union.

[a] Residents of the District of Columbia received the presidential vote in 1961.

[b] Fewer total votes for a given state within a party system indicate admission of the state during the party system or nonvoting in certain southern states in 1864, 1868, and 1872.

Sources: Compiled by the editors from *Congressional Quarterly's Guide to U.S. Elections*, 5th ed. (Washington, D.C.: CQ Press, 2005), 750–804; Table 1-9, this volume; and previous editions of *Vital Statistics on American Politics*.

Table 1-9 Presidential General Election Returns, by State, 2008

| State | Popular vote | | | | | | | Plurality[a] | | Electoral vote | |
| | Obama (Democratic) | | McCain (Republican) | | Other | | Total vote | | | Dem. | Rep. |
	Vote	%	Vote	%	Vote	%		Vote	%		
Alabama	813,479	38.7	1,266,546	60.3	19,794	0.9	2,099,819	453,067	21.6		9
Alaska	123,594	37.9	193,841	59.4	8,762	2.7	326,197	70,247	21.5		3
Arizona	1,034,707	45.1	1,230,111	53.6	28,657	1.2	2,293,475	195,404	8.5		10
Arkansas	422,310	38.9	638,017	58.7	26,290	2.4	1,086,617	215,707	19.9		6
California	8,274,473	61.0	5,011,781	37.0	275,646	2.0	13,561,900	3,262,692	24.1	55	
Colorado	1,288,568	53.7	1,073,584	44.7	39,197	1.6	2,401,349	214,984	9.0	9	
Connecticut	1,000,994	60.7	628,873	38.1	18,693	1.1	1,648,560	372,121	22.6	7	
Delaware	255,459	61.9	152,374	36.9	4,579	1.1	412,412	103,085	25.0	3	
District of Columbia	245,800	92.5	17,367	6.5	2,686	1.0	265,853	228,433	85.9	3	
Florida	4,282,074	51.0	4,045,624	48.2	63,046	0.8	8,390,744	236,450	2.8	27	
Georgia	1,844,137	47.0	2,048,744	52.2	31,559	0.8	3,924,440	204,607	5.2		15
Hawaii	325,871	71.8	120,566	26.6	7,131	1.6	453,568	205,305	45.3	4	
Idaho	236,440	36.1	403,012	61.5	15,580	2.4	655,032	166,572	25.4		4
Illinois	3,419,673	61.9	2,031,527	36.8	71,851	1.3	5,523,051	1,388,146	25.1	21	
Indiana	1,374,039	49.9	1,345,648	48.9	31,367	1.1	2,751,054	28,391	1.0	11	
Iowa	828,940	53.9	682,379	44.4	25,804	1.7	1,537,123	146,561	9.5	7	
Kansas	514,765	41.7	699,655	56.6	21,452	1.7	1,235,872	184,890	15.0		6
Kentucky	751,985	41.2	1,048,462	57.4	26,061	1.4	1,826,508	296,477	16.2		8
Louisiana	782,989	39.9	1,148,275	58.6	29,497	1.5	1,960,761	365,286	18.6		9
Maine	421,923	57.7	295,273	40.4	13,967	1.9	731,163	126,650	17.3	4	
Maryland	1,628,995	61.9	959,694	36.5	42,258	1.6	2,630,947	669,301	25.4	10	
Massachusetts	1,904,097	61.8	1,108,854	36.0	68,034	2.2	3,080,985	795,243	25.8	12	
Michigan	2,872,579	57.4	2,048,639	41.0	80,548	1.6	5,001,766	823,940	16.5	17	
Minnesota	1,573,354	54.1	1,275,409	43.8	61,606	2.1	2,910,369	297,945	10.2	10	
Mississippi	554,662	43.0	724,597	56.2	10,606	0.8	1,289,865	169,935	13.2		6

Missouri	1,441,911	49.3	49.4	1,445,814	37,480	1.3	2,925,205	3,903	0.1		11
Montana	231,667	47.3	49.5	242,763	15,679	3.2	490,109	11,096	2.3		3
Nebraska	333,319	41.6	56.5	452,979	14,983	1.9	801,281	119,660	14.9	1[b]	4
Nevada	533,736	55.1	42.7	412,827	21,285	2.2	967,848	120,909	12.5	5	
New Hampshire	384,826	54.1	44.5	316,534	9,610	1.4	710,970	68,292	9.6	4	
New Jersey	2,215,422	57.3	41.7	1,613,207	39,608	1.0	3,868,237	602,215	15.6	15	
New Mexico	472,422	56.9	41.8	346,832	10,904	1.3	830,158	125,590	15.1	5	
New York	4,769,700	62.8	36.1	2,742,298	82,815	1.1	7,594,813	2,027,402	26.7	31	
North Carolina	2,142,651	49.7	49.4	2,128,474	39,664	0.9	4,310,789	14,177	0.3	15	
North Dakota	141,278	44.6	53.3	168,601	6,742	2.1	316,621	27,323	8.6		3
Ohio	2,933,388	51.5	46.9	2,674,491	90,381	1.6	5,698,260	258,897	4.5	20	
Oklahoma	502,496	34.4	65.6	960,165	—	—	1,462,661	457,669	31.3		7
Oregon	1,037,291	56.7	40.4	738,475	52,098	2.9	1,827,864	298,816	16.3	7	
Pennsylvania	3,276,363	54.7	44.3	2,651,812	62,889	1.0	5,991,064	624,551	10.4	21	
Rhode Island	296,571	63.1	35.2	165,391	7,805	1.7	469,767	131,180	27.9	4	
South Carolina	862,449	44.9	53.9	1,034,896	23,624	1.2	1,920,969	172,447	9.0		8
South Dakota	170,924	44.7	53.2	203,054	7,997	2.1	381,975	32,130	8.4		3
Tennessee	1,087,437	41.8	56.9	1,479,178	33,134	1.3	2,599,749	391,741	15.1		11
Texas	3,528,633	43.7	55.5	4,479,328	69,834	0.9	8,077,795	950,695	11.8		34
Utah	327,670	34.4	62.6	596,030	28,670	3.0	952,370	268,360	28.2		5
Vermont	219,262	67.5	30.4	98,974	6,810	2.1	325,046	120,288	37.0	3	
Virginia	1,959,532	52.6	46.3	1,725,005	38,723	1.0	3,723,260	234,527	6.3	13	
Washington	1,750,848	57.7	40.5	1,229,216	56,814	1.9	3,036,878	521,632	17.2	11	
West Virginia	304,127	42.6	55.7	398,061	12,058	1.7	714,246	93,934	13.2		5
Wisconsin	1,677,211	56.2	42.3	1,262,393	43,813	1.5	2,983,417	414,818	13.9	10	
Wyoming	82,868	32.5	64.8	164,958	6,832	2.7	254,658	82,090	32.2		3
Total	69,459,909	52.9	45.7	59,930,608	1,844,923	1.4	131,235,440	9,529,301	7.3	365	173

Note: "—" indicates not available. Percentage for "Plurality" calculated by the editors. Data for earlier years can be found in previous editions of *Vital Statistics on American Politics.*

[a] "Plurality" indicates the vote margin between the leader and the second-place finisher.
[b] Obama won one electoral vote in Nebraska by carrying the Second Congressional District. See note, Figure 1-4, for details.

Source: "The Rhodes Cook Letter," December 2008, 21 (*www.rhodescook.com*).

Figure 1-4   Presidential General Election Map, 2008

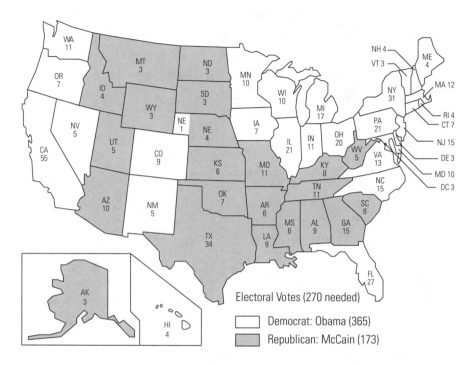

Note: Most states award electoral votes statewide on a winner-take-all basis. Maine and Nebraska award electoral votes by a district system, one for the candidate carrying each congressional district, two for the candidate carrying the state. In 2008 Nebraska (five electoral votes) awarded four electoral votes to McCain and one electoral vote to Obama for carrying the Second Congressional District. Maine awarded all four electoral votes to Obama.

Source: Table 1-9, this volume.

Table 1-10 House and Senate Election Results, by Congress, 1788–2008

| | | House | | | | | Senate | | | | | |
| | | | | | Gains/losses[c] | | | | | Gains/losses[c] | | |
Election year	Congress	Dem.[a]	Rep.[b]	Other	Dem.	Rep.	Dem.[a]	Rep.[b]	Other	Dem.	Rep.	President[d]
1788	1st	26	38		a	b	9	17		a	b	Washington (F)
1790	2nd	33	37		a	b	13	16		a	b	
1792	3rd	57	48		24	11	13	17		0	1	Washington (F)
1794	4th	52	54		−5	6	13	19		0	2	
1796	5th	48	58		−4	4	12	20		−1	1	J. Adams (F)
1798	6th	42	64		−6	6	13	19		1	−1	
1800	7th	69	36		27	−28	18	13		5	−6	Jefferson (DR)
1802	8th	102	39		33	3	25	9		7	−4	
1804	9th	116	25		14	−14	27	7		2	−2	Jefferson (DR)
1806	10th	118	24		2	−1	28	6		1	−1	
1808	11th	94	48		−24	24	28	6		0	0	Madison (DR)
1810	12th	108	36		14	−12	30	6		2	0	
1812	13th	112	68		4	32	27	9		−3	3	Madison (DR)
1814	14th	117	65		5	−3	25	11		−2	2	
1816	15th	141	42		24	−23	34	10		9	−1	Monroe (DR)
1818	16th	156	27		15	−15	35	7		1	−3	
1820	17th	158	25		2	−2	44	4		9	−3	Monroe (DR)
1822	18th	187	26		29	1	44	4		0	0	
1824	19th	105	97		a	b	26	20		a	b	J. Q. Adams (DR)
1826	20th	94	119		−11	22	20	28		−6	8	
1828	21st	139	74		a	b	26	22		a	b	Jackson (D)
1830	22nd	141	58	14	2	−16	25	21	2	−1	−1	
1832	23rd	147	53	60	6	−5	20	20	8	a	b	Jackson (D)
1834	24th	145	98		−2	45	27	25		a	b	
1836	25th	108	107	24	−37	9	30	18	4	3	−7	Van Buren (D)

(Table continues)

Table 1-10 *(Continued)*

Election year	Congress	House Dem.[a]	House Rep.[b]	House Other	House Gains/losses[c] Dem.	House Gains/losses[c] Rep.	Senate Dem.[a]	Senate Rep.[b]	Senate Other	Senate Gains/losses[c] Dem.	Senate Gains/losses[c] Rep.	President[d]
1838	26th	124	118		16	11	28	22	2	−2	4	
1840	27th	102	133	6	−22	15	28	22	1	0	0	Harrison (W)
1842	28th	142	79	1	40	−54	25	28		−3	6	Tyler (W)
1844	29th	143	77	6	1	−2	31	25	1	6	−3	Polk (D)
1846	30th	108	115	4	−35	38	36	21	2	5	−4	
1848	31st	112	109	9	4	−6	35	25	3	−1	4	Taylor (W)
1850	32nd	140	88	5	28	−21	35	24	2	0	−1	Fillmore (W)
1852	33rd	159	71	4	19	−17	38	22	5	3	−2	Pierce (D)
1854	34th	83	108	43	−76	37	40	15	8	a	b	
1856	35th	118	92	26	35	−16	36	20	4	−4	5	Buchanan (D)
1858	36th	92	114	31	−26	22	36	26	7	0	6	
1860	37th	42	106	28	−50	−8	11	31		−25	5	Lincoln (R)
1862	38th	80	103		38	−3	12	39		1	8	
1864	39th	46	145		−34	42	10	42		−2	3	Lincoln (R)
1866	40th	49	143		3	−2	11	42		1	0	A. Johnson (R)
1868	41st	73	170		24	27	11	61		0	19	Grant (R)
1870	42nd	104	139		31	−31	17	57		6	−4	
1872	43rd	88	203	3	−16	64	19	54		2	−3	Grant (R)
1874	44th	181	107		93	−96	29	46		10	−8	
1876	45th	156	137	14	−25	30	36	39	1	7	−7	Hayes (R)
1878	46th	150	128	11	−6	−9	43	33		7	−6	
1880	47th	130	152	6	−20	24	37	37		−6	4	Garfield (R)
1882	48th	200	119	2	70	−33	36	40	2	−1	3	Arthur (R)
1884	49th	182	140	2	−18	21	34	41		−2	1	Cleveland (D)
1886	50th	170	151	4	−12	11	37	39		3	−2	

Year	Congress											President
1888	51st	156	173	1	−14	22	37	47	2	0	8	Harrison (R)
1890	52nd	231	88	14	75	−85	39	47	3	2	0	Cleveland (D)
1892	53rd	220	126	8	−11	38	44	38	5	5	−9	McKinley (R)
1894	54th	104	246	7	−116	120	30	44	10	−14	6	
1896	55th	134	206	16	30	−40	34	46	11	4	2	McKinley (R)
1898	56th	163	185	9	29	−21	26	53	3	−8	7	
1900	57th	153	198	5	−10	13	29	56		3	3	T. Roosevelt (R)
1902	58th	178	207		25	9	32	58		3	2	T. Roosevelt (R)
1904	59th	136	250		−42	43	32	58		0	0	
1906	60th	164	222		28	−28	29	61		−3	3	
1908	61st	172	219		8	−3	32	59		3	−2	Taft (R)
1910	62nd	228	162	1	56	−57	42	49	1	10	−10	
1912	63rd	290	127	18	62	−35	51	44	1	9	−5	Wilson (D)
1914	64th	231	193	8	−59	66	56	39	1	5	−5	
1916	65th	210	216	9	−21	23	53	42	1	−3	3	Wilson (D)
1918	66th	191	237	7	−19	21	47	48		−6	6	
1920	67th	132	300	1	−59	63	37	59		−10	11	Harding (R)
1922	68th	207	225	3	75	−75	43	51	2	6	−8	
1924	69th	183	247	5	−24	22	40	54	1	−3	3	Coolidge (R)
1926	70th	195	237	3	12	−10	47	48	1	7	−6	
1928	71st	167	267	1	−28	30	39	56	1	−8	8	Hoover (R)
1930	72nd	220	214	1	53	−53	47	48	1	8	−8	
1932	73rd	313	117	5	93	−97	59	36	1	12	−12	F. Roosevelt (D)
1934	74th	322	103	10	9	−14	69	25	2	10	−11	
1936	75th	333	89	13	11	−14	75	17	4	6	−8	F. Roosevelt (D)
1938	76th	262	169	4	−71	80	69	23	4	−6	6	
1940	77th	267	162	6	5	−7	66	28	2	−3	5	F. Roosevelt (D)
1942	78th	222	209	4	−45	47	57	38	1	−9	10	
1944	79th	243	190	2	21	−19	57	38		0	0	F. Roosevelt (D)
1946	80th	188	246	1	−55	56	45	51		−12	13	Truman (D)
1948	81st	263	171	1	75	−75	54	42		9	−9	Truman (D)

(Table continues)

Table 1-10 (Continued)

Election year	Congress	House Dem.[a]	House Rep.[b]	House Other	House Gains/losses[c] Dem.	House Gains/losses[c] Rep.	Senate Dem.[a]	Senate Rep.[b]	Senate Other	Senate Gains/losses[c] Dem.	Senate Gains/losses[c] Rep.	President[d]
1950	82nd	234	199	2	−29	28	48	47	1	−6	5	
1952	83rd	213	221	1	−21	22	47	48	1	−1	1	Eisenhower (R)
1954	84th	232	203		19	−18	48	47	1	1	−1	
1956	85th	234	201		2	−2	49	47		1	0	Eisenhower (R)
1958	86th	283	154		49	−47	64	34		15	−13	
1960	87th	263	174		−20	20	64	36		0	2	Kennedy (D)
1962	88th	258	176	1	−5	2	67	33		3	−3	
1964	89th	295	140		37	−36	68	32		1	−1	L. Johnson (D)
1966	90th	248	187		−47	47	64	36		−4	4	
1968	91st	243	192		−5	5	58	42		−6	6	Nixon (R)
1970	92nd	255	180		12	−12	55	45		−3	3	
1972	93rd	243	192		−12	12	57	43		2	−2	Nixon (R)
1974	94th	291	144		48	−48	61	38		4	−5	Ford (R)
1976	95th	292	143		1	−1	62	38		1	0	Carter (D)
1978	96th	277	158		−15	15	59	41		−3	3	
1980	97th	243	192		−34	34	47	53		−12	12	Reagan (R)
1982	98th	269	166		26	−26	46	54		−1	1	
1984	99th	253	182		−16	16	47	53		1	−1	Reagan (R)
1986	100th	258	177		5	−5	55	45		8	−8	
1988	101st	259	174		1	−3	55	45		0	0	G. H. W. Bush (R)
1990	102nd	267	167	1	8	−7	56	44		1	−1	
1992	103rd	258	176	1	−9	9	57	43		1	−1	Clinton (D)
1994	104th	204	230	1	−54	54	47	53		−10	10	
1996	105th	207	227	1	3	−3	45	55		−2	2	Clinton (D)

1998	211	223	1		4	−4	45	55	1	0	0		G. W. Bush (R)
2000	212	221	2		1	−2	50	50	1	5	−5		G. W. Bush (R)
2002	205	229	1		−7	8	48	51	1	−2	1		
2004	201	232	1		−4	3	44	55	1	−4	4		G. W. Bush (R)
2006	233	202			32	−30	50	49		6	−6		
2008	256	178		2	23	−24	55	41	2	5	−8		Obama (D)

Note: For parties, see Figure 1-3, this volume.

[a] "Democratic" column indicates Democratic partisans in 1828 and later, "Administration" in 1824 and 1826, "Democratic Republicans" from 1790 to 1822, and "Opposition" in 1788. Consequently, and because of changes within the "Republican" column noted in note b, gains/losses in the "Democratic" column are calculated only for 1792–1822, 1826, 1830, 1836–1852, and 1856 and later.

[b] The "Republican" column indicates Republican partisans in 1854 and later, "Whigs" from 1834 to 1852, "Anti-Masons" in 1832, "National Republicans" in 1828 and 1830, "Jacksonians" in 1824 and 1826, "Federalists" from 1790 to 1822, and "Administration" in 1788. Consequently, gains/losses in the "Republican" column are calculated only for 1792–1822, 1826, 1830, 1836–1852, and 1856 and later.

[c] The seat totals reflect the makeup of the House and Senate at the start of each Congress. Special elections that shifted party ratios between elections are not noted. Because of changes in the overall number of seats in the Senate and House, in the number of seats won by third parties, and in the number of vacancies, a Republican loss is not always matched precisely by a Democratic gain, or vice versa. Partisan seat shares at the start of each Congress need not match postelection seat shares: deaths, resignations, and special elections can cause further changes in party makeup. In the 1930 election, for example, Republicans won majority control, but when Congress organized, special elections held to fill fourteen vacancies resulted in a Democratic majority.

[d] President elected in the year indicated or, if a midterm election year, nonelected president in office at the time of the midterm election.

Sources: Seat gains and losses calculated by the editors. Other data: 1788–1858: U.S. Bureau of the Census, *Historical Statistics of the United States, Colonial Times to 1970* (Washington, D.C.: Government Printing Office, 1975), 1083–1084; 1860–2000: *Congressional Quarterly's Guide to U.S. Elections*, 4th ed. (Washington, D.C.: CQ Press, 2001), 1569–1571; 2002–2008: *CQ Weekly* (2002), 2988; (2003), 8; (2004), 2602, 2621; (2005), 185; (2007), 121; (2009), 27.

Table 1-11 Party Victories in U.S. House Elections, by State, 1860–2008

	Total 1860–1895			Total 1896–1931			Total 1932–1965			Total 1966–2008		
State	Dem.	Rep.	Other	Dem.	Rep.	Other	Dem.	Rep.	Other	Dem.	Rep.	Other
Alabama	92	19	8	170	0	8	146	5	0	83	74	0
Alaska	—	—	—	—	—	—	4	0	0	2	20	0
Arizona	—	—	—	11	0	0	26	7	0	37	79	0
Arkansas	54	5	6	124	0	0	109	0	0	59	29	0
California[a]	29	46	8	30	133	15	234	212	0	605	421	0
Colorado	1	9	3	21	34	6	43	26	0	60	65	0
Connecticut	33	36	5	11	77	0	58	44	0	79	49	0
Delaware	15	3	2	5	14	0	9	8	0	5	17	0
Florida	18	8	1	57	4	0	111	8	0	212	209	0
Georgia	111	11	12	207	0	1	170	1	0	157	80	0
Hawaii	—	—	—	0	0	1	6	0	0	42	2	0
Idaho	0	4	0	5	42	2	20	14	0	7	37	0
Illinois	118	191	20	136	333	1	220	221	0	252	226	0
Indiana	104	105	17	97	139	0	85	108	0	116	108	0
Iowa	16	131	11	10	193	0	35	105	0	47	79	0
Kansas	0	62	12	30	114	0	16	90	0	26	75	0
Kentucky	133	20	38	151	54	0	122	25	0	71	74	0
Louisiana	69	20	2	136	0	2	139	0	0	101	66	0
Maine	3	76	7	4	71	0	8	41	0	26	18	0
Maryland	74	15	18	63	49	0	87	25	0	116	60	0
Massachusetts	31	165	17	60	211	2	103	136	0	207	34	0
Michigan	33	118	13	12	214	2	112	187	0	206	176	0
Minnesota	11	51	5	8	146	12	44	91	16	104	72	0
Mississippi	70	17	3	142	0	0	110	1	0	75	31	0
Missouri	143	43	38	202	88	0	157	49	0	136	70	0
Montana	1	3	0	13	14	1	23	12	0	17	18	0

Nebraska	3	28	5	36	63	9	21	50	0	5	61	0
Nevada	4	9	4	5	10	4	14	3	0	20	20	0
New Hampshire	11	33	3	3	33	0	3	31	0	11	33	0
New Jersey	53	58	5	66	137	0	84	158	0	178	129	0
New Mexico	—	—	—	7	5	0	29	0	0	23	35	0
New York	236	312	66	328	397	6	387	368	1	480	279	0
North Carolina	78	32	19	157	11	9	189	9	0	156	99	0
North Dakota	0	4	0	0	44	0	2	33	0	16	9	0
Ohio	146	186	39	123	264	0	163	238	0	187	272	0
Oklahoma	—	—	—	70	27	0	112	14	0	70	58	0
Oregon	7	13	2	2	44	0	22	41	0	74	28	0
Pennsylvania	158	300	38	83	522	17	255	291	0	266	236	0
Rhode Island	8	32	2	13	34	0	32	2	0	36	8	0
South Carolina	62	30	6	127	0	0	97	2	0	72	60	0
South Dakota	6	11	0	3	42	2	7	27	0	15	15	0
Tennessee	83	52	13	139	39	4	121	37	1	110	83	0
Texas	110	1	3	295	7	0	365	8	0	401	201	0
Utah	—	—	—	7	23	0	23	11	0	19	39	0
Vermont	0	42	5	0	36	0	1	16	0	2	12	8
Virginia	81	23	23	167	15	0	147	15	0	100	128	1
Washington	0	6	0	8	61	2	54	55	0	118	59	0
West Virginia	37	15	6	23	75	0	84	16	0	74	8	0
Wisconsin	40	94	9	18	176	4	46	105	21	104	93	0
Wyoming	1	2	0	1	17	0	3	14	0	4	18	0
Total	2,283	2,441	494	3,386	4,012	110	4,458	2,960	39	5,389	4,172	9

Note: Entries indicate the number of U.S. House seats won by the party in the state. "—" indicates that the state was not yet admitted to the Union. The period beginning in 1966 does not include special elections; candidates endorsed by both major and minor parties are counted as major-party candidates.

[a] When it could be determined, candidates who ran as both Republican and Democrat were classified by their usual party affiliation.

Sources: 1860–1964: *Congressional Quarterly's Guide to U.S. Elections*, 2nd ed. (Washington, D.C.: Congressional Quarterly, 1985), 1118–1119; 1966–2004: *Congressional Quarterly's Guide to U.S. Elections*, 5th ed. (Washington, D.C.: CQ Press, 2005), 1190, 1191, 1210, 1275, 1280, 1638–1641; 2006–2008: *CQ Weekly* (2006), 3076–3078, 3132, 3186, 3238, 3381; (2008), 3043–3052, 3102, 3206, 3293, 3374.

Table 1-12   Popular Vote and Seats in House Elections, by Party, 1896–2008

Year	Democratic candidates Percentage of all votes	Percentage of all seats	Republican candidates Percentage of all votes	Percentage of all seats	Difference between Democratic percentage of all seats and all votes[a]
1896	43.3	37.6	46.7	57.9	−5.6
1898	46.7	45.7	45.7	51.8	−1.0
1900	44.7	43.0	51.2	55.6	−1.7
1902	46.7	46.2	49.3	53.8	−0.5
1904	41.7	35.2	53.8	64.8	−6.5
1906	44.2	42.5	50.7	57.5	−1.7
1908	46.1	44.0	49.7	56.0	−2.1
1910	47.4	58.3	46.5	41.4	10.9
1912	45.3	66.7	34.0	29.2	21.3
1914	43.1	53.5	42.6	44.7	10.3
1916	46.3	48.3	48.4	49.7	2.0
1918	43.1	43.9	52.5	54.5	0.8
1920	35.8	30.5	58.6	69.3	−5.4
1922	44.7	47.6	51.7	51.7	2.8
1924	40.4	42.1	55.5	56.8	1.7
1926	40.5	44.8	57.0	54.5	4.3
1928	42.4	37.8	56.5	61.9	−4.5
1930	44.6	49.7	52.6	50.1	5.1
1932	54.5	72.0	41.4	26.9	17.4
1934	53.9	74.0	42.0	23.7	20.1
1936	55.8	76.6	39.6	20.5	20.7
1938	48.6	60.2	47.0	38.9	11.6
1940	51.3	61.4	45.6	37.2	10.1
1942	46.1	51.0	50.6	48.0	5.0
1944	50.6	55.9	47.2	43.7	5.3
1946	44.2	43.2	53.5	56.6	−1.0
1948	51.9	60.5	45.5	39.3	8.6
1950	49.0	53.8	49.0	45.7	4.7
1952	49.7	49.0	49.3	50.8	0.8
1954	52.5	53.3	47.0	46.7	0.8
1956	51.1	53.8	48.7	46.2	2.7
1958	56.3	64.8	43.5	35.2	8.5
1960	54.2	60.2	45.4	39.8	6.0
1962	52.3	59.3	47.4	40.5	7.0
1964	57.4	67.8	42.1	32.2	10.4
1966	50.9	57.0	48.2	43.0	6.1
1968	50.2	55.9	48.5	44.1	5.7
1970	53.4	58.6	45.1	41.4	5.2
1972	51.7	55.9	46.4	44.1	4.2
1974	57.6	66.9	40.6	33.1	9.9
1976	56.2	67.1	42.1	32.9	10.9
1978	53.4	63.7	44.7	36.3	10.3
1980	50.4	55.9	48.0	44.1	5.5
1982	55.6	61.8	42.9	38.2	6.2
1984	52.1	58.2	47.0	41.8	6.0

Table 1-12   *(Continued)*

Year	Democratic candidates		Republican candidates		*Difference between Democratic percentage of all seats and all votes*[a]
	Percentage of all votes	Percentage of all seats	Percentage of all votes	Percentage of all seats	
1986	54.5	59.3	44.6	40.7	4.8
1988	53.3	59.8	45.5	40.2	6.5
1990	52.9	61.4	45.0	38.4	8.5
1992	50.8	59.3	45.6	40.5	8.5
1994	45.4	46.7	52.4	53.1	1.2
1996	48.5	47.6	48.9	52.2	−1.0
1998	47.8	48.5	48.9	51.3	0.7
2000	47.4	48.7	48.7	50.8	1.3
2002	45.2	47.1	51.6	52.6	1.9
2004	47.4	46.4	50.1	53.3	−1.0
2006	52.8	53.6	44.9	46.4	0.7
2008	53.9	59.1	42.9	40.9	5.2

Note: In recent years, there has been "built-in" inaccuracy in that some states have chosen not to count votes in uncontested races or, in the case of Florida, to put uncontested races on the ballot.

[a] Calculated before rounding.

Sources: Votes, 1896–1970: U.S. Bureau of the Census, *Historical Statistics of the United States, Colonial Times to 1970* (Washington, D.C.: Government Printing Office, 1975), part 2, 1084; votes, 1972–1974: U.S. Bureau of the Census, *Statistical Abstract of the United States, 1976* (Washington, D.C.: Government Printing Office, 1976), 460; votes, 1976–1996: *Congressional Quarterly Weekly Report* (1977), 488; (1979), 571; (1981), 713; (1983), 387; (1985), 687; (1987), 484; (1989), 1063; (1991), 487; (1993), 965; (1995), 1079; (1997), 444; votes, 1998 and 2002: "The Rhodes Cook Letter," November 2002, 5; votes, 2000: calculated by the editors using unpublished data provided by Congressional Quarterly; votes, 2004: "The Rhodes Cook Letter," January 2005, 14; votes, 2006: "The Rhodes Cook Letter," December 2006, 16–17; votes, 2008: "The Rhodes Cook Letter," February 2009, 3 (*www.rhodescook.com*); seats: Table 1-10, this volume.

Table 1-13   Divided Government in the United States, by Congress, 1861–2011

Years	Congress	Unified/ divided	President (party)	Senate majority	House majority
1861–1863	37th	unified	Lincoln (R)	R	R
1863–1865	38th	unified	Lincoln (R)	R	R
1865–1867	39th	unified	Lincoln (R)	R	R
1867–1869	40th	unified	Grant (R)	R	R
1869–1871	41st	unified	Grant (R)	R	R
1871–1873	42nd	divided	Grant (R)	R	D
1873–1875	43rd	unified	Grant (R)	R	R
1875–1877	44th	divided	Grant (R)	R	D
1877–1879	45th	divided	Hayes (R)	R	D
1879–1881	46th	divided	Hayes (R)	D	D
1881–1883	47th	unified	Garfield (R)	even[a]	R
1883–1885	48th	divided	Arthur (R)	R	D
1885–1887	49th	divided	Cleveland (D)	R	D
1887–1889	50th	divided	Cleveland (D)	R	D
1889–1891	51st	unified	Harrison (R)	R	R
1891–1893	52nd	divided	Harrison (R)	R	D
1893–1895	53rd	unified	Cleveland (D)	D	D
1895–1897	54th	divided	Cleveland (D)	R	R
1897–1899	55th	unified	McKinley (R)	R	R
1899–1901	56th	unified	McKinley (R)	R	R
1901–1903	57th	unified	McKinley (R)	R	R
1903–1905	58th	unified	T. Roosevelt (R)	R	R
1905–1907	59th	unified	T. Roosevelt (R)	R	R
1907–1909	60th	unified	T. Roosevelt (R)	R	R
1909–1911	61st	unified	Taft (R)	R	R
1911–1913	62nd	divided	Taft (R)	R	D
1913–1915	63rd	unified	Wilson (D)	D	D
1915–1917	64th	unified	Wilson (D)	D	D
1917–1919	65th	divided	Wilson (D)	D	R
1919–1921	66th	divided	Wilson (D)	R	R
1921–1923	67th	unified	Harding (R)	R	R
1923–1925	68th	unified	Harding (R)	R	R
1925–1927	69th	unified	Coolidge (R)	R	R
1927–1929	70th	unified	Coolidge (R)	R	R
1929–1931	71st	unified	Hoover (R)	R	R
1931–1933	72nd	divided	Hoover (R)	R	D
1933–1935	73rd	unified	F. Roosevelt (D)	D	D
1935–1937	74th	unified	F. Roosevelt (D)	D	D
1937–1939	75th	unified	F. Roosevelt (D)	D	D
1939–1941	76th	unified	F. Roosevelt (D)	D	D
1941–1943	77th	unified	F. Roosevelt (D)	D	D
1943–1945	78th	unified	F. Roosevelt (D)	D	D
1945–1947	79th	unified	F. Roosevelt (D)	D	D
1947–1949	80th	divided	Truman (D)	R	R
1949–1951	81st	unified	Truman (D)	D	D
1951–1953	82nd	unified	Truman (D)	D	D
1953–1955	83rd	unified	Eisenhower (R)	R	R
1955–1957	84th	divided	Eisenhower (R)	D	D
1957–1959	85th	divided	Eisenhower (R)	D	D

Table 1-13   *(Continued)*

Years	Congress	Unified/ divided	President (party)	Senate majority	House majority
1959–1961	86th	divided	Eisenhower (R)	D	D
1961–1963	87th	unified	Kennedy (D)	D	D
1963–1965	88th	unified	Kennedy (D)	D	D
1965–1967	89th	unified	L. Johnson (D)	D	D
1967–1969	90th	unified	L. Johnson (D)	D	D
1969–1971	91st	divided	Nixon (R)	D	D
1971–1973	92nd	divided	Nixon (R)	D	D
1973–1975	93rd	divided	Nixon (R)	D	D
1975–1977	94th	divided	Ford (R)	D	D
1977–1979	95th	unified	Carter (D)	D	D
1979–1981	96th	unified	Carter (D)	D	D
1981–1983	97th	divided	Reagan (R)	R	D
1983–1985	98th	divided	Reagan (R)	R	D
1985–1987	99th	divided	Reagan (R)	R	D
1987–1989	100th	divided	Reagan (R)	D	D
1989–1991	101st	divided	G. H. W. Bush (R)	D	D
1991–1993	102nd	divided	G. H. W. Bush (R)	D	D
1993–1995	103rd	unified	Clinton (D)	D	D
1995–1997	104th	divided	Clinton (D)	R	R
1997–1999	105th	divided	Clinton (D)	R	R
1999–2001	106th	divided	Clinton (D)	R	R
2001–2003	107th	unified	G. W. Bush (R)	even[a]	R
2003–2005	108th	unified	G. W. Bush (R)	R	R
2005–2007	109th	unified	G. W. Bush (R)	R	R
2007–2009	110th	divided	G. W. Bush (R)	D	D
2009–2011	111th	unified	Obama (D)	D	D

	Summary[b]	
	Unified	Divided
1861–1896	9 (50%)	9
1897–1932	14 (78%)	4
1933–1966	13 (76%)	4
1967–2010	8 (36%)	14

Note: "R" indicates Republican; "D" indicates Democrat.

[a] Divided or unified government is as of the start of each Congress. In the Forty-seventh Congress (1881), the Senate was initially composed of thirty-seven Republicans and thirty-seven Democrats, one independent (David Davis of Illinois, who voted with the Democrats), and one variously described as an independent or a Readjuster (William Mahone of Virginia, who voted with the Republicans). Vice President Chester A. Arthur's deciding vote resulted in the Republicans organizing the Senate. In the 107th Congress, the Senate was composed of fifty Republicans and fifty Democrats. On January 20, the Republicans organized the Senate. When James M. Jeffords of Vermont switched to independent effective June 6 and caucused with the Democrats, control shifted to the Democrats. This is the only instance for the years indicated in which party control shifted in one chamber after the start of a Congress and led to a change in the organization of that chamber. See the source on party changes in the Eighty-third Congress.

[b] 1861–1896 covers the elections of 1860–1894; 1897–1932 covers the elections of 1896–1930; 1933–1966 covers the elections of 1932–1964; 1967–2010 covers the elections of 1966–2008.

Sources: Table 1-10, this volume. Information on party switching and party control in evenly divided Congresses is from "Party Division in the Senate, 1789–Present" (*www.senate.gov*).

Table 1-14   Split Presidential and House Election Outcomes in
Congressional Districts, 1900–2008

Year	Total number of districts[a]	Number of districts with split results[b]	Percentage of total
1900	295	10	3.4
1904	310	5	1.6
1908	314	21	6.7
1912	333	84	25.2
1916	333	35	10.5
1920	344	11	3.2
1924	356	42	11.8
1928	359	68	18.9
1932	355	50	14.1
1936	361	51	14.1
1940	362	53	14.6
1944	367	41	11.2
1948	422	90	21.3
1952	435	84	19.3
1956	435	130	29.9
1960	437	114	26.1
1964	435	145	33.3
1968	435	139	32.0
1972	435	192	44.1
1976	435	124	28.5
1980	435	143	32.8
1984	435	196	45.0
1988	435	148	34.0
1992	435	100	23.0
1996	435	111	25.5
2000	435	86	19.8
2004	435	59	13.6
2008	435	83	19.1

[a] For years 1900–1948, data on every congressional district are not available.
[b] Congressional districts carried by a presidential candidate of one party and a House candidate of another party.

Sources: Norman J. Ornstein, Thomas E. Mann, and Michael J. Malbin, eds., *Vital Statistics on Congress, 1993–1994* (Washington, D.C.: Congressional Quarterly, 1994), 64; *Congressional Quarterly Weekly Report (CQ Weekly)* (1997), 862; (2000), 1062; (2005), 879; (2009), 659.

Table 1-15   Mean Turnover in the House of Representatives from Various Causes, by Decade and Party System, 1789–2008

Period	Total turnover	Deaths	Retired[a]	Not renom- inated	General election defeat	Unknown[b]
1790s	0.379	0.017	0.164	0.002	0.027	0.170
1800s	0.361	0.018	0.154	0.001	0.032	0.157
1810s	0.488	0.025	0.181	0.008	0.065	0.209
1820s	0.401	0.018	0.142	0.002	0.079	0.159
1830s	0.483	0.029	0.175	0.006	0.117	0.156
1840s	0.594	0.030	0.253	0.009	0.098	0.205
1850s	0.580	0.018	0.252	0.015	0.140	0.154
1860s	0.492	0.025	0.237	0.026	0.119	0.086
1870s	0.482	0.020	0.220	0.035	0.147	0.060
1880s	0.442	0.023	0.189	0.045	0.130	0.056
1890s	0.394	0.026	0.170	0.043	0.126	0.028
1900s	0.276	0.028	0.114	0.033	0.086	0.015
1910s	0.290	0.029	0.112	0.028	0.114	0.006
1920s	0.223	0.035	0.076	0.026	0.085	0.000
1930s	0.283	0.039	0.084	0.047	0.114	0.000
1940s	0.245	0.025	0.084	0.032	0.104	0.000
1950s	0.168	0.025	0.073	0.014	0.056	0.000
1960s	0.166	0.016	0.073	0.021	0.057	0.000
1970s	0.190	0.010	0.112	0.014	0.053	0.000
1980s	0.120	0.010	0.069	0.007	0.033	0.000
1990s	0.167	0.007	0.106	0.013	0.042	0.000
2000s	0.126	0.007	0.077	0.009	0.033	0.000
Overall, 1789–2008	0.299	0.022	0.127	0.022	0.084	0.043
Grouped by party system						
First, 1789–1824	0.415	0.020	0.162	0.004	0.048	0.180
Second, 1825–1854	0.524	0.026	0.206	0.007	0.111	0.175
Third, 1855–1896	0.476	0.022	0.215	0.036	0.137	0.067
Fourth, 1897–1932	0.275	0.032	0.103	0.034	0.098	0.008
Fifth, 1933–1964	0.218	0.027	0.080	0.026	0.084	0.000
Sixth, 1965–2008	0.151	0.009	0.088	0.012	0.041	0.000

Note: Figures are proportions of the original House membership for each Congress failing to return to the following Congress, averaged across all Congresses within a decade (or a party system). Decades are defined by the first year of a Congress (for example, the 1980s spans 1981–1982 through 1989–1990); each decade mean is based on five Congresses, except for the 1790s (six) and the 2000s (four). Results reflect the final disposition of challenged elections. Data are current through January 2009.

[a] Includes retirements from public office, retirements to seek or accept other elective offices (including the Senate), retirements to accept federal executive branch appointments, resignations, and expulsions.
[b] "Unknown" are cases in which the member was not a candidate in the next general election, but it could not be determined whether he or she deliberately chose not to seek reelection or was denied renomination.

Sources: Revised from John W. Swain, Stephen A. Borrelli, Brian C. Reed, and Sean F. Evans, "A New Look at Turnover in the U.S. House of Representatives, 1789–1998," *American Politics Quarterly* 28 (2000): 435–457; other data supplied by the authors.

Table 1-16   House and Senate Seats That Changed Party, 1954–2008

Chamber/ year	Total changes	Incumbent defeated		Open seat	
		Democrat to Republican	Republican to Democrat	Democrat to Republican	Republican to Democrat
House					
1954	26	3	18	2	3
1956	20	7	7	2	4
1958	50	1	35	0	14
1960	37	23	2	6	6
1962	19	9	5	2	3
1964	57	5	39	5	8
1966	47	39	1	4	3
1968	11	5	0	2	4
1970	25	2	9	6	8
1972	23	6	3	9	5
1974	55	4	36	2	13
1976	22	7	5	3	7
1978	33	14	5	8	6
1980	41	27	3	10	1
1982	31	1	22	3	5
1984	22	13	3	5	1
1986	21	1	5	7	8
1988	9	2	4	1	2
1990	21	6	9	0	6
1992	43	16	8	11	8
1994	61	35	0	22	4
1996	35	3	18	10	4
1998	17	1	5	5	6
2000	18	2	4	6	6
2002	12	2	2	4	4
2004	10	3	2	2	3
2006	30	0	22	0	8
2008	31	5	14	0	12
Senate					
1954	8	2	4	1	1
1956	8	1	3	3	1
1958	13	0	11	0	2
1960	2	1	0	1	0
1962	8	2	3	0	3
1964	4	1	3	0	0
1966	3	1	0	2	0
1968	9	4	0	3	2
1970	6	3	2	1	0
1972	10	1	4	3	2
1974	6	0	2	1	3
1976	14	5	4	2	3
1978	13	5	2	3	3
1980	12	9	0	3	0
1982	4	1	1	1	1

Table 1-16   *(Continued)*

Chamber/ year	Total changes	Incumbent defeated		Open seat	
		Democrat to Republican	Republican to Democrat	Democrat to Republican	Republican to Democrat
1984	4	1	2	0	1
1986	10	0	7	1	2
1988	7	1	3	2	1
1990	1	0	1	0	0
1992	4	2	2	0	0
1994	8	2	0	6	0
1996	4	0	1	3	0
1998	6	1	2	2	1
2000	8	1	5	1	1
2002	4	2	1	1	0
2004	8	1	0	5	2
2006	6	0	6	0	0
2008	8[a]	0	5[a]	0	3

Note: This table reflects shifts in party control from before to after the November elections. It does not include shifts from the creation of districts or redistricting that result in incumbents from different districts running against each other in the same district.

[a] Reflects the win of the November 2008 Senate election in Minnesota by Democrat Al Franken. Incumbent Norm Coleman apparently lost the election by 225 votes, filed suit challenging the final tally, and conceded June 30, 2009, after an adverse Minnesota State Supreme Court decision.

Sources: 1954–1992: Norman J. Ornstein, Thomas E. Mann, and Michael J. Malbin, eds., *Vital Statistics on Congress, 1993–1994* (Washington, D.C.: Congressional Quarterly, 1994), 54, 56; 1994–2000: *Congressional Quarterly Weekly Report (CQ Weekly)* (1994), 3232–3233, 3240; (1996), 3228, 3238, 3402; (1998), 3004, 3010–3011; (2000), 2646–2647, 2652–2654; 2002: *2003 Congressional Staff Directory* (Washington, D.C.: CQ Press, 2003), 7, 215; 2004: *2005 Congressional Staff Directory* (Washington, D.C.: CQ Press, 2005), 7, 237; 2006: *CQ Weekly* (2006), 3066, 3068–3075, 3132, 3186, 3238, 3381; 2008: *CQ Weekly* (2008), 3043–3052, 3056, 3102, 3153, 3206, 3293, 3374; (2009), 216.

Table 1-17   Losses by President's Party in Midterm Elections, 1862–2006

Year	Party holding presidency	President's party: gain/loss of seats in House	President's party: gain/loss of seats in Senate
1862	R	−3	8
1866	R	−2	0
1870	R	−31	−4
1874	R	−96	−8
1878	R	−9	−6
1882	R	−33	3
1886	D	−12	3
1890	R	−85	0
1894	D	−116	−14
1898	R	−21	7
1902	R	9[a]	2
1906	R	−28	3
1910	R	−57	−10
1914	D	−59	5
1918	D	−19	−6
1922	R	−75	−8
1926	R	−10	−6
1930	R	−53	−8
1934	D	9	10
1938	D	−71	−6
1942	D	−45	−9
1946	D	−55	−12
1950	D	−29	−6
1954	R	−18	−1
1958	R	−47	−13
1962	D	−5	3
1966	D	−47	−4
1970	R	−12	3
1974	R	−48	−5
1978	D	−15	−3
1982	R	−26	1
1986	R	−5	−8
1990	R	−7	−1
1994	D	−54	−10
1998	D	4	0
2002	R	8	1
2006	R	−30	−6

Note: Each entry is the difference between the number of seats held by the president's party at the start of Congress after the midterm election and the number of seats held by that party at the start of Congress after the preceding general election. Special elections that shifted partisan seat totals between elections are not noted. Because of changes in the overall number of seats in the Senate and House, in the number of seats won by third parties, and in the number of vacancies, a Republican loss is not always matched precisely by a Democratic gain, or vice versa.

[a] Although the Republicans gained nine seats in the 1902 elections, they actually lost ground to the Democrats, who gained twenty-five seats after the increase in the overall number of representatives after the 1900 census.

Source: Table 1-10, this volume.

Table 1-18   House and Senate Incumbents Retired, Defeated, or Reelected, 1946–2008

| Chamber/ year | Retired[a] | Number seeking reelection | Defeated | | Reelected | |
			Primaries	General election	Total	Percentage of those seeking reelection
House						
1946	32	398	18	52	328	82.4
1948	29	400	15	68	317	79.3
1950	29	400	6	32	362	90.5
1952	42	389	9	26	354	91.0
1954	24	407	6	22	379	93.1
1956	21	411	6	16	389	94.6
1958	33	396	3	37	356	89.9
1960[b,c]	27	405	6	25	375	92.6
1962[d]	24	402	12	22	368	91.5
1964	33	397	8	45	344	86.6
1966	23	411	8	41	362	88.1
1968[e]	24	408	4	9	395	96.8
1970[c]	30	401	10	12	379	94.5
1972[c,f]	40	392	14	13	366	93.4
1974	43	391	8	40	343	87.7
1976	47	384	3	13	368	95.8
1978	49	382	5	19	358	93.7
1980[c]	34	398	6	31	361	90.7
1982	31	387	4	29	354	91.5
1984	22	411	3	16	392	95.4
1986	40	394	3	6	385	97.7
1988	23	409	1	6	402	98.3
1990	27	407	1	15	391	96.1
1992	65	368	19	24	325	88.3
1994[c]	48	387	4	34	349	90.2
1996	49	384	2	21	361	94.0
1998	33	402	1	6	395	98.3
2000	32	403	3	6	394	97.8
2002	35	398	8	8	382	96.0
2004	29	404	2	7	395	97.8
2006[g]	27	404	2	22	380	94.1
2008	32	403	4	19	380	94.3
Senate						
1946	9	30	6	7	17	56.7
1948	8	25	2	8	15	60.0
1950	4	32	5	5	22	68.8
1952	4	31	2	9	20	64.5
1954	6	32	2	6	24	75.0
1956	6	29	0	4	25	86.2
1958	6	28	0	10	18	64.3
1960	4	29	0	1	28	96.6
1962	4	35	1	5	29	82.9
1964	2	33	1	4	28	84.8
1966	3	32	3	1	28	87.5
1968[c]	6	28	4	4	20	71.4
1970	4	31	1	6	24	77.4

(Table continues)

Table 1-18   *(Continued)*

Chamber/ year	Retired [a]	Number seeking reelection	Defeated Primaries	Defeated General election	Reelected Total	Reelected Percentage of those seeking reelection
1972	6	27	2	5	20	74.1
1974	7	27	2	2	23	85.2
1976	8	25	0	9	16	64.0
1978	10	25	3	7	15	60.0
1980[c]	5	29	4	9	16	55.2
1982	3	30	0	2	28	93.3
1984	4	29	0	3	26	89.7
1986	6	28	0	7	21	75.0
1988	6	27	0	4	23	85.2
1990	3	32	0	1	31	96.9
1992	7	28	1	4	23	82.1
1994	8	26	0	2	24	92.2
1996	13	21	1	1	19	90.5
1998	5	29	0	3	26	89.7
2000	5	29	0	6	23	79.3
2002	6	28	1	3	24	85.7
2004	8	26	0	1	25	96.2
2006[h]	4	29	1	6	23	79.3
2008[i]	5	30	0	5	25	83.3

[a] Does not include persons who died or resigned from office before the election.

[b] Harold B. McSween, D-La., lost the Democratic primary in 1960 and is counted as an incumbent defeated in the primary. However, his victorious primary opponent, Earl K. Long, died after winning the primary, and McSween was appointed to replace Long in the general election by the Eighth District Democratic Committee. McSween won the general election and is counted as an incumbent winning the general election.

[c] In this year, an incumbent candidate lost the party primary and is counted as an incumbent defeated in the primary. The candidate then ran in the general election on a minor-party label or as a write-in candidate and lost again, but is not also counted (here or in Table 1-19) as an incumbent defeated in the general election. House: 1960, Ludwig Teller, D-N.Y.; 1970, Philip Philbin, D-Mass.; 1972, Emanuel Celler, D-N.Y.; 1980, John Buchanan, R-Ala.; 1994, David A. Levy, R-N.Y. Senate; 1968, Ernest Gruening, D-Alaska; 1980, Jacob K. Javits, R-N.Y.

[d] Clem Miller, D-Calif., was killed in a plane crash on October 7, 1962, but his name remained on the 1962 general election ballot. He won the election posthumously and is counted here as an incumbent winning the general election.

[e] Adam Clayton Powell, D-N.Y., won a special election on April 11, 1967, but he was prevented from taking the oath of office and did not take his seat in Congress. Therefore, he is not counted here (or in Table 1-19) as an incumbent in the 1968 general election.

[f] Bella Abzug, D-N.Y., lost the Democratic primary in 1972 and is counted as an incumbent defeated in the primary. However, her victorious primary opponent, William F. Ryan, died after winning the primary, and Abzug was appointed to replace him in the general election by the local party committee. Abzug won the general election and is counted as an incumbent winning the general election.

[g] In 2006 three representatives withdrew from the general election after winning their primaries: Tom DeLay, R-Texas; Mark Foley, R-Fla.; and Bob Ney, R-Ohio. Because they did not run in the general election, they are not counted as incumbents seeking reelection (here or in Table 1-19).

[h] Joseph I. Lieberman, D-Conn., lost the Democratic primary in 2006 and is counted as an incumbent defeated in the primary. He ran as an independent in the general election and won. He is counted as an incumbent winning the general election.

[i] Reflects the win of the November 2008 Senate election in Minnesota by Democrat Al Franken. Incumbent Norm Coleman apparently lost the election by 225 votes, filed suit challenging the final tally, and conceded June 30, 2009, after an adverse Minnesota State Supreme Court decision.

Source: Congressional Quarterly.

Table 1-19 Incumbent Reelection Rates: Representatives, Senators, and Governors, General Elections, 1960–2008

Year/office	Number of incumbents			Incumbents winning election[a]	Incumbents reelected with 60+ percent of the major-party vote[a]
	Ran	Won	Lost		
1960					
House[b,c]	400	375	25	93.5%	59.3%
Senate	29	28	1	96.6	44.8
Governor	14	8	6	57.1	14.3
1962					
House[d]	390	368	22	96.2	61.0[e]
Senate	34	29	5	85.3	32.4
Governor	26	15	11	57.7	7.7
1964					
House	389	344	45	88.4	58.1
Senate	32	28	4	87.5	46.9
Governor	14	12	2	85.7	50.0
1966					
House	403	362	41	90.0	67.0
Senate	29	28	1	96.6	44.8
Governor	22	15	7	68.2	22.7
1968					
House[f]	404	395	9	98.8	70.8
Senate[c]	24	20	4	83.3	45.8
Governor	14	10	4	71.4	21.4
1970					
House[c]	391	379	12	96.9	76.7
Senate	30	24	6	79.3	33.3
Governor	22	17	5	77.3	9.1
1972					
House[c,g]	379	366	13	96.6	76.3
Senate	25	20	5	80.0	48.0
Governor	9	7	2	77.8	44.4
1974					
House	383	343	40	89.6	66.6
Senate	25	23	2	92.0	44.0
Governor	21	16	5	76.2	42.9
1976					
House	381	368	13	96.6	72.7
Senate	25	16	9	64.0	44.0
Governor	7	5	2	71.4	28.6
1978					
House	377	358	19	95.0	75.3
Senate	22	15	7	68.2	31.8
Governor	20	15	5	75.0	30.0
1980					
House[c]	392	361	31	92.1	73.2
Senate[c]	25	16	9	64.0	38.5
Governor	10	7	3	70.0	40.0
1982					
House	383	354	29	92.4	69.9
Senate	30	28	2	93.3	46.7
Governor	24	19	5	79.2	45.8

(Table continues)

Table 1-19   *(Continued)*

	Number of incumbents			Incumbents winning election[a]	Incumbents reelected with 60+ percent of the major-party vote[a]
Year/office	Ran	Won	Lost		
1984					
House	408	392	16	96.1	77.2
Senate	29	26	3	89.7	65.5
Governor	6	4	2	66.7	50.0
1986					
House	391	385	6	98.5	84.4
Senate	28	21	7	75.0	50.0
Governor	17	15	2	88.2	52.9
1988					
House	408	402	6	98.5	87.0
Senate	27	23	4	85.2	55.6
Governor	9	8	1	88.9	33.3
1990					
House	406	391	15	96.3	74.9
Senate	32	31	1	96.9	62.5
Governor	23	17	6	73.9	47.8
1992					
House	349	325	24	93.1	65.6
Senate	27	23	4	85.2	48.1
Governor	4	4	0	100.0	100.0
1994					
House[c]	383	349	34	91.9	67.2
Senate	26	24	2	92.3	38.5
Governor	21	17	4	81.0	38.1
1996					
House	382	361	21	94.5	67.8
Senate	20	19	1	95.0	30.0
Governor	7	7	0	100.0	71.4
1998					
House	401	395	6	98.5	77.3
Senate	29	26	3	89.6	65.5
Governor	26	24	2	92.3	50.0
2000					
House	400	394	6	98.5	78.0
Senate	29	23	6	79.3	58.6
Governor	6	5	1	83.3	0.0
2002					
House	390	382	8	97.9	86.4
Senate	27	24	3	88.9	65.4
Governor	16	12	4	75.0	25.0
2004					
House	402	395	7	98.3	85.3
Senate	26	25	1	96.2	69.2
Governor	6	4	2	66.7	33.3
2006					
House[h]	402	380	22	94.5	75.1
Senate[i]	29	23	6	79.3	58.6
Governor	26	25	1	96.1	46.2

Table 1-19   *(Continued)*

Year/office	Number of incumbents			Incumbents winning election[a]	Incumbents reelected with 60+ percent of the major-party vote[a]
	Ran	Won	Lost		
2008					
House	399	380	19	95.2	76.4
Senate[j]	30	25	5	83.3	56.7
Governor	8	8	0	100.0	87.5

Note: Percentage gaining more than 60 percent of the vote (among incumbents who ran) is calculated on the basis of the vote for the two major parties. Incumbents running unopposed are considered to have won with over 60 percent of the major-party vote. "Off-off" year gubernatorial elections, held in Kentucky, Louisiana, Mississippi, New Jersey, and Virginia, are not included in the above totals. For these gubernatorial election outcomes, see *Congressional Quarterly's Guide to U.S. Elections*, 5th ed. (Washington, D.C.: CQ Press, 2005).

[a] Percentage is calculated based on all incumbents running in the general election.

[b] Harold B. McSween, D-La., lost the Democratic primary in 1960 and is counted as an incumbent defeated in the primary in Table 1-18. However, his victorious primary opponent, Earl K. Long, died after winning the primary, and McSween was appointed to replace Long in the general election by the Eighth District Democratic Committee. McSween won the general election and is counted as an incumbent winning the general election.

[c] In this year, an incumbent candidate lost the party primary and is counted as an incumbent defeated in the primary in Table 1-18. The candidate then ran in the general election on a minor-party label or as a write-in candidate and lost again, but is not also counted (here or in Table 1-18) as an incumbent defeated in the general election. House: 1960, Ludwig Teller, D-N.Y.; 1970, Philip Philbin, D-Mass.; 1972, Emanuel Celler, D-N.Y.; 1980, John Buchanan, R-Ala.; 1994, David A. Levy, R-N.Y. Senate; 1968, Ernest Gruening, D-Alaska; 1980, Jacob K. Javits, R-N.Y.

[d] Clem Miller, D-Calif., was killed in a plane crash on October 7, 1962, but his name remained on the 1962 general election ballot. He won the election posthumously and is counted here as an incumbent winning the general election.

[e] Data not available for Alabama. The percentage is calculated excluding the number of incumbents winning House seats in Alabama for this year.

[f] Adam Clayton Powell, D-N.Y., won a special election on April 11, 1967, but he was prevented from taking the oath of office and did not take his seat in Congress. Therefore, he is not counted here (or in Table 1-18) as an incumbent in the 1968 general election.

[g] Bella Abzug, D-N.Y., lost the Democratic primary in 1972 and is counted as an incumbent defeated in the primary in Table 1-18. However, her victorious primary opponent, William F. Ryan, died after winning the primary, and Abzug was appointed to replace him in the general election by the local party committee. Abzug won the general election and is counted as an incumbent winning the general election.

[h] In 2006 three representatives withdrew from the general election after winning their primaries: Tom DeLay, R-Texas; Mark Foley, R-Fla.; and Bob Ney, R-Ohio. Because they did not run in the general election, they are not counted as incumbents seeking reelection (here or in Table 1-18).

[i] Joseph I. Lieberman, D-Conn., lost the Democratic primary in 2006 and is counted as an incumbent defeated in the primary in Table 1-18. He ran as an independent in the general election and won. He is counted as an incumbent winning the general election.

[j] Reflects the win of the November 2008 Senate election in Minnesota by Democrat Al Franken. Incumbent Norm Coleman apparently lost the election by 225 votes, filed suit challenging the final tally, and conceded June 30, 2009, after an adverse Minnesota State Supreme Court decision.

Source: Congressional Quarterly.

Table 1-20 Congressional Districts with a Racial or Ethnic Minority Representative or a "Majority-Minority" Population, 2009

| State | District number | Non-Hispanic (percent) Single race | | | | Two or more races | Hispanic (percent) | Representative elected in 2008 | Party | Representative's race/ethnicity |
		White	Black	Asian	Other					
Racial or ethnic minority representatives in congressional districts without a majority-minority population										
Colorado	3	74.6	0.7	0.5	1.6	1.2	21.5	Salazar, John T.	D	Hispanic
Indiana	7	63.0	29.4	1.3	0.5	1.5	4.4	Carson	D	Black
Minnesota	5	71.2	12.8	5.1	1.8	3.0	6.0	Ellison	D	Black
Missouri	5	66.3	24.2	1.3	0.7	1.9	5.6	Cleaver	D	Black
Ohio	7	88.7	7.5	1.0	0.4	1.3	1.1	Austria	R	Asian
Oklahoma	4	77.6	6.6	1.7	5.7	3.6	4.8	Cole	R	American Indian
Oregon	1	81.1	1.1	5.0	1.1	2.3	9.4	Wu	D	Asian
Wisconsin	4	50.4	33.0	2.7	0.9	1.8	11.2	Moore	D	Black
Congressional districts with a majority-minority population										
Alabama	7	35.5	61.7	0.6	0.2	0.6	1.3	Davis, Artur	D	Black
Arizona	4	29.3	7.5	1.3	2.6	1.5	58.0	Pastor	D	Hispanic
Arizona	7	38.6	2.8	1.3	5.5	1.3	50.6	Grijalva	D	Hispanic
California	5	43.4	14.4	14.9	1.9	4.7	20.8	Matsui	D	Asian
California	7	43.2	16.8	13.3	1.3	3.9	21.4	Miller, George	D	White
California	8	42.9	8.6	28.7	1.1	2.9	15.7	Pelosi	D	White
California	9	35.2	26.0	15.4	1.1	3.6	18.7	Lee	D	Black
California	12	48.2	2.5	28.5	1.4	3.6	15.7	Speier	D	White
California	13	38.4	6.3	28.2	1.5	4.5	21.1	Stark	D	White
California	15	47.1	2.4	29.2	0.8	3.2	17.2	Honda	D	Asian
California	16	31.9	3.4	23.4	0.9	2.8	37.6	Lofgren	D	White
California	17	46.3	2.6	4.8	1.0	2.5	42.9	Farr	D	White

State	District							Name	Party	Race
California	18	39.1	5.6	8.9	1.2	3.2	41.9	Cardoza	D	White
California	20	21.4	7.2	5.6	1.0	1.7	63.1	Costa	D	White
California	21	46.4	2.1	4.9	1.1	2.2	43.4	Nunes	R	White
California	23	48.7	1.9	4.9	0.8	2.0	41.7	Capps	D	White
California	27	44.9	4.5	10.5	0.6	3.1	36.5	Sherman	D	White
California	28	31.4	4.1	5.9	0.5	2.4	55.6	Berman	D	White
California	29	39.1	5.9	23.7	0.5	4.7	26.1	Schiff	D	White
California	31	9.8	4.2	13.8	0.5	1.5	70.2	Becerra	D	Hispanic
California	32	14.8	2.6	18.4	0.5	1.4	62.3	Solis	D	Hispanic
California	33	19.9	29.9	12.1	0.7	2.8	34.6	Watson	D	Black
California	34	11.4	4.4	5.5	0.6	0.9	77.2	Roybal-Allard	D	Hispanic
California	35	10.4	34.1	5.6	0.8	1.8	47.4	Waters	D	Black
California	36	48.4	4.1	13.4	1.0	2.9	30.3	Harman	D	White
California	37	16.6	24.8	11.1	1.9	2.4	43.2	Richardson	D	Black
California	38	13.6	3.6	10.2	0.6	1.4	70.6	Napolitano	D	Hispanic
California	39	21.0	6.1	9.5	0.7	1.5	61.2	Sanchez, Linda	D	Hispanic
California	40	49.3	2.2	15.6	0.9	2.4	29.6	Royce	R	White
California	43	23.4	12.4	3.1	0.9	1.9	58.3	Baca	D	Hispanic
California	47	17.3	1.5	13.9	0.7	1.3	65.3	Sanchez, Loretta	D	Hispanic
California	51	21.3	9.4	12.4	1.2	2.4	53.3	Filner	D	White
Florida	3	38.4	49.3	1.6	0.6	2.1	8.0	Brown, Corinne	D	Black
Florida	11	48.3	27.4	2.0	0.6	1.7	20.0	Castor	D	White
Florida	17	18.4	55.2	1.5	0.5	3.1	21.2	Meek, Kendrick	D	Black
Florida	18	29.7	5.7	0.9	0.3	0.7	62.7	Ros-Lehtinen	R	Hispanic
Florida	21	21.0	6.5	1.8	0.2	0.8	69.7	Diaz-Balart, Lincoln	R	Hispanic
Florida	23	29.4	51.2	1.2	0.6	3.9	13.7	Hastings	D	Black
Florida	25	24.3	10.0	1.6	0.4	1.4	62.4	Diaz-Balart, Mario	R	Hispanic
Georgia	2	47.7	47.5	0.5	0.4	0.8	3.0	Bishop, Sanford	D	Black
Georgia	4	29.6	52.6	4.9	0.5	1.7	10.7	Johnson, Hank	D	Black
Georgia	5	34.4	55.7	2.2	0.3	1.1	6.2	Lewis, John	D	Black
Georgia	13	46.7	41.0	2.8	0.5	1.4	7.6	Scott, David	D	Black
Hawaii	1	17.7	1.9	53.6	6.9	14.4	5.4	Abercrombie	D	White
Hawaii	2	28.0	1.5	28.0	11.8	21.7	9.0	Hirono	D	Asian

(Table continues)

Table 1-20 (Continued)

| State | District number | Non-Hispanic (percent) | | | | Two or more races | Hispanic (percent) | Representative elected in 2008 | Party | Representative's race/ethnicity |
| | | Single race | | | | | | | | |
		White	Black	Asian	Other					
Illinois	1	27.3	65.2	1.4	0.2	1.0	4.8	Rush	D	Black
Illinois	2	25.6	62.0	0.6	0.2	1.2	10.4	Jackson	D	Black
Illinois	4	18.4	3.7	1.7	0.3	1.4	74.5	Gutierrez	D	Hispanic
Illinois	7	27.3	61.6	3.8	0.3	1.2	5.8	Davis, Danny K.	D	Black
Louisiana	2	28.3	63.7	2.7	0.5	1.0	3.8	Cao	D	Asian
Maryland	4	27.6	56.8	5.6	0.5	2.0	7.5	Edwards	D	Black
Maryland	7	34.2	58.8	3.5	0.4	1.3	1.7	Cummings	D	Black
Massachusetts	8	48.9	21.9	8.1	1.8	3.5	15.9	Capuano	D	White
Michigan	13	28.9	60.5	1.2	0.5	1.8	7.2	Kilpatrick	D	Black
Michigan	14	32.1	61.1	1.2	0.5	3.3	1.8	Conyers	D	Black
Mississippi	2	34.5	63.2	0.4	0.2	0.5	1.2	Thompson, Bennie G.	D	Black
Missouri	1	45.8	49.7	1.5	0.3	1.3	1.3	Clay	D	Black
New Jersey	10	21.4	56.6	3.6	0.7	2.8	15.0	Payne	D	Black
New Jersey	13	32.3	11.3	5.5	0.8	2.4	47.6	Sires	D	Hispanic
New Mexico	1	48.5	2.3	1.7	3.1	1.6	42.6	Heinrich	D	White
New Mexico	2	44.3	1.6	0.5	5.1	1.2	47.3	Teague	D	White
New Mexico	3	41.4	1.1	0.7	19.1	1.4	36.3	Luján	D	Hispanic
New York	5	44.2	5.1	24.5	0.5	2.1	23.5	Ackerman	D	White
New York	6	12.8	52.1	8.9	3.2	6.1	16.9	Meeks	D	Black
New York	7	27.6	16.5	12.8	0.9	2.7	39.5	Crowley	D	White
New York	10	16.2	60.2	2.7	1.2	2.6	17.2	Towns	D	Black
New York	11	21.4	58.5	4.1	0.8	3.0	12.1	Clarke	D	Black
New York	12	23.3	8.8	15.9	1.0	2.5	48.5	Velázquez	D	Hispanic
New York	15	16.4	30.5	2.8	0.7	1.8	47.9	Rangel	D	Black

State	District							Representative	Party	Race
New York	16	2.9	30.3	1.6	0.9	1.6	62.8	Serrano	D	Hispanic
New York	17	41.3	30.4	4.5	0.7	2.6	20.4	Engel	D	White
North Carolina	1	44.4	50.5	0.5	0.8	0.8	3.1	Butterfield	D	Black
North Carolina	12	44.6	44.6	2.1	0.5	1.1	7.1	Watt	D	Black
Ohio	11	38.8	55.5	1.6	0.3	1.4	2.3	Fudge	D	Black
Pennsylvania	1	33.1	44.9	4.8	0.4	1.8	15.0	Brady	D	White
Pennsylvania	2	29.9	60.7	4.3	0.4	1.7	3.0	Fattah	D	Black
South Carolina	6	40.3	56.7	0.5	0.4	0.7	1.5	Clyburn	D	Black
Tennessee	9	34.9	59.5	1.5	0.3	0.9	3.0	Cohen	D	White
Texas	9	17.4	37.0	10.7	0.4	1.7	32.8	Green, Al	D	Black
Texas	15	19.7	1.7	0.5	0.2	0.3	77.6	Hinojosa	D	Hispanic
Texas	16	17.4	2.9	0.9	0.4	0.7	77.7	Reyes	D	Hispanic
Texas	18	19.7	40.1	3.3	0.3	1.0	35.6	Jackson-Lee	D	Black
Texas	20	23.4	6.6	1.4	0.4	1.1	67.1	Gonzalez	D	Hispanic
Texas	23	30.0	2.8	0.9	0.4	0.7	65.1	Rodriguez	D	Hispanic
Texas	27	27.6	2.5	0.8	0.3	0.7	68.1	Ortiz	D	Hispanic
Texas	28	20.3	1.1	0.4	0.2	0.4	77.5	Cuellar	D	Hispanic
Texas	29	21.9	9.7	1.3	0.3	0.7	66.1	Green, Gene	D	White
Texas	30	21.9	41.4	1.3	0.4	0.9	34.2	Johnson, Eddie Bernice	D	Black
Virginia	3	37.7	56.0	1.4	0.7	1.6	2.6	Scott, Robert C.	D	Black

Note: "D" indicates Democratic; "R" indicates Republican. Majority-minority districts are those in which the non-Hispanic white population does not constitute a majority of the total population. Population values are based on the 2000 census. The six population categories sum to 100 percent. Non-Hispanic white, non-Hispanic black, and non-Hispanic other are single-race counts, indicating persons who considered themselves only one race, not two or more races. The percentage for all non-Hispanics who considered themselves to be of two or more races is indicated separately. Data for earlier years can be found in previous editions of *Vital Statistics on American Politics.*

Sources: U.S. Census Bureau, "110th Congressional District Summary Files" (*www.census.gov*); *CQ Weekly* (2006), 3008; (2008), 2998, 3043–3052, 3374.

Table 1-21   Latino Elected Officials in the United States, 1996–2007

	1996	2000	2005	2007
Members of Congress	17	19	25	26
State officials	6	8	9	6
State legislators	156	190	232	238
County officials	358	398	498	512
Municipal officials	1,295	1,469	1,651	1,640
Judicial and law enforcement	546	465	678	685
School board members	1,240	1,392	1,760	1,847
Special district officials	125	119	188	175
Total	3,743	4,060	5,041	5,129

Note: After the 2008 election, there were 27 Latino members of Congress and 243 state legislators.

Source: National Association of Latino Elected Officials, *2007 National Directory of Latino Elected Officials (www.naleo.org)*.

Table 1-22 Blacks, Hispanics, and Women as a Percentage of State Legislators and State Voting-Age Population

State	Total number of legislators	Blacks				Hispanics				Women			
		Legislators	Percentage	Percentage VAP	Ratio[a]	Legislators	Percentage	Percentage VAP	Ratio[a]	Legislators	Percentage	Percentage VAP	Ratio[a]
Alabama	140	34	24.3	25.8	0.941	0	0.0	2.1	0.000	18	12.9	51.9	0.249
Alaska	60	1	1.7	3.8	0.449	0	0.0	3.7	0.000	12	20.0	49.2	0.406
Arizona	90	1	1.1	4.0	0.274	14	15.6	31.5	0.496	27	30.0	50.3	0.597
Arkansas	135	15	11.1	15.7	0.708	0	0.0	4.1	0.000	32	23.7	51.2	0.463
California	120	9	7.5	6.5	1.151	27	22.5	37.4	0.602	33	27.5	50.4	0.546
Colorado	100	3	3.0	4.0	0.741	3	3.0	18.4	0.163	39	39.0	50.0	0.780
Connecticut	187	13	7.0	10.2	0.684	8	4.3	11.5	0.375	59	31.6	51.4	0.615
Delaware	62	5	8.1	20.9	0.387	1	1.6	7.0	0.228	15	24.2	51.9	0.467
Florida	160	23	14.4	15.8	0.913	15	9.4	20.9	0.450	38	23.8	51.2	0.465
Georgia	236	55	23.3	29.9	0.778	3	1.3	8.4	0.155	45	19.1	51.4	0.372
Hawaii	76	0	0.0	2.5	0.000	0	0.0	6.3	0.000	25	32.9	50.7	0.649
Idaho	105	0	0.0	0.9	0.000	1	1.0	12.9	0.078	26	24.8	50.0	0.496
Illinois	177	28	15.8	14.8	1.070	12	6.8	14.0	0.484	48	27.1	50.9	0.533
Indiana	150	12	8.0	8.9	0.903	1	0.7	5.0	0.141	33	22.0	50.8	0.433
Iowa	150	4	2.7	2.6	1.045	0	0.0	5.9	0.000	34	22.7	50.6	0.449
Kansas	165	7	4.2	5.9	0.718	4	2.4	8.6	0.278	48	29.1	50.7	0.574
Kentucky	138	7	5.1	7.5	0.678	0	0.0	1.8	0.000	21	15.2	51.4	0.296
Louisiana	144	29	20.1	31.6	0.636	0	0.0	3.8	0.000	22	15.3	51.9	0.295
Maine	186	0	0.0	1.0	0.000	0	0.0	2.1	0.000	54	29.0	51.3	0.565
Maryland	188	42	22.3	29.2	0.763	4	2.1	7.0	0.300	59	31.4	52.0	0.604
Massachusetts	200	7	3.5	6.8	0.512	5	2.5	7.1	0.350	52	26.0	51.5	0.505
Michigan	148	19	12.8	14.1	0.908	3	2.0	3.2	0.625	37	25.0	51.0	0.490
Minnesota	201	1	0.5	4.5	0.111	2	1.0	4.2	0.241	70	34.8	50.2	0.693
Mississippi	174	50	28.7	36.9	0.779	0	0.0	2.3	0.000	25	14.4	52.0	0.277
Missouri	197	18	9.1	11.3	0.809	1	0.5	3.0	0.169	41	20.8	51.4	0.405
Montana	150	0	0.0	0.6	0.000	1	0.7	2.7	0.261	39	26.0	50.1	0.519
Nebraska	49	1	2.0	4.3	0.466	0	0.0	7.2	0.000	10	20.4	50.5	0.404
Nevada	63	7	11.1	8.0	1.391	5	7.9	23.6	0.334	20	31.7	49.4	0.642
New Hampshire	424	6	1.4	1.2	1.153	1	0.2	2.0	0.101	160	37.7	50.7	0.744
New Jersey	120	15	12.5	14.2	0.882	8	6.7	17.0	0.394	35	29.2	51.2	0.570

(Table continues)

Table 1-22 (*Continued*)

State	Total number of legislators	Blacks Legislators	Blacks Percentage	Blacks Percentage VAP	Blacks Ratio[a]	Hispanics Legislators	Hispanics Percentage	Hispanics Percentage VAP	Hispanics Ratio[a]	Women Legislators	Women Percentage	Women Percentage VAP	Women Ratio[a]
New Mexico	112	2	1.8	2.8	0.642	48	42.9	47.1	0.911	34	30.4	51.1	0.595
New York	212	33	15.6	17.2	0.906	18	8.5	15.6	0.544	52	24.5	51.6	0.475
North Carolina	170	27	15.9	21.4	0.741	2	1.2	6.6	0.182	43	25.3	51.7	0.490
North Dakota	141	0	0.0	1.0	0.000	0	0.0	1.7	0.000	22	15.6	50.1	0.311
Ohio	132	17	12.9	11.9	1.085	0	0.0	3.1	0.000	27	20.5	51.3	0.399
Oklahoma	149	6	4.9	7.7	0.635	1	0.7	7.9	0.089	17	11.4	51.1	0.223
Oregon	90	3	3.3	2.0	1.661	1	1.1	10.7	0.103	25	27.8	50.6	0.550
Pennsylvania	253	20	7.9	10.6	0.744	1	0.4	4.7	0.085	37	14.6	51.5	0.284
Rhode Island	113	4	3.5	6.4	0.550	3	2.7	11.2	0.240	25	22.1	51.7	0.428
South Carolina	170	36	21.2	27.9	0.761	0	0.0	4.0	0.000	17	10.0	51.9	0.193
South Dakota	105	0	0.0	1.1	0.000	0	0.0	2.2	0.000	20	19.0	50.4	0.377
Tennessee	132	19	14.4	16.3	0.883	1	0.8	4.6	0.175	24	18.2	51.5	0.354
Texas	181	16	8.8	11.7	0.750	37	20.4	39.8	0.513	43	23.8	50.5	0.471
Utah	104	0	0.0	1.2	0.000	4	3.8	9.1	0.419	23	22.1	49.6	0.446
Vermont	180	0	0.0	0.9	0.000	0	0.0	1.4	0.000	67	37.2	50.7	0.733
Virginia	140	16	11.4	19.5	0.585	1	0.7	6.5	0.108	24	17.1	51.6	0.331
Washington	147	2	1.4	3.6	0.391	3	2.0	9.4	0.212	47	32.0	50.5	0.634
West Virginia	134	2	1.5	3.4	0.442	0	0.0	1.1	0.000	22	16.4	51.1	0.321
Wisconsin	132	8	6.1	5.8	1.045	1	0.8	7.3	0.110	29	22.0	50.5	0.436
Wyoming	90	0	0.0	1.2	0.000	2	2.2	6.1	0.363	16	17.8	49.5	0.360
United States	7,382	623	8.4	12.6	0.664	242	3.3	15.6	0.211	1,791	24.3	51.0	0.476

Note: Hispanics may be of any race. The black voting-age population (VAP) figures are for the black-alone racial category. The counts of black legislators are as of January 2008; of Hispanic legislators as of November 2008 (postelection); of female legislators as of January 2009.

[a] The ratio between the group's indicated percentage of state legislators and the group's percentage of the state voting-age population. Calculated before rounding.

Sources: Total number of legislators and women legislators: Center for American Women and Politics, "Women in State Legislatures 2009" (*www.cawp.rutgers.edu*); black legislators: unpublished data from the Joint Center for Political and Economic Studies, Black Elected Officials Roster (*www.jointcenter.org*); Hispanic legislators: National Association of Latino Elected and Appointed Officials, "Latinos Achieve New Political Milestones in Congress and State Houses" (*www.naleo.org*); voting-age population percentages calculated by the editors from U.S. Census Bureau, "Current Population Reports, Voting and Registration in the Election of November 2008" (*www.census.gov*).

Table 1-23   Presidential Primaries, 1912–2008

Year	*Democratic Party* Number of primaries	Votes cast	Percentage of delegates selected through primaries	*Republican Party* Number of primaries	Votes cast	Percentage of delegates selected through primaries
1912	12	974,775	32.9	13	2,261,240	41.7
1916	20	1,187,691	53.5	20	1,923,374	58.9
1920	16	571,671	44.6	20	3,186,248	57.8
1924	14	763,858	35.5	17	3,525,185	45.3
1928	16	1,264,220	42.2	15	4,110,288	44.9
1932	16	2,952,933	40.0	14	2,346,996	37.7
1936	14	5,181,808	36.5	12	3,319,810	37.5
1940	13	4,468,631	35.8	13	3,227,875	38.8
1944	14	1,867,609	36.7	13	2,271,605	38.7
1948	14	2,151,865	36.3	12	2,653,255	36.0
1952	16	4,928,006	38.7	13	7,801,413	39.0
1956	19	5,832,592	42.7	19	5,828,272	44.8
1960	16	5,687,742	38.3	15	5,537,967	38.6
1964	16	6,247,435	45.7	16	5,935,339	45.6
1968	15	7,535,069	40.2	15	4,473,551	38.1
1972	21	15,993,965	65.3	20	6,188,281	56.8
1976	27	16,052,652	76.0	26	10,374,125	71.0
1980	34	18,747,825	71.8	34	12,690,451	76.0
1984	29	18,009,217	52.4	25	6,575,651	71.0
1988	36	22,961,936	66.6	36	12,165,115	76.9
1992	39	20,239,385	66.9	38	12,696,547	83.9
1996	35	10,996,395	65.3	42	14,233,939	84.6
2000	40	14,045,745	64.6	43	17,156,117	83.8
2004	40	16,535,823	67.5	26[a]	8,008,070	55.5
2008	39	33,668,508	67.4	42	20,836,547	82.2

Note: Only those primaries in which pledged delegates are selected by the primary results are included in the counts.

[a]Republican presidential primaries in five states—Connecticut, Florida, Mississippi, New York, and South Dakota—with 309 delegates were cancelled because only George W. Bush qualified for the primary. Consequently, these five states are not included in the primary count, and the delegates from these states (12.3 percent of the total) are not included in the percentage of delegates selected through primaries.

Sources: 1912–2004: *Congressional Quarterly's Guide to U.S. Elections,* 5th ed. (Washington, D.C.: CQ Press, 2005), 318; 2008: derived by the editors from "The Rhodes Cook Letter," June 2008, 10–14 (*www.rhodescook.com*); and Rhodes Cook, *Race for the Presidency: Winning the 2008 Nomination* (Washington, D.C.: CQ Press, 2008), viii–x.

Table 1-24 State Methods for Choosing National Convention Delegates, 1968–2008

State	1968	1972	1976	1980	1984	1988	1992	1996	2000	2004	2008
Alabama	DP	↓	OP	↓	↓	↓	↓	↓	↓	↓	↓
Alaska	CL	↓	↓	↓	↓	↓	↓	↓	↓	↓	↓
Arizona	(D)CS (R)CL	CL	↓	↓	↓	↓	↓	(D)CL (R)P	P	(D)P (R)CL	P
Arkansas	CS	CL	OP	(D)OP (R)CL	CL	OP	↓	↓	↓	↓	↓
California	P	↓	↓	↓	↓	↓	↓	↓	↓	(D)PI (R)P	↓
Colorado	CL	↓	↓	↓	↓	↓	OP	↓	↓	CL	↓
Connecticut	CL	↓	↓	P	(D)P (R)CL	P	↓	↓	↓	↓	↓
Delaware	CL	↓	↓	↓	↓	↓	↓	(D)CL (R)P	(D)X (R)CL	(D)P (R)CL	P
District of Columbia	P	↓	↓	↓	↓	↓	↓	↓	↓	(D)X (R)CL	P
Florida	P	↓	↓	↓	↓	↓	↓	↓	↓	↓	↓
Georgia	(D)CS (R)CL	CL	OP	↓	↓	↓	↓	↓	↓	↓	↓
Hawaii	CL	↓	↓	↓	↓	↓	↓	↓	↓	↓	↓
Idaho	CL	↓	OP	(D)CL (R)OP	(D)PI (R)OP	(D)X (R)OP	↓	↓	(D)X (R)OP,CS	(D)CL (R)OP	OP
Illinois	DP,CL	P	OP	↓	DP	↓	↓	↓	(D)OP (R)DP,CS	(D)OP (R)DP	(D)OP (R)DP

State											
Indiana	OP	↓	↓	↓	↓	↓	↓	↓	(D)OP (R)OP,CS	OP	OP
Iowa	CL	↓	↓	↓	↓	↓	PI	↓	↓	↓	↓
Kansas	CL	↓	↓	PI	CL	P	↓	↓	↓	CL	↓
Kentucky	CL	↓	P	↓	CL	↓	↓	P	↓	↓	↓
Louisiana	CS	CL	↓	P	↓	↓	↓	(D)P (R)CL	P	↓	↓
Maine	CL	↓	↓	↓	↓	↓	↓	PI	↓	CL	↓
Maryland	(D)CS (R)CL	P	↓	↓	DP	P	↓	↓	(D)P (R)PI	(D)P (R)PI	P
Massachusetts	PI	↓	↓	↓	CL	(D)CL (R)X	P	↓	↓	↓	↓
Michigan	CL	OP	↓	(D)CL (R)OP	CL	↓	↓	(D)CL (R)OP	↓	(D)PI (R)CL	P
Minnesota	CL	↓	↓	↓	CL	↓	↓	↓	↓	↓	↓
Mississippi	CL	↓	↓	(D)CL (R)DP	CL	OP	↓	↓	↓	↓	↓
Missouri	(D)CL,CS (R)CL	CL	↓	↓	↓	OP	CL	↓	OP	↓	↓
Montana	CL	↓	OP	↓	DP	(D)OP (R)X	↓	↓	↓	↓	↓
Nebraska	OP	↓	↓	↓	P	↓	↓	PI	(D)P (R)X	↓	CL,X
Nevada	CL	↓	P	↓	CL	↓	↓	(D)CL (R)P	CL	↓	↓
New Hampshire	PI	↓	↓	↓	↓	↓	↓	↓	↓	↓	↓
New Jersey	PI	↓	↓	↓	DP	↓	↓	(D)PI (R)DP	↓	↓	PI

(Table continues)

Table 1-24 (*Continued*)

State	1968	1972	1976	1980	1984	1988	1992	1996	2000	2004	2008
New Mexico	CL	P	CL	P	↓	↓	↓	↓	↓	(D)CL (R)P	↓
New York	DP,CS	↓	DP	(D)P (R)DP,CS	(D)DP (R)DP,CS	↓	↓	↓	(D)P (R)DP,CS	P	↓
North Carolina	CL	P	↓	↓	↓	↓	(D)P (R)OP	(D)P (R)PI	PI	CL	PI
North Dakota	CL	↓	↓	↓	DP	(D)X (R)OP	↓	↓	CS	CL	↓
Ohio	OP	↓	↓	↓	PI	↓	↓	↓	OP	↓	↓
Oklahoma	CL	↓	↓	↓	↓	P	↓	↓	↓	↓	↓
Oregon	P	↓	↓	↓	↓	↓	↓	↓	↓	↓	↓
Pennsylvania	P,CS	P	↓	↓	DP	↓	↓	↓	(D)P (R)DP,CS		↓
Rhode Island	(D)CS (R)CL	PI	↓	↓	↓	↓	↓	↓	↓	↓	↓
South Carolina	CL	↓	(D)CL (R)OP	↓	↓	↓	OP	(D)CL (R)OP	OP	(D)OP (R)CL	OP
South Dakota	P	↓	↓	↓	↓	↓	↓	↓	↓	↓	↓
Tennessee	CL	OP	↓	↓	↓	↓	↓	↓	↓	↓	↓
Texas	CL	↓	OP	P	(D)CL (R)OP	OP	↓	↓	(D)OP,CS (R)OP	↓	↓
Utah	CL	↓	↓	↓	↓	↓	↓	↓	PI	(D)PI (R)CL	OP
Vermont	CL	↓	X	↓	↓	↓	↓	OP	↓	↓	↓

Virginia	CL	←	←	←	←	←	(D)OP (R)X	CL	←	(D)OP (R)CL	(D)CL (R)OP	OP
Washington	(D)CL,CS (R)CL	←	(D)CL (R)P	←	CL	←	←	CL	P	(D)CL (R)OP,CL	(D)X (R)P,CL	(D)CL (R)OP
West Virginia	P	←	←	←	←	←	←	(D)P (R)PI	←	(D)P (R)DP	←	(D)PI (R)PI,CS
Wisconsin	OP	←	(D)X (R)OP	(D)PI (R)OP	OP	←	←	OP	(D)P (R)PI	←	←	←
Wyoming	CL	←	←	←	←	←	←	←	←	←	←	←
(Puerto Rico)	(D)CL	CL	(D)PI (R)CL	(D)PI (R)OP	PI	OP	←	←	←	←	(D)CL (R)OP	←

Note: "←" indicates method same as in previous presidential election; "CL" indicates delegates chosen by state and local caucuses and conventions; "CS" indicates delegates chosen by state party committee; "(D)" indicates Democrats; "DP" indicates delegates chosen directly by voters in primaries with nonbinding presidential preference poll; "OP" indicates delegates chosen or bound by presidential preference primaries open to all registered voters with no regard for party preregistration (or voters can switch party affiliation at the polls on primary day); "P" indicates delegates chosen or bound by presidential preference primaries open only to voters pre-registered as members of the particular parties; "PI" indicates delegates chosen or bound by presidential preference primaries open only to voters preregistered as members of the particular parties or as independents; "(R)" indicates Republicans; "X" indicates having nonbinding presidential preference primaries, but delegates are chosen by party caucus and conventions. States with primaries but without voter registration by party are coded "OP."

Sources: 1968–1984: Austin Ranney, ed., *The American Elections of 1984* (Durham, N.C.: Duke University Press, 1985), 330–332 (copyright © American Enterprise Institute for Public Policy Research, reprinted by permission); 1988: derived by the editors from Kevin Coleman, "A Summary of National and State Party Rules and State Laws Concerning the Election of Delegates to the 1988 Democratic and Republican National Conventions," Report no. 88–102 GOV, Congressional Research Service, Washington, D.C., 1988; 1992: derived by the editors from Congressional Quarterly, *The First Hurrah: A 1992 Guide to the Nomination of the President* (Washington, D.C.: Congressional Quarterly, 1991); *Congressional Quarterly Weekly Report* (1991), 3478; and Thomas M. Durbin and L. Paige Whitaker, *Nomination and Election of the President and Vice President of the United States, 1992: Including the Manner of Selecting Delegates to National Party Conventions* (Washington, D.C.: Government Printing Office, 1992); 1996: derived by the editors from *Congressional Quarterly Weekly Report* (1995), 2485–2599; 2000–2008: derived by the editors from Rhodes Cook, *Race for the Presidency* (Washington, D.C.: CQ Press, 2000, 2004, and 2008). Because the sources of these methods are published prior to the nomination season and because last-minute changes are made in some states' methods, occasionally later publications have led to revisions of a classification for an earlier year.

Figure 1-5   Democratic and Republican Presidential Nominations, Campaign Lengths, 1968–2008

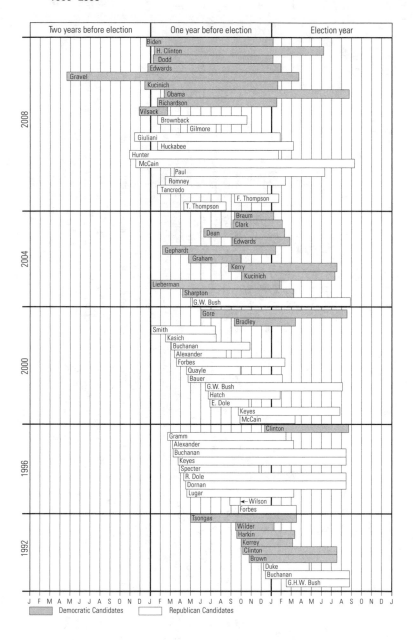

Figure 1-5   (Continued)

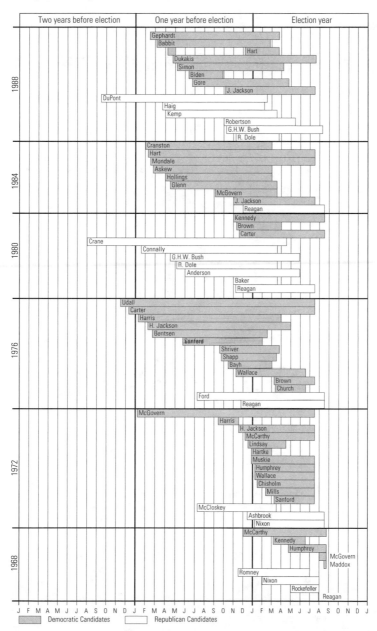

Note: Beginning of campaigns is determined by date of the formal announcement.

Sources: 1968–1984: *Congressional Quarterly, Elections '80* (Washington, D.C.: *Congressional Quarterly, 1980), and Congressional Quarterly's Guide to U.S. Elections,* 2nd ed. (Washington, D.C.: Congressional Quarterly, 1985), 387; 1988–1996: *Congressional Quarterly Weekly Report* (1987), 2732; (1988), 1894, 1896, 1899; (1991), 3735; (1992), 66, 361, 556, 633, 1086; (1995), 2, 13, 15, 3025, 3606; (1996), 641, 716; 2000–2008: compiled by the editors from news reports, various sources.

Table 1-25 Presidential Primary Returns, 2008

Democratic	Date	Turnout	Clinton	Edwards	Obama	Others
New Hampshire	Jan. 8	287,557	39%	17%	36%	8%
Michigan[a]	Jan. 15	594,398	55	—	—	45
South Carolina	Jan. 26	532,151	26	18	55	0
Florida[a]	Jan. 29	1,749,920	50	14	33	3
Alabama	Feb. 5	536,626	42	1	56	1
Arizona	Feb. 5	455,635	50	5	42	2
Arkansas	Feb. 5	314,234	70	2	26	2
California	Feb. 5	5,066,993	51	4	43	2
Connecticut	Feb. 5	354,539	47	1	51	2
Delaware	Feb. 5	96,374	42	1	53	3
Georgia	Feb. 5	1,060,851	31	2	66	1
Illinois	Feb. 5	2,038,614	33	2	65	1
Massachusetts	Feb. 5	1,258,923	56	2	41	2
Missouri	Feb. 5	822,734	48	2	49	1
New Jersey	Feb. 5	1,141,199	54	1	44	1
New York	Feb. 5	1,862,445	57	1	40	1
Oklahoma	Feb. 5	417,207	55	10	31	4
Tennessee	Feb. 5	624,764	54	4	40	1
Utah	Feb. 5	131,403	39	3	57	1
Louisiana	Feb. 9	384,346	36	3	57	4
District of Columbia	Feb. 12	123,994	24	0	75	1
Maryland	Feb. 12	878,174	36	1	61	2
Virginia	Feb. 12	986,203	35	1	64	0
Washington[b]	Feb. 19	691,381	46	2	51	1
Wisconsin	Feb. 19	1,113,753	41	1	58	1
Ohio	March 4	2,354,721	53	2	45	—
Rhode Island	March 4	186,439	58	1	40	1
Texas	March 4	2,874,986	51	1	47	1
Vermont	March 4	154,960	39	1	59	1
Mississippi	March 11	434,071	37	1	61	1
Pennsylvania	April 22	2,336,480	55	—	45	—
Indiana	May 6	1,278,274	51	—	49	—

	Date	Turnout							
North Carolina	May 6	1,580,726			42			56	2
Nebraska[b]	May 13	93,757			47			49	4
West Virginia	May 13	357,301			67		7	26	3
Kentucky	May 20	701,768			65		2	30	1
Oregon	May 20	640,630			41			59	6
Idaho[b]	May 27	42,802			38			56	
Puerto Rico	June 1	384,578			68			32	2
Montana	June 3	181,906			41			56	
South Dakota	June 3	97,797			55			45	

Republican

	Date	Turnout	Giuliani	Huckabee	McCain	Paul	Romney	F. Thompson	Others
New Hampshire	Jan. 8	239,699	8%	11%	37%	8%	32%	1%	3%
Michigan	Jan. 15	869,169	3	16	30	6	39	4	3
South Carolina	Jan. 19	445,499	2	30	33	4	15	16	0
Florida	Jan. 29	1,949,498	15	13	36	3	31	1	0
Alabama	Feb. 5	552,155	0	41	37	3	18	0	1
Arizona	Feb. 5	541,035	3	9	47	4	35	2	0
Arkansas	Feb. 5	229,153	0	60	20	5	14	0	1
California	Feb. 5	2,932,811	4	12	42	4	35	2	0
Connecticut	Feb. 5	151,604	2	7	52	4	33	0	1
Delaware	Feb. 5	50,239	2	15	45	4	33	—	2
Georgia	Feb. 5	963,541	1	34	32	3	30	0	0
Illinois[b]	Feb. 5	899,422	1	16	47	5	29	—	0
Massachusetts	Feb. 5	500,550	1	4	41	3	51	0	0
Missouri	Feb. 5	588,427	1	32	33	4	29	1	1
New Jersey	Feb. 5	566,201	3	8	55	5	28	1	1
New York	Feb. 5	642,894	4	11	52	6	28	—	—
Oklahoma	Feb. 5	335,054	1	33	37	3	25	—	—
Tennessee	Feb. 5	553,815	1	34	32	6	24	3	1
Utah	Feb. 5	296,061	0	1	5	3	89	0	1
Louisiana	Feb. 9	161,169	1	43	42	5	6	1	1

(Table continues)

Table 1-25 *(Continued)*

Republican

	Date	Turnout	Giuliani	Huckabee	McCain	Paul	Romney	F. Thompson	Others
District of Columbia	Feb. 12	6,211	2	16	68	8	6	—	—
Maryland	Feb. 12	320,989	1	29	55	6	7	1	1
Virginia	Feb. 12	489,252	0	41	50	4	4	1	—
Washington	Feb. 19	529,932	1	24	49	8	16	1	1
Wisconsin	Feb. 19	410,607	0	37	55	5	2	1	1
Ohio	March 4	1,095,917	—	31	60	5	3	2	—
Rhode Island	March 4	26,996	—	22	65	7	4	—	3
Texas	March 4	1,362,322	0	38	51	5	2	1	3
Vermont	March 4	39,483	2	14	71	7	5	—	1
Mississippi	March 11	143,286	1	13	79	4	2	2	1
Pennsylvania[b]	April 22	816,928	—	11	73	16	—	—	—
Indiana	May 6	412,748	—	10	78	8	5	—	—
North Carolina	May 6	517,583	—	12	74	7	—	—	7
Nebraska[b]	May 13	135,712	—	—	87	13	—	—	—
West Virginia	May 13	117,936	2	10	76	5	4	—	2
Kentucky	May 20	197,793	2	8	72	7	5	—	6
Oregon	May 20	351,916	—	—	81	15	—	—	4
Idaho	May 27	125,570	—	—	70	24	—	—	7
Montana[b]	June 3	95,232	—	—	76	21	—	—	7
New Mexico	June 3	110,814	—	—	86	14	—	—	2
South Dakota	June 3	60,964	—	7	70	17	3	—	3

Note: "—" indicates that the candidate was not listed on the ballot. Percentages are rounded and thus do not always sum to 100. Primary results are based on official state returns for Idaho, Kentucky, and North Carolina and for all states that voted before May. Data for earlier years can be found in previous editions of *Vital Statistics on American Politics*.

[a] This state set a primary date that was not approved by the Democratic National Committee. As a result, some candidates chose not to campaign in the state. Half of the delegations from these contests were eventually seated.
[b] Nonbinding primaries.

Source: "The Rhodes Cook Letter," June 2008, 11–14 (*www.rhodescook.com*).

Table 1-26 Presidential Caucus Results, 2008

Democratic

	Date	Turnout	Clinton	Edwards	Obama	Others
Iowa	Jan. 3	239,000	29%	30%	38%	3%
Nevada	Jan. 19	117,599	51	4	45	0
Alaska	Feb. 5	8,880	25	0	75	0
Colorado	Feb. 5	119,831	32	0	66	1
Idaho	Feb. 5	21,224	17	1	80	3
Kansas	Feb. 5	36,731	26	0	74	0
Minnesota	Feb. 5	214,066	32	1	66	1
New Mexico	Feb. 5	149,379	49	1	48	2
North Dakota	Feb. 5	19,012	37	1	61	1
Nebraska	Feb. 9	38,670	32	0	68	0
Washington	Feb. 9	244,458	31	0	68	1
Maine	Feb. 10	44,340	40	0	60	1
Hawaii	Feb. 19	37,182	24	0	76	0
Texas	March 4	1,000,000	44	0	56	0
Wyoming	March 8	8,753	38	0	61	1

Republican

	Date	Turnout	Giuliani	Huckabee	McCain	Paul	Romney	F. Thompson	Others
Iowa	Jan. 3	119,188	3%	34%	13%	10%	25%	13%	0%
Wyoming[a]	Jan. 5	3,200	a	a	a	a	a	a	a
Nevada	Jan. 19	43,578	4	8	13	13	51	8	2
Hawaii[b]	Jan. 25–Feb. 7	b	b	b	b	b	b	b	b
Maine	Feb. 1–3	5,446	0	6	21	18	52	0	3

(Table continues)

65

Table 1-26 (*Continued*)

Republican

	Date	Turnout	Giuliani	Huckabee	McCain	Paul	Romney	F. Thompson	Others
Alaska	Feb. 5	13,703	0	22	16	17	44	0	2
Colorado	Feb. 5	70,229	0	13	18	8	60	0	0
Minnesota	Feb. 5	62,828	0	20	22	16	41	0	1
Montana	Feb. 5	1,630	0	15	22	25	38	0	0
North Dakota	Feb. 5	9,785	0	20	23	21	36	0	0
West Virginia[c]	Feb. 5	1,089	0	33	16	10	41	0	0
Kansas	Feb. 9	19,516	0	60	24	11	3	0	2
Washington	Feb. 9	—	0	23	25	22	16	0	15

Note: "——" indicates not available. Percentages are rounded and thus do not always sum to 100. Caucus results are based on final or nearly final tallies from the state parties, and reflect either a direct vote for the candidates or delegates elected to the next stage of the process. The turnout figures for the Iowa and Texas Democratic caucuses as well as for the Wyoming Republican caucus are estimates from the state parties. The Montana, West Virginia, and Wyoming Republican caucuses were conducted with a closed universe of voters who were selected earlier. Data for earlier years can be found in previous editions of *Vital Statistics on American Politics*.

[a] The contest was for national convention delegates.
[b] The contest was for state convention delegates.
[c] The percentages reflect the result on the first ballot at the state convention, as reported by the *Charleston Gazette*. Mike Huckabee defeated Mitt Romney on the second ballot, 52 percent to 48 percent, to win all eighteen delegates at stake. The West Virginia turnout reflects the number of votes cast on the second ballot, according to the *Gazette*.

Source: "The Rhodes Cook Letter," June 2008, 11–14 (*www.rhodescook.com*).

Table 1-27   Location and Size of National Party Conventions, 1932–2008

	Democrats		Republicans	
Year	Location	Delegate votes	Location	Delegate votes
1932	Chicago	1,154	Chicago	1,154
1936	Philadelphia	1,100	Cleveland	1,003
1940	Chicago	1,100	Philadelphia	1,000
1944	Chicago	1,176	Chicago	1,056
1948	Philadelphia	1,234	Philadelphia	1,094
1952	Chicago	1,230	Chicago	1,206
1956	Chicago	1,372	San Francisco	1,323
1960	Los Angeles	1,521	Chicago	1,331
1964	Atlantic City	2,316	San Francisco	1,308
1968	Chicago	2,622	Miami Beach	1,333
1972	Miami Beach	3,016	Miami Beach	1,348
1976	New York	3,008	Kansas City	2,259
1980	New York	3,331	Detroit	1,994
1984	San Francisco	3,933	Dallas	2,235
1988	Atlanta	4,161	New Orleans	2,277
1992	New York	4,288	Houston	2,210
1996	Chicago	4,289	San Diego	1,990
2000	Los Angeles	4,339	Philadelphia	2,066
2004	Boston	4,353	New York	2,509
2008	Denver	4,419	St. Paul	2,380

Note: The number of delegates (persons attending) may be larger because of fractional votes.

Sources: 1932–2004: *Congressional Quarterly's Guide to U.S. Elections*, 5th ed. (Washington, D.C.: Congressional Quarterly, 2005), 433–434, 436; 2008: "The Rhodes Cook Letter," August 2008, 11 (*www. rhodescook.com*).

Table 1-28 Profile of National Convention Delegates, 1968–2008 (percent)

	1968 D	1968 R	1972 D	1972 R	1976 D	1976 R	1980 D	1980 R	1984 D	1984 R	1988 D	1988 R	1992 D	1992 R	1996 D	1996 R	2000 D	2000 R	2004 D	2004 R	2008 D	2008 R
Female	13	16	40	29	33	31	49	29	49	44	48	33	48	43	50	36	48	35	50	43	49	32
Black	5	2	15	4	11	3	15	3	18	4	23	4	16	5	19	3	19	4	18	6	23	2
Hispanic	—	—	—	—	—	—	5	1	6	4	6	3	7	4	9	3	12	6	12	7	11	5
Lawyer	28	22	12	—	16	15	13	15	17	14	16	17	14	—	10	11	9	9	13	—	17	16
Teacher	8	2	11	—	12	4	15	4	16	6	14	5	9	—	9	2	7	2	13	—	8	—
Union member	—	—	16	—	21	3	27	4	25	4	25	3	26	—	35	4	31	4	25	3	24	5
Attending first convention	67	66	83	78	80	78	87	69	78	69	65	68	62	—	61	65	49	54	57	55	57	58
Protestant	—	—	42	—	47	73	47	72	49	71	50	69	47	—	47	62	47	63	43	65	43	57
Catholic	—	—	26	—	34	18	37	22	29	22	30	22	30	—	30	25	30	27	32	26	26	30
Jewish	—	—	9	—	9	3	8	3	8	2	7	2	10	—	6	3	8	2	8	2	9	3
Liberal	—	—	—	—	40	3	46	2	48	1	43	0	48	1	43	0	36	1	41	1	43	0
Moderate	—	—	—	—	47	45	42	36	42	35	43	35	44	32	48	27	56	34	52	33	50	26
Conservative	—	—	—	—	8	48	6	58	4	60	5	58	5	63	5	70	5	63	3	63	3	72
Under age 30	3	4	22	6	15	7	11	5	8	4	4	3	4	—	6	2	4	3	7	4	7	3
Median age (years)	49	49	42	—	43	48	44	49	43	51	46	51	46	—	49	52	51	53	—	54	54	54

Note: "D" indicates Democrat; "R" indicates Republican; "—" indicates not available. Data for additional years can be found in previous editions of *Vital Statistics on American Politics.*

Sources: 1992 (Democrat median age, teacher, attending first convention): "New York *Newsday* Democratic Delegate Survey"; Democrats (all other), 1968–2008: CBS News/*New York Times* Poll, "Overview of the Democratic Delegates, 1968–2008," August 24, 2008 (*www.cbsnews.com*); Republicans, 1968–2008: CBS News/*New York Times* Poll, "Overview of the Republican Delegates, 1968–2008," August 31, 2008 (*www.cbsnews.com*).

Table 1-29 Legislative Districting: Deviations from Equality in Congressional and State Legislative Districts (percent)

	Congressional districts				State legislative districts — Senate				State legislative districts — House			
State	1960s	1980s	1990s	2000s	1960s	1980s	1990s	2000s	1960s	1980s	1990s	2000s
Alabama	38.6	2.45	a	0.00	665.4	8.50	9.22	9.73	317.7	9.80	10.20	9.93
Alaska	AL	AL	AL	AL	467.3	9.77	11.70	9.32	75.6	9.99	15.50	9.96
Arizona	107.2	0.08	a	0.00	704.7	8.40	9.85	3.79	151.4	8.40	9.85	3.79
Arkansas	54.2	0.73	0.73	0.04	88.4	9.15	9.27	9.81	150.9	9.15	9.52	9.87
California	451.4	0.08	0.49	0.00	1,528.4	4.60	1.60	0.00	118.9	3.60	1.80	0.00
Colorado	104.5	a	a	0.00	117.6	3.98	4.90	4.95	107.6	4.94	4.96	4.88
Connecticut	87.7	0.46	0.05	0.00	200.6	3.92	7.98	8.03	937.8	8.35	8.78	9.20
Delaware	AL	AL	AL	AL	251.0	9.78	10.18	9.96	444.3	25.10	9.58	9.98
Florida	102.5	0.13	a	0.00	710.7	1.05	0.86	0.03	592.5	0.46	4.99	2.79
Georgia	139.9	—	0.93	0.01	746.1	9.99	9.95	1.94	954.9	9.94	9.95	1.96
Hawaii	AL	a	a	0.32	217.3	18.60	9.86	38.90	151.5	8.60	9.78	20.10
Idaho	45.8	0.04	a	0.60	611.0	5.35	9.88	9.70	139.2	5.35	9.88	9.70
Illinois	65.2	0.03	a	0.00	295.2	1.75	a	0.00	220.7	2.80	a	0.00
Indiana	96.0	2.96	a	0.02	130.9	4.04	2.19	3.80	162.2	4.45	3.36	1.92
Iowa	22.7	0.05	0.05	0.02	419.2	0.71	1.45	1.46	490.7	1.78	1.97	1.89
Kansas	38.2	0.34	0.01	0.00	599.5	6.50	6.89	9.27	381.8	9.90	9.72	9.95
Kentucky	60.0	1.39	a	0.00	208.6	7.52	6.13	9.53	185.9	13.47	9.91	10.00
Louisiana	66.8	0.42	0.04	0.04	259.6	8.40	9.78	9.95	364.2	9.69	9.97	9.88
Maine	8.6	a	a	0.00	114.0	10.18	4.16	3.57	167.8	10.94	43.74b	9.33
Maryland	123.6	0.35	a	0.00	443.5	9.80	9.84	9.91	258.0	15.70	10.67	9.89
Massachusetts	23.9	1.09	a	0.39	88.6	—	4.75	9.33	213.9	—	9.92	9.68
Michigan	156.7	a	a	0.00	306.1	16.24	15.83	9.92	142.4	16.34	16.13	9.92

(Table continues)

Table 1-29 (Continued)

| State | Congressional districts | | | | State legislative districts | | | | | | | |
| | | | | | Senate | | | | House | | | |
	1960s	1980s	1990s	2000s	1960s	1980s	1990s	2000s	1960s	1980s	1990s	2000s
Minnesota	25.2	0.01	a	0.00	143.0	4.61	3.42	1.35	348.6	3.93	5.90	1.56
Mississippi	72.2	—	0.02	0.00	251.9	4.61	8.96	9.30	359.8	4.90	9.97	9.98
Missouri	29.7	0.18	0.20	0.00	46.1	6.10	8.42	6.81	184.8	9.30	8.96	6.08
Montana	37.4	—	AL	AL	648.6	—	9.51	9.82	161.6	—	9.97	9.85
Nebraska	26.8	0.23	0.20	0.00	99.5	9.43	3.81	9.21	c	c	c	c
Nevada	AL	0.60	a	0.00	754.6	8.20	2.28	9.91	730.9	9.70	4.55	1.97
New Hampshire	18.6	0.24	0.07	0.10	101.3	7.60	12.36	9.50	383.7	13.74	14.53	9.26
New Jersey	81.7	0.69	a	0.00	305.2	7.70	4.60	1.83	93.2	7.70	4.60	1.83
New Mexico	AL	0.87	0.16	0.03	876.7	9.83	9.58	9.60	189.7	9.87	9.89	9.70
New York	29.5	1.64	a	0.00	81.6	5.29	4.29	9.78	120.6	8.17	9.43	9.43
North Carolina	55.6	1.76	AL	0.00	249.6	9.46	9.94	9.96	204.7	9.66	9.97	9.98
North Dakota	10.8	AL	AL	AL	288.6	9.93	8.71	10.00	103.7	9.93	8.71	10.00
Ohio	121.1	0.68	a	0.00	72.8	8.88	13.60	8.81	122.6	9.67	13.60	12.46
Oklahoma	83.8	0.58	a	0.00	629.2	5.60	3.93	4.71	293.9	10.98	6.13	2.05
Oregon	58.2	0.15	a	0.00	74.3	3.73	1.69	1.77	69.7	5.34	1.89	1.90
Pennsylvania	59.6	0.24	0.01	0.00	222.1	1.93	1.86	3.98	249.8	2.82	4.94	5.54
Rhode Island	14.0	0.02	0.02	0.00	248.9	—	13.00	9.91	215.4	10.47	14.70	9.88
South Carolina	65.3	0.28	a	0.00	400.6	—	1.00	9.87	108.1	9.88	5.20	4.99
South Dakota	92.6	AL	AL	AL	170.9	12.90	9.47	9.69	145.2	12.40	9.47	9.69
Tennessee	101.8	2.40	a	0.00	183.2	10.22	13.92	9.98	211.8	1.66	9.96	9.99
Texas	167.0	0.28	a	0.00	355.8	1.82	9.98	9.71	111.9	9.95	9.99	9.74

Utah	57.2	AL	0.02	0.00	154.9	7.80	7.60	7.02	224.4	5.41	7.94	8.00
Vermont	0.43	AL	AL	AL	120.3	16.18	16.36	14.28	2,088.4	19.33	17.62	18.99
Virginia	57.1	1.81	a	0.00	235.9	10.65	8.53	4.00	308.8	5.11	9.67	3.90
Washington	41.2	0.06	a	0.00	217.5	5.40	a	0.30	158.4	5.70	a	0.30
West Virginia	32.0	0.50	0.09	0.22	372.4	8.96	9.98	10.92	188.9	9.94	9.96	9.98
Wisconsin	74.3	0.14	a	0.00	110.7	1.23	0.52	0.98	171.7	1.74	0.92	1.60
Wyoming	AL	AL	AL	AL	221.4	63.70	9.60	9.51	120.6	89.40	9.97	9.81

Note: "AL" indicates at-large district (only one congressional representative); "—" indicates not available. Figures represent the absolute sum of the maximum percentage deviations (positive and negative) from the average district population. 1960s data are from 1962; 1980s data are as of April 1983; 1990s data are as of August 1994. The 1980 state house plans for Delaware and Rhode Island contained errors that increased total deviation, but had not been corrected. 2000s data are as of March 2005.

a Less than 0.01 percent.
b Apart from two districts, the deviation is 8.15.
c Nebraska's state legislature is unicameral.

Sources: 1960s: Robert G. Dixon Jr., *Democratic Representation: Reapportionment in Law and Politics* (New York: Oxford University Press, 1968), appendixes A and B (copyright © 1985, Regents of the University of California, all rights reserved); 1980s: Election Data Services, Inc.; 1990s: Supreme Judicial Court of Maine, *In re Apportionment of 1993* (Docket #JC-93-229) and unpublished data from the National Conference of State Legislators, Illinois State Board of Elections, Michigan Information Center (Department of Management and Budget), and Tennessee Office of Local Government; 2000s: National Conference of State Legislators (*www.ncsl.org*).

Table 1-30   Jurisdictions Subject to Federal Preclearance of Election Law
Changes and to Minority Language Provisions of the Voting
Rights Act

Coverage under preclearance provisions	Coverage under minority language provisions	
Alabama	Alaska	Nevada (2)
Alaska	Arizona	New Jersey (5)
Arizona	California (21)	New Mexico (26)
California (4)	Colorado (11)	New York (7)
Florida (5)	Connecticut (4)[a]	North Carolina (1)
Georgia	Florida (9)	North Dakota (3)
Louisiana	Hawaii (3)	Oklahoma (1)
Michigan (2)[a]	Idaho (4)	Oregon (1)
Mississippi	Illinois (1)	Pennsylvania (1)
New Hampshire (10)[a]	Iowa (1)	Rhode Island (1)[a]
New York (3)	Louisiana (1)	South Dakota (8)
North Carolina (40)	Massachusetts (5)[a]	Texas
South Carolina	Michigan (3)[a]	Utah (1)
South Dakota (2)	Mississippi (6)	Wisconsin (1)
Texas		
Virginia[b]		

Note: "Preclearance" means that changes in election laws must be approved by the U.S. Justice Department. "Language provisions" require covered jurisdictions to provide bilingual voting materials to members of specified minority language groups. Numbers in parentheses indicate the number of counties in the state affected by the provisions. If there are no parentheses, coverage is statewide.

[a] Number of towns, townships, cities, boroughs, or areas.
[b] Thirteen counties and four cities have "bailed out" from coverage pursuant to Section 4 of the Voting Rights Act. One other Virginia county (Pulaski) filed a bailout action in the District Court of the District of Columbia. The Department of Justice signed a consent decree approved by a single judge but not the three-judge court as required by the Voting Rights Act.

Sources: U.S. Department of Justice, Voting Section, "Section 5 Covered Jurisdictions" and "About Language Minority Voting Rights" (*www.usdoj.gov*).

Table 1-31 Term Limits on State Legislators

State[a]	Lower house (years)[b]	Upper house (years)[b]	Year adopted	Percent support	Year of first impact Lower house	Year of first impact Upper house	Mechanism[c]	Break in service[d]
Arizona	8	8	1992	74	2000	2000	S	2 years
Arkansas	6	8	1992	60	1998	2000	S	lifetime
California	6	8	1990	52	1996	1998	S	lifetime
Colorado	8	8	1990	71	1998	1998	S	4 years
Florida	8	8	1992	77	2000	2000	B	2 years
Louisiana	12	12	1995	76	2007	2007	S	4 years
Maine	8	8	1993	68	1996	1996	S	2 years
Michigan	6	8	1992	59	1998	2002	S	lifetime
Missouri[e]	8	8	1992	75	2002	2002	S	lifetime
Montana	8/16	8/16	1992	67	2000	2000	B	contingent
Nebraska	f	8[f]	2000	56	f	2006	S	2 years
Nevada[g]	12	12	1996	70	2010	2010	S	lifetime
Ohio	8	8	1992	68	2000	2000	S	4 years
Oklahoma	12 years total in legislature		1990	67	2004	2004	S	lifetime
South Dakota	8	8	1992	64	2000	2000	S	2 years

Note: States have varying provisions for counting partial terms stemming from appointment or special election. In many states, limits are defined in terms of times elected rather than years served or contain a clause such as "or, but for resignation, would have served."

[a] In addition to the states listed here, Washington, Oregon, and Wyoming passed state legislative term limits in 1992 and Massachusetts, Idaho, and Utah in 1994, but they were overturned by the courts in the first four states (in 1998, 2002, 2004, and 1997, respectively) and by the legislatures in Idaho (in 2002) and Utah (in 2003). In Oregon, some legislators were "termed out" in 1998 and 2000.

(Table continues)

Table 1-31 (*Continued*)

[b] Number of years an individual may serve before term limits are applied. A pair of numbers indicates that an individual may not serve more than a certain number of years over a longer period—for example, six of twelve years—whether or not those years are consecutive.

[c] Strict term limits (S) prohibit service in the legislature. Ballot access restrictions (B) prevent a candidate's name from being placed on the ballot, but do not prevent a candidate from being elected on write-in votes.

[d] Length of time an individual must "sit out" before serving (or having ballot access) again in the same house. The time is "contingent" when the term limit law specifies that an individual may serve no more than a certain number of years over a longer period.

[e] Because of special elections, term limits were effective in 2000 for eight members of the House and in 1998 for one senator.

[f] Nebraska's legislature is unicameral.

[g] The Nevada Legislative Council and attorney general have ruled that Nevada's term limits cannot be applied to those legislators elected in the same year term limits were passed (1996). They first apply to persons elected in 1998.

Sources: National Conference of State Legislatures (*www.ncsl.org*) and texts of state measures.

Table 1-32   Members of Congress under Self-Imposed Term Limits, 1998–2010

Year[a]	Member	State	District/chamber	Party	Kept pledge
1998					
	Coats	Indiana	Senate	R	yes
	Furse	Oregon	1	D	yes
	Inglis	South Carolina	4	R	yes
				2R, 1D	
2000					
	Burns	Montana	Senate	R	no/reelected
	Canady	Florida	12	R	yes
	Chenoweth	Idaho	1	R	yes
	Coburn	Oklahoma	2	R	yes/elected to Senate
	Fowler	Florida	4	R	yes
	McInnis	Colorado	3	R	no/reelected
	Meehan	Massachusetts	5	D	no/reelected
	Metcalf	Washington	2	R	yes
	Nethercutt	Washington	5	R	no/reelected
	Salmon	Arizona	1	R	yes
	Sanford	South Carolina	1	R	yes
				10R, 1D	
2002					
	Baldacci	Maine	2	D	yes
	Cooksey	Louisiana	5	R	yes
	Lewis	Kentucky	2	R	no/reelected
	Miller	Florida	13	R	yes
	Riley	Florida	3	R	yes
	Schaffer	Colorado	4	R	yes
	Thune	South Dakota	AL	R	yes/elected to Senate
	Weldon	Florida	15	R	no/reelected
	Wellstone	Minnesota	Senate	D	no[b]
				7R, 2D	
2004					
	Bond	Missouri	Senate	R	no/reelected
	Boswell	Iowa	3	D	no/reelected
	Calvert	California	43	R	no/reelected
	Campbell	Colorado	Senate	R	yes
	Capps	California	22	D	no/reelected
	Deal	Georgia	9	R	no/reelected
	DeMint	South Carolina	4	R	yes/elected to Senate
	Ganske	Iowa	4	R	yes
	Goodlatte	Virginia	6	R	no/reelected
	Goss	Florida	14	R	c
	Green	Wisconsin	8	R	no/reelected
	Hoekstra	Michigan	2	R	no/reelected
	Knollenberg	Michigan	11	R	no/reelected
	LaTourette	Ohio	19	R	no/reelected
	Lucas	Kentucky	4	D	yes
	Maloney	Connecticut	5	D	yes
	Napolitano	California	34	D	no/reelected
	Ose	California	3	R	yes
	Radanovich	California	19	R	no/reelected
	Smith	Michigan	7	R	yes

(Table continues)

Table 1-32   *(Continued)*

Year[a]	Member	State	District/chamber	Party	Kept pledge
	Tancredo	Colorado	6	R	no/reelected
	Toomey	Pennsylvania	15	R	yes
				17R, 5D	
2006					
	Bryant	Tennessee	7	R	[d]
	Cubin	Wyoming	AL	R	no/reelected
	English	Pennsylvania	3	R	no/reelected
	Flake	Arizona	6	R	no/reelected
	Frist	Tennessee	Senate	R	yes
	Graham	South Carolina	Senate	R	yes[e]
	Gutknecht	Minnesota	1	R	no[f]
	Hilleary	Tennessee	4	R	yes
	Hutchison	Texas	Senate	R	no/reelected
	Johnson	Illinois	15	R	no/reelected
	Keller	Florida	8	R	no/reelected
	Largent	Oklahoma	1	R	yes
	LoBiondo	New Jersey	2	R	no/reelected
	Souder	Indiana	3	R	no/reelected
	Wamp	Tennessee	3	R	no/reelected
				15R	
2008					
	Allard	Colorado	Senate	R	yes
	Collins	Maine	Senate	R	no/reelected
	Hutchinson	Arkansas	Senate	R	no[g]
	Thompson	Tennessee	Senate	R	[h]
				4R	
2010					
	Brownback	Kansas	Senate	R	yes[i]
	Bunning	Kentucky	Senate	R	
	Fitzgerald	Illinois	Senate	R	[j]
	Voinovich	Ohio	Senate	R	
				4R	
	Total		52 House	59R, 9D	
			16 Senate		

Note: "R" indicates Republican; "D" indicates Democrat; "AL" indicates "at large." Members who kept their pledge did not run for reelection to the chamber they were in when they made the pledge. They may have resigned or run for another office at the time their pledge ended or before.

[a] The year that the member's time in Congress ended or will end if he or she is not defeated earlier and the self-imposed term limit is observed.

[b] Sen. Paul Wellstone died while campaigning for reelection.

[c] Rep. Porter Goss announced that he would break his term limits pledge, but he was appointed head of the Central Intelligence Agency by President George W. Bush.

[d] Rep. Ed Bryant ran for reelection in 2002 and was defeated.

[e] Sen. Lindsay Graham was elected to the U.S. House in 1994 and pledged to serve no more than six terms. In 2002 he ran for the U.S. Senate and won.

[f] Rep. Gil Gutknecht ran for reelection in 2006 and was defeated.

[g] Sen. Tim Hutchinson ran for reelection in 2002 and was defeated.

[h] Sen. Fred Thompson retired in 2004.

[i] Sen. Sam Brownback announced that he would not run for reelection in 2010 (Brownback press release, December 19, 2008).

[j] Sen. Peter G. Fitzgerald retired in 2004.

Source: U.S. Term Limits (*www.ustl.org*); updated by the editors.

Table 1-33   Members "Termed Out" of State Legislatures, 1998–2008

State	Chamber	Membership	1998	2000	2002	2004	2006	2008
					Members termed out in			
Arizona	House	60	—	15	9	5	3	7
	Senate	30	—	7	6	2	3	2
Arkansas	House	100	49	25	14	36	29	28
	Senate	35	—	13	11	0	1[a]	4
California	Assembly	80	16	19	20	18	26	24
	Senate	40	11	8	7	8[b]	12	10
Colorado	House	65	18	10	7	7[c]	11	8
	Senate	35	9	11	5	5	4	7
Florida	House	120	—	55	14	7	19	28
	Senate	40	—	11	12	0	5	5
Maine	House	151	11	17	28	21	19	15
	Senate	35	1	7	8	7	1	6
Michigan	House	110	63	21	23	37	23	44
	Senate	38	—	—	27	d	6	0
Missouri	House	163	—	8	73	15	10	21
	Senate	34	1	—	12	10	3	4
Montana	House	100	—	33	7	6	16	17
	Senate	50	—	14	15	10	5	10
Nebraska	Senate[e]	49	—	—	—	—	20	13
Ohio	House	99	—	45	9	7[f]	14	21
	Senate	33	—	6	4	5[f]	7	4
Oklahoma	House	101	—	—	—	28	15	7
	Senate	48	—	—	—	13	7	5
Oregon[g]	House	60	22	17	—	—	—	—
	Senate	30	2	5	—	—	—	—
South Dakota	House	70	—	20	7	3	7	13
	Senate	35	—	13	4	7	2	6
Total		1,811	203	380	322[h]	257	268	309

Note: "—" indicates term limits were not yet applicable.

[a] A second senator would have been termed out in 2006, but died in office in February 2006.
[b] A ninth senator would have been termed out in 2004, but died in office in May 2004.
[c] An eighth member would have been termed out in 2004, but resigned to take an appointment to the public utilities commission.
[d] The Michigan Senate did not have elections in 2004.
[e] Nebraska has a unicameral, nonpartisan legislature in which all members are called senators.
[f] In Ohio, two representatives and one senator who otherwise would have been termed out resigned prior to the end of their terms. They are not included in these numbers.
[g] Term limits were overturned by the state supreme court in 2002.
[h] Does not include eight "termed out" legislators who resigned in midterm.

Source: National Conference of State Legislatures (*www.ncsl.org*).

Table 1-34 Types of Voting Equipment Used in U.S. Elections, November 2008

Type of voting equipment used	Number of counties	Percent	Number of precincts	Percent	Voting-age population	Percent	Number of registered voters	Percent
Punch card[a]	11	0.4	259	0.1	232,531	0.1	163,023	0.1
Lever machine[b]	62	2.0	15,317	8.4	14,809,734	6.7	11,363,178	6.7
Paper ballots	56	1.8	757	0.4	362,844	0.2	280,047	0.2
Optical scan[c]	1,836	58.9	105,848	57.7	129,311,832	58.5	94,926,873	56.2
Electronic[d]	1,068	34.3	56,350	30.7	67,621,282	30.6	55,142,920	32.6
Mixed	84	2.7	4,899	2.7	8,544,287	3.9	7,124,765	4.2
Total	3,117	100.1	183,430	100.0	220,882,510	100.0	169,000,806	100.0

Note: Data for earlier years can be found in previous editions of *Vital Statistics on American Politics.*

[a] Voters mark their ballots by punching holes in paper cards.
[b] Voters depress mechanical levers underneath or alongside candidates' names.
[c] Voters fill in circles, ovals, or squares that are printed on the ballot or complete a broken arrow. Ballots are then read with optical scanning equipment. Also called mark-sense ballots.
[d] Voters cast ballots by pressing buttons or images on a computer screen. Often called Direct Recording Electronic (DRE) machines.

Source: Election Data Services Inc., Washington, D.C. (*www.electiondataservices.com*).

2

Campaign Finance and Political Action Committees

- **Contribution Limits**
- **Presidential Campaign Financing**
- **Party Expenditures**
- **Political Action Committees (PACs)**

One of the most important aspects of election campaigns and political activities more generally is money: who gives it, who spends it, who regulates it, and what effect it has. Surprisingly, a huge quantity of information is available on the subject. This abundance stems chiefly from the large number of elections in the United States and the effort over the past three-and-a-half decades to collect data about them and make these data available to the public. The Bipartisan Campaign Reform Act (BCRA) of 2002, a recent attempt to regulate the role of money in campaigns, enacted new contribution limits (Table 2-1), changed the law on "soft" money (Table 2-8), and otherwise reworked campaign finance law.

This chapter presents information on the amounts of money collected and spent by individual presidential candidates (Tables 2-3 and 2-4), along with more aggregated information about expenditures by the political parties (Tables 2-6 through 2-8). The most recent campaign expenditures for all 435 representatives and 100 senators can be found in Chapter 5 on Congress (Tables 5-11 and 5-12).

One could, in fact, easily be inundated by numbers on campaign finance. The publications of the Federal Election Commission (FEC) alone run to multiple volumes every two years, with detailed accountings of the receipts and expenditures of candidates in federal elections. Additional volumes are produced, though inconsistently and much less systematically, by various state agencies. Because such information is so voluminous, it is often summarized as it is here: how much was spent by various types of political action committees (Table 2-11), which PACs are the biggest contributors (Table 2-13), and so on.

This wealth of information has been collected since the mid-1970s, when the FEC was established. Although studies of campaign costs were conducted before then, present time series are often limited to this span of about thirty-five years. Laws regulating campaign contributions, expenditures, and interest group activities change so frequently that longer time series are often unobtainable and would be misleading if they could be compiled. For example, the growth of PACs dates from 1974 because changes in the laws at that time allowed their establishment (Table 2-9). Similarly, data on public funding of presidential campaigns date from 1976 (Table 2-5).

Concern about money is not limited strictly to candidate spending. Indeed, researchers and watchdog groups are probably more concerned about interest group spending and about where candidates' funds come from and what, if anything, that money buys. Fortunately, more and more data are now available on interest group finances and on candidates' fund-raising as well as on expenditures. Much of the data are related to PACs, the dominant organizations through which interest groups raise and spend money (Table 2-10). The information presented here is related primarily to the general categories of PACs (Tables 2-9, 2-11, 2-12, and 2-14); the list of the largest PAC contributors illustrates the variety of organizations that fall into these categories (Table 2-13).

Because money is at the heart of interest group activities, matters of campaign finance law are directly relevant in this chapter. At the federal level, these regulations consist mainly of fairly straightforward contribution limits—limits that were recently changed by the BCRA (Table 2-1). At the state level, there is a myriad of contribution and expenditure limits (Table 2-2).

Of course, not all questions about efforts to influence the electoral or the political process involve money (directly anyway). Other aspects of interest group activity that can be quantified are depicted in Chapters 5 and 11, such as the growth and decline of labor unions (Table 11-8) and interest groups' ratings of members of Congress on how favorable their votes were to the groups' interests (Tables 5-11 and 5-12).

For obvious reasons, no one is able to collect systematically what would surely be the most captivating data on organized interests—that is, any bribes, threats, and blackmail that may insinuate themselves into campaign finance. Although political analysts now have access to a larger body of material on campaign finances and related matters than ever before, much of this information is buried in hard-to-digest volumes or in bland lists of what interests are represented in various politicians' support groups. Yet such data provide unprecedented knowledge and research potential about the scope and possible influence of organized interests.

Table 2-1 Contribution Limits under the Bipartisan Campaign Reform Act of 2002

Donors	Recipients				
	Candidate committees	PAC[a]	State, district, and local party committees[b]	National party committees[c]	Special limits
Individual	$2,400 per election[d,e]	$5,000 per year	$10,000 per year combined limit	$30,400 per year[d]	Biennial limit of $115,500 per two-year cycle ($45,600 to all candidates and $69,900 to all PACs and parties[f])[d]
State, district, and local party committees[b]	$5,000 per election combined limit	$5,000 per year combined limit	Unlimited transfers to other party committees	Unlimited transfers to other party committees	
National party committees[c]	$5,000 per election	$5,000 per year	Unlimited transfers to other party committees	Unlimited transfers to other party committees	$42,600 to Senate candidate per campaign[d,g]
PAC multicandidate[h]	$5,000 per election	$5,000 per year	$5,000 per year combined limit	$15,000 per year	
PAC not multicandidate[h]	$2,400 per election[d]	$5,000 per year	$10,000 per year combined limit	$30,400 per year[d]	

[a] These limits apply to both separate segregated funds (SSFs) and political action committees (PACs). Affiliated committees share the same set of limits on contributions made and received.

[b] A state party committee shares its limits with local and district party committees in that state unless a local or district committee's independence can be demonstrated. These limits apply to multicandidate committees only.

[c] A party's national committee, Senate campaign committee, and House campaign committee are each considered national party committees, and each has separate limits, except with respect to Senate candidates—see special limits column.

[d] These limits will be indexed for inflation. Amounts shown are for the 2009–2010 election cycle.

[e] Each of the following is considered a separate election with a separate limit: primary election, caucus or convention with the authority to nominate, general election, runoff election, and special election.

[f] No more than $45,600 of this amount may be contributed to state and local parties and PACs.

[g] This limit is shared by the national committee and the Senate campaign committee.

[h] A multicandidate committee is a political action committee that has been registered for at least six months, has received contributions from more than fifty contributors and—with the exception of a state party committee—has made contributions to at least five federal candidates.

Source: Federal Election Commission, "Contributions," January 2009 (*www.fec.gov*).

Table 2-2   Contribution Limits on Funding of State Election Campaigns

State	Individuals	Corporations	Labor unions	Political action committees	State parties
Alabama	no	yes[a]	no	no	no
Alaska	yes	prohibited	prohibited	yes	yes
Arizona[b]	yes	prohibited[a]	prohibited[a]	yes	yes
Arkansas	yes	yes	yes	yes	yes
California	yes	yes	yes	yes	no
Colorado	yes	prohibited[a]	prohibited[a]	yes	yes
Connecticut[b]	yes	prohibited[a]	yes[a]	yes	yes
Delaware	yes	yes	yes	yes	yes
Florida	yes	yes	yes	yes	yes
Georgia	yes	yes	yes	yes	yes
Hawaii	yes	yes	yes	yes	yes
Idaho	yes	yes	yes	yes	yes
Illinois	no	no	no	no	no
Indiana	no	yes	yes	no	no
Iowa	no	prohibited	no	no	no
Kansas	yes	yes	yes	yes	no[c]
Kentucky	yes	prohibited	yes	yes	yes[d]
Louisiana	yes	yes	yes	yes	no
Maine[b]	yes	yes	yes	yes	yes
Maryland	yes	yes	yes	yes	yes
Massachusetts	yes	prohibited	yes	yes	yes
Michigan	yes	prohibited[a]	prohibited[a]	yes	yes
Minnesota	yes	prohibited	yes	yes	yes
Mississippi	no	yes	no	no	no
Missouri	no	no	no	no	no
Montana	yes	prohibited[a]	yes	yes	yes
Nebraska	no	yes	yes	yes	yes
Nevada	yes	yes	yes	yes	yes
New Hampshire	yes	yes	prohibited	yes	yes
New Jersey	yes	yes	yes	yes	yes
New Mexico[d]	yes	yes	yes	yes	yes
New York	yes	yes	yes	yes	no[c]
North Carolina	yes	prohibited[a]	prohibited[a]	yes	no
North Dakota	no	prohibited[a]	prohibited[a]	no	no
Ohio	yes	prohibited[a]	prohibited[a]	yes	yes
Oklahoma	yes	prohibited[a]	prohibited[a]	yes	yes
Oregon	no	no	no	no	no
Pennsylvania	no	prohibited[a]	prohibited[a]	no	no
Rhode Island	yes	prohibited	prohibited	yes	yes
South Carolina	yes	yes	yes	yes	yes
South Dakota	yes	prohibited	prohibited[a]	no	no
Tennessee	yes	prohibited	yes	yes	yes
Texas	no	prohibited[a]	prohibited[a]	no	no
Utah	no	no	no	no	no

Table 2-2   *(Continued)*

State	Individuals	Corporations	Labor unions	Political action committees	State parties
Vermont[e]	yes	yes	yes	yes	no
Virginia	no	no	no	no	no
Washington	yes	yes	yes	yes	yes
West Virginia	yes	prohibited[a]	yes	yes	yes
Wisconsin	yes	prohibited	prohibited	yes	yes
Wyoming	yes	prohibited	prohibited	no	no

Note: Limits on sizes of contributions and other restrictions (for example, from government employees, regulated industries) vary widely across states. For details, see first source.

[a] Direct corporate and union contributions are prohibited, and the use of treasury funds or dues is prohibited. In these states, the law specifically says that nothing prevents the employees or officers of a corporation from making political contributions through a PAC, using funds from an account that is segregated from corporate accounts. Such contributions are subject to the same limitations placed on other PACs.

[b] Candidates participating in "Clean Elections" public financing may not accept contributions after qualifying for public funds.

[c] Unlimited, except for contested primary elections in Kansas (subject to limitations) and primaries in New York (prohibited).

[d] Effective November 3, 2010, contribution limits will be imposed on each category of funding. See the first source for more details.

[e] Full public financing is available to qualifying candidates for governor or lieutenant governor. A candidate who wishes to receive public funding may not solicit or accept any private contributions except qualifying contributions.

Sources: National Conference of State Legislatures, "State Limits on Contributions to Candidates" (*www.ncsl.org*); unpublished data.

Table 2-3 Presidential Prenomination Campaign Finance, 2008

Party/candidate	Federal matching funds	Individual contributions minus refunds	Political action committee contributions minus refunds	Candidate contributions and loans minus repayments	Transfers-in[a]	Other receipts[b]	Total receipts	Total disbursements
Republicans								
Brownback	$0	$3,530,942	$49,435	$25	$575,000	$87,069	$4,242,471	$4,210,774
Gilmore	0	349,736	8,000	0	0	30,408	388,145	371,940
Giuliani	0	55,008,874	397,259	800,000	2,038,269	412,489	58,656,891	58,642,902
Huckabee	0	15,991,901	54,423	0	0	13,663	16,059,987	16,025,153
Hunter	453,527	2,343,898	41,273	0	36,000	0	2,874,699	2,821,048
McCain	0	190,411,677	1,301,134	0	22,825,545	5,052,695	219,591,051	202,082,251
Paul	0	34,336,199	18,302	0	0	180,402	34,534,903	30,455,936
Romney	0	59,786,640	350,802	44,663,736	20,160	335,214	105,156,552	105,120,314
Tancredo	2,145,126[c]	3,979,701	6,525	125	100,000	-13,252	6,218,225	6,049,501
Thompson, F.	0	23,202,419	176,555	0	0	69,506	23,448,481	23,247,270
Thompson, T.	0	967,322	10,174	234,760	0	998	1,213,254	1,213,254
Total, Republicans	2,598,653	389,909,310	2,413,883	45,698,646	25,594,974	6,169,192	472,384,657	450,240,342
Democrats								
Biden	2,027,072	7,767,364	210,745	0	1,900,000	12,624	11,917,805	11,279,292
Clinton	0	196,842,746	1,439,279	13,175,000	10,029,145	2,373,055	223,859,225	215,825,248
Dodd	1,447,568[d]	8,889,713	750,698	0	4,739,005	-89,222	15,737,763	15,149,053
Edwards	12,882,864	35,126,205	0	0	0	1,570,942	48,158,668	43,996,279
Gravel	100,000[e]	448,053	502	3,000	0	0	551,555	498,518
Kucinich	1,070,521	4,375,584	14,200	10,347	0	9,209	5,479,860	5,479,120

Obama[f]	0	657,117,793	480	0	86,950,000	1,668,000	745,736,273	729,288,031
Richardson	0	22,053,014	278,829	2,300	0	65,608	22,399,751	22,401,549
Total, Democrats	17,528,025	932,620,472	2,694,733	13,190,647	103,618,150	5,610,215	1,073,840,899	1,043,917,090
Grand total	20,126,678	1,322,529,782	5,108,616	58,889,293	129,213,124	11,779,406	1,546,225,556	1,494,157,432

Note: Amounts are through December 31, 2008. Data for earlier years can be found in previous editions of *Vital Statistics on American Politics.*

[a] "Transfers-in" is the total amount of all transfers from previous federal campaigns or any other committees authorized by each candidate.
[b] "Other receipts" include party contributions minus refunds and other loans minus repayment.
[c] Tancredo received funds in early 2009 ($83,775).
[d] Dodd received a total of $1,961,742, but only the amount of $1,447,568 was specifically identified in his reports.
[e] Gravel received funds in early 2009 ($115,966).
[f] Because the Obama campaign used a single committee for both primary and general election financial activity, the Obama figures include both primary and general election funds.

Source: Federal Election Commission, "2008 Presidential Campaign Financial Activity Summarized: Receipts Nearly Double 2004 Total," June 8, 2009 (*www.fec.gov*).

Table 2-4 Presidential Campaign Finance, Aggregated Contributions from Individual Donors to Leading Presidential Candidates, 2004 and 2008

Candidate	Total number of itemized individual donors	Total amount of itemized contributions	Net individual contributions	Percentage of individual contributions from donors aggregating to		
				$200 or less	$201–999	$1,000 or more
2004						
Democrats						
Kerry	209,894	$164,134,439	$215,915,455	20	24	56
Dean	57,448	27,947,961	51,360,995	38	30	28
Edwards	18,589	20,173,933	21,880,659	7	14	78
Republicans						
Bush, G. W	190,640	183,235,226	256,081,557	25	13	60
2008						
Democrats						
Obama	403,341	301,118,063	452,852,990	26	27	47
Clinton	170,777	167,048,346	210,901,574	16	21	63
Edwards	33,135	31,060,174	38,638,348	15	22	63
Republicans						
McCain	169,783	154,806,518	206,363,245	21	20	59
Romney	44,795	52,972,073	63,065,340	14	13	73
Giuliani	39,489	51,211,030	61,022,495	15	9	76
Paul	32,234	18,372,743	34,336,193	39	29	32
Thompson, F.	17,058	13,905,983	23,369,742	38	18	44
Huckabee	13,728	10,449,883	15,991,901	29	24	47

Note: Amounts are through August 31, 2004, and August 31, 2008.

Source: Michael J. Malbin, "Small Donors, Large Donors and the Internet: The Case for Public Financing after Obama," Campaign Finance Institute, April 2009, 16 (www.CampaignFinanceInstitute.org); derived by Campaign Finance Institute from data from Federal Election Commission.

Table 2-5 Public Funding of Presidential Elections, 1976–2008 (millions)

Year	Spending limits		Maximum entitlement, primary matching funds[b]	Public funds for each major-party convention[c]	Public funds for each major-party nominee for general election[d]	Coordinated party spending limit[e]
	Primary[a]	Primary plus 20%[a]				
1976	$10.9	$13.1	$5.5	$2.2	$21.8	$3.2
1980	14.7	17.7	7.4	4.4	29.4	4.6
1984	20.2	24.2	10.1	8.1	40.4	6.9
1988	23.1	27.7	11.5	9.2	46.1	8.3
1992	27.6	33.1	13.8	11.0	55.2	10.3
1996	30.9	37.1	15.5	12.4	61.8	12.0
2000	33.8	40.5	16.9	13.5	67.6	13.7
2004	37.3	44.8	18.7	14.9	74.6	16.2
2008	42.1	50.5	21.0	16.8	84.1	19.1

Note: Amounts are in current dollars. The following third party candidates received public funds for general elections: John B. Anderson (independent), $4.2 million in 1980; H. Ross Perot (Reform Party), $29.1 million in 1996; and Pat Buchanan (Reform Party), $12.6 million in 2000. Perot declined public funds in 1992.

[a] $10 million + COLA. (COLA is the cost-of-living adjustment over the base year of 1974.) Campaigns are also allowed to exempt fund-raising costs up to 20 percent of the overall limit, which, in effect, raises their total spending limit by 20 percent. Legal and accounting costs, up to 15 percent of the overall limit, if incurred to comply with the law, are also exempt from the limit.

[b] Eligible candidates in the presidential primaries may receive public funds to match the individual contributions they raise. Contributions from political action committees (PACs) and party committees are not matchable. Although an individual has been able to give up to $1,000 to a primary candidate (before the Bipartisan Campaign Reform Act of 2002 raised that limit to $2,000), only the first $250 of that contribution is matchable. Presidential candidates become eligible for matching funds by raising more than $5,000 in matchable contributions in each of twenty different states. Candidates must agree to use these public funds only for campaign expenses.

[c] $4 million + COLA. Originally, the limit was $2 million + COLA. The base was raised to $3 million for the 1980 convention, then to $4 million for the 1984 convention. The Reform Party received $2.523 million for its presidential nominating convention in 2000.

[d] $20 million + COLA. Legal and accounting costs incurred to comply with the law are exempt from the limit and may be defrayed from private monies raised in separate compliance funds (subject to contribution limitations and prohibitions). The Republican and Democratic candidates who win their party's nominations for president are each eligible to receive a grant to cover all the expenses of their general election campaigns. Nominees who accept the funds must agree not to raise private contributions (from individuals, PACs, or party committees) and to limit their campaign expenditures to the amount of public funds they receive. They may use the funds only for campaign expenses. A third-party presidential candidate may qualify for some public funds after the general election if he or she receives at least 5 percent of the popular vote.

[e] $.02 × voting-age population of U.S. + COLA. This is the amount the national party may spend on behalf of its nominee. The party may work in conjunction with the campaign, but the money is raised, spent, and reported by the national party committee.

Source: Federal Election Commission Press Office.

Table 2-6 Financial Activity of the National Political Parties, 1991–2008 (millions)

Party	1991–1992	1993–1994	1995–1996	1997–1998	1999–2000	2001–2002	2003–2004	2005–2006	2007–2008
Democratic									
Raised	$163.3	$132.8	$221.6	$160.0	$275.2	$217.2	$678.8	$483.1	$763.3
Spent	157.5	131.3	214.3	155.3	265.8	208.7	655.6	472.4	746.5
Contributions	1.9	2.2	2.2	1.2	1.4	2.3	1.8	4.1	2.5
Coordinated expenditures[a]	28.1	21.2	22.6	18.6	21.0	7.1	33.1	20.7	38.0
Independent expenditures[b]	—	—	1.5	1.5	2.3	1.7	176.5	108.1	156.1
Republican									
Raised	264.9	244.1	416.5	285.0	465.8	424.1	782.4	602.3	792.9
Spent	251.7	232.1	408.5	275.9	427.0	427.0	752.6	608.2	766.1
Contributions	3.0	3.0	3.7	2.6	2.3	4.7	2.6	1.9	8.6
Coordinated expenditures[a]	33.9	20.6	31.0	15.7	29.6	16.0	29.1	14.2	32.0
Independent expenditures[b]	—	—	10.0	0.3	1.6	1.9	88.0	115.6	196.6

Note: "—" indicates not available. Amounts in current dollars. This table includes only federal activity. Total receipts and disbursements do not include monies transferred among committees. Building funds and state and local election spending are not reported to the Federal Election Commission. Data for earlier years can be found in previous editions of *Vital Statistics on American Politics.*

[a] Party committees are also allowed to spend money in behalf of federal candidates, in addition to the money party committees may contribute directly. This spending may be coordinated with a candidate.
[b] The 1996 election cycle was the first in which party committees were permitted to make independent expenditures.

Source: Federal Election Commission, "Democratic National Party Federal Financial Activity through the End of the 2007–2008 Election Cycle" and "Republican National Party Federal Financial Activity through the End of the 2007–2008 Election Cycle" (*www.fec.gov*).

Table 2-7 Party Contributions and Coordinated Expenditures, by Office and Party, 1991–2008

Year/party	Senate		House	
	Contributions	Expenditures	Contributions	Expenditures
1991–1992				
Democratic	$689,953	$11,915,878	$1,234,593	$5,883,678
Republican	807,397	16,509,940	2,197,611	6,906,729
1993–1994				
Democratic	664,700	13,220,395	1,499,943	8,519,892
Republican	753,551	11,549,856	2,198,148	9,063,415
1995–1996				
Democratic	690,260	8,717,875	1,525,150	6,783,902
Republican	1,016,699	11,014,061	2,627,868	8,240,158
1997–1998				
Democratic	271,833	9,410,063	945,589	4,598,377
Republican	504,246	9,372,899	2,109,332	6,300,036
1999–2000				
Democratic	362,970	5,083,060	990,909	3,339,023
Republican	527,542	10,840,561	1,755,609	5,240,038
2001–2002				
Democratic	560,641	1,235,561	1,023,047	2,938,812
Republican	1,121,198	9,862,432	2,375,312	5,803,316
2003–2004				
Democratic	616,414	10,191,088	783,971	3,616,613
Republican	810,260	9,355,364	1,482,024	3,529,949
2005–2006				
Democratic	596,800	5,796,005	2,429,919	2,409,914
Republican	386,782	8,784,685	785,435	4,519,856
2007–2008				
Democratic	558,600	3,822,927	1,027,145	1,654,217
Republican	135,000	1,530,625	736,191	6,491,220

Note: Includes direct contributions made by party committees to congressional candidates and coordinated expenditures made in their behalf. Amounts in current dollars. Data for 1991–2004 are through December 31 of the election cycle. Data for 2005–2008 are through November 31 of the election cycle. Data for earlier years can be found in previous editions of *Vital Statistics on American Politics.*

Sources: 1991–1992: Federal Election Commission, "Democrats Increase Spending by 89% in the '92 Cycle," press release, January 1994; 1993–1994: "FEC Issues Final Report on Political Party Activity for 1993–94," press release, November 1995; 1995–1996: "FEC Reports Major Increase in Party Activity for 1995–96," press release, March 19, 1997; 1997–1998: "FEC Reports on Political Party Activity for 1997–98," press release, April 9, 1999; 1999–2000: "FEC Reports Increase in Party Fundraising for 2000," press release, May 15, 2001; 2001–2002: "Party Committees Raise More than $1 Billion in 2001–2002," press release, March 20, 2003; 2003–2004: "Party Financial Activity Summarized for the 2004 Election Cycle," press release, March 2, 2005, corrected March 14, 2005 (*www.fec.gov*); 2005–2008: Campaign Finance Institute (*www.CampaignFinanceInstitute.org*); derived from data filed with Federal Election Commission.

Table 2-8   National Party Campaign Finance: "Soft" and "Hard" Money, 1993–2008 (millions)

Type of money/party	1993–1994	1995–1996	1997–1998	1999–2000	2001–2002	2003–2004	2005–2006	2007–2008
Nonfederal, "soft" money[a]								
Democratic								
Raised	$49.1	$123.9	$92.8	$245.2	$246.1	b	b	b
Spent	50.4	121.8	93.0	244.8	250.7	b	b	b
Republican								
Raised	52.5	138.2	131.6	249.9	250.0	b	b	b
Spent	48.4	149.7	127.7	252.8	258.9	b	b	b
Federal, "hard" money								
Democratic								
Raised	132.8	221.6	160.0	275.2	217.2	$678.8	$483.1	$763.3
Spent	131.3	214.3	155.3	265.8	208.7	655.6	472.4	746.5
Republican								
Raised	244.1	416.5	285.0	465.8	424.1	782.4	602.3	792.9
Spent	232.1	408.5	275.9	427.0	427.0	752.6	608.2	766.1
Total, "soft" and "hard" money								
Democratic								
Raised	181.9	345.5	252.8	520.4	463.3	678.8	483.1	763.3
Spent	181.7	336.1	248.3	510.6	459.4	655.6	472.4	746.5
Republican								
Raised	296.6	554.7	416.6	715.7	674.1	782.4	602.3	792.9
Spent	280.5	558.2	403.6	679.8	685.9	752.6	608.2	766.1

Note: Amounts in current dollars. Totals do not include transfers among national party committees.

[a] Before 2003–2004, party committees could, without affecting their other contribution and expenditure limits, spend unlimited amounts ("soft" money) on grassroots activities specified in campaign finance law (for example, voter drives by volunteers in support of the parties' presidential nominees and campaign materials for volunteer distribution). Soft money could also be used to pay for issue advocacy and generic party advertising, to support the construction and maintenance of party headquarters, to pay a portion of the overhead expenses of party organizations, and to meet other shared expenses that benefited candidates in both federal and nonfederal elections. A portion could be transferred as well from national committees to state and local party committees, and some could be contributed directly to candidates in nonfederal races.
[b] The Bipartisan Campaign Reform Act (BCRA) of 2002 and court rulings prohibited political parties from raising soft money starting with the 2003–2004 election cycle.

Sources: "Soft" money: Federal Election Commission, "Party Committees Raise More than $1 Billion in 2001–2002," press release, March 20, 2003; "hard" money: Federal Election Commission, "Democratic National Party Federal Financial Activity through the End of the 2007–2008 Election Cycle" and "Republican National Party Federal Financial Activity through the End of the 2007–2008 Election Cycle" (*www.fec.gov*).

Table 2-9 Number of Political Action Committees (PACs), by Type, 1974–2009

Year	Corporate	Labor	Trade/ membership/health	Cooperative	Corporation without stock	Nonconnected[b]	Total
			Connected[a]				
1974	89	201	318	—	—	—	608
1975	139	226	357	—	—	—	722
1976	433	224	489	—	—	—	1,146
1977	550	234	438	8	20	110	1,360
1978	785	217	453	12	24	162	1,653
1979	950	240	514	17	32	247	2,000
1980	1,206	297	576	42	56	374	2,551
1981	1,329	318	614	41	68	531	2,901
1982	1,469	380	649	47	103	723	3,371
1983	1,538	378	643	51	122	793	3,525
1984	1,682	394	698	52	130	1,053	4,009
1986	1,744	384	745	56	151	1,077	4,157
1988	1,816	354	786	59	138	1,115	4,268
1990	1,795	346	774	59	136	1,062	4,172
1992	1,735	347	770	56	142	1,145	4,195
1994	1,660	333	792	53	136	980	3,954
1996	1,642	332	838	41	123	1,103	4,079
1998	1,567	321	821	39	115	935	3,798
2000	1,548	318	844	38	115	972	3,835
2002	1,508	316	891	41	116	1,019	3,891
2004	1,538	310	884	35	102	999	3,868
2006	1,622	290	925	37	103	1,233	4,210
2008	1,601	273	925	38	97	1,300	4,234
2009	1,598	272	995	49	103	1,594	4,611

Note: "—" indicates not available. Counts are as of December 31 for 1974–1998 (except 1975, which is as of November 24) and as of January 1 for 2000–2009. Counts for other years can be found in earlier editions of *Vital Statistics on American Politics.* The counts reflect federally registered PACs. Registration does not necessarily imply financial activity. Trade/membership/health category for 1974–1976 includes all PACs except corporate and labor; no further breakdown available.

[a] Connected PACs are associated with a sponsoring organization that may pay operating and fund-raising expenses. They are typically subdivided by the type of sponsor: corporate (with stockholders), labor (unions), trade/membership/health (professional groups and associations of corporations), cooperatives (primarily agricultural), and corporations without stock.

[b] Nonconnected PACs do not have a sponsoring organization.

Source: Federal Election Commission, "Number of Federal PACs Increases," press release, March 9, 2009 (*www.fec.gov*).

Table 2-10 PACs: Receipts, Expenditures, and Contributions, 1975–2008

Election cycle[a]	Receipts[b] (millions)	Expenditures[b] (millions)	Contributions to congressional candidates[c] (millions)	Percentage of receipts contributed to congressional candidates
1975–1976	$54.0	$52.9	$22.6	42
1977–1978	80.0	77.4	34.1	43
1979–1980	137.7	131.2	60.2	44
1981–1982	199.5	190.2	87.6	44
1983–1984	288.7	266.8	113.0	39
1985–1986	353.4	340.0	139.8	40
1987–1988	384.6	364.2	159.2	41
1989–1990	372.1	357.6	159.1	43
1991–1992	385.5	394.8	188.9	49
1993–1994	391.8	388.1	189.6	48
1995–1996	437.4	429.9	217.8	50
1997–1998	502.6	470.8	219.9	44
1999–2000	604.9	579.4	259.8	43
2001–2002	685.3	656.5	282.0	41
2003–2004	915.7	842.9	310.5	34
2005–2006	1,085.5	1,055.3	372.1	34
2007–2008	1,212.4	1,180.0	412.8	34

Note: Amounts in current dollars.

[a] Data cover January 1 of the odd-numbered year to December 31 of the even-numbered year.
[b] Receipts and expenditures for 1975–1984 exclude funds transferred between affiliated committees.
[c] Primarily contributions to candidates for election in the even-numbered year, made during the two-year election cycle. Some contributions — $27 million in 2007–2008 — went to candidates running for office in future years, or to debt retirement for candidates in past cycles.

Sources: 1975–1976: Joseph E. Cantor, "Political Action Committees: Their Evolution and Growth and Their Implications for the Political System," Report no. 83, Congressional Research Service, Washington, D.C., 1982, 87–88; 1977–1978: Federal Election Commission, "FEC Releases First PAC Figures for 1985–86," press release, May 21, 1987, 1; 1979–1988: "PAC Activity Falls in 1990 Elections," press release, March 31, 1991, 10; 1989–2008: "Growth in PAC Financial Activity Slows," press release, April 24, 2009 (*www.fec.gov*).

Table 2-11 Spending, by Type of PAC, 1977–2008 (millions)

Election cycle[a]	Corporate	Labor	Trade/membership/ health	Non-connected	Other connected[b]	Total
1977–1978	$15.2	$18.6	$23.8	$17.4	$2.4	$77.4
1979–1980	31.4	25.1	32.0	38.6	4.0	131.2
1981–1982	43.3	34.8	41.9	64.3	5.8	190.2
1983–1984	59.2	47.5	54.0	97.4	8.7	266.8
1985–1986	79.3	57.9	73.3	118.4	11.1	340.0
1987–1988	89.9	74.1	83.7	104.9	11.7	364.2
1989–1990	101.1	84.6	88.1	71.4	12.5	357.6
1991–1992	112.4	94.6	97.5	76.2	14.1	394.8
1993–1994	116.8	88.4	94.1	75.1	13.7	388.1
1995–1996	130.6	99.8	105.4	81.3	12.9	429.9
1997–1998	137.6	98.2	114.4	107.8	12.9	470.8
1999–2000	158.3	128.7	137.2	139.7	15.5	579.4
2001–2002	178.3	158.0	141.3	165.7	13.3	656.5
2003–2004	221.6	182.9	170.1	255.2	13.1	842.9
2005–2006	277.8	197.4	208.9	354.5	16.7	1,055.3
2007–2008	298.6	265.0	229.5	364.6	22.3	1,180.0

Note: Amounts in current dollars. Expenditures exclude transfers of funds between affiliated committees for 1977–1984. Detail may not add to totals because of rounding.

[a] Data cover January 1 of the odd-numbered year to December 31 of the even-numbered year.
[b] This category combines the Federal Election Commission categories of cooperatives and corporations without stock.

Sources: 1977–1978: Norman J. Ornstein, Thomas E. Mann, and Michael J. Malbin, eds., *Vital Statistics on Congress, 1987–1988* (Washington, D.C.: Congressional Quarterly, 1987), 105; 1979–1984: Federal Election Commission, "PAC Activity in 1994 Elections Remains at 1992 Levels," press release, March 31, 1995, 12; 1985–1988: "PAC Activity Increases for 2002 Elections," press release, March 27, 2003; 1989–2008: "Growth in PAC Financial Activity Slows," press release, April 24, 2009 (www.fec.gov).

Table 2-12 Contributions and Independent Expenditures, by Type of PAC, 1999–2008

Election cycle/PAC type	Number[a]	Receipts[b]	Contributions to federal candidates[c]		Independent expenditures[d]	
			Amount	Percentage of receipts	Amount	Percentage of receipts
1999–2000						
Corporate	1,365	$164,454,559	$91,525,699	56	$137,535	0.1%
Labor	236	136,011,151	51,573,364	38	2,825,840	2.1
Trade/membership/health	662	142,870,952	71,802,756	50	11,143,902	7.8
Cooperative	37	3,716,550	2,360,236	64	4,958	0.1
Corporations without stock	94	13,591,109	5,270,336	39	1,340,384	9.9
Nonconnected	670	144,266,748	37,297,383	26	5,589,170	3.9
Total	3,064	604,911,069	259,829,774	43	21,041,789	3.5
2001–2002						
Corporate	1,359	191,656,789	99,577,798	52	52,190	0.0
Labor	215	167,820,067	53,897,795	32	3,559,519	2.1
Trade/membership/health	697	145,781,414	75,146,673	52	8,092,148	5.6
Cooperative	36	3,680,041	2,656,875	72	0	0.0
Corporations without stock	86	9,714,903	4,399,446	45	82,601	0.9
Nonconnected	700	166,652,339	46,362,859	28	2,221,561	1.3
Total	3,093	685,305,553	282,041,446	41	14,008,019	2.0
2003–2004						
Corporate	1,402	238,984,115	115,641,547	48	223,729	0.1
Labor	206	191,651,043	52,103,572	27	20,737,373	10.8
Trade/membership/health	722	181,837,429	83,221,870	46	18,138,069	10.0
Cooperative	34	4,187,378	2,872,363	69	4,993	0.1
Corporations without stock	75	9,639,838	4,182,321	43	111,095	1.2
Nonconnected	819	289,423,580	52,467,328	18	18,159,133	6.3
Total	3,258	915,723,383	310,489,001	34	57,374,392	6.3

2005–2006					
Corporate	1,464	278,345,927	135,925,970	49	0.1
Labor	204	218,185,504	55,815,069	26	4.6
Trade/membership/health	745	218,448,147	101,803,507	47	8.7
Cooperative	35	6,166,566	3,454,915	56	0.1
Corporations without stock	89	11,441,713	4,885,718	43	3.3
Nonconnected	887	352,947,674	70,217,568	20	2.3
Total	3,424	1,085,535,531	372,102,747	34	3.5
2007–2008					
Corporate	1,470	313,350,975	158,323,496	51	0.1
Labor	203	262,055,837	62,675,294	24	22.4
Trade/membership/health	794	240,983,640	112,897,919	47	18.6
Cooperative	39	10,283,949	6,861,823	67	0.0
Corporations without stock	84	13,025,360	5,461,525	42	4.5
Nonconnected	1,023	372,720,837	66,627,495	18	8.3
Total	3,613	1,212,420,598	412,847,552	34	11.1

Note: Amounts in current dollars. Data for earlier years can be found in previous editions of *Vital Statistics on American Politics.*

[a] The numbers shown are those PACs that actually made contributions.
[b] Not adjusted for money transferred between affiliated committees. Receipts are for all PACs whether or not they made contributions to candidates in the election cycle.
[c] Figures include contributions to all federal candidates, including those who did not run for office during the years indicated.
[d] Independent expenditures include money spent for candidates and against candidates.

Sources: Federal Election Commission, "PAC Activity Increases in 2000 Election Cycle," press release, May 31, 2001; "PAC Activity Increases for 2002 Elections," press release, March 27, 2003; "PAC Activity Increases for 2004 Elections," press release, April 13, 2005; "PAC Activity Continues Climb in 2006," press release, October 5, 2007; "Growth in PAC Financial Activity Slows," press release, April 24, 2009 (*www.fec.gov*).

Table 2-13   Top Twenty PACs in Overall Spending and in Contributions to
Federal Candidates, 2007–2008

Rank	PAC	Overall spending
1	ACTBLUE	$53,547,065
2	Service Employees International Union Committee on Political Education (SEIU COPE)	45,956,641
3	Moveon.org PAC	38,123,090
4	Emily's List	25,061,526
5	Fred Thompson Political Action Committee	24,316,838
6	American Federation of State, County, and Municipal Employees—P E O P L E	19,319,462
7	National Rifle Association of America Political Victory Fund	15,588,823
8	UAW-V-CAP (UAW Voluntary Community Action Program)	13,116,234
9	DRIVE (Democrat Republican Independent Voter Education) PAC for International Brotherhood of Teamsters	13,077,646
10	National Association of Realtors PAC	11,893,487
11	1199 Service Employees International Union Federal Political Action Fund	11,783,975
12	American Federation of Teachers, AFL-CIO Committee on Political Education	10,705,693
13	National Republican Trust PAC	10,024,954
14	International Brotherhood of Electrical Workers PAC	8,953,424
15	United Food and Commercial Workers International Union Active Ballot Club	7,751,148
16	International Brotherhood of Electrical Workers Local 98 Committee on Political Education	7,388,940
17	Lyndon Larouche Political Action Committee	7,351,626
18	Communications Workers of America-COPE Political Contributions Committee	6,451,003
19	American Association for Justice PAC (AAJ PAC)	5,769,003
20	Voice of Teachers for Education/Committee on Political Education of NY State United Teachers (VOTE/COPE) of NYSUT	5,723,434

Rank	PAC	Contributions to federal candidates
1	National Association of Realtors PAC	$4,013,900
2	International Brotherhood of Electrical Workers PAC	3,333,650
3	AT&T Inc. Federal PAC	3,122,200
4	National Beer Wholesalers Association PAC	2,869,000
5	Dealers Election Action Committee of the National Automobile Dealers Association	2,864,000
6	American Bankers Association PAC (BANKPAC)	2,811,550
7	International Association of Firefighters Interested in Registration and Education PAC	2,709,900
8	American Association for Justice PAC (AAJ PAC)	2,700,500
9	Honeywell International PAC	2,515,616

Table 2-13   *(Continued)*

Rank	PAC	*Contributions to federal candidates*
10	BUILD Political Action Committee of the National Association of Home Builders	2,480,000
11	Machinists Non-Partisan Political League of the International Association of Machinists and Aerospace Workers	2,326,600
12	CULAC: PAC of Credit Union National Association	2,310,049
13	Service Employees International Union Committee on Political Education (SEIU COPE)	2,289,250
14	American Federation of Teachers, AFL-CIO Committee on Political Education	2,265,250
15	National Air Traffic Controllers Association PAC	2,236,475
16	DRIVE (Democrat Republican Independent Voter Education) PAC for International Brotherhood of Teamsters	2,202,300
17	Engineers Political Education Committee (EPEC)/ International Union of Operating Engineers	2,191,475
18	Airline Pilots Association PAC	2,115,500
19	American Federation of State, County, and Municipal Employees—P E O P L E	2,112,593
20	United Parcel Service Inc. PAC	2,082,707

Note: Amounts in current dollars. Information for earlier years can be found in previous editions of *Vital Statistics on American Politics.*

Source: Federal Election Commission, "Growth in PAC Financial Activity Slows," press release, April 24, 2009 (*www.fec.gov*).

Table 2-14 PAC Congressional Campaign Contributions, by Type of PAC and Incumbency Status of Candidate, 1991–2008 (millions)

Election cycle/ PAC type	House						Senate					
	Candidate party		Type of contest				Candidate party		Type of contest			
	Dem.	Rep.	Incumbent	Challenger	Open seat[a]	Total	Dem.	Rep.	Incumbent	Challenger	Open seat[a]	Total
1991–1992												
Corporate	$24.3	$20.5	$36.9	$2.9	$5.0	$44.9	$9.9	$13.5	$16.8	$2.4	$4.2	$23.4
Trade/membership/health	23.9	16.2	30.5	3.0	6.5	40.2	7.1	6.3	9.3	1.7	2.4	13.5
Labor	29.8	1.7	20.7	4.5	6.2	31.7	8.9	0.4	4.2	2.9	2.2	9.3
Nonconnected	6.9	3.7	6.5	1.6	2.4	10.6	4.6	2.9	4.4	1.5	1.5	7.4
Total[b]	88.1	43.7	98.7	12.4	20.7	132.2	31.8	23.9	36.3	8.7	10.7	55.7
1993–1994												
Corporate	24.8	20.4	37.9	3.1	4.3	45.3	9.2	15.1	15.2	2.0	7.1	24.2
Trade/membership/health	22.7	17.1	31.0	3.4	5.4	39.9	5.6	7.4	8.3	1.1	3.5	12.9
Labor	32.5	1.4	24.2	4.2	5.6	34.1	7.4	0.3	4.0	1.7	1.9	7.7
Nonconnected	7.5	4.4	7.6	1.9	2.4	11.9	3.3	2.8	3.6	0.8	1.7	6.1
Total[b]	90.9	45.0	104.9	13.0	18.2	136.2	26.6	26.5	32.6	5.8	14.7	53.1
1995–1996												
Corporate	16.2	36.8	45.8	2.0	5.3	53.2	4.9	18.5	13.7	2.6	7.1	23.4
Trade/membership/health	16.8	28.4	35.5	3.8	6.1	45.4	4.1	10.3	7.7	1.7	5.1	14.5
Labor	37.3	2.7	22.2	11.9	6.0	40.2	7.0	0.7	2.4	1.5	3.8	7.7
Nonconnected	6.8	8.7	9.6	3.6	2.5	15.7	2.7	5.2	3.8	1.3	2.8	7.9
Total[b]	79.4	79.7	117.7	21.7	20.5	159.9	19.4	36.1	28.7	7.4	19.3	55.5

1997–1998												
Corporate	16.7	35.0	45.4	2.1	4.2	51.7	8.3	17.9	20.6	2.7	3.0	26.3
Trade/membership/health	18.0	29.4	39.0	3.1	5.3	47.5	5.5	9.4	11.3	1.6	1.9	14.9
Labor	34.5	3.3	26.6	5.4	5.7	37.9	6.0	0.7	4.6	1.0	1.1	6.7
Nonconnected	7.7	12.4	11.7	4.2	4.3	20.2	3.3	4.6	5.6	1.3	1.0	7.9
Total[b]	79.1	82.8	127.0	15.2	19.8	162.1	24.1	33.6	43.8	6.8	7.2	57.8
1999–2000												
Corporate	22.2	40.7	55.4	2.4	5.3	63.1	7.5	19.3	20.7	1.5	4.6	26.8
Trade/membership/health	22.5	33.0	46.4	3.5	5.7	55.7	5.1	10.6	11.7	1.2	2.8	15.7
Labor	40.3	3.6	30.7	8.1	5.3	44.0	7.0	0.5	3.2	2.8	1.5	7.5
Nonconnected	11.5	15.8	15.3	5.8	6.2	27.4	3.6	5.9	5.8	1.5	2.2	9.5
Total[b]	99.2	96.2	152.7	20.2	23.0	195.9	23.9	37.4	42.7	7.2	11.4	61.3
2001–2002												
Corporate	24.1	46.1	61.7	1.7	6.9	70.3	10.3	19.0	21.6	4.3	3.4	29.3
Trade/membership/health	23.4	35.2	48.4	2.2	8.0	58.6	6.4	10.1	11.7	3.1	1.7	16.5
Labor	40.7	4.5	32.3	5.3	7.7	45.3	7.8	0.8	5.1	2.4	1.1	8.6
Nonconnected	14.3	18.5	18.9	4.9	8.9	32.7	6.5	7.1	7.6	4.2	1.8	13.6
Total[b]	104.6	107.2	165.7	14.2	32.1	212.0	31.9	38.1	47.7	14.3	8.1	70.0
2003–2004												
Corporate	25.5	56.3	75.2	2.0	4.6	81.8	11.4	20.9	24.2	1.3	6.7	32.2
Trade/membership/health	23.4	41.4	57.1	2.4	5.4	64.9	6.9	11.0	12.8	1.1	4.0	18.0
Labor	37.8	5.6	33.7	5.3	4.6	43.5	7.3	1.0	5.1	0.9	2.3	8.4
Nonconnected	11.6	24.3	22.2	6.1	7.6	35.9	6.7	9.1	8.1	2.2	5.4	15.8
Total[b]	100.5	130.7	192.9	16.0	22.5	231.4	33.2	42.8	51.6	5.7	18.8	76.1

(Table continues)

Table 2-14 (*Continued*)

| | House | | | | | | Senate | | | | | |
| | Candidate party | | Type of contest | | | | Candidate party | | Type of contest | | | |
Election cycle/ PAC type	Dem.	Rep.	Incum-bent	Chal-lenger	Open seat[a]	Total	Dem.	Rep.	Incum-bent	Chal-lenger	Open seat[a]	Total
2005–2006												
Corporate	32.0	66.7	92.7	1.7	4.2	98.7	12.7	23.4	31.8	1.7	2.6	37.2
Trade/membership/ health	30.5	50.7	72.0	3.4	5.7	81.2	7.5	12.4	16.2	1.8	2.0	20.6
Labor	42.5	5.7	32.8	10.3	5.1	48.3	6.4	0.7	4.1	2.1	0.9	7.5
Nonconnected[b]	18.3	33.0	32.6	10.5	8.2	51.3	7.8	10.5	11.3	4.3	2.7	18.9
Total[b]	126.1	159.7	235.9	26.3	23.5	286.0	35.3	48.0	64.9	10.1	8.3	86.1
2007–2008												
Corporate	57.4	54.4	103.2	5.0	3.6	111.8	17.9	26.7	38.8	2.8	3.1	44.7
Trade/membership/ health	48.0	40.0	76.1	7.2	4.8	88.0	10.0	14.5	19.8	2.6	2.0	24.4
Labor	50.0	3.9	37.9	11.3	4.6	53.8	7.7	0.7	4.2	3.0	1.2	8.4
Nonconnected[b]	25.3	19.6	27.9	11.6	5.4	44.9	9.3	10.7	13.1	4.4	2.5	20.0
Total[b]	185.7	122.5	253.6	35.7	18.8	308.2	46.0	54.1	77.9	13.0	9.1	100.0

Note: Amounts are current dollar amounts contributed during the two-year election cycle indicated to all candidates in primary, general, runoff, and special elections. Figures are for all House and Senate candidates, not just those up for election in the two-year cycle. Data for earlier years can be found in previous editions of *Vital Statistics on American Politics.*

[a] "Open seat" refers to candidates in elections in which an incumbent did not seek reelection.
[b] Includes PACs classified by the Federal Election Commission as cooperatives and corporations without stock.

Sources: 1991–1992: "PAC Activity Rebounds in 1991–1992 Election Cycle," press release, April 29, 1993, 4–5; 1993–1994: "PAC Activity in 1994 Elections Remains at 1992 Levels," press release, March 31, 1995, 4, 5; 1995–1996: "PAC Activity Increases in the 1995–96 Election Cycle," press release, April 22, 1997; 1997–1998: "FEC Releases Information on PAC Activity for 1997–98," press release, June 9, 1999; 1999–2000: "PAC Activity Increases in 2000 Election Cycle," press release, May 31, 2001; 2001–2002: "PAC Activity Increases for 2002 Elections," press release, March 27, 2003; 2003–2004: "PAC Activity Increases for 2004 Elections," press release, April 13, 2005; 2005–2006: "PAC Activity Continues Climb in 2006," press release, October 5, 2007; 2007–2008: "Growth in PAC Financial Activity Slows," press release, April 24, 2009 (*www.fec.gov*).

3

Public Opinion and Voting

- **Partisanship**
- **Ideology**
- **Voting by Groups**
- **Presidential and Congressional Approval**
- **Confidence in Government and the Economy**
- **Most Important Problem**
- **Specific Issues**

Public opinion data are everywhere. For example, preelection polls give the pundits and the voters an idea of who is ahead and who is behind. Other polls give candidates and officeholders a glimpse into what the public thinks and how it would react to changes in public policies. Survey data are also used, in a more partisan way, by politicians, commentators, and interest groups to support their positions. And, in a slightly different form, they are used even more widely by advertisers and manufacturers to gauge consumer reactions to new products and services. Reflecting this frequent and varied use of surveys, this chapter presents public opinion on issues ranging from the very broad, such as the government and the economy, to the specific, such as gun control and the death penalty.

This chapter also includes tables and figures on how specific groups of voters cast their ballots in elections. Chapter 1 presented overall election results, indicating which party or individual won an election, whereas this chapter shows votes by region, gender, race, religion, and so on, as well as for groups of ideologues, such as liberals and conservatives, partisan groups, and sometimes special groups such as first-time voters. Because these data are analogous to public opinion data in that they come from sample surveys and indicate group opinions rather than overall election outcomes, they are included in this chapter.

Figures 3-1 through 3-4 and Tables 3-1 through 3-3 cover two of the most frequently cited components of public opinion—partisanship and political ideology. These characteristics merit emphasis because of their practical political significance. They are of interest not only to analysts who wish to understand scientifically why people behave as they do, but also to those who assess long-term political and social trends, as well as those who track day-to-day politics.

From another perspective, these results are important because they illustrate the reliability and validity of public opinion polling, as well as the hazards of gauging personal opinion. Figures 3-1 and 3-2, showing self-proclaimed party identification, are reasonably similar for the period they jointly cover. If public opinion data were totally unreliable, as some contend, such similarity would be unlikely. Moreover, these figures illustrate two aspects of reliability and validity. First, polling as few as fifteen hundred people is a window to the opinion of the entire population; the two separate polling organizations represented in Figures 3-1 and 3-2 would not obtain such similarity over decades of interviewing if their results represented only those actually interviewed. (Of course, one must choose the fifteen hundred respondents according to scientific sampling procedures, as do all the major polling organizations.) Second, poll results are not completely dependent on exact question wording. The Pew question (Figure 3-1) focuses on the immediate situation ("In politics today . . . "), while the American National Election Studies question (Table 3-1) is broader ("Generally speaking . . . "), suggesting that the Pew question might pick up more short-term fluctuations in partisanship. Yet the results are quite similar.

Both the American National Election Studies and Pew surveys probe those who claim to be independents to determine whether they lean toward one party or the other. The responses to this probe as well as other evidence (Table 3-7) raise the question of whether independents are really closet partisans. How that question is answered, as the contrast between the two plots in Figures 3-1 and 3-2 shows, has major implications for conclusions about the relative strengths of the parties. As emphasized in earlier introductions, even simple data descriptions involve interpretation.

Because surveys are not exact counts of the whole population, "sampling error" is often reported to convey the range within which the true population result lies. For example, results are said to be accurate to within plus or minus 3 percent. Yet even with greater precision (achieved by increasing the size of the sample), survey results still require interpretation. Suppose one could ask every American adult simultaneously whether he or she is a Democrat, an independent, or a Republican. There would then be no sampling error; because everyone was asked, the information would describe the entire U.S. population at that particular time. But that leads back to an equally vexing question: what does it mean to be an independent?

The "don't know" responses to the ideology question about liberal or conservative self-identification in Table 3-3—and in the other public opinion tables—illustrate a similar point. Whether pollsters ask about a general position or a specific issue, some proportion of the sample—often as much as 15 percent and sometimes much more—responds "don't know." It is not immediately apparent how to interpret such responses. Some people have information about the subject matter but no opinion; some have no information and no opinion; and a few have no information but have an opinion anyway. The pollster's decision about how to treat such responses can make a large difference. For example, in a preelection poll should a pollster assume that those respondents who have not yet chosen candidates to support will eventually (1) split votes between candidates in similar proportions as those who have already decided, (2) not vote, (3) divide evenly between the candidates, or (4) overwhelmingly support particular candidates?

For public officials seeking guidance on public sentiment, no simple reading suffices because they must assess intensity as well as direction. Those pursuing a theoretical understanding of politics face the same problem. Take the matter of gun control. For more than forty years, a majority of Americans— usually 70–80 percent—have favored stronger gun control as represented by a survey question about requiring a permit to own a gun (Table 3-14). If that is true, why is it more stringent gun control laws have not been enacted? The answer has to do, in part, with the strength of feeling—and organization—of the anti-gun control lobby. Those supporting Second Amendment rights (as they would probably prefer to be known) have historically been much better organized and have outspent those who would restrict gun ownership, presumably because gun advocates feel more strongly about the issue. Understanding the importance of public opinion in politics requires more than a simple nose count. The salience of an opinion to the person holding it also counts.

Another factor in polling is that a particular survey result usually says little in isolation. The soundest interpretations depend on several surveys stretching over time, often over a period of years. Consider the decline and partial recovery in public confidence in government (Figure 3-8). The confidence level at a particular time is a mere point, difficult or impossible to interpret. Yet that point, when viewed with comparable points from similar surveys over the years, indicates a trend—decline, upsurge, constancy, whatever. Consequently, reports of public opinion increasingly emphasize extended time series, as is done here (Figures 3-11, 3-12, 3-15, and 3-16, and Tables 3-11 through 3-17). Such time series data can be usefully supplemented by cross sections (Table 3-2). Such within-survey contrasts convey whether and how groups differ in attitudes. Where long time series are impossible because of the nature of the event—such as the U.S. military actions in Iraq (Figure 3-18) and the war on terrorism (Table 3-18)—comparison of multiple time series can aid interpretation.

The issues most salient in the public's mind vary across time. This fact itself has been measured by asking people what they regard as the nation's most important problem (Figures 3-11 and 3-12). Yet many issues are of perennial interest, and over-time assessments (which sometimes require the use of earlier editions of this volume) often date back to the 1940s (Tables 3-11 and 3-16). From the point of view of elections, the significance of public opinion lies chiefly in how the public translates its feelings into summary judgments of the president (Figure 3-6), Congress (Figure 3-7), and government and society as a whole (Figures 3-8 and 3-9). Yet another set consists of favorable versus unfavorable opinions of the two parties (Figure 3-13). Finally, public satisfaction with the status quo and evaluations of the economy, both personal and national and present and future, are perennial concerns in politics (Figures 3-9 and 3-10).

Of course, the most direct and important judgments about political leaders, candidates, and parties occur in elections, but election results tell us only the overall results (and outcome in different geographical areas). Surveys are the prime means of looking into the behavior of individuals and groups. This chapter reveals how various kinds of individuals voted for president, both in the general election (Table 3-4) and in presidential primaries (Tables 3-5 and 3-6), and for Congress (Table 3-8). These data also answer questions of great theoretical and practical interest, such as the extent to which individuals vote in accordance with their general party preference and in straight or split tickets (Tables 3-7, 3-9, and 3-10).

A final note. Even a firm understanding of public opinion can be contradicted by events because one cannot blindly equate opinion with behavior. The growth of racial tolerance in the South is a telling counterpoint to a political atmosphere formerly committed to white supremacy. As one respondent, a segregationist, told a pollster in the mid-1960s: "You asked me what I favored, not what I will accept graciously, not what I thought was right."[1]

Note

1. Donald R. Matthews and James W. Prothro, *Negroes and the New Southern Politics* (New York: Harcourt, Brace and World, 1966), 363. See also Robert Weissberg's thoughtful discussion of different types of tolerance, especially his distinction between "hearts and minds" tolerance and various forms of behavioral tolerance. Weissberg, *Political Tolerance: Balancing Community and Diversity* (Thousand Oaks, Calif.: Sage Publications, 1998).

Table 3-1   Partisan Identification, American National Election Studies, 1952–2008 (percent)

	Democrat			Inde-pen-dent	Republican			Apo-litical	Total	Number of inter-views
Year	Strong	Weak	Inde-pendent		Inde-pendent	Weak	Strong			
1952	22	25	10	6	7	14	14	3	101	1,784
1954	22	25	9	7	6	14	13	4	100	1,130
1956	21	23	6	9	8	14	15	4	100	1,757
1958	27	22	7	7	5	16	11	4	99	1,439
1960	20	25	6	10	7	14	16	2	100	1,156
1962	23	23	7	8	6	16	12	4	99	1,287
1964	27	25	9	8	6	14	11	1	101	1,550
1966	18	28	9	12	7	15	10	1	100	1,278
1968	20	25	10	11	9	15	10	1	101	1,553
1970	20	24	10	13	8	15	9	1	100	1,501
1972	15	26	11	13	10	13	10	1	99	2,694
1974	17	21	13	15	9	14	8	3	100	1,567
1976	15	25	12	15	10	14	9	1	101	2,233
1978	15	24	14	14	10	13	8	3	101	2,283
1980	18	23	11	13	10	14	9	2	100	1,612
1982	20	24	11	11	8	14	10	2	100	1,411
1984	17	20	11	11	12	15	12	2	100	2,236
1986	18	22	10	12	11	15	10	2	100	2,166
1988	17	18	12	11	13	14	14	2	101	2,032
1990	20	19	12	10	12	15	10	2	100	1,966
1992	18	18	14	12	12	14	11	1	100	2,471
1994	15	19	13	11	12	15	15	1	101	1,787
1996	18	19	14	9	12	15	12	1	100	1,709
1998	19	18	14	11	11	16	10	2	101	1,274
2000	19	15	15	12	13	12	12	0	98	1,785
2002	16	17	15	8	13	16	14	1	100	1,498
2004	16	16	17	10	12	12	16	0	99	1,212
2008	19	15	17	11	11	13	13	0	99	2,299

Note: Question: "Generally speaking, do you consider yourself a Republican, a Democrat, an Independent, or what?" If Republican or Democrat: "Would you call yourself a strong (R/D) or a not very strong (R/D)?" If Independent or other: "Do you think of yourself as closer to the Republican or Democratic party?" There was no update of the American National Election Studies series in 2006.

Source: Calculated by the editors from American National Election Studies data, Center for Political Studies, University of Michigan, Ann Arbor (*www.electionstudies.org*).

106

Figure 3-1 Partisan Identification, American National Election Studies, 1952–2008

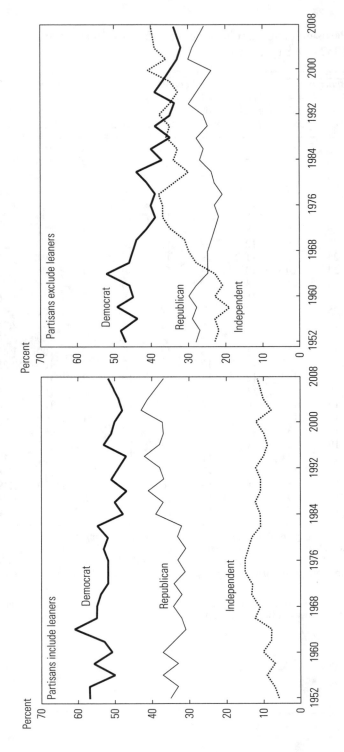

Note: See Table 3-1, this volume, for question. "Leaners" are independents who consider themselves closer to one party. There was no update of the American National Election Studies series in 2006.

Source: Calculated by the editors from American National Election Studies data, Center for Political Studies, University of Michigan, Ann Arbor (*www.electionstudies.org*).

Figure 3-2 Partisan Identification, Pew Surveys, 1987–2009

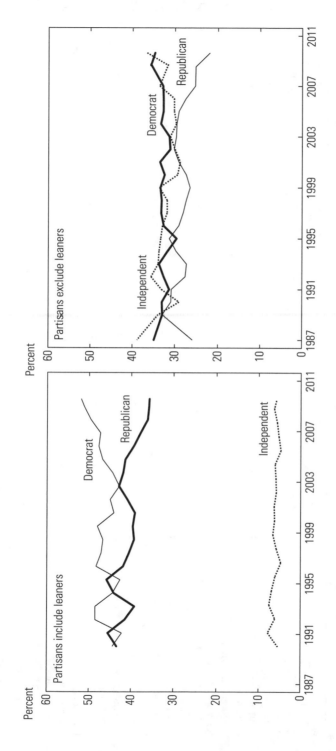

107

Note: Data for 2009 is through April. Related data for additional years can be found in previous editions of *Vital Statistics on American Politics.* Question: "In politics today, do you consider yourself a Republican, Democrat, or Independent?" If answered other than Republican or Democrat: "As of today do you lean more to the Republican Party or more to the Democratic Party?"

Source: Pew Research Center for the People and the Press, "Trends in Political Values and Core Attitudes: 1987–2009," May 21, 2009, 136–137 (*http://people-press.org*).

Table 3-2 Partisan Identification, by Groups, 2004 and 2008 (percent)

	2004				2008				Democratic gain since 2004	Sample size, 2008
	Democrat	Independent	Republican	Democratic advantage	Democrat	Independent	Republican	Democratic advantage		
Sex										
Men	43	9	48	−5	47	11	42	5	4	8,308
Women	51	9	40	11	55	11	34	21	4	9,235
Age										
18–29 years	50	9	40	10	58	10	33	25	8	1,710
30–49 years	45	8	47	−2	50	10	39	11	5	5,416
50–64 years	48	8	44	4	51	11	38	13	3	5,647
65 years and over	50	9	42	8	49	11	40	9	−1	4,408
Race and ethnicity										
White	42	8	50	−8	46	10	44	2	4	14,391
All others	70	12	18	52	73	12	15	58	3	3,152
Black	83	8	9	74	86	8	7	79	3	1,776
Hispanic	56	10	34	22	62	11	27	35	6	926
Region										
East	52	9	40	12	55	11	34	21	3	3,194
Midwest	46	10	45	1	50	12	38	12	4	4,513
South	45	8	46	−1	49	10	41	8	4	6,405
West	48	8	43	5	53	10	37	16	5	3,431
Education										
Less than high school	57	11	32	25	60	13	27	33	3	930

High school graduate	48	10	43	5	52	11	38	14	4	4,786
Some college	44	9	48	−4	50	11	39	11	6	4,541
College graduate	44	7	50	−6	47	10	43	4	3	4,179
Postgraduate	51	7	42	9	53	9	38	15	2	3,020
Income										
<$20,000	60	10	30	30	63	12	24	39	3	1,973
$20,000–29,999	56	9	35	21	58	10	32	26	2	1,460
$30,000–49,999	47	8	45	2	54	9	36	18	7	3,076
$50,000–74,999	43	6	51	−8	51	8	41	10	8	2,854
$75,000–99,999	40	6	54	−14	48	8	45	3	8	2,212
$100,000+	42	7	52	−10	45	8	47	−2	3	3,335
Community type										
Urban	56	9	35	21	58	11	32	26	2	4,751
Suburban	44	9	48	−4	49	11	40	9	5	7,301
Rural	43	9	47	−4	45	12	43	2	2	3,069
Religious preference										
Total, white Protestant	36	7	57	−21	37	10	53	−16	1	7,843
White, evangelical Protestant	28	6	66	−38	30	8	62	−32	2	3,947
White, mainline Protestant	43	8	49	−6	45	11	44	1	2	3,896
White, non-Hispanic Catholic	45	8	47	−2	49	10	40	9	4	3,146
Union household										
Yes	56	8	36	20	58	12	30	28	2	581
No	46	9	46	0	50	11	39	11	4	3,217

(Table continues)

Table 3-2 *(Continued)*

	2004				2008				Democratic gain since 2004	Sample size, 2008
	Democrat	Independent	Republican	Democratic advantage	Democrat	Independent	Republican	Democratic advantage		
Homeowner										
Yes	44	8	47	−3	47	10	43	4	3	5,579
No	59	9	32	27	62	12	26	36	3	1,491
Marital status										
Married	40	8	51	−11	45	10	45	0	5	9,643
Divorced/ separated	54	9	36	18	60	11	29	31	6	2,296
Widowed	55	9	36	19	55	13	32	23	0	1,363
Never married	59	9	32	27	61	11	28	33	2	2,002
Living with partner	—	—	—	—	61	10	29	32	—	858
Parent or guardian										
Yes	44	8	48	−4	47	12	41	6	3	1,579
No	49	9	42	7	53	13	35	18	4	3,855
Total	47	9	44	3	51	11	38	13	4	17,543

Note: "—" indicates not available. Percentages are from pooled surveys of 17,543 registered voters interviewed by the Pew Research Center from January through August of 2004 and 2008. Not all characteristics were available in each of the pooled surveys, making sample sizes vary. A Democratic gain is not always matched precisely by a Republican loss, or vice versa. Related data for additional years can be found in previous editions of *Vital Statistics on American Politics*. For question, see Figure 3-2, this volume. Percentages in the table count leaners as partisans.

Source: Pew Research Center for the People and the Press, "Convention Backgrounder: A Closer Look at the Parties in 2008," August 22, 2008, 5–6 *(http://people-press.org).*

Table 3-3 Liberal or Conservative Self-Identification, 1973–2008 (percent)

Year	Extremely liberal	Liberal	Slightly liberal	Moderate	Slightly conservative	Conservative	Extremely conservative	Don't know	Number of interviews
1973	4	14	13	36	13	13	3	6	1,484
1975	3	12	13	38	16	11	2	5	1,478
1978	2	9	16	37	18	13	2	4	1,509
1980	3	8	14	40	19	12	3	1	1,451
1982	2	9	15	39	14	13	4	4	1,498
1983	2	8	12	40	18	13	2	3	802
1984	2	9	12	39	19	13	3	3	1,463
1985	2	11	11	37	18	14	3	4	1,526
1986	2	9	11	39	17	15	3	4	1,468
1987	2	12	13	37	16	12	2	4	1,436
1988	2	12	12	35	17	16	2	4	1,472
1989	3	12	12	37	16	13	2	5	1,532
1990	3	10	13	34	18	14	4	4	1,369
1991	2	10	14	39	14	14	3	3	1,512
1993	2	12	13	35	17	16	3	3	1,598
1994	2	11	13	35	16	16	3	3	2,981
1996	2	10	12	36	16	16	3	5	2,898
1998	2	12	12	36	15	15	3	5	2,824
2000	4	11	10	38	14	15	3	5	2,797
2002	3	11	12	38	15	16	3	3	1,362
2004	3	9	12	37	16	17	4	2	1,325
2006	3	11	11	37	14	15	4	3	1,323
2008	3	12	11	37	14	16	4	4	2,010

Note: GSS interviews are conducted in the spring of the year indicated, usually March–June. Question: "We hear a lot of talk these days about liberals and conservatives. I'm going to show you a seven-point scale on which the political views that people might hold are arranged from extremely liberal—point 1—to extremely conservative—point 7. Where would you place yourself on this scale?" Data for additional years can be found in previous editions of *Vital Statistics on American Politics*.

Source: General Social Survey, National Opinion Research Center, University of Chicago.

112

Figure 3-3 Liberal, Moderate, and Conservative Self-Identification, 1973–2008

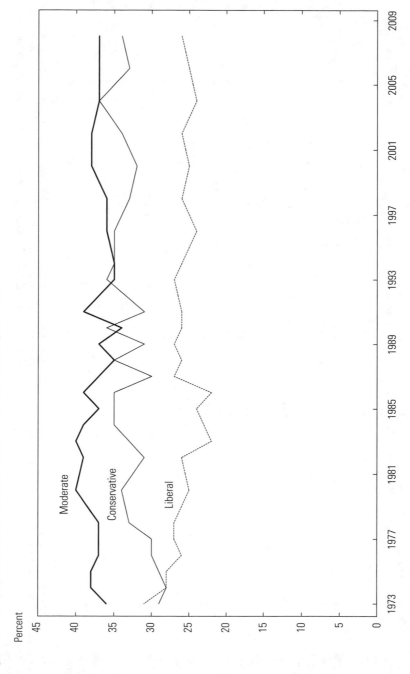

Note: See Table 3-3, this volume.

Source: Table 3-3, this volume.

Figure 3-4 Ideological Self-Identification of College Freshmen, 1970–2008

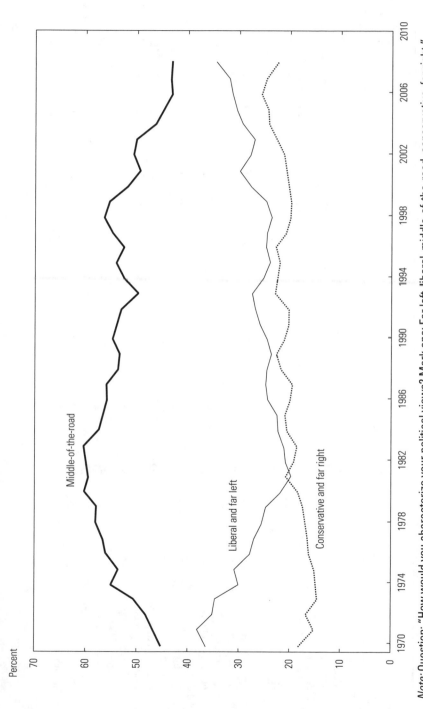

Percent

Middle-of-the-road

Liberal and far left

Conservative and far right

Note: Question: "How would you characterize your political views? Mark one: Far left, liberal, middle-of-the-road, conservative, far right."

Sources: Alexander Astin et al., *The American Freshman: Thirty Year Trends* (Los Angeles: Higher Education Research Institute, University of California, Los Angeles, 1997); *The American Freshman: National Norms for Fall 1997–* (Los Angeles: Higher Education Research Institute, University of California, Los Angeles, annual).

Table 3-4 Presidential Vote in General Elections, by Groups, Network Exit Polls, 1992–2008 (percent)

	Percentage of voters					1992			1996			2000			2004		2008	
	1992	1996	2000	2004	2008	D	R	I	D	R	I	D	R	I	D	R	D	R
Sex																		
Men	47	48	48	46	47	41	38	21	43	44	10	42	53	3	44	55	49	48
Women	53	52	52	54	53	45	37	17	54	38	7	54	43	2	51	48	56	43
Race/ethnicity																		
White	87	83	82	77	74	39	40	20	43	46	9	42	54	3	41	58	43	55
Black	8	10	10	11	13	83	10	7	84	12	4	90	8	1	88	11	95	4
Hispanic/Latino	3	5	4	8	9	61	25	14	72	21	6	67	31	2	53	44	67	31
Age																		
Under 30 years	21	17	17	17	18	43	34	22	53	34	10	48	46	5	54	45	66	32
30–44 years	36	33	33	29	29	41	38	21	48	41	9	48	49	2	46	53	52	46
45–59 years	23	26	28	30	37[a]	41	40	19	48	41	9	48	49	2	48	51	50[a]	49[a]
60 years and older	21	24	22	24	16[b]	50	38	12	48	44	7	51	47	2	46	54	45[b]	53[b]
Education																		
Not high school graduate	7	6	5	4	4	54	28	18	59	28	11	59	39	1	50	49	63	35
High school graduate	25	24	21	22	20	43	36	21	51	35	13	48	49	1	47	52	52	46
College incomplete	29	27	32	32	31	41	37	21	48	40	10	45	51	3	46	54	51	47
College graduate	39	43	24	42	45	44	39	17	47	44	7	48	48	3	49	49	53	45
Religion																		
White Protestant	38	34	47	41	42	34	47	19	38	53	8	34	63	2	32	67	34	65
White fundamentalist	17	24	14	23	26	23	62	15	26	65	8	18	80	2	21	78	24	74
Catholic	27	29	26	27	27	44	35	20	53	37	9	49	47	2	47	52	54	45
Jewish	4	3	4	3	2	80	11	9	78	16	3	79	19	1	74	25	78	21

Region																		
East	24	23	23	22	21c	47	35	18	55	34	9	56	39	3	56	43	59c	40c
Midwest	27	26	26	26	24	42	37	21	48	41	10	48	49	2	48	51	54	44
South	29	30	31	32	32	41	43	16	46	46	7	43	55	1	42	58	45	54
West	20	20	21	20	23	43	34	23	48	40	8	48	46	4	50	49	57	40
Union household	19	23	26	24	21	55	24	21	59	30	9	59	37	3	59	40	59	39
Family income																		
Under $15,000	14	11	7	8	6	58	23	19	59	28	11	57	37	4	63	36	73	25
$15,000–29,999	24	23	16	15	12	45	35	20	53	36	9	54	41	3	57	42	60	37
$30,000–49,999	30	27	24	22	19	41	38	21	48	40	10	49	48	2	50	49	55	43
$50,000–74,999	20	21	25	23	21	40	41	18	47	45	7	46	51	2	43	56	48	49
Over $75,000	13	18	28	32	41	36	48	16	41	51	7	44	53	2	43	57	50	49
Party																		
Democratic	38	39	39	37	39	77	10	13	84	10	5	86	11	2	89	11	89	10
Independent	27	26	27	26	29	38	32	30	43	35	17	45	47	6	49	48	52	44
Republican	35	35	35	37	32	10	73	17	13	80	6	8	91	1	6	93	9	90
Ideology																		
Liberal	21	20	20	21	22	68	14	18	78	11	7	80	13	6	85	13	89	10
Moderate	49	47	50	45	44	47	31	21	57	33	9	52	44	2	54	45	60	39
Conservative	30	33	29	34	34	18	64	18	20	71	8	17	81	1	15	84	20	78
Previous presidential vote																		
Democratic	27	47	46	37	37	83	5	12	85	9	4	82	15	2	90	10	89	9
Independent/third party	2	14	6	3	4	66	5	30	22	44	33	27	64	7	71	21	66	24
Republican	55	38	31	43	46	21	59	20	13	82	4	7	91	1	9	91	17	82
Congressional vote																		
Democratic	46	49	49	49	54	74	11	15	84	8	7	85	11	3	88	11	88	10
Republican	54	49	49	50	44	10	72	18	15	76	8	12	86	1	9	91	9	89

(Table continues)

Table 3-4 *(Continued)*

	Percentage of voters					1992			1996			2000			2004		2008	
	1992	1996	2000	2004	2008	D	R	I	D	R	I	D	R	I	D	R	D	R
First-time voter	11	9	9	11	11	46	32	22	54	34	11	52	43	4	53	46	69	30
Total	100	100	100	100	100	43	38	19	49	41	8	48	48	2	48	51	53	45

Note: "D" indicates Democrat; "R" indicates Republican; "I" indicates H. Ross Perot's candidacy in 1992 and 1996 and Ralph Nader's in 2000. Data based on questionnaires completed by voters leaving polling places around the nation on election day. Differing questions and question formats make comparability across elections of some of these groups problematic. For example, in some years the "white fundamentalist" category is "evangelicals," "born-again Christians," or members of the "religious right." See sources for details. The number of respondents in 1992 was 15,490; in 1996, 16,637; in 2000, 13,279; in 2004, 13,660; and in 2008, 17,836. Data for earlier years can be found in previous editions of *Vital Statistics on American Politics*.

^a Age category is 45–64 years for 2008.
^b Age category is 65 years and older for 2008.
^c Region is "Northeast" for 2008.

Sources: Percentages calculated by the editors from Voter Research and Surveys, General Election Exit Polls, National Files, 1992; Voter News Service, General Election Exit Polls, National Files, 1996 and 2000; National Election Pool General Election Exit Polls, 2004, National Data; CNN Presidential Election National Exit Poll, 2008 (*www.cnn.com*); obtained through the Inter-university Consortium for Political and Social Research (*www.icpsr.umich.edu*). Neither the collectors of the original data nor the Consortium bear any responsibility for the results presented here.

117

Figure 3-5 Presidential Preferences during 2008

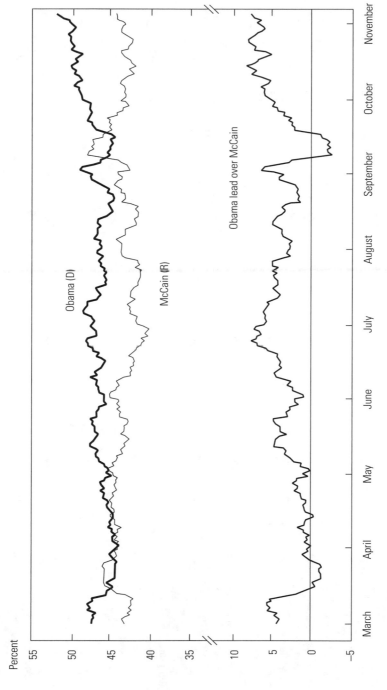

Note: Figure shows five-day moving average from national polls gauging support for Sen. Barack Obama and Sen. John McCain for president. Starting October 11, and through the final weeks of election 2008, only nonpartisan affiliated polls were included in the averages.

Source: Real Clear Politics (*www.realclearpolitics.com*).

Table 3-5 Vote in Democratic Presidential Primaries, by Groups, 1988–2008 (percent)

Group	Percentage of primary voters — 1988	1992	2000	2004	2008	1988 Dukakis	1988 Jackson	1988 Others	1992 Clinton	1992 Brown	1992 Tsongas	2000 Bradley	2000 Gore	2004 Edwards	2004 Kerry	2004 Others	2008 Clinton	2008 Obama
Sex																		
Men	47	47	43	46	43	41	29	30	50	21	20	27	71	25	54	21	43	50
Women	53	53	57	54	57	43	30	26	51	20	21	22	76	26	55	20	52	43
Race/ethnicity																		
White	75	80	69	73	65	54	12	35	47	23	25	29	69	28	53	19	55	39
Black	21	14	17	16	19	4	92	4	70	15	8	12	86	19	56	25	15	82
Hispanic	3	4	10	8	12	48	30	20	51	30	15	11	89	13	70	17	61	35
Age																		
Under 30 years	14	12	9	10	14	35	38	27	47	24	19	26	72	25	48	27	38	58
30–44 years	31	33	26	23	—	37	36	26	45	26	22	24	74	25	52	23	—	—
45–59 years	25	25	31	34	—	42	30	28	51	19	20	27	71	27	56	18	—	—
60 years and older	30	30	33	33	18[a]	53	19	29	59	15	18	21	77	25	63	12	59[a]	34[a]
Religion																		
Catholic	30	50	29	29	—	60	18	22	55	14	21	26	72	23	61	16	—	—
White Protestant	36	30	49	—	—	43	10	47	44	24	24	26	71	—	—	—	—	—
Jewish	7	6	8	5	—	75	8	17	75	15	33	31	68	17	70	13	—	—
Party																		
Democratic	72	67	84	73	76	43	33	24	57	19	17	21	77	23	60	17	51	45
Independent	20	29	14	22	19	44	20	34	36	25	27	42	55	31	42	28	40	52
Ideology																		
Liberal	27	35	47	46	47	41	41	19	47	26	20	21	72	22	58	20	47	48
Moderate	47	45	41	39	40	47	25	28	54	18	19	22	77	28	54	18	50	45
Conservative	22	20	12	15	13	38	23	38	48	17	23	27	68	30	43	26	47	44

	—	—	28	32	—	—	43	29	28	50	21	20	24	75	23	58	19	—	—
Union household																			
Total	100	100	100	100	—	—	—	—	—	—	—	—	22	74	25	54	21	—	—

Note: "—" indicates not available. Entries are derived from exit poll data in thirty-three contested delegate selection primaries in 1988, twenty-nine in 1992, twenty in 2000, and eighteen in 2004; for 2008, exit poll data include thirty-six contested delegate selection primaries and three caucuses (Iowa, Nevada, and New Mexico). No exit poll in Louisiana in 1984; in Montana, Oregon, and District of Columbia in 1988; in Arizona, Michigan, Utah, and Washington State in 2000; in Michigan, New Mexico, and Utah in 2004; and in Idaho, Nebraska, Puerto Rico, District of Columbia, and Washington State in 2008.

[a] Age 65 years and older for 2008.

Sources: Percentages calculated by the editors from CBS News/*New York Times* Primary Election Day Exit Polls, 1984 and 1988; Voter Research and Surveys, Presidential Primary Exit Polls, 1992; Voter News Service, Presidential Primary Exit Polls, 2000; Edison Media Research, Mitofsky International, National Election Pool Democratic Presidential Preference Primary Exit Polls, 2004; and ABC News Presidential Primary Exit Polls (*http://abcnews.go.com*), 2008; obtained through the Inter-university Consortium for Political and Social Research (*www.icpsr.org*). Neither the collectors of the original data nor the Consortium bear any responsibility for the results presented here.

Table 3-6 Vote in Republican Presidential Primaries, by Groups, 2000 and 2008 (percent)

Group	Percentage of voters		2000		2008		
	2000	2008	G. W. Bush	McCain	Huckabee	McCain	Romney
Sex							
Men	51	54	55	38	21	43	25
Women	49	46	60	35	24	41	25
Race/ethnicity							
White	—	89	—	—	22	42	25
Black	—	2	—	—	27	42	17
Hispanic	—	6	—	—	19	46	19
Age							
Under 30 years	10	11	56	34	29	34	21
30–44 years	26	—	59	33	—	—	—
45–59 years	31	—	55	39	—	—	—
60 years and older	34	23[a]	60	37	16[a]	48[a]	26[a]
Party							
Democrat	6	3	18	77	22	48	16
Independent	25	21	38	55	19	42	20
Republican	70	76	67	27	23	42	26
Ideology							
Liberal	11	9	40	54	15	55	16
Moderate	33	27	46	50	14	55	18
Conservative	55	63	68	25	27	35	29
Evangelical or member of religious right							
No	72	56	52	43	10	49	28
Yes	23	44	74	17	39	33	20
Time of vote decision							
In last three days	18	25	48	42	24	39	27
Within last week	17	—	49	44	—	—	—

Earlier this year	48	—	50	46	—	—	—
Last year	18	—	69	26	—	—	—
Military veteran							
Yes	—	22	—	—	19	47	25
No	—	78	—	—	23	41	25
Percentage of total vote	100	100	58	36	22	42	25

Note: "—" indicates not available. The small percentage of votes going to other candidates is not shown. For 2000, based on combined vote totals and results from exit polls conducted in twenty-five primary states between February 1 and March 14 by Voter News Service. Some questions were not asked in each state. There was no exit poll in Washington State. There were no exit polls for the 2004 primaries. For 2008, based on twenty-seven primaries and two caucuses (Iowa and Nevada) held between January 8 and March 11. There were no exit polls for primaries held in Rhode Island, the District of Columbia, and Washington State. In 2004 President Bush was uncontested for renomination.

[a] Age category is 65 years and older for 2008.

Sources: Calculated by the editors from data in previous editions of *Vital Statistics on American Politics* and exit poll data as reported by CNN (*www.cnn.com*), ABC News (*http://abcnews.go.com*), and MSNBC (*www.msnbc.msn.com*).

Table 3-7 Strength of Party Identification and the Presidential Vote, 1952–2008 (percent)

Year/candidate	Strong Democrat	Weak Democrat	Independent Democrat	Independent	Independent Republican	Weak Republican	Strong Republican	Total
1952								
Stevenson (D)	84	62	61	20	7	6	2	42
Eisenhower (R)	16	38	39	80	93	94	98	58
1956								
Stevenson (D)	85	63	67	17	6	7	0	40
Eisenhower (R)	15	37	33	83	94	93	100	60
1960								
Kennedy (D)	91	72	90	46	12	13	2	49
Nixon (R)	9	28	10	54	88	87	98	51
1964								
L. Johnson (D)	95	82	90	77	25	43	10	68
Goldwater (R)	5	18	10	23	75	57	90	32
1968								
Humphrey (D)	92	68	64	30	5	11	3	46
Nixon (R)	8	32	36	70	95	89	97	54
1972								
McGovern (D)	73	48	61	30	13	9	3	36
Nixon (R)	27	52	39	70	87	91	97	64
1976								
Carter (D)	92	75	76	44	14	22	3	51
Ford (R)	8	25	24	56	86	78	97	49
1980								
Carter (D)	89	65	60	26	13	5	5	44
Reagan (R)	11	35	40	74	87	95	95	56
1984								
Mondale (D)	89	68	79	28	7	6	3	42
Reagan (R)	11	32	21	72	93	94	97	58

1988								
Dukakis (D)	94	72	88	35	15	17	2	47
G. H. W. Bush (R)	6	28	12	65	85	83	98	53
1992								
Clinton (D)	97	84	92	65	15	20	3	58
G. H. W. Bush (R)	3	16	8	35	85	80	98	42
1996								
Clinton (D)	98	91	93	49	23	23	5	58
Dole (R)	2	9	7	51	77	77	95	42
2000								
Gore (D)	97	85	78	45	14	16	2	52
G. W. Bush (R)	3	15	22	55	86	84	98	48
2004								
Kerry (D)	98	85	88	58	15	11	3	50
G. W. Bush (R)	2	15	12	42	85	89	97	50
2008								
Obama (D)	95	86	91	57	18	12	4	55
McCain (R)	5	14	9	43	82	88	96	45

Note: "D" indicates Democrat; "R" indicates Republican. Results are from surveys in which voters are asked with which party they identify and for whom they voted. For the party identification questions, see Table 3-1, this volume. Votes for candidates other than Democratic or Republican were excluded.

Source: Calculated by the editors from American National Election Studies data, Center for Political Studies, University of Michigan, Ann Arbor (*www. electionstudies.org*).

124

Table 3-8 Congressional Vote in General Elections, by Groups, 1998–2008 (percent)

Group	Percentage of voters						1998		2000		2002		2004		2006		2008	
	1998	2000	2002	2004	2006	2008	D	R	D	R	D	R	D	R	D	R	D	R
Sex																		
Men	49	48	49	46	49	47	45	52	44	54	43	54	45	53	50	47	52	46
Women	51	52	51	54	51	53	51	46	53	45	49	49	52	46	55	43	56	42
Race/ethnicity																		
White	82	81	81	77	79	74	42	55	43	55	39	58	42	57	47	51	45	53
Black	10	10	9	12	10	13	88	11	88	11	90	9	89	10	89	10	93	5
Hispanic/Latino	5	6	7	8	8	8	59	35	64	35	61	37	55	44	69	30	68	29
Asian	1	2	1	2	2	2	54	42	58	40	64	34	56	41	62	37	63	31
Age																		
Under 30 years	13	16	11	16	12	18	48	48	49	48	49	47	55	44	60	38	63	34
30–44 years	29	33	29	29	24	29	49	49	47	50	44	53	47	51	53	45	53	44
45–59 years	30	29	33	30	34	38[a]	50	46	49	49	46	52	49	49	53	46	51[a]	46[a]
60 years and older	28	22	27	25	29	15[b]	44	54	51	47	48	50	46	53	50	48	49[b]	48[b]
Education																		
Not a high school graduate	5	5	4	4	3	4	57	41	57	41	62	36	49	48	64	35	67	30
High school graduate	22	21	22	22	21	21	49	47	49	49	51	47	49	50	55	44	55	43
College incomplete	27	32	31	32	31	31	51	53	47	51	45	52	47	51	51	47	53	45
College graduate	46	42	42	43	45	45	47	50	48	50	43	54	49	49	53	46	52	45

Region																		
East	22	23	22	22	22	23[c]	54	42	56	40	52	46	57	40	63	35	61[c]	38[c]
Midwest	29	27	27	26	27	25	46	52	49	50	46	51	49	50	52	47	53	45
South	24	29	32	32	30	34	44	53	43	55	41	56	43	56	45	53	48	50
West	25	21	19	20	21	18	48	48	49	49	48	48	48	50	54	43	58	39
Religion																		
White Protestant	32	46	58	41	44	42	33	64	35	63	30	68	34	65	37	61	35	63
White fundamentalist	14	15	9	23	24	26	24	73	21	77	21	77	25	74	28	70	28	70
Catholic	27	26	27	27	26	26	51	45	50	48	53	45	49	50	55	44	55	42
Jewish	3	4	3	3	2	2	78	21	74	24	62	35	76	22	87	12	81	19
Union household	22	27	23	24	23	21	61	35	60	38	62	36	61	37	64	34	64	34
Family income																		
Under $15,000	8	6	7	8	7	6	57	39	58	39	64	33	64	34	67	30	74	25
$15,000–29,999	18	16	15	15	12	12	53	44	56	42	55	42	58	39	61	36	63	35
$30,000–49,999	26	24	22	22	21	19	48	49	50	48	48	49	51	47	56	43	57	40
$50,000–74,999	25	25	24	23	22	22	44	54	47	51	45	53	44	54	50	48	51	46
Over $75,000	24	28	32	33	39	41	45	52	43	55	37	61	43	56	49	50	49	49
Party																		
Democratic	37	39	38	38	38	40	87	11	87	11	89	10	90	9	93	7	92	7
Independent	27	26	22	25	26	28	45	48	46	49	45	48	49	46	57	39	51	43
Republican	36	36	40	38	36	33	9	90	8	91	6	93	7	93	8	91	9	89
Ideology																		
Liberal	19	21	17	21	20	22	81	16	81	16	78	18	83	14	87	11	87	11
Moderate	50	50	49	45	47	44	54	43	53	45	53	45	56	43	60	38	61	37
Conservative	31	30	34	34	32	34	17	80	19	80	18	79	17	81	20	78	23	75

(Table continues)

Table 3-8 (Continued)

Group	Percentage of voters						1998		2000		2002		2004		2006		2008	
	1998	2000	2002	2004	2006	2008	D	R	D	R	D	R	D	R	D	R	D	R
Previous presidential vote																		
Democratic	48	46	38	37	43	37	80	17	80	18	86	12	86	12	92	7	88	8
Independent/third party	9	8	4	3	4	4	35	54	32	61	61	29	70	19	66	23	63	28
Republican	38	33	53	43	49	46	9	89	10	88	14	84	13	86	15	83	19	80
First-time voter	5	9	—	11	—	11	50	43	50	48	—	—	53	46	—	—	63	35
Total	100	100	100	100	100	100	48	49	49	49	46	51	49	50	53	45	54	44

Note: "D" indicates Democrat; "R" indicates Republican. Percentages based on Democratic, Republican, and other (not shown) votes. "—" indicates not available. Data based on questionnaires completed by voters leaving polling places around the nation on election day. Differing questions and question formats make comparability across elections of some of these groups problematic. For example, in some years the "white fundamentalist" category is "evangelicals," "born-again Christians," or members of the "religious right." See sources for details. The number of respondents in 1998 was 11,387; in 2000, 11,578; in 2002, 17,872; in 2004, 12,649; in 2006, 13,251; and in 2008, 16,521. Data for earlier years can be found in previous editions of *Vital Statistics on American Politics*.

[a] Age category is 45–64 years for 2008.
[b] Age category is 65 years and older for 2008.
[c] Region is "Northeast" for 2008.

Sources: Percentages calculated by the editors from Voter News Service, General Election Exit Polls, National Files, 1998, 2000, 2002, 2004, and 2006, obtained through the Inter-university Consortium for Political and Social Research (*www.icpsr.umich.edu*); CNN U.S. House National Exit Poll, 2008 (*www.cnn.com*). Neither the collectors of the original data nor the Consortium bears any responsibility for the results presented here.

Table 3-9 Party-Line Voting in Presidential and Congressional Elections, 1952–2008 (percent)

Year	Presidential elections			U.S. Senate elections			U.S. House elections		
	Party-line voters[a]	Defectors[b]	Independents	Party-line voters[a]	Defectors[b]	Independents	Party-line voters[a]	Defectors[b]	Independents
1952	77	18	5	79	16	5	80	15	5
1956	76	15	9	80	12	8	82	9	9
1958				84	11	5	84	11	5
1960	79	13	8	79	12	9	80	11	8
1962				—	—	—	83	11	6
1964	79	15	5	78	16	6	79	15	5
1966				76	17	7	76	17	7
1968	69	24	7	73	20	7	74	19	7
1970				77	13	10	76	16	9
1972	67	25	8	69	22	9	74	17	8
1974				74	18	8	74	18	8
1976	73	16	11	69	19	12	72	19	9
1978				71	20	9	67	23	10
1980	68	24	8	71	21	8	69	23	8
1982				77	17	6	76	17	6
1984	79	13	8	72	20	9	70	23	7
1986				76	20	4	72	22	6
1988	81	12	7	72	20	7	74	19	7
1990				73	23	6	76	19	5
1992	68	24	9	74	20	7	71	21	7
1994				77	17	6	77	17	6
1996	78	16	5	77	16	7	77	17	5
1998				77	16	8	72	22	6
2000	79	12	8	79	13	7	76	17	7
2002				81	15	3	76	20	4
2004	85	10	5	81	14	5	79	15	6
2008	84	9	7	81	12	7	80	13	6

Note: "—" indicates not available. In presidential elections, the base for percentages is all voters. In Senate and House elections, the base for percentages is all voters supporting Democratic or Republican candidates. There was no update of the American National Election Studies series in 2006.

[a] Democratic or Republican identifiers who vote for the candidate of their party. Party identification is based on surveys in which voters are asked with which party they identify. See Table 3-1, this volume, for question. "Independent partisans," or "leaners," are included here as party-line voters or defectors.

[b] Democratic or Republican identifiers who do not vote for the candidate of their party.

Source: Calculated by the editors from American National Election Studies data, Center for Political Studies, University of Michigan, Ann Arbor (*www.electionstudies.org*).

Table 3-10   Split-Ticket Voting, 1952–2008 (percent)

Year	President-House	Senate-House	State-local
1952	13	9	26
1956	16	10	29
1958		10	31
1960	14	9	27
1962		—	42
1964	14	18	41
1966		21	50
1968	17	21	47
1970		20	51
1972	30	22	58
1974		24	61
1976	25	23	—
1978		35	—
1980	28	31	59
1982		24	55
1984	25	20	52
1986		28	—
1988	25	27	—
1990		25	—
1992	22	25	—
1994		24	—
1996	18	19	—
1998		23	—
2000	19	18	—
2002		21	—
2004	17	16	—
2008	17	16	—

Note: "—" indicates not available. Entries are the percentages of voters who "split" their ticket by supporting candidates of different parties for the offices indicated. Those who cast ballots for other than Democratic and Republican candidates are excluded in presidential and congressional calculations. The state-local figure is based on a general question: "Did you vote for other state and local offices? Did you vote a straight ticket or did you vote for candidates from different parties?"

Source: Calculated by the editors from American National Election Studies data, Center for Political Studies, University of Michigan, Ann Arbor (*www.electionstudies.org*).

Figure 3-6 Presidential Approval, 1993–2009

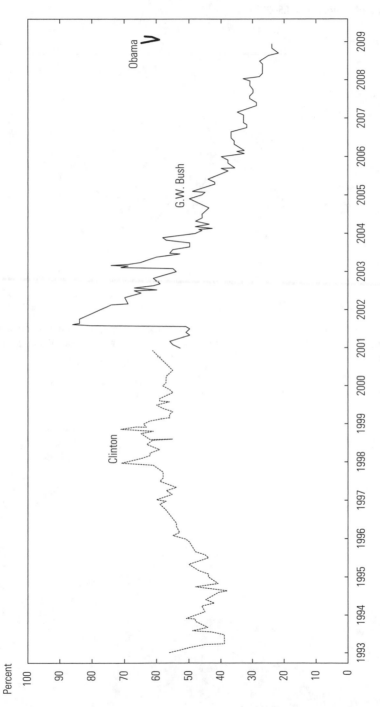

Note: Question: "Do you approve or disapprove of the way _____ (Bill Clinton/George W. Bush/Barack Obama) is handling his job as president?" Related data for additional years can be found in previous editions of *Vital Statistics on American Politics.*

Source: Clinton: Pew Research Center for the People and the Press, "It's the Economy Again!: Clinton Nostalgia Sets in, Bush Reaction Mixed," January 11, 2001, 27–28; Bush: "Reviewing the Bush Years and the Public's Final Verdict: Bush and Public Opinion," December 18, 2008, 24–25; Obama: "Trends in Political Values and Core Attitudes: 1987–2009," May 21, 2009, 117 (*http://people-press.org*).

Figure 3-7   Rating of Congress, 1985–2009

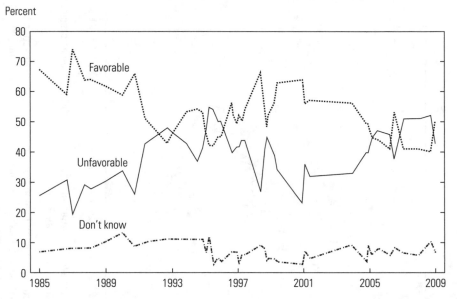

Note: Question: "I'd like to get your opinion of some groups and organizations. Is your overall opinion of Congress very favorable, mostly favorable, mostly unfavorable, or very unfavorable?" Related data for additional years can be found in previous editions of *Vital Statistics on American Politics.*

Source: Pew Research Center for the People and the Press, "Trends in Political Values and Core Attitudes: 1987–2009," May 21, 2009, 123, 125 (*http://people-press.org*).

Figure 3-8   Individual Confidence in Government, 1952–2008

Percentage difference index

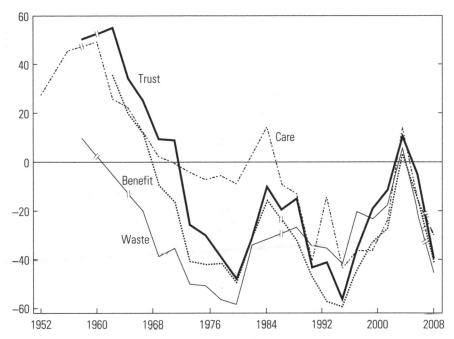

Note: Broken line indicates question not asked that year in the biennial American National Election Studies. Questions: (Care) "I don't think public officials care much about what people like me think." (Trust) "How much of the time do you think you can trust the government in Washington to do what is right—just about always, most of the time, or only some of the time?" (Benefit) "Would you say the government is pretty much run by a few big interests looking out for themselves or that it is run for the benefit of all people?" (Waste) "Do you think that people in the government waste a lot of money we pay in taxes, waste some of it, or don't waste very much of it?" The percentage difference index is calculated by subtracting the percentage giving a nontrusting response from the percentage giving a trusting response. There was no update of the American National Election Studies series in 2006.

Source: American National Election Studies, Center for Political Studies, University of Michigan, Ann Arbor (*www.electionstudies.org*).

Figure 3-9 Satisfaction with "The Way Things Are Going," 1988–2009

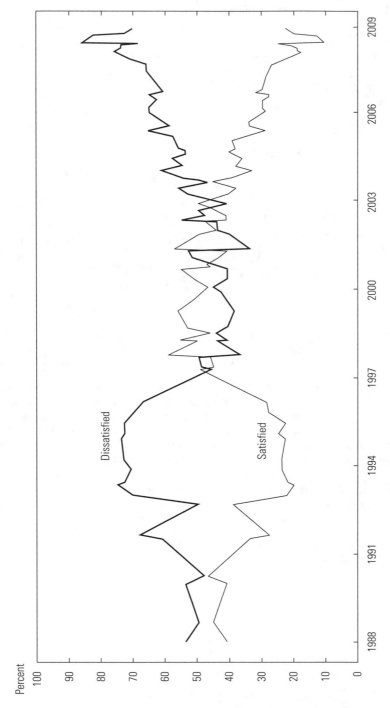

Note: Question: "All in all, are you satisfied or dissatisfied with the way things are going in this country today?" Related data for additional years can be found in previous editions of *Vital Statistics on American Politics.*

Source: Pew Research Center for the People and the Press, "Trends in Political Values and Core Attitudes: 1987–2009," May 21, 2009, 118 (*http://people-press.org*).

Figure 3-10 Consumer Confidence, 1960–2008

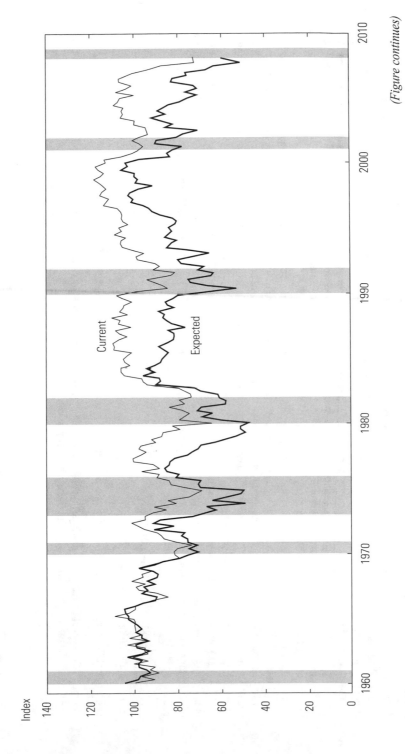

(Figure continues)

Figure 3-10 (continued)

Note: Shaded areas indicate periods of economic recession, as determined by the National Bureau of Economic Research (*www.nber.org*). The curves reflect data from surveys conducted quarterly from 1960 through 1977, and monthly since 1978 (though aggregated by quarter). "Current" indicates the Index of Current Economic Conditions (ICC) and "Expected" the Index of Consumer Expectations (ICE).

The current index includes the following survey questions: (X1) "We are interested in how people are getting along financially these days. Would you say that you (and your family living there) are better off or worse off financially than you were a year ago?" (X5) "About the big things people buy for their homes—such as furniture, a refrigerator, stove, television, and things like that. Generally speaking, do you think now is a good or a bad time for people to buy major household items?"

The expected index includes the following survey questions: (X2) "Now looking ahead—do you think that a year from now you (and your family living there) will be better off financially, or worse off, or just about the same as now?" (X3) "Now turning to business conditions in the country as a whole—do you think that during the next twelve months we'll have good times financially, or bad times, or what?" (X4) "Looking ahead, which would you say is more likely—that in the country as a whole we'll have continuous good times during the next five years or so, or that we will have periods of widespread unemployment or depression?"

As a first step in calculating each index, a relative score is calculated from the percent giving favorable replies minus the percent giving unfavorable replies, plus 100 percent, for each question used. Each relative score is rounded to the nearest whole number. Using the following equation for each index, the relative scores of the appropriate survey questions are summed, divided by the 1966 base period constant for the index, and 2 is added (a constant to correct for sample design changes from the 1950s).

$$ICC = ((X1 + X5)/ 2.6424) + 2.0$$

$$ICE = ((X2 + X3 + X4)/ 4.1134) + 2.0$$

The Index of Consumer Sentiment is a weighted average of the current and expected indexes.

Sources: "Surveys of Consumers," Reuters/University of Michigan (*www.sca.isr.umich.edu*); recession periods determined by the National Bureau of Economic Research (*www.nber.org*). Reprinted with permission.

Figure 3-11   The Most Important Problem: Foreign Affairs, 1987–2009

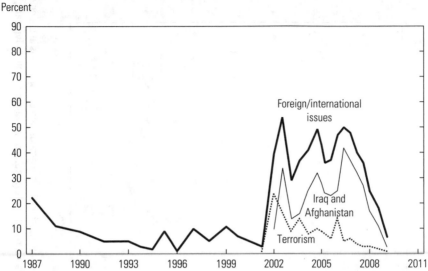

Note: Question: "What do you think is the most important problem facing the country today?" Verbatim responses recorded. Multiple responses allowed.

Source: Pew Research Center for the People and the Press (*http://people-press.org*).

Figure 3-12   The Most Important Problem: Domestic Issues, 1987–2009

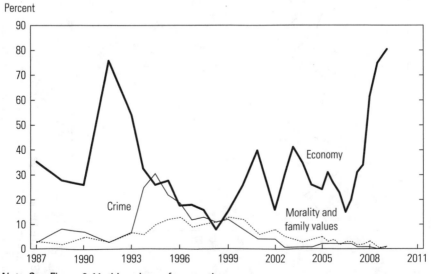

Note: See Figure 3-11, this volume, for question.

Source: Pew Research Center for the People and the Press (*http://people-press.org*).

136

Figure 3-13 Favorable Opinions of the Democratic and Republican Parties, 1992–2009

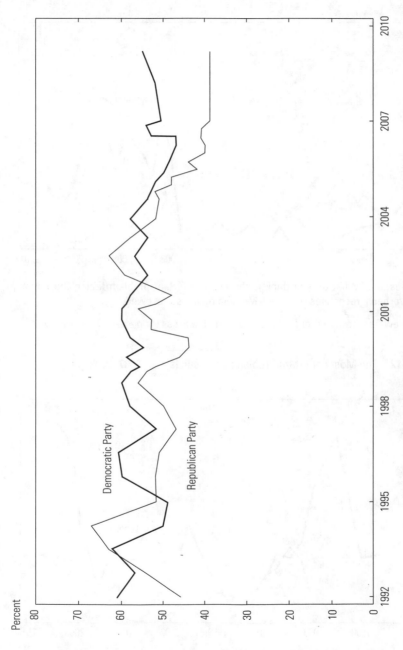

Note: Shown is the percentage "very" or "mostly" favorable to the question "I'd like to get your opinion of some groups and organizations in the news. Is your overall opinion of the [Democratic] [Republican] Party very favorable, mostly favorable, mostly unfavorable, or very unfavorable?" Typically, 5–10 percent of the respondents volunteer that they cannot rate the parties.

Source: Pew Research Center for the People and the Press (*http://people-press.org*).

Figure 3-14   Condition of Nation's Economy and Citizens' Personal Financial Situations over the Last Year, 1980–2008 (percent)

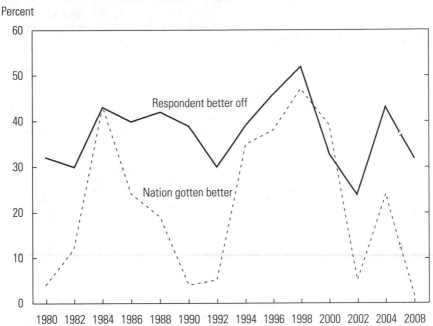

Note: Questions: Nation's economy: "How about (1996–later: Now thinking about) the economy (1990, 1994–later: in the country as a whole)?" All years except 2000: "Would you say that over the past year the nation's economy has gotten better, stayed (all years except 1984: about) the same, or gotten worse?" (2000:) "Would you say that over the past year the nation's economy has gotten worse, stayed about the same, or gotten better?"; personal financial situation: 1962–1998, 2004: "We are interested in how people are getting along financially these days. Would you say that (1962, 1966–1974: you [and your family]; 1976 and later: you [and your family living here]) are better off or worse off financially than you were a year ago?"; 2000–2002: "We are interested in how people are getting along financially these days. Would you say that you (and your family [2000 face-to-face only: living here]) are better off, worse off, or just about the same financially as you were a year ago?"

Source: Calculated by the editors from American National Election Studies data, Center for Political Studies, University of Michigan, Ann Arbor (*www.electionstudies.org*).

Table 3-11   Public Opinion on Civil Liberties, 1940–2008 (percent)

Issue/year	Allow[a]	Don't forbid[b]
Public speeches against democracy		
1940	25	46
1974	56	72
1976	55	80
1976	52	79

Issue/year	Allow to speak	Allow to teach college	Keep book in library
Atheist[c]			
1954	37	12	35
1964[d]	—	—	61
1972	66	41	61
1973[a]	66	42	62
1973[b]	62	39	57
1974	62	42	60
1976	65	42	60
1977	63	40	59
1978	63	—	60
1980	66	46	62
1982	65	46	61
1984	68	46	64
1985	65	46	61
1987	70	47	67
1988	70	46	64
1989	72	52	68
1990	73	51	67
1991	73	51	68
1993	71	53	68
1994	73	53	70
1996	74	56	68
1998	75	58	70
2000	75	57	68
2002	77	60	72
2004	76	64	72
2006	77	60	71
2008	76	61	71
Admitted communist[c]			
1954	27	6	27
1972	53	33	53
1973[a]	61	40	59
1973[b]	53	30	54
1974	58	42	59
1976	55	42	57
1977	56	39	56
1978	60	—	61

Table 3-11   *(Continued)*

Issue/year	Allow to speak	Allow to teach college	Keep book in library
1980	55	41	57
1982	56	43	57
1984	59	46	60
1985	58	46	58
1987	60	46	62
1988	61	48	60
1989	65	51	63
1990	65	53	64
1991	68	54	67
1993	70	57	68
1994	67	55	67
1996	64	58	65
1998	67	57	67
2000	66	57	66
2002	69	59	69
2004	69	63	70
2006	67	60	68
2008	65	58	67
Racist[c]			
1943[e]	17	—	—
1976	61	41	60
1977	59	41	62
1978	62	—	64
1980	62	42	64
1982	59	43	60
1984	57	40	63
1985	56	42	60
1987	60	43	64
1988	61	41	61
1989	62	46	65
1990	64	45	65
1991	62	41	65
1993	61	45	65
1994	62	43	66
1996	61	46	64
1998	62	47	63
2000	60	46	63
2002	62	52	65
2004	62	46	65
2006	61	46	64
2008	59	45	63
Admitted homosexual[c]			
1973	61	48	54
1974	63	51	56
1976	63	53	56

(Table continues)

Table 3-11   *(Continued)*

Issue/year	Allow to speak	Allow to teach college	Keep book in library
1977	62	50	55
1980	66	55	58
1982	65	55	56
1984	68	58	59
1985	67	58	56
1987	68	57	58
1988	70	57	61
1989	77	64	66
1990	75	65	65
1991	77	63	69
1993	79	69	67
1994	80	71	69
1996	81	75	69
1998	81	75	70
2000	81	76	71
2002	83	78	75
2004	83	79	73
2006	82	78	74
2008	82	79	76

Note: "—" indicates not available.

[a] Question: "Do you think the United States should allow public speeches against democracy?"
[b] Question: "Do you think the United States should forbid public speeches against democracy?"
[c] Question: "There are always some people whose ideas are considered bad or dangerous by other people. For instance, somebody who (is against all churches and religion/admits he is a communist/believes that blacks are genetically inferior/admits that he is a homosexual). If such a person wanted to make a speech in your (city/town/community), should he be allowed to speak or not? Should such a person be allowed to teach in a college or university or not? If some people in your community suggested that a book he wrote (against churches and religion/promoting communism/which said blacks are inferior/in favor of homosexuality) should be taken out of your public library, would you favor removing this book or not?" (Slight variations in wording across groups.)
[d] In 1964 the question was as follows: "Suppose a man admitted in public that he did not believe in God. Do you think a book he wrote should be removed from a public library?"
[e] In 1943 the question was as follows: "In peacetime, do you think anyone in the United States should be allowed to make speeches against certain races in this country?"

Sources: Public speeches against democracy: Howard Schuman and Stanley Presser, *Questions and Answers in Attitude Surveys* (New York: Academic Press, 1981), 277; Atheist...: 1943, 1964, and 1973a: National Opinion Research Center surveys; 1954: Samuel A. Stouffer, *Communism, Conformity, and Civil Liberties* (Garden City, N.Y.: Doubleday, 1955), 32–34, 40–43; 1973b: Clyde Z. Nunn et al., *Tolerance for Nonconformity* (San Francisco: Jossey-Bass, 1978), 40–43; data for all other years from General Social Survey, National Opinion Research Center, University of Chicago.

Table 3-12   Public Opinion on the Death Penalty, 1972–2008 (percent)

Year	Favor	Oppose	Don't know
1972	53	39	8
1973	60	35	5
1974	63	32	5
1975	60	33	7
1976	66	29	5
1977	68	26	6
1978	67	28	5
1980	68	27	5
1982	74	21	5
1983	74	21	5
1984	72	23	5
1985	75	20	5
1986	72	23	5
1987	69	25	6
1988	71	22	7
1989	74	21	5
1990	75	20	6
1991	72	22	6
1993	72	21	7
1994	75	19	6
1996	72	21	7
1998	68	25	7
2000	64	28	8
2002	67	29	4
2004	65	30	5
2006	64	30	5
2008	64	31	5

Note: GSS interviews are conducted in the spring of the year indicated, usually March–June. Question: "Do you favor or oppose the death penalty for persons [or: "people"] convicted of murder?" Data for additional years can be found in previous editions of *Vital Statistics on American Politics.*

Source: General Social Survey, National Opinion Research Center, University of Chicago.

Table 3-13   Public Opinion on Abortion, 1965–2008 (percent)

			Abortion should be legal under these circumstances				
Year	Mother's health	Rape	Birth defect	Low income	Single mother	As form of birth control	Any reason
1965	70	56	55	21	17	15	—
1972	84	75	75	46	41	38	—
1973	90	81	82	52	47	47	—
1974	91	83	82	52	48	45	—
1975	88	80	80	50	46	43	—
1976	89	81	82	51	48	45	—
1977	89	81	83	51	47	44	36
1978	88	80	80	45	39	38	32
1980	88	80	81	50	46	45	39
1982	90	84	82	49	45	46	38
1983	87	78	76	41	36	37	32
1984	88	76	78	45	42	41	37
1985	88	78	77	42	40	39	36
1987	86	77	76	43	40	40	37
1988	86	77	76	40	38	39	35
1989	88	80	79	46	43	43	39
1990	90	81	78	45	43	43	42
1991	88	83	80	46	43	42	41
1993	86	79	77	47	45	44	42
1994	88	81	79	48	46	46	45
1996	88	80	78	44	43	44	42
1998	84	76	74	41	39	39	38
2000	85	76	75	39	36	38	37
2002	89	76	75	42	39	41	40
2004	83	73	69	39	40	39	38
2006	84	73	70	40	37	40	38
2008	85	72	70	41	40	43	40

Note: "—" indicates not available. Question: "Please tell me whether or not you think it should be possible for a pregnant woman to obtain a legal abortion [in the order asked in the survey] if there is a strong chance of serious defect in the baby? If she is married and does not want any more children? If the woman's own health is seriously endangered by the pregnancy? If the family has a very low income and cannot afford any more children? If she became pregnant as a result of rape? If she is not married and does not want to marry the man? The woman wants it for any reason?" Data for additional years can be found in previous editions of *Vital Statistics on American Politics*.

Sources: 1965: National Opinion Research Center surveys; 1972–2008: General Social Survey, National Opinion Research Center, University of Chicago.

Figure 3-15   Public Opinion on Interracial Dating, 1987–2009

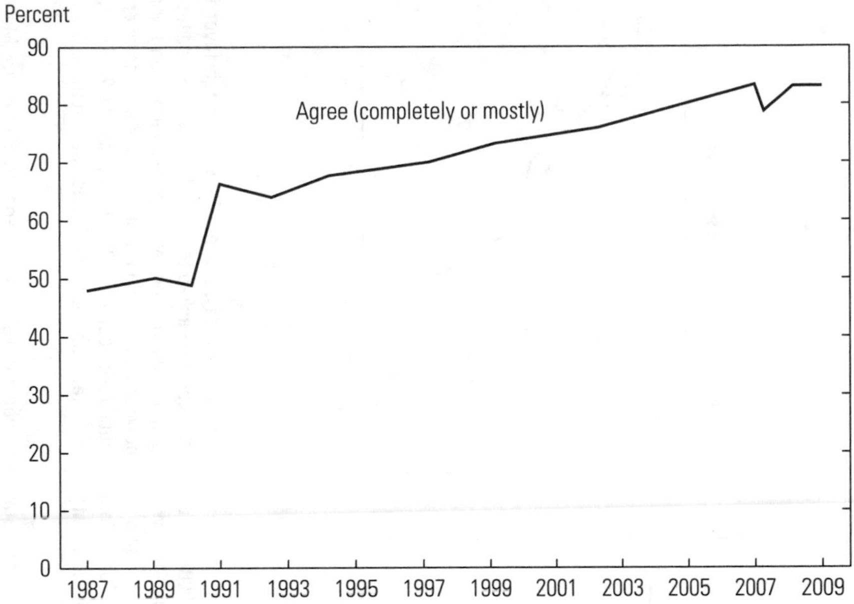

Note: Shown is the percentage agreeing "completely" or "mostly" to the statement "It's all right for blacks and whites to date each other."

Source: Pew Research Center for the People and the Press (*http://people-press.org*).

144

Figure 3-16 Public Opinion, 1995–2009, and States' Actions on Same-Sex Marriage

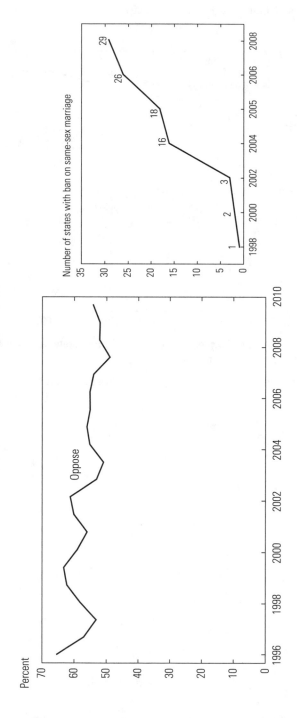

Note: As of June 4, 2009. Public opinion shown is the percentage responding "strongly oppose" or "oppose" to the question "Do you strongly favor, favor, oppose, or strongly oppose allowing gay and lesbian couples to marry legally?" In 2007 and earlier, the question asked about "allowing gays and lesbians to marry legally." Typically, 8–12 percent of the respondents volunteer that they don't know. In addition to the number of states with a ban on same-sex marriage shown above, more states have laws limiting the legal definition of marriage to a union between a man and a woman. Six states permit same-sex marriage. These six states and the effective dates are Massachusetts (May 17, 2004), Connecticut (November 12, 2008), Iowa (April 24, 2009), Vermont (September 1, 2009), Maine (September 2009), and New Hampshire (January 1, 2010). The first three resulted from court decisions, the last three from state legislative action. Maine's decision may be subject to a referendum.

Sources: State information: Pew Forum on Religion and Public Life, "States with Voter-Approved Constitutional Bans on Same-Sex Marriage, 1998–2008" (*http://pewforum.org*); public opinion: Pew Research Center for the People and the Press (*http://people-press.org*).

Figure 3-17   Religious Affiliation of the U.S. Population and Political Ideology and Views on Homosexuality, by Religious Affiliation, 2007

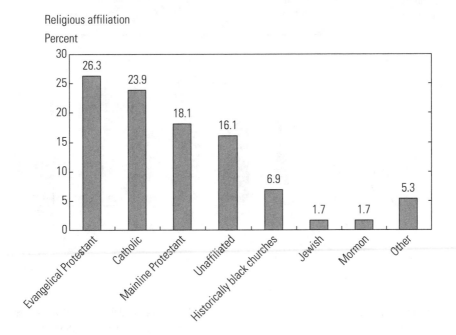

Religious affiliation

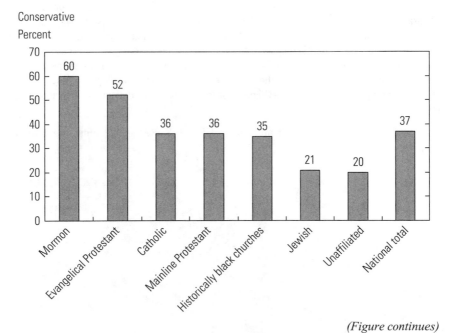

Conservative

(Figure continues)

Figure 3-17   (continued)

Homosexuality should be accepted
Percent

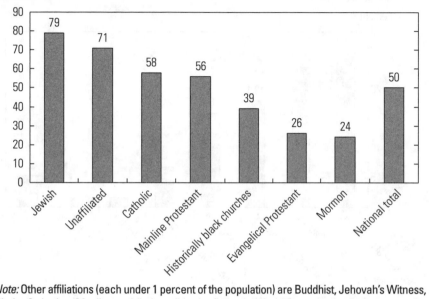

Note: Other affiliations (each under 1 percent of the population) are Buddhist, Jehovah's Witness, Hindu, Orthodox, Muslim, and "others." In the figure labeled "Conservative," shown are the percentages responding "very conservative" or "conservative" in response to the question "In general, would you describe your political views as very conservative, conservative, moderate, liberal, or very liberal?" In the figure labeled "Homosexuality should be accepted," shown are those responding "accepted" in response to the question "Now I'm going to read you a few pairs of statements. For each pair, tell me whether the first statement or the second statement comes closer to your own views—even if neither is exactly right. 1 – Homosexuality is a way of life that should be accepted by society or 2 – Homosexuality is a way of life that should be discouraged by society."

Source: Pew Forum on Religion and Public Life, "U.S. Religious Landscape Survey" (*http://pewforum.org*).

Table 3-14   Public Opinion on Gun Control, 1972–2008 (percent)

Year	Favor	Oppose	Don't know
1972	70	27	3
1973	74	25	2
1974	75	23	1
1975 (Feb.)	71	28	1
1975	73	25	3
1976 (Feb.)	73	24	4
1976	72	27	1
1977	71	27	2
1980	69	29	2
1982	72	26	2
1984	71	27	3
1985	72	27	1
1987	69	29	2
1988	74	24	3
1989	78	20	2
1990	79	19	2
1991	81	18	1
1993	81	18	2
1994	78	21	1
1996	80	18	2
1998	82	16	2
2000	79	18	2
2002	81	19	1
2004	80	19	1
2006	78	20	1
2008	77	21	1

Note: GSS interviews are conducted in the spring of the year indicated, usually March–June. Question: "Would you favor or oppose a law which would require a person to obtain a police permit before he or she could buy a gun?" Data for additional years can be found in previous editions of *Vital Statistics on American Politics*.

Sources: February 1975, February 1976: Survey Research Center, University of Michigan; others: General Social Survey, National Opinion Research Center, University of Chicago.

Table 3-15   Public Opinion on the Courts, 1972–2008 (percent)

Year	Too harsh	About right	Not harsh enough	Don't know
1972	8	16	66	11
1973	5	13	73	9
1974[a]	5	6	60	29
1974	6	10	78	6
1975	4	10	79	7
1976	3	10	82	6
1977	3	8	83	5
1978	3	7	85	5
1980	3	7	84	5
1981 (Jan.)	3	13	77	7
1982[a]	4	5	76	14
1982	3	6	86	4
1983	4	6	85	4
1984	3	11	82	4
1985	3	10	84	3
1986	3	8	85	4
1987	3	12	80	5
1988	4	10	82	4
1989	3	9	84	5
1990	4	10	82	4
1991	4	11	80	5
1993	4	9	82	5
1994	3	8	85	4
1996	5	10	78	7
1998	6	13	75	6
2000	7	15	69	8
2002	9	17	67	6
2004	9	20	65	6
2006	9	21	64	5
2008	12	19	63	6

Note: GSS interviews are conducted in the spring of the year indicated, usually March–June. Question: "In general, do you think the courts in this area deal too harshly or not harshly enough with criminals?" Data for additional years can be found in previous editions of *Vital Statistics on American Politics.*

[a] In 1974 and 1982, half of the General Social Survey sample was asked the question as noted above and half the sample was asked the same question but with the phrase "or don't you have enough information about the courts to say" added at the end. The "don't know" column for these rows includes those saying "not enough information."

Sources: 1981: *Los Angeles Times* survey; others: General Social Survey, National Opinion Research Center, University of Chicago.

Table 3-16   Public Opinion on U.S. Involvement in World Affairs, 1987–2009
(percent)

	Agree		Disagree		
Date	Completely	Mostly	Mostly	Completely	*Don't know*
May 1987	32	55	7	1	5
May 1988	47	43	6	1	3
February 1989	51	42	3	1	3
May 1990	39	50	6	1	4
November 1991	54	38	4	2	2
June 1992	47	44	5	2	2
May 1993	33	54	9	1	3
July 1994	51	39	7	2	1
November 1997	48	43	6	2	1
September 1999	45	43	8	2	2
August 2002	49	41	5	3	2
August 2003	50	40	6	2	2
January 2007	42	44	7	3	4
April 2009	51	39	5	2	3

Note: Question: "Now I am going to read you another series of statements on some different topics. For each statement, please tell me if you completely agree with it, mostly agree with it, mostly disagree with it, or completely disagree with it. It's best for the future of our country to be active in world affairs." Related data for additional years can be found in previous editions of *Vital Statistics on American Politics.*

Source: Pew Research Center for the People and the Press, "Trends in Political Values and Core Attitudes: 1987–2009," May 21, 2009, 145 (*http://people-press.org*).

Table 3-17   Public Opinion on Peace through Military Strength, 1987–2009 (percent)

Date	Agree		Disagree		Don't know
	Completely	Mostly	Mostly	Completely	
May 1987	14	40	30	10	6
May 1988	22	37	25	12	4
February 1989	22	39	26	10	3
May 1990	17	35	31	13	4
November 1991	21	31	29	16	3
June 1992	21	33	30	13	3
May 1993	16	38	33	10	3
July 1994	20	35	27	17	1
November 1997	23	34	29	11	3
September 1999	23	32	30	12	3
August 2002	26	36	24	10	4
August 2003	23	30	29	15	3
January 2007	18	31	30	17	4
April 2009	22	31	27	15	5

Note: Question: "Now I am going to read you another series of statements on some different topics. For each statement, please tell me if you completely agree with it, mostly agree with it, mostly disagree with it, or completely disagree with it. The best way to ensure peace is through military strength." Related data for additional years can be found in previous editions of *Vital Statistics on American Politics.*

Source: Pew Research Center for the People and the Press, "Trends in Political Values and Core Attitudes: 1987–2009," May 21, 2009, 144 (*http://people-press.org*).

Figure 3-18 Public Opinion on U.S. Military Involvement in Iraq, 2003–2009

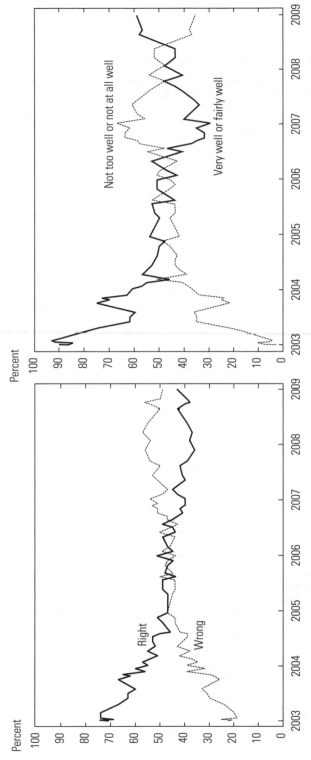

Note: Questions: "Do you think the U.S. made the right decision or the wrong decision in using military force against Iraq?" "How well is the U.S. military effort in Iraq going—very well, fairly well, not too well, or not at all well?" Related data for additional years can be found in previous editions of *Vital Statistics on American Politics.*

Source: Pew Research Center for the People and the Press, "America's Pre-Inauguration Mood: Strong Confidence in Obama—Country Seen as Less Politically Divided," January 15, 2009, 40–42 (*http://people-press.org*).

Table 3-18   Public Opinion on Terrorism, 2001–2009

Ability to launch another major attack on the U.S.

Date	Greater	The same	Less	Don't know, refused
August 2002	22	39	34	5
July 2004	24	39	34	3
July 2005	28	40	29	3
January 2006	17	39	39	5
August 2006	25	37	33	5
December 2006	23	41	31	5
February 2008	16	41	39	4
September 2008	18	43	36	3
February 2009	17	44	35	4

U.S. government reducing the threat of terrorism

Date	Very well	Fairly well	Not too well	Not at all well	Don't know
October 10–14, 2001	48	40	6	2	4
October 15–21, 2001	38	46	9	4	3
November 2001	35	46	9	5	5
June 2002	16	60	16	4	4
August 2003	19	56	16	7	2
July 2004	18	53	17	8	4
July 2005	17	53	19	8	3
January 2006	16	50	20	9	5
February 2006	16	52	20	10	2
August 2006	22	52	16	8	2
December 2006	17	48	21	11	3
January 2007	17	37	27	17	2
February 2008	21	45	19	12	3
February 2009	22	49	16	6	7

Source: Pew Research Center for the People and the Press, "No Change in Views of Torture, Warrantless Wiretaps," February 18, 2009, 8–9 (*http://people-press.org*).

Note: Questions: "Overall, do you think the ability of terrorists to launch another major attack on the U.S. is greater, the same, or less than it was at the time of the September 11th terrorist attacks?" "In general, how well do you think the U.S. government is doing in reducing the threat of terrorism?"

4

The Media

- **National Reach**
- **Presence in Washington**
- **Public Use**
- **Coverage and Viewership of Presidential Campaigns, Conventions, and Debates**
- **Newspaper Endorsements**

The mass media thrive on numbers. Nearly every American adult has heard of the audience ratings games—serious games with millions of dollars and many individual careers at stake—played by television, newspapers, radio, and magazines. Will the top-ranked television show remain first in the ratings, and how much will it help the show that follows it? Will a new e-zine be profitable? Will a radio station increase its audience ratings—and what kind of audience will it attract—by playing more hard rock? How many extra copies and how much more advertising will a weekly news magazine sell with excerpts of a soon-to-be-published political memoir—and how much can the publisher afford to pay for those excerpts? So much money is at stake that media organizations spend millions of dollars each year to find the answers to such questions.

Politics, as it relates to the media, also involves numbers. What is the reach or penetration of different media (Tables 4-1 and 4-2)? Some questions simply involve market share and audience, much like the questions just noted: How many and what kinds of people rely on which media for news (Tables 4-4 through 4-9)? What is the availability of information about specific parts of government, and how has it changed over time (Figure 4-1 and Table 4-3)? How much attention do people pay to political campaign coverage, political party conventions, campaign debates, and so on (Tables 4-12 and 4-14 through 4-16)? To what extent do people now get their news from cable networks and the Internet and to what extent from other sources (Tables 4-4 through 4-9, and 4-11)? The broadcast networks have reduced coverage of the national nominating conventions (Table 4-14). Who actually watched each party's 2008 convention (Table 4-15)? Somewhat more complicated is the question of how much confidence people have in what the media report (Table 4-13). Of course, all of these matters, while important, are relatively straightforward. More complex and controversial are other matters that involve numbers. Some critics charge, for example, that the media have a political bias and that people pick the news channel that fits their political leanings (Tables 4-9 and 4-10 and Figures 4-3 and 4-4).

Although data specifically about politics and the media are not as plentiful as one might think (for example, some information, such as candidates' private surveys, is proprietary), more is available now than in the past. Television coverage extends more than fifty years (with extended coverage since the 1960s), and congressional proceedings have been televised for more than two decades (since 1979 in the House and 1986 in the Senate). Thus researchers should now be in a position to do more extensive studies of the media and politics than they were before. Predictably, there has been a spurt in such studies. Perhaps as a consequence of the closer attention, there is an increasingly strong sense of media influence on individual voters and on the political system generally.

As for media coverage of presidential campaigns, the greater amounts of data now available include the saliency of the campaign in the news (Figure 4-2) and the coverage given candidates for the nomination and general election (Figures 4-3 and 4-4). Some information is now available for several election cycles, including the public's use of media to follow the campaigns (Table 4-12), and the electorate's viewing of the nominating conventions (Table 4-14) and presidential and vice-presidential debates (Table 4-16). Long-standing tabulations are also available of newspaper endorsements of the presidential candidates (Table 4-17 and Figure 4-5).

The media themselves are increasingly well preserved and documented in ways that make them highly accessible. Magazines are saved and are well indexed. Major newspapers are widely available and also well indexed, and small newspapers—increasingly available online—combine to give widespread coverage of politics as practiced and perceived throughout the country. CBS News has published transcripts and indexes of its news programs since 1975 to facilitate research. LexisNexis, an online subscription service, contains transcripts of various news programs. Network television news programs since 1968 have been stored at Vanderbilt University; the archives are indexed and available to researchers. These efforts at preservation mean that studies can be undertaken of both past and contemporary events. Indeed, some of the most interesting studies of politics and the media are yet to come, because they will be able to cover long expanses of time.

As in all areas of research, data about the media are rarely self-interpreting. One specific problem here is that the media both shape the news and reflect it. The shift in emphasis from parties to candidates (see, for example,

Tables 1-14 and 3-10 on split-ticket voting) is a case in point. To some degree, this shift simply reflects, on the one hand, the weakening hold of political parties over American voters, a process that began as long ago as the beginning of the twentieth century, well before the advent of television. On the other hand, the power of television to bring individual candidates directly into one's living room has accelerated the declining influence of party organizations in particular and of party affiliation more generally.

Problems of interpretation—especially whether the media cause or simply reflect events—thus make inferences about media influence difficult. The usual response to such problems of inference is to bring additional data to bear on the subject. With more data now available, researchers can safely anticipate better answers to questions about media audiences, coverage, emphasis, and influence as they relate to the political process.

Table 4-1   Reach and Use of Selected Media, 1950–2009

Year	Percentage of households with			Percentage of adults who use Internet[c]	Percentage of TV households with		Average hours viewing per TV home per day[e]
	Telephone service[a]	Television sets[b]	Internet		Cable TV	Satellite television[d]	
1950	62.0	9.0	—	—	—	—	4.6
1960	78.5	87.1	—	—	—	—	5.1
1970	87.0	95.3	—	—	6.7	—	5.9
1975	—	97.1	—	—	12.6	—	6.1
1980	93.0	97.9	—	—	19.9	—	6.6
1981	—	98.1	—	—	22.3	—	6.8
1982	—	98.1	—	—	29.8	—	6.8
1983	—	98.1	—	—	34.0	—	7.0
1984	91.8	98.1	—	—	39.3	—	7.1
1985	91.8	98.1	—	—	42.8	—	7.2
1986	92.2	98.1	—	—	45.6	—	7.1
1987	92.5	98.1	—	—	47.7	—	7.0
1988	92.9	98.1	—	—	49.4	—	7.1
1989	93.0	98.2	—	—	52.8	—	7.0
1990	93.3	98.2	—	—	56.4	—	6.9
1991	93.6	98.2	—	—	58.9	—	7.0
1992	93.9	98.3	—	—	60.2	—	7.1
1993	94.2	98.3	—	—	61.4	—	7.2
1994	93.9	98.3	—	—	62.4	—	7.3
1995	93.9	98.3	—	14	63.4	—	7.3
1996	93.8	98.3	—	23	65.3	6.0	7.2
1997	93.9	98.4	—	36	66.5	7.6	7.2
1998	94.1	98.3	—	35	67.2	9.0	7.2
1999	94.0	98.2	—	—	67.5	9.1	7.4
2000	94.6	98.2	42.5	62	68.0	11.4	7.6
2001	94.6	98.2	51.0	66	68.0	13.9	7.7
2002	95.5	98.2	52.9	63	69.4	16.5	7.7
2003	95.5	98.2	55.1	71	69.8	18.2	8.0
2004	94.2	98.2	56.8	71	68.1	19.2	8.0
2005	92.5	98.2	58.5	72	67.5	20.8	8.2
2006	92.9	98.2	60.2	71	66.4	24.5	8.2
2007	—	98.2	62.0	74	64.1	28.0	8.2
2008	—	98.2	63.6	74	61.3[f]	28.7	8.3
2009	—	98.9	65.2[g]	—	—	—	—

Note: "—" indicates not available.

[a] For occupied housing units. 1950–1980, as of April 1; thereafter, as of March 1.
[b] 1970–1975, as of September of prior year; all other years, as of January of year shown.
[c] Questions have varied over the years, but usually a variant of "Do you use the Internet, at least occasionally?"
[d] Includes a small number of other delivery systems. November of year shown.
[e] Annual average.
[f] "Wired cable" for 2008. In overlapping years, percentages with wired cable are slightly lower than previous estimates for cable households.
[g] Estimated.

Sources: Telephone service: U.S. Census Bureau, *Statistical Abstract of the United States, 2009* (Washington, D.C.: Government Printing Office, 2008), "Utilization of Selected Media" (table), and earlier editions of *Statistical Abstract*; television, cable, satellite television, viewing: Television Bureau of Advertising (*www.tvb.org*), various years, reprinted with permission; Internet households: MAGNA On-Demand Quarterly, App. 4 (*www.MagnaInsights.com*); Internet users: 1995–1998, Pew Center for the People and the Press; 2000–2008: Pew Internet and American Life Project, "Usage Over Time Spreadsheet" (*www.pewinternet.org*).

Table 4-2   Newspaper Circulation, Daily Papers, 1850–2007

Year	Number	Circulation (thousands)	Circulation as a percentage of population
1850	254	758	3.3
1860	387	1,478	4.7
1870	574	2,602	6.5
1880	971	3,566	7.1
1890	1,610	8,387	13.3
1900	2,226	15,102	19.8
1904	2,452	19,633	23.4
1909	2,600	24,212	26.2
1914	2,580	28,777	28.6
1919	2,441	33,029	31.0
1921	2,334	33,742	31.7
1923	2,271	35,471	30.6
1925	2,116	37,407	32.3
1927	2,091	41,368	35.7
1929	2,086	42,015	34.1
1931	2,044	41,294	33.6
1933	1,903	37,630	29.6
1935	2,037	40,871	32.1
1937	2,065	43,345	34.1
1939	2,040	42,966	32.4
1947	1,854	53,287	37.0
1950	1,772	53,800	35.3
1954	1,820	56,410	34.6
1958	1,778	58,713	33.6
1960	1,763	58,900	32.6
1963	1,766	63,831	33.7
1965	1,751	60,400	31.1
1967	—	66,527	33.5
1970	1,748	62,100	30.3
1975	1,756	60,700	28.1
1978	1,756	62,000	27.9
1979	1,763	62,200	27.6
1980	1,745	62,200	27.3
1981	1,730	61,400	26.7
1982	1,711	62,500	26.9
1983	1,701	62,600	26.7
1984	1,688	63,300	26.8
1985	1,676	62,800	26.3
1986	1,657	62,500	26.0
1987	1,645	62,826	25.9
1988	1,642	62,695	25.6
1989	1,626	62,649	25.3
1990	1,611	62,328	24.9
1991	1,586	60,687	24.4
1992	1,570	60,164	23.1

(Table continues)

Table 4-2   *(Continued)*

Year	Number	Circulation (thousands)	Circulation as a percentage of population
1993	1,556	59,812	22.6
1994	1,548	59,305	22.2
1995	1,533	58,193	21.9
1996	1,520	56,983	21.1
1997	1,509	56,728	20.7
1998	1,489	56,182	20.3
1999	1,483	55,979	20.2
2000	1,480	55,773	19.8
2001	1,468	55,578	19.2
2002	1,457	55,186	18.9
2003	1,456	55,185	18.6
2004	1,457	54,626	18.6
2005	1,452	53,345	18.0
2006	1,437	52,329	17.5
2007	1,422	50,742	16.8

Note: "—" indicates not available. Data are for English language newspapers only. In 1900 and earlier, figures include a small number of periodicals. In 1970 and later, the number of newspapers is for February of the following year, and circulation figures are as of September 30 of the year indicated.

Sources: Daily papers, 1850–1967: U.S. Bureau of the Census, *Historical Statistics of the United States* (Washington, D.C.: Government Printing Office, 1975), 810; 1970–2007: *Editor & Publisher International Yearbook* (New York: Editor & Publisher, annual); population, 1850–1990, 1998–1999, 2004–2007: U.S. Bureau of the Census, *Statistical Abstract of the United States* (Washington, D.C.: Government Printing Office, annual); 1991–1997, 2000–2003: estimated by *Editor & Publisher,* reprinted with permission.

Figure 4-1   Growth of Congressional Press Corps, 1864–2008

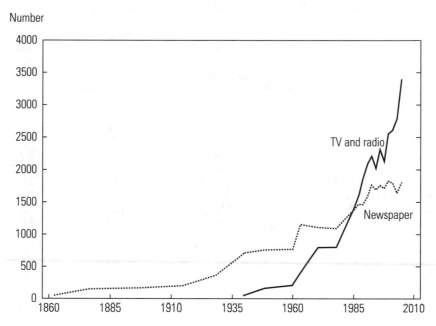

Note: Press corps members are those correspondents entitled to admission to the Senate and House press galleries and radio and television galleries. Before 1986, the number of press corps members was recorded about every ten years. Since 2000, the numbers are from the revised, online edition of the *Official Congressional Directory* (see source) for the year indicated.

Sources: Samuel Kernell, *Going Public: New Strategies of Presidential Leadership* (Washington, D.C.: CQ Press, 1986), 57; updated by the editors from successive volumes of U.S. Congress Joint Committee on Printing, *Official Congressional Directory* (Washington, D.C.: Government Printing Office); as of 2000 from the online version (*www.access.gpo.gov*).

Table 4-3   Presidential News Conferences, 1913–2009

President	Total number of solo press conferences	Total number of press conferences	Average number of press conferences per month
Wilson (1913–1921)	159	159	1.7
Harding (1921–1923)	—	—	—
Coolidge (1923–1929)	521	521	7.8
Hoover (1929–1933)	267	268	5.6
F. Roosevelt (1933–1945)	984	1,020	7.0
Truman (1945–1953)	311	324	3.4
Eisenhower (1953–1961)	192	193	2.0
Kennedy (1961–1963)	65	65	1.9
L. Johnson (1963–1969)	118	135	2.2
Nixon (1969–1974)	39	39	0.6
Ford (1974–1977)	39	40	1.3
Carter (1977–1981)	59	59	1.2
Reagan (1981–1989)	46	46	0.5
G. H. W. Bush (1989–1993)	84	143	3.0
Clinton (1993–2001)	62	193	2.0
G. W. Bush (2001–2009)	50	208	2.2
Obama (2009–)	6	12	3.0

Note: "—" indicates data not available. Obama count is through May 19, 2009. Counting news conferences—even distinguishing between solo and joint conferences—requires judgment because of the variety of contacts presidents have with the press. In almost all cases, the solo counts exclude those news conferences in which the president appears jointly with foreign leaders or other U.S. officials. For details, see Martha Joynt Kumar, "'Does This Constitute a Press Conference?' Defining and Tabulating Modern Presidential Press Conferences," *Presidential Studies Quarterly* (March 2003). In addition to the more formal press conferences counted in the table, presidents submit to interviews with individual and groups of reporters, such as those with individual television anchors. A third type of presidential session with reporters is a short question-and-answer session with reporters that takes place mostly in the Oval Office, Roosevelt Room, Cabinet Room, or Diplomatic Room, where space is at a premium and a pool of reporters represents the whole of the press corps. The number of such interviews for recent presidents are Clinton, 374; Bush, 415; and Obama, 43. Some interview transcripts are found in the *Public Papers of the Presidents of the United States*, but many are not—the news organization conducting the interview controls the transcript and chooses whether to release it. The short question-and-answer sessions numbered 1,042 for Clinton, 468 for Bush, and 20 for Obama. For details, see Martha Joynt Kumar, *Managing the President's Message: The White House Communications Operation* (Baltimore: Johns Hopkins University Press, 2007).

Sources: Martha Joynt Kumar, "Source Material: Presidential Press Conferences: The Evolution of an Enduring Forum," *Presidential Studies Quarterly* (March 2005); data supplied by Kumar, May 2009.

Table 4-4   Use of Television for News, 1990–2008 (percent)

Date	Local TV news[a]	Network TV news[b]	Cable news channels[c]	Cable News Network (CNN)[d]	Fox News Cable Channel[e]	MSNBC[f]	CNBC[g]
			Regularly or sometimes watch				
January 1990	—	—	—	51	—	—	—
June 1990	—	—	—	57	—	—	—
February 1993	92	81	—	—	—	—	—
May 1993	93	88	—	69	—	—	—
March 1995	90	76	—	58	—	—	—
April 1996	88	71	—	59	—	—	—
February 1997	88	72	—	58	—	—	—
April 1998	86	67	—	57	47	31	39
August 1999	—	73	—	—	—	—	—
April 2000	80	58	—	55	45	38	42
April 2002	81	61	68	56	48	45	43
April 2004	82	62	71	55	54	42	41
April 2006	77	54	65	54	51	40	37
May 2008	77	54	67	57	50	46	38

Note: "—" indicates not available. Data for other months can be found in previous editions of *Vital Statistics on American Politics.*

[a] Question: "How often do you watch the local news about your viewing area which usually comes on before the national news in the evening and again later at night—regularly, sometimes, hardly ever, or never?" (Prior to 2002, the question was: "How often do you watch the local news about your viewing area? This usually comes on before the national news and then later at night at 10 or 11.")

[b] Question: "How often do you watch the national nightly network news on CBS, ABC, or NBC? This is different from local news shows about the area where you live—regularly, sometimes, hardly ever, or never?"

[c] Question: "How often do you watch cable news channels such as CNN, MSNBC, or the Fox News Cable Channel—regularly, sometimes, hardly ever, or never?"

[d] Question: "How often do you watch CNN—regularly, sometimes, hardly ever, or never?" (Prior to 2008, the question was: "How often do you watch Cable News Network (CNN)—regularly, sometimes, hardly ever, or never?")

[e] Question: "How often do you watch the Fox News Cable Channel—regularly, sometimes, hardly ever, or never?"

[f] Question: "How often do you watch MSNBC—regularly, sometimes, hardly ever, or never?"

[g] Question: "How often do you watch CNBC—regularly, sometimes, hardly ever, or never?"

Source: Pew Research Center for the People and the Press (*http://people-press.org*).

Table 4-5 Use of Internet and Newspapers for News, 1990–2008 (percent)

Date	Ever go online?[a]		Frequency of going online to get news[b]						Read newspaper regularly?[c]	
	Yes	No	Every day	3–5 days/week	1–2 days/week	Every few weeks	Less often	No/never (volunteered)	Yes	No
November 1990	—	—	—	—	—	—	—	—	74	26
July 1991	—	—	—	—	—	—	—	—	73	27
June 1992	—	—	—	—	—	—	—	—	75	25
October 1994	—	—	—	—	—	—	—	—	73	27
March 1995	—	—	—	—	—	—	—	—	71	29
June 1995	14	86	6	9	15	13	28	29	69	34
April 1996	21	79	—	—	—	—	—	—	71	28
April 1998	36	64	18	17	20	15	21	9	68	32
September 1998	42	58	23	16	21	14	19	7	—	—
November 1998	—	—	—	—	—	—	—	—	70	30
December 1998	42	58	25	17	22	10	18	8	—	—
August 1999	52	48	22	15	19	15	20	9	—	—
October 1999	50	50	25	14	22	11	20	8	—	—
April 2000	54	46	27	15	19	12	18	9	63	37
April 2002	62	38	25	16	16	13	21	9	63	37
April 2004	66	34	27	18	15	12	17	11	60	40
April 2006	67	33	27	20	17	12	16	8	59	41
May 2008	67	33	37	18	16	8	13	8	54	46

Note: "—" indicates not available.

[a] Question: "Do you ever go online to access the Internet or to send and receive e-mail?" (Prior to 2006, the question was "Do you ever go online to access the Internet or World Wide Web or to send and receive e-mail?")

[b] Question: (Asked only of those who "ever" go online) "How frequently do you go online to get news… Would you say every day, 3 to 5 days per week, 1 or 2 days per week, once every few weeks, or less often?"

[c] Question: "Do you happen to read any daily newspaper or newspapers regularly, or not?"

Source: Pew Research Center for the People and the Press (*http://people-press.org*).

Table 4-6   Use of Newspaper, Radio, and Television for News, 1993–2008 (percent)

	1993	1996	1998	2000	2002	2004	2006	2008
Listened/read yesterday								
Newspaper[a]	58[b]	50	48	47	41	42	40	34
Radio news[c]	47[b]	44	49	43	41	40	36	35
Regularly watch								
Cable TV news[d]	—	—	—	—	33	38	34	39
Local TV news[e]	77	65	64	56	57	59	54	52
Nightly network news[f]	60	42	38	30	32	34	28	29
Morning network news[g]	—	—	23	20	22	22	23	22

Note: "—" indicates not available.

[a] Question: "Did you get a chance to read a daily newspaper yesterday, or not?"
[b] Data from 1994.
[c] Question: "About how much time did you spend listening to any news on the radio yesterday, or didn't you happen to listen to the news on the radio yesterday?"
[d] Question: "Tell me if you watch cable news channels such as CNN, MSNBC, or the Fox News Cable Channel—regularly, sometimes, hardly ever, or never."
[e] Question: "Tell me if you watch the local news about your viewing area which usually comes on before or after the national news in the evening and again later at night—regularly, sometimes, hardly ever, or never."
[f] Question: "Tell me if you watch the national nightly network news on CBS, ABC, or NBC—regularly, sometimes, hardly ever, or never."
[g] Question: "Now I'd like to know how often you watch or listen to certain TV and radio programs. For each that I read, tell me if you watch or listen to it regularly, sometimes, hardly ever or never...*The Today Show, Good Morning America,* or *The Early Show.*"

Source: Pew Research Center for the People and the Press, "Audience Segments in a Changing News Environment" (2008 Pew Research Center Biennial News Consumption Survey), 3 (*http://people-press.org*).

Table 4-7   Media Use, by Groups, 2008 (percent)

	Newspaper[a]	News online[b]	TV news[c]	Radio news[d]	Nightly network news[e]	Cable news channels[f]	Local news[g]
Total	34	29	57	35	29	40	52
Sex							
Men	36	32	57	39	27	44	48
Women	32	26	57	31	31	35	55
Age							
18–29 years	19	31	41	28	20	36	36
30–49 years	28	36	54	41	23	38	51
50–64 years	40	29	64	37	34	42	60
65 years and older	55	13	75	29	46	44	63
Sex/age							
Men under 30 years	20	30	44	30	24	42	31
Women under 30 years	18	32	37	25	17	29	41
Men 30–49 years	31	39	52	45	21	43	49
Women 30–49 years	25	32	55	36	24	33	53
Men 50 years and older	49	27	68	39	35	46	58
Women 50 years and older	43	19	68	30	42	40	63
Race/ethnicity							
White	37	30	56	35	29	39	52
Nonwhite	24	26	59	34	30	43	52
Black	24	21	68	33	32	47	61
Hispanic[h]	23	26	51	35	29	45	44
Education							
College graduate	45	47	57	46	28	45	47
Some college	34	36	55	32	28	42	52
High school graduate	30	18	59	33	33	36	58
Less than high school graduate	20	5	53	20	25	32	47
Family income							
Less than $30,000	23	18	56	24	30	35	53
$30,000–49,999	37	25	58	36	28	46	57
$50,000–74,999	36	34	59	37	31	41	54
$75,000–99,999	39	41	58	46	28	40	52
$100,000 or more	42	45	58	43	28	45	46
Region							
East	37	28	56	36	29	39	48
Midwest	36	28	58	35	27	38	54
South	33	29	57	35	30	41	55
West	31	31	55	34	30	39	48
Party identification							
Democrat	36	28	61	33	37	44	59
Independent	32	30	53	35	26	33	48
Republican	36	32	58	41	25	48	49

Table 4-7   *(Continued)*

	Newspaper[a]	News online[b]	TV news[c]	Radio news[d]	Nightly network news[e]	Cable news channels[f]	Local news[g]
Cable TV							
Subscriber	35	30	58	35	30	45	53
Nonsubscriber	26	24	48	33	25	17	45
Online use							
Internet user	35	41	55	39	27	42	50
Not an Internet user	32	5	60	26	33	35	56

Note: Percentages are those responding "yes" for newspaper, news online, and TV news; "did listen" for radio news; and "regularly" for nightly network news, cable news channels, and local news.

[a] Question: "Did you get a chance to read a daily newspaper yesterday, or not?"
[b] Question: "Did you get any news online through the Internet yesterday, or not?"
[c] Question: "Did you watch the news or a news program on television yesterday, or not?"
[d] Question: "About how much time did you spend listening to any news on the radio yesterday, or didn't you happen to listen to the news on the radio yesterday?"
[e] Question: "Tell me if you watch the national nightly network news on CBS, ABC, or NBC—regularly, sometimes, hardly ever, or never."
[f] Question: "Tell me if you watch cable news channels such as CNN, MSNBC, or the Fox News Cable Channel—regularly, sometimes, hardly ever, or never."
[g] Question: "Tell me if you watch the local news about your viewing area which usually comes on before or after the national news in the evening and again later at night—regularly, sometimes, hardly ever, or never."
[h] Hispanics may be of any race.

Source: Pew Research Center for the People and the Press, "Audience Segments in a Changing News Environment" (2008 Pew Research Center Biennial News Consumption Survey), 64–67 (*http://people-press.org*).

Table 4-8   Network and Cable Television Audiences Compared, 2008 (percent)

	Regularly watch	
	Nightly network news	Cable news channels
Sex		
Men	27	44
Women	31	35
Age		
18–29 years	21	36
30–49 years	22	38
50–64 years	34	42
65 years and older	46	44
Education		
Less than high school graduate	25	32
High school graduate	33	36
Some college	27	42
College graduate	28	45
Total	29	39

Note: For question, see Table 4-4, footnotes b and c, this volume.

Source: Pew Research Center for the People and the Press, "Audience Segments in a Changing News Environment" (2008 Pew Research Center Biennial News Consumption Survey), 14 (*http://people-press.org*).

Table 4-9   Partisan Profile of TV News Audiences, 2006 and 2008 (percent)

| | Percentage of those who regularly watch who are | | | |
	Democrats	Independents	Republicans	Don't know
2006				
CNN	45	26	22	7
Fox News Channel	31	22	38	9
MSNBC	48	26	19	7
NewsHour	47	22	21	10
Nightly network news	40	24	28	8
General public	32	30	28	10
2008				
CNN	51	23	18	8
Fox News Channel	33	22	39	6
MSNBC	45	27	18	10
NewsHour	46	23	21	10
Nightly network news	45	26	22	7
General public	36	29	25	10

Note: Table entries are the shares of each audience who identify themselves as Republicans, Democrats, and Independents. Those who lean toward a party are counted as partisans. Questions: "How often do you watch *The NewsHour with Jim Lehrer*—regularly, sometimes, hardly ever, or never?" Party identification: see Figure 3-2, this volume. See Table 4-4, this volume, for the other questions.

Source: Pew Research Center for the People and the Press, "Audience Segments in a Changing News Environment" (2008 Pew Research Center Biennial News Consumption Survey), 15 (*http://people-press.org*).

Table 4-10   Preference for News with a Point of View, 2004–2008 (percent)

	Prefer news from		
	My point of view	No point of view	Don't know
2004	25	67	8
2006	23	68	9
2008	23	66	11
Education			
High school or less	28	58	14
Some college	19	74	7
College graduate	19	74	7
Partisanship and ideology			
Liberal Democrat	31	64	5
Conservative or moderate	27	64	9
Democrat			
Independent	15	77	8
Liberal or moderate Republican	21	71	8
Conservative Republican	33	58	9

Note: Question: "Thinking about the different kinds of political news available to you, what do you prefer… getting news from sources that share your political point of view or getting news from sources that don't have a particular political point of view?"

Source: Pew Research Center for the People and the Press, "Audience Segments in a Changing News Environment" (2008 Pew Research Center Biennial News Consumption Survey), 37 (*http://people-press.org*).

Table 4-11 Sources of Campaign News, 1992–2008 (percent)

	1992	1996	2000	2002[a]	2004	2006[a]	2008
Main source of campaign news[b]							
Television	82	72	70	66	76	69	68
Newspapers	57	60	39	33	46	34	33
Radio	12	19	15	13	22	17	16
Internet	—	3	11	7	21	15	36
Magazines	9	11	4	1	6	2	3
Campaign news from the Internet[c]							
Yes	—	10	30	—	41	—	56
No	—	90	70	—	59	—	44

Note: "—" indicates not available.

[a] The 2002 and 2006 results are based on all adults. Other years are based on adults who voted.
[b] Question: "How have you been getting most of your news about 2008 November elections?" Respondents were allowed to give two responses.
[c] Question: "Did you happen to get any news or information about "____" elections from the Internet, or not?"

Sources: Campaign news sources, 2002 and 2006: "Election 2006 Online," Pew Internet and American Life Project (*www.pewinternet.org*); campaign news sources, 1992–2000, 2004, 2008, and campaign news from the Internet, "Republicans Want More Conservative Direction for GOP," Pew Research Center for the People and the Press (*http://people-press.org*).

Table 4-12 Public's Use of Media to Follow Presidential Campaigns, 1952–2008 (percent)

Media	1952	1956	1960	1964	1968	1972	1976	1980	1984	1988	1992	1996	2000	2004	2008
Read newspaper articles about the election															
Regularly	—	—	44	40	37	26	28	—	—	—	—	—	—	—	—
Often[a]	39	69	12	14	12	14	17	27	24	—	—	—	—	—	—
From time to time[b]	40	—	16	18	19	16	24	29	34	—	—	—	—	—	—
Once in a great while[c]	—	—	7	6	7	4	10	17	19	—	—	—	—	—	—
None	21	31	21	22	25	40	22	27	23	—	—	—	—	—	—
Paid attention to newspaper articles about the presidential campaign															
Great deal	—	—	—	—	—	—	—	—	8	6	9	5	6	8	9
Quite a bit	—	—	—	—	—	—	—	—	14	12	15	11	10	14	18
Some	—	—	—	—	—	—	—	—	28	22	20	19	19	21	31
Very little	—	—	—	—	—	—	—	—	20	9	6	7	6	6	9
None	—	—	—	—	—	—	—	—	31	52	50	58	60	51	33
Listened to speeches or discussions on radio															
Good many[d]	34	—	15	12	12	8	12	14	10	5	7	7	8	15	13
Several[e]	—	45	17	23	16	21	20	22	20	10	11	14	14	18	19
One or two[f]	35	—	10	12	12	13	16	15	16	17	18	18	15	18	15
None	30	55	58	52	59	59	52	50	55	69	64	61	62	49	53
Watched programs about the campaign on television															
Good many[d]	32	—	47	41	42	33	37	28	25	—	31	15	24	27	29
Several[e]	—	74	29	34	34	41	38	37	37	—	39	32	35	37	37
One or two[f]	19	—	11	13	13	16	15	22	24	—	19	28	23	22	20
None	49	26	13	11	11	9	10	13	14	—	11	25	18	14	14

Paid attention to television news about the presidential campaign														
Great deal	—	—	—	—	—	—	—	—	—	—	17	15	20	27
Quite a bit	—	—	—	—	—	—	—	—	—	—	24	26	29	31
Some	—	—	—	—	—	—	—	—	—	—	28	29	28	23
Very little	—	—	—	—	—	—	—	—	—	—	11	13	11	8
None	—	—	—	—	—	—	—	—	—	—	20	17	13	11
Read about the campaign in magazines														
Good many[d]	15	—	12	10	9	7	12	7	7	—	—	—	—	—
Several[e]	—	31	15	16	12	15	24	19	16	—	—	—	—	—
One or two[f]	26	—	13	13	15	14	15	12	11	—	—	—	—	—
None	60	69	59	61	64	64	49	62	66	—	—	—	—	—
Paid attention to magazine articles about the presidential campaign														
Great deal	—	—	—	—	—	—	—	—	3	3	4	3	4	3
Quite a bit	—	—	—	—	—	—	—	—	4	6	7	7	7	8
Some	—	—	—	—	—	—	—	—	7	11	10	15	12	17
Very little	—	—	—	—	—	—	—	—	2	3	3	7	6	7
None	—	—	—	—	—	—	—	—	84	76	77	68	72	65

Note: "—" indicates question not asked or response category not offered.

a "Quite a lot, pretty much" in 1952; "yes" in 1956; "good many" in 1980–1984.
b "Not very much" in 1952; "several" in 1980–1984.
c "One or two" in 1980–1984.
d "Quite a lot, pretty much" in 1952.
e "Yes" in 1956.
f "Not very much" in 1952.

Source: Calculated by the editors from the American National Election Studies data, Center for Political Studies, University of Michigan, Ann Arbor (*www.electionstudies.org*).

Table 4-13   Credibility of Television and Print Media, 1998–2008 (percent)

	1998	2000	2002	2004	2006	2008	Not rated, 2008[a]
TV news outlets							
60 Minutes (CBS)	35	34	34	33	27	29	9
ABC News	30	30	24	24	22	24	7
BBC	—	—	—	—	—	21	35
CBS News	28	29	26	24	22	22	8
CNN	42	39	37	32	28	30	9
C-SPAN	32	33	30	27	25	26	29
Fox News Channel	—	26	24	25	25	23	11
Local TV news	34	33	27	25	23	28	4
MSNBC	—	28	28	22	21	24	13
NBC News	30	29	25	24	23	24	5
NewsHour (PBS)	29	24	26	23	23	23	37
National Public Radio	19	25	23	23	22	27	30
Print news outlets							
Associated Press	18	21	17	18	17	16	14
National Enquirer	3	4	3	5	6	5	15
New York Times	—	—	—	21	20	18	21
Newsweek	24	24	20	19	18	16	19
People	10	10	9	7	8	8	18
Time	27	29	23	22	21	21	18
U.S. News	—	—	26	24	21	20	20
USA Today	23	23	19	19	18	16	18
Wall Street Journal	41	41	33	24	26	25	21
Your daily newspaper	29	25	21	19	19	22	9

Note: "—" indicates not available. The 1998–2008 percentages are, of respondents who could rate each organization, those who believe all or most of what the organization says. Question: "As I name some organizations, please rate how much you think you can believe each that I name on a scale of 4 to 1. On this four-point scale, '4' means you can believe all or most of what the organization says, and '1' means you believe almost nothing of what they say. First, how would you rate the believability of _____ on this scale of 4 to 1?"

[a] "Not rated" combines "never heard of" and "can't rate" responses.

Sources: Pew Research Center for the People and the Press, "Audience Segments in a Changing News Environment" (2008 Pew Research Center Biennial News Consumption Survey), 56–57; and "May 2008 Political/Believability Survey," Final Topline, May 21–25, 2008, 22–26 (*http://people-press.org*).

Figure 4-2   Share of News Coverage Devoted to Presidential Campaign, 2008

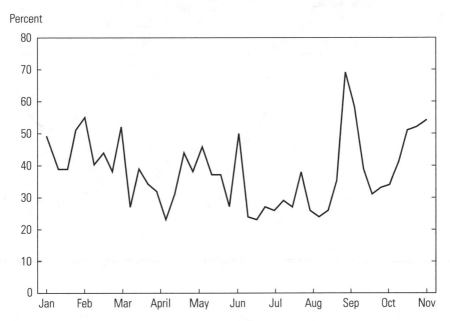

Note: News stories are considered to be about the presidential election if 50 percent or more of the story is devoted to discussion of the ongoing presidential campaign. Figures are based on the Campaign Coverage Index and the News Coverage Index from the Pew Research Center's Project for Excellence in Journalism. The project monitors on a rotating basis forty-eight different news outlets each week in five media sectors—newspaper, online, network TV, cable TV, and radio. For details, see source. Related data for additional years can be found in previous editions of *Vital Statistics on American Politics*.

Source: Pew Research Center's Project for Excellence in Journalism, "Campaign Coverage Index" (*http://journalism.org*).

Figure 4-3 Media Exposure of Clinton, McCain, and Obama in the 2008 Presidential Nominations

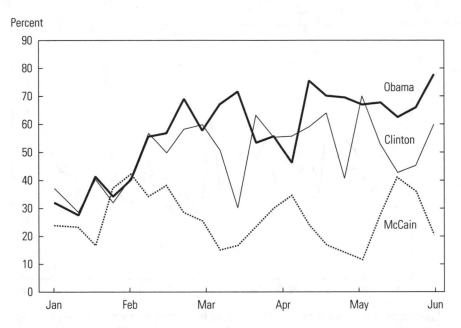

Note: Plotted are the percentages of campaign news stories in which the candidate was the subject of 25 percent or more of the story. More than one candidate may be so featured in a single news story. For details on the content analysis, see note to Figure 4-2, this volume. Analysis of the tone of campaign news coverage from January through early March 2008 revealed that Obama and Clinton, but not McCain, received similar positive-in-tone news coverage: Obama, 69 percent positive; Clinton, 67 percent; and McCain, 43 percent (Pew Research Center's Project for Excellence in Journalism, "Character and the Primaries of 2008," May 29, 2008). Earlier, between January and May 2007, Obama had more favorable coverage than Clinton or McCain: Obama, 47 percent positive; Clinton, 27 percent; and McCain, 12 percent (Pew Research Center's Project for Excellence in Journalism, "The Invisible Primary—Invisible No Longer," October 29, 2007). Related data for additional years can be found in previous editions of *Vital Statistics on American Politics.*

Source: Pew Research Center's Project for Excellence in Journalism, "Campaign Coverage Index" (*http://journalism.org*).

Figure 4-4   Media Exposure of McCain and Obama in the 2008 Presidential General Election

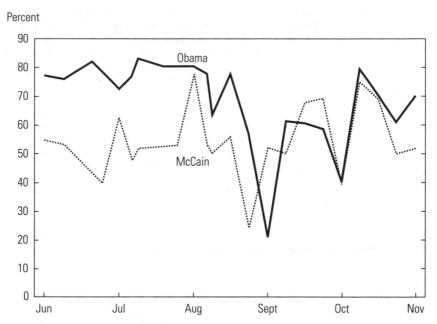

Note: Plotted are the percentages of campaign news stories in which the candidate was the subject of 25 percent or more of the story. More than one candidate may be so featured in a single news story. For details on the content analysis, see note to Figure 4-2, this volume. Analysis of the tone of campaign news coverage from September 8 through October 16 revealed that Obama received 36 percent positive coverage, 35 percent neutral, and 29 percent negative; McCain received 14 percent positive coverage, 29 percent neutral, and 57 percent negative (Pew Research Center's Project for Excellence in Journalism, "Winning the Media Campaign," October 22, 2008). Related data for additional years can be found in previous editions of *Vital Statistics on American Politics.*

Source: Pew Research Center's Project for Excellence in Journalism, "Campaign Coverage Index" (*http://journalism.org*).

Table 4-14   National Nominating Conventions: Television Coverage and Viewership, 1952–2008

Year/party	Audience rating[a] (percent)	Average hours viewed by household	Network hours telecast[b]
1952			
Republican	—	10.5	57.5
Democratic	—	13.1	61.1
1956			
Republican	—	6.4	22.8
Democratic	—	8.4	37.6
1960			
Republican	28.0	6.2	25.5
Democratic	29.2	8.3	29.3
1964			
Republican	21.8	7.0	36.5
Democratic	28.8	6.4	23.5
1968			
Republican	26.4	6.5	34.0
Democratic	28.5	8.5	39.1
1972			
Republican	23.4	3.5	19.8
Democratic	18.3	5.8	36.7
1976			
Republican	31.5	6.3	29.5
Democratic	25.2	5.2	30.4
1980			
Republican	21.6	3.8	22.7
Democratic	27.0	4.4	24.1
1984			
Republican	19.2	1.9	11.9
Democratic	23.4	2.5	12.9
1988			
Republican	18.3	2.2	12.6
Democratic	19.8	2.3	12.8
1992			
Republican	20.5	—	7.3
Democratic	22.0	—	8.0
1996			
Republican	16.5	—	5.0
Democratic	17.2	—	5.0
2000			
Republican	13.9	—	5.2
Democratic	15.3	—	5.3
2004			
Republican	15.3	—	3.0
Democratic	14.3	—	3.0

Table 4-14   *(Continued)*

Year/party	Audience rating[a] (percent)	Average hours viewed by household	Network hours telecast[b]
2008			
Republican	21.9	1.4	3.0[c]
Democratic	19.9	1.4	4.0

Note: "—" indicates not available.

[a] Sum of the percentage of television households viewing the convention during an average minute of common coverage time periods. Through 1988, based on viewing of ABC, CBS, and NBC; for 1992 and 1996, based on viewing the three networks plus PBS and CNN (the 1996 Republican convention was also televised on the Family Channel, but that is not included in the rating); for 2000, includes the three networks, CNN, Fox News Channel, and MSNBC; for 2004, includes the three networks, CNN, Fox News Channel, and MSNBC; for 2008, includes the three networks, CNN, Fox News Channel, MSNBC, BET (Democratic convention only), TV One (Democratic convention only), Univision (day four only), and Telemundo (day four only). C-SPAN viewing not included.

[b] Number of hours during which one or more of ABC, CBS, or NBC was broadcasting the convention. CNN, Fox News Channel, and MSNBC provided extensive coverage, often entailing regular news programming anchored from the convention site.

[c] Four hours of network coverage of the Republican convention was originally planned. However, because of Hurricane Gustav the convention's first night was scaled back and networks aired storm coverage instead.

Sources: Audience rating, 1960–2004: The Nielsen Company, "Historical TV Ratings," August 27, 2008 (*http://blog.nielsen.com*); audience rating, 2008: "Audience Estimates for the 2008 Republican Convention," The Nielsen Company, September 5, 2008; hours viewed, hours telecast, 1952–1964: *Network Television Audiences to Primaries, Conventions, Elections* (Northbrook, Ill.: A. C. Nielsen, 1976), 8, 9, 21; hours viewed, hours telecast, 1968–1992: A. C. Nielsen Co., *Nielsen Tunes in to Politics (1960–1992)* (New York: Nielsen Media Research, 1993), 1–3; hours telecast, 1996: John Carmody, "Convention Low-Show," *Washington Post*, August 19, 1996, B1; hours telecast, 2000: Robin Toner, "The Conventions Are Over, the Party's Just Starting," *New York Times*, August 20, 2000, iv; hours telecast, 2004: Michael Janofsky, "Each Convention to Get 3 Hours of Prime Time on TV Networks," *New York Times*, July 13, 2004, A16; hours telecast, 2008: "Networks Rethink Conventions," *Baltimore Sun*, August 25, 2008, 11A, and "Media Alert: Republican National Convention Coverage," The Nielsen Company, September 1, 2008; hours viewed, 2008: The Nielsen Company, "Nielsen Examines TV Viewers to the Political Convention," September 2008, 3.

Table 4-15   National Nominating Conventions: Television Viewing, by Selected Characteristics, 2008

	Democratic National Convention only	Republican National Convention only	Both	Total
Viewers, age				
18–24 years	9.0	8.5	6.6	24.1
25–34 years	13.2	12.0	14.1	39.3
35–44 years	13.8	15.1	18.1	47.0
45–54 years	15.9	16.4	22.5	54.8
55 years and over	15.2	14.9	33.1	63.2
Income, household				
Under $20,000	16.9	11.9	29.1	57.9
$20,000 to under 30,000	14.9	12.8	32.0	59.7
$30,000 to under 40,000	17.6	13.8	31.0	62.4
$40,000 to under 50,000	15.7	15.6	30.1	61.4
$50,000 to under 60,000	15.9	15.3	32.0	63.2
$60,000 to under 75,000	17.4	16.9	32.9	67.2
$75,000 to under 100,000	16.2	15.7	36.5	68.4
Over $100,000	11.6	17.9	43.5	73.0
Education, head of household				
1–3 years of high school	16.5	11.2	28.2	55.9
4 years of high school or high school graduate	15.6	15.1	31.4	62.1
1–3 years of college	16.0	14.8	32.4	63.2
4 or more years of college	14.6	16.4	38.5	69.5
Race and ethnicity, household				
White	13.6	16.2	34.5	64.3
Black	27.4	8.1	35.7	71.2
Hispanic	19.8	14.0	28.8	62.6
Other	16.7	14.2	27.7	58.6
All households	15.7	15.0	33.8	64.5
All individuals 18 years and over	13.9	13.9	21.5	49.3

Note: Table entries reflect the viewing percentages for each characteristic. Viewership was calculated for the final hour of coverage each evening, August 25 through August 28 (Democratic National Convention), and September 2 through September 4 (Republican National Convention). (Republican coverage was only three nights because of the effects of Hurricane Gustav.) A household or person had to watch a minimum of six noncontinuous minutes to qualify as a viewer. Based on viewing of ABC, CBS, NBC, CNN, Fox News Channel, and MSNBC. For August 28 and September 4, Telemundo and Univision were added. For the Democratic National Convention, BET and TV1 were added. For details, see source. Totals calculated by the editors.

Source: "Nielsen Examines TV Viewers to the Political Conventions," September 2008, 1, 8, 9, 13 (*http://blog.nielsen.com*).

Table 4-16   Television Viewership of Presidential and Vice Presidential Debates, 1960–2008

Year	Candidates	Date	Audience rating[a] (percent)	Viewers (millions)
1960	Kennedy–Nixon	Sept. 26	59.5	66.4
		Oct. 7	59.1	61.9
		Oct. 13	61.0	63.7
		Oct. 21	57.8	60.4
1976	Carter–Ford	Sept. 23	53.5	69.7
		Oct. 6	52.4	63.9
		Oct. 22	47.8	62.7
	Mondale–Dole	Oct. 15	35.5	43.2
1980	Carter–Reagan	Oct. 28	58.9	80.6
1984	Mondale–Reagan	Oct. 7	45.3	65.1
		Oct. 21	46.0	67.3
	Ferraro–G. H. W. Bush	Oct. 11	43.6	56.7
1988	Dukakis–G. H. W. Bush	Sept. 25	36.8	65.1
		Oct. 13	35.9	67.3
	Bentsen–Quayle	Oct. 5	33.6	46.9
1992	Clinton–G. H. W. Bush–Perot	Oct. 11	38.3	62.4
		Oct. 15	46.3	69.9
		Oct. 19	45.2	66.9
	Gore–Quayle–Stockdale	Oct. 13	36.0	51.2
1996	Clinton–Dole	Oct. 6	31.6	46.1
		Oct. 16	26.1	36.3
	Gore–Kemp	Oct. 9	19.7	26.6
2000	Gore–G. W. Bush	Oct. 3	31.7	46.6
		Oct. 11	26.8	37.5
		Oct. 17	25.9	37.7
	Lieberman–Cheney	Oct. 5	21.0	29.1
2004	Kerry–G. W. Bush	Sept. 30	39.4	62.5
		Oct. 8	29.6	46.7
		Oct. 13	32.6	51.2
	Edwards–Cheney	Oct. 5	28.1	43.6
2008	Obama–McCain	Sept. 26	31.6	52.4
		Oct. 7	38.8	63.2
		Oct. 15	35.0	56.5
	Biden–Palin	Oct. 2	41.7	70.0

Note: Vice presidential candidates are in italics. 1976–1988 debates include ABC, CBS, and NBC only; 1992 includes ABC, CBS (not Oct. 11), NBC, and CNN; 1996 includes ABC, CBS, NBC, CNN, and Fox (only Oct. 6); 2000 includes ABC, CBS, NBC (some affiliates on tape delay Oct. 3), CNN, Fox (some affiliates on tape delay Oct. 3, not included Oct. 5 or Oct. 11), Fox News Channel, and MSNBC; 2004 includes ABC, CBS, NBC, CNN, Fox (not Oct. 5 or Oct. 13), Fox News Channel, and MSNBC; 2008 includes ABC, CBS, Fox (not Oct. 15), NBC, Telefutura (not Oct. 7 or Oct. 15), Telemundo, Univision (not Sept. 26 or Oct. 2), BBC-America, CNBC, CNN, Fox News Channel, MSNBC, and MUN2 (only Oct. 15). PBS and C-SPAN data not included. Combined audience estimates are based on comparable durations. Debates during the primary and caucus season attract far fewer viewers. The April 16, 2008, Democratic debate in Pennsylvania, broadcast on ABC, attracted an average of 10.7 million viewers and was the most watched debate of any during the 2008 presidential nomination season.

[a] Percentage of television households viewing the debates during an average minute.

Source: Nielsen Media Research.

Table 4-17   Newspaper Endorsements of Presidential Candidates,
1940–2008

Year/candidate endorsed	Papers		Circulation	
	Number	Percent	Number	Percent
1940				
Willkie (R)	813	64	—	—
F. Roosevelt (D)	289	23	—	—
Uncommitted	171	13	—	—
1944				
Dewey (R)	796	60	26,654,996	69
F. Roosevelt (D)	291	22	6,902,243	18
Uncommitted	237	18	5,356,807	14
1948				
Dewey (R)	771	65	35,152,807	79
Truman (D)	182	15	4,489,851	10
Thurmond	45	4	537,730	1
Wallace	3	0	60,233	0
Uncommitted	182	15	4,454,557	10
1952				
Eisenhower (R)	933	67	40,129,237	80
Stevenson (D)	202	15	5,466,781	11
Uncommitted	250	18	4,417,102	9
1956				
Eisenhower (R)	740	62	34,538,755	72
Stevenson (D)	189	15	6,122,491	13
Uncommitted	270	23	7,079,846	15
1960				
Nixon (R)	731	58	38,006,203	71
Kennedy (D)	208	16	8,448,677	16
Uncommitted	328	26	7,135,954	13
1964				
Goldwater (R)	359	35	8,977,214	21
L. Johnson (D)	440	42	26,997,400	62
Uncommitted	237	23	7,638,727	18
1968				
Nixon (R)	634	61	34,559,385	70
Humphrey (D)	146	14	9,572,948	19
1972				
Nixon (R)	753	71	30,560,535	77
McGovern (D)	56	5	3,044,534	8
Uncommitted	245	23	5,864,548	15
1976				
Ford (R)	411	62	20,951,798	62
Carter (D)	80	12	7,607,739	23
Uncommitted	168	26	5,074,069	15
1980				
Reagan (R)	443	42	17,561,333	49
Carter (D)	126	12	7,782,078	22

Table 4-17   *(Continued)*

Year/candidate endorsed	Papers		Circulation	
	Number	Percent	Number	Percent
Anderson	40	4	1,614,740	4
Uncommitted	439	42	9,131,940	25
1984				
Reagan (R)	381	58	18,357,512	52
Mondale (D)	62	9	7,568,639	21
Uncommitted	216	33	9,611,058	27
1988				
G. H. W. Bush (R)	241	31	18,186,225	40
Dukakis (D)	103	13	11,644,600	25
Uncommitted	428	55	16,224,807	35
1992[a]				
G. H. W. Bush (R)	121	15	7,134,599	18
Clinton (D)	149	18	10,961,415	27
Uncommitted	542	67	22,225,342	55
1996[b]				
Dole (R)	111	19	4,741,645	13
Clinton (D)	65	11	4,581,337	13
Uncommitted	415	70	26,173,692	74
2000				
G. W. Bush (R)	93	48	—	—
Gore (D)	44	23	—	—
Uncommitted	56	29	—	—
2004				
G. W. Bush (R)	205	48	15,743,799	41
Kerry (D)	213	50	20,882,889	55
Uncommitted	12[c]	3	1,650,819[c]	4
2008				
McCain (R)	159	34	9,301,511	29
Obama (D)	287	61	23,086,607	71
Uncommitted	26	6	—	—

Note: "D" indicates Democrat; "R" indicates Republican; "—" indicates not available. In 2000 *Editor & Publisher* changed the survey method used to conduct its quadrennial poll of newspaper endorsements. This change resulted in a much smaller number of responses, with an unknown but probably larger bias. *Editor & Publisher* did not indicate the circulation of newspapers endorsing candidates or remaining uncommitted in 2000. It also did not indicate the circulation of newspapers that were uncommitted in 2008. Data for additional years can be found in previous editions of *Vital Statistics on American Politics.*

[a] One newspaper—circulation 9,075—endorsed H. Ross Perot, independent.
[b] One newspaper—circulation 3,300—endorsed Harry Browne, Libertarian.
[c] Based on the 2008 listing, which indicated those uncommitted in 2004.

Sources: Editor & Publisher, October 26, 1940, 7; November 4, 1944, 9; October 30, 1948, 11; November 1, 1952, 9; November 3, 1956, 11; November 5, 1960, 10; October 31, 1964, 10; November 2, 1968, 9; November 7, 1972, 9; October 30, 1976, 5; November 1, 1980, 10; November 3, 1984, 9; November 5, 1988, 9; October 24, 1992, 9; October 26, 1996, 8; November 6, 2000, 9; November 5, 2004; November 7, 2008 (*www.editorandpublisher.com*). Reprinted with permission of Nielsen Business Media Inc.

Figure 4-5 Newspaper Endorsements of Presidential Candidates: Democratic, Republican, and Uncommitted, 1932–2008

Percent

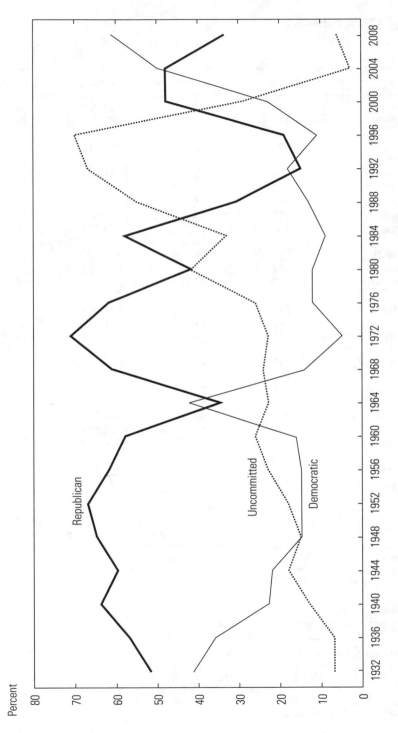

Note: Plotted are percentages of newspapers endorsing each party's nominees or remaining uncommitted.

Sources: Harold W. Stanley and Richard G. Niemi, eds., *Vital Statistics on American Politics 2007–2008* (Washington, D.C.: CQ Press, 2008), table 4-17, this volume.

5

Congress

- **Apportionment**
- **Membership Characteristics**
- **Committees**
- **Bills and Laws**
- **Voting Patterns**
- **Current Members**

Statistics about Congress abound. Capsule descriptions of senators and representatives and their districts run to more than a thousand pages for each Congress (see, for example, *Politics in America,* published by CQ Press, and the *Almanac of American Politics,* published by the National Journal Group). Elections are held every two years, generating mounds of electoral and financial data. Moreover, the annual number of record votes totals more than five hundred in the House and nearly three hundred in the Senate. It is thus hardly surprising that votes for Congress, votes in Congress, members of Congress themselves, and all those who surround them or contribute to their activities have been subjected to extensive statistical scrutiny.

Election-related material is one of the largest collections of data about Congress, and various aspects of these data are provided in several chapters of this book. Election results, including material associated specifically with congressional elections such as losses by the president's party at midterm are provided in Chapter 1; information on the funding of congressional campaigns is provided in Chapter 2. Chapter 3 covers individual voting behavior in congressional elections, as well as public judgments of the institution—so-called congressional approval (see Figure 3-7).

Congress also generates many other kinds of statistics. Simply apportioning members among the states (Table 5-1 and Figure 5-1) has led to a surprising amount of controversy and statistical calculation, which has resulted in a fascinating book-length treatment.[1] As the composition of Congress changes to include more women and minorities, these and other characteristics have also been tabulated and analyzed (Tables 5-2 through 5-5).

Likewise, as Congress has become a larger and more complex operation, analysts have become more interested in its structure and workload. These aspects of Congress are represented here with information about the numbers of committees and their leadership (Table 5-6), numbers of measures considered and passed (Figure 5-2 and Table 5-7), and numbers of votes (Table 5-8). Although these items might at first be considered insignificant or analytically useless tabulations, analyses of the relationships among congressional voting, voter behavior, and legislative output suggest otherwise.

Voting by the members of Congress is of obvious interest. Indeed, cohesion within and contrasts between the political parties were the topics of some of the first statistical treatments of political subjects.[2] Increased numbers of roll calls and other record votes (Table 5-8) have done nothing to dampen this tradition. Party unity and presidential support by individual representatives and senators (Tables 5-11 and 5-12) and for groups (Tables 5-9, 5-10, and Figure 5-3) have become a standard part of congressional analyses.

For the statistically minded, the study of Congress has long been an inviting prospect. The traditional topics are still interesting because the turnover in personnel, the ongoing change in congressional leadership and of the president, the changes in regional strength, and so on make Congress anything but static. In addition, the reforms of congressional procedures and of campaign finance since the Watergate scandal in the 1970s, the technological changes that have resulted in electronic voting and the televising of proceedings in both chambers, and the changes in the size and scope of the government bureaucracy that Congress must deal with are reason enough to scrutinize anew the data underlying one's understanding of Congress.

Notes

1. Michel Balinski and H. P. Young, *Fair Representation* (New Haven, Conn.: Yale University Press, 1982).
2. Stuart Rice, *Quantitative Methods in Politics* (New York: Knopf, 1928).

Table 5-1 Apportionment of Membership of the House of Representatives, 1789–2000

State	1789[a]	1790	1800	1810	1820	1830	1840	1850	1860	1870	1880	1890	1900	1910	1930[b]	1940	1950	1960	1970	1980	1990	2000
Alabama	—	—	—	—	3	5	7	7	6	8	8	9	9	10	9	9	9	8	7	7	7	7
Alaska	—	—	—	—	—	—	—	—	—	—	—	—	—	—	—	—	—	1	1	1	1	1
Arizona	—	—	—	—	—	—	—	—	—	—	—	—	—	1	1	2	2	3	4	5	6	8
Arkansas	—	—	—	—	—	—	1	2	3	4	5	6	7	7	7	7	6	4	4	4	4	4
California	—	—	—	—	—	—	—	2	3	4	6	7	8	11	20	23	30	38	43	45	52	53
Colorado	—	—	—	—	—	—	—	—	—	—	1	2	3	4	4	4	4	4	5	6	6	7
Connecticut	5	7	7	7	6	6	4	4	4	4	4	4	5	5	6	6	6	6	6	6	6	5
Delaware	1	1	1	2	1	1	1	1	1	1	1	1	1	1	1	1	1	1	1	1	1	1
Florida	—	—	—	—	—	—	—	1	1	2	2	2	3	4	5	6	8	12	15	19	23	25
Georgia	3	2	4	6	7	9	8	8	7	9	10	11	11	12	10	10	10	10	10	10	11	13
Hawaii	—	—	—	—	—	—	—	—	—	—	—	—	—	—	—	—	—	2	2	2	2	2
Idaho	—	—	—	—	—	—	—	—	—	—	—	1	1	2	2	2	2	2	2	2	2	2
Illinois	—	—	—	—	1	3	7	9	14	19	20	22	25	27	27	26	25	24	24	22	20	19
Indiana	—	—	—	—	3	7	10	11	11	13	13	13	13	13	12	11	11	11	11	10	10	9
Iowa	—	—	—	—	—	—	—	2	6	9	11	11	11	11	9	8	8	7	6	6	5	5
Kansas	—	—	—	—	—	—	—	—	—	3	7	8	8	8	7	6	6	5	5	5	4	4
Kentucky	—	2	6	10	12	13	10	10	9	10	11	11	11	11	9	9	8	7	7	7	6	6
Louisiana	—	—	—	—	3	3	4	4	5	6	6	6	7	8	8	8	8	8	8	8	7	7
Maine	—	—	—	—	7	8	7	6	5	5	4	4	4	4	3	3	3	2	2	2	2	2
Maryland	6	8	9	9	9	8	6	6	5	6	6	6	6	6	6	6	7	8	8	8	8	8
Massachusetts	8	14	17	20	13	12	10	11	10	11	12	13	14	16	15	14	14	12	12	11	10	10
Michigan	—	—	—	—	—	—	3	4	6	9	11	12	12	13	17	17	18	19	19	18	16	15
Minnesota	—	—	—	—	—	—	—	—	2	3	5	7	9	10	9	9	9	8	8	8	8	8
Mississippi	—	—	—	—	1	2	4	5	5	6	7	7	8	8	7	7	6	5	5	5	5	4
Missouri	—	—	—	—	1	2	5	7	9	13	14	15	16	16	13	13	11	10	10	9	9	9
Montana	—	—	—	—	—	—	—	—	—	—	—	1	1	2	2	2	2	2	2	2	1	1

(Table continues)

Table 5-1 *(Continued)*

State	1789[a]	1790	1800	1810	1820	1830	1840	1850	1860	1870	1880	1890	1900	1910	1930[b]	1940	1950	1960	1970	1980	1990	2000
Nebraska	—	—	—	—	—	—	—	—	—	1	3	6	6	6	5	4	4	3	3	3	3	3
Nevada	—	—	—	—	—	—	—	—	—	1	1	1	1	1	1	1	1	1	1	2	2	3
New Hampshire	3	4	5	6	6	5	4	3	3	3	2	2	2	2	2	2	2	2	2	2	2	2
New Jersey	4	5	6	6	6	6	5	5	5	7	7	8	10	12	14	14	14	15	15	14	13	13
New Mexico	—	—	—	—	—	—	—	—	—	—	—	—	—	1	1	2	2	2	2	3	3	3
New York	6	10	17	27	34	40	34	33	31	33	34	34	37	43	45	45	43	41	39	34	31	29
North Carolina	5	10	12	13	13	13	9	8	7	8	9	9	10	10	11	12	12	11	11	11	12	13
North Dakota	—	—	—	—	—	—	—	—	—	—	—	1	2	3	2	2	2	2	1	1	1	1
Ohio	—	—	—	6	14	19	21	21	19	20	21	21	21	22	24	23	23	24	23	21	19	18
Oklahoma	—	—	—	—	—	—	—	—	—	—	—	—	—	8	9	8	6	6	6	6	6	5
Oregon	—	—	—	—	—	—	—	—	1	1	1	2	2	3	3	4	4	4	4	5	5	5
Pennsylvania	8	13	18	23	26	28	24	25	24	27	28	30	32	36	34	33	30	27	25	23	21	19
Rhode Island	1	2	2	2	2	2	2	2	2	2	2	2	2	3	2	2	2	2	2	2	2	2
South Carolina	5	6	8	9	9	9	7	6	4	5	7	7	7	7	6	6	6	6	6	6	6	6
South Dakota	—	—	—	—	—	—	—	—	—	—	—	2	2	3	2	2	2	2	2	1	1	1
Tennessee	—	—	3	6	9	13	11	10	8	10	10	10	10	10	9	10	9	9	8	9	9	9
Texas	—	—	—	—	—	—	—	2	4	6	11	13	16	18	21	21	22	23	24	27	30	32
Utah	—	—	—	—	—	—	—	—	—	—	—	—	1	2	2	2	2	2	2	3	3	3
Vermont	—	2	4	6	5	5	4	3	3	3	2	2	2	2	1	1	1	1	1	1	1	1
Virginia	10	19	22	23	22	21	15	13	11	9	10	10	10	10	9	9	10	10	10	10	11	11
Washington	—	—	—	—	—	—	—	—	—	—	—	2	3	5	6	6	7	7	7	8	9	9
West Virginia	—	—	—	—	—	—	—	—	—	3	4	4	5	6	6	6	6	5	4	4	3	3
Wisconsin	—	—	—	—	—	—	—	3	6	8	9	10	11	11	10	10	10	10	9	9	9	8
Wyoming	—	—	—	—	—	—	—	—	—	—	—	1	1	1	1	1	1	1	1	1	1	1
Representatives apportioned by census count	65	105	141	181	213	240	223	234	241	292	325	356	386	435	435	435	435	435	435	435	435	435

Apportionment population^c (^d)	3,615,823	4,879,820	6,584,231	8,972,396	11,930,987	15,908,376	21,766,691	29,550,038	38,115,641	49,371,340	61,908,906	74,562,608	91,603,772	122,093,455	131,006,184	149,895,183	178,559,217	204,053,025	225,867,174	249,022,783	281,424,177
Apportionment ratio^e	30,000^f	34,436	34,609	36,377	42,124	49,712	71,338	93,020	122,614	130,533	151,912	173,901	193,167	210,583	280,675	301,164	344,587	410,481	469,088	519,235	572,466	646,952

Note: "—" indicates state not yet admitted to Union. States mentioned in the decennial apportionment law or report are listed for that year. Several territories were counted in the census and admitted after the census year, but before the apportionment law. These states are included in that apportionment decade. The remaining states were admitted during the decade after an apportionment law or report. All new states were admitted with one seat unless noted. These states were, after the 1790 apportionment, Tennessee; after 1800, Ohio; after 1810, Alabama, Illinois, Indiana, Louisiana, and Mississippi; after 1830, Arkansas and Michigan; after 1840, California, Florida, Iowa, and Wisconsin; after 1870, Colorado; after 1880, Idaho, Montana, North Dakota, South Dakota, Washington, and Wyoming; after 1890, Utah; after 1900, Oklahoma; after 1950, Alaska and Hawaii. Twenty members were assigned to Massachusetts in the 1810 apportionment; seven of these were credited to Maine when that area became a state. Virginia had eleven representatives in 1860; three of these were credited to West Virginia when that area became a state. The only exception to the census apportionment or new state admittance manner of securing a representative was when California was given one additional representative for the Thirty-seventh Congress (1861–1863).

a Original apportionment made in Constitution, pending first census.

b No apportionment was made in 1920.

c Excludes the population of District of Columbia; the population of the territories; prior to 1940, the number of American Indians not taxed; and, prior to 1870, two-fifths of the slave population. In 1970 and 1990 includes selected segments of Americans abroad.

d No census prior to 1790.

e The ratio of apportionment population to the number of representatives apportioned by census.

f The minimum ratio of population to representative, as stated in Article I, section 2, of the U.S. Constitution.

Sources: Apportionment of membership, 1788–1990: Kenneth C. Martis and Greg A. Elmes, *The Historical Atlas of State Power in Congress, 1790–1990* (Washington, D.C.: Congressional Quarterly, 1993); apportionment population, 1790–1990: U.S. Census Bureau, "Population Base for Apportionment and the Number of Representatives Apportioned: 1790 to 1990" (*www.census.gov*); 2000: U.S. Census Bureau, "Apportionment Population and Number of Representatives, by State: Census 2000" (*www.census.gov*). Apportionment ratios calculated by the editors.

188

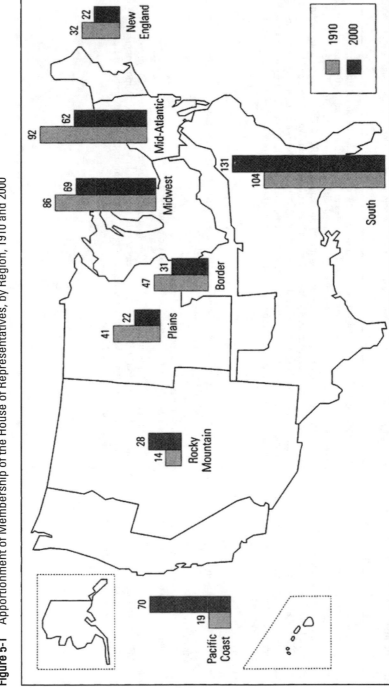

Figure 5-1 Apportionment of Membership of the House of Representatives, by Region, 1910 and 2000

New England
22
32

Mid-Atlantic
62
92

Midwest
69
86

South
131
104

Border
31
47

Plains
22
41

Rocky Mountain
28
14

Pacific Coast
70
19

1910
2000

Source: Table 5-1, this volume.

Table 5-2 Members of Congress: Female, Black, Hispanic, Marital Status, and Age, 1971–2009

Congress		Female	Black	Hispanic	Not married[a]	Age					
						Under 40	40–49	50–59	60–69	70–79	80 and over
Representatives											
92nd	(1971)	12	12	5	26	40	133	152	86	19	3
93rd	(1973)	14	15	5	34	45	132	154	80	20	2
94th	(1975)	18	16	5	54	69	138	137	75	14	2
95th	(1977)	18	16	5	56	81	121	147	71	15	0
96th	(1979)	16	16	6	69	86	125	145	63	14	0
97th	(1981)	19	16	6	86	94	142	132	54	12	1
98th	(1983)	21	20	10	68	86	145	132	57	13	1
99th	(1985)	22	19	11	69	71	154	131	59	17	2
100th	(1987)	23	22	11	64	63	153	137	56	24	2
101st	(1989)	25	23	11	—	41	163	133	74	20	2
102nd	(1991)	28	25	10	—	39	153	133	86	20	4
103rd	(1993)	47	38	17	—	47	152	129	91	13	3
104th	(1995)	47	39	18	—	53	153	136	80	12	1
105th	(1997)	51	37	18	—	47	145	147	82	10	2
106th	(1999)	56	39	19	—	32	131	171	80	20	0
107th	(2001)	59	36	19	—	36	118	175	78	26	0
108th	(2003)	59	37	23	—	26	111	175	102	21	0
109th	(2005)	65	40	23	—	25	97	176	111	23	3
110th	(2007)	71	40	23	—	20	93	171	117	30	4
111th	(2009)	78	41	25	—	23	84	156	128	40	3
Senators											
92nd	(1971)	1	1	1	3	4	24	32	23	16	1
93rd	(1973)	0	1	1	4	3	25	37	23	11	1
94th	(1975)[b]	0	1	1	6	5	21	35	24	15	0
95th	(1977)	0	1	0	9	6	26	35	21	10	2

(Table continues)

Table 5-2 (Continued)

Congress		Female	Black	Hispanic	Not married[a]	Age					
						Under 40	40–49	50–59	60–69	70–79	80 and over
96th	(1979)	1	0	0	5	10	31	33	17	8	1
97th	(1981)	2	0	0	7	9	35	36	14	6	0
98th	(1983)	2	0	0	10	7	28	39	20	3	3
99th	(1985)	2	0	0	8	4	27	38	25	4	2
100th	(1987)	2	0	0	11	5	30	36	22	5	2
101st	(1989)	2	0	0	—	0	30	40	22	6	2
102nd	(1991)	2	1	0	—	0	22	47	24	5	2
103rd	(1993)	6	1	0	—	1	16	49	22	11	1
104th	(1995)	8	1	0	—	1	14	41	27	16	1
105th	(1997)	9	1	0	—	1	21	39	26	12	1
106th	(1999)	9	0	0	—	2	16	42	27	11	2
107th	(2001)	13	0	0	—	0	17	43	31	7	2
108th	(2003)	14	0	0	—	2	16	33	36	11	2
109th	(2005)	14	1	2	—	0	17	29	33	16	5
110th	(2007)	16	1	3	—	0	11	30	34	20	5
111th	(2009)	17	0	3	—	0	7	32	37	18	4

Note: "—" indicates not available. As of beginning of first session of each Congress. Figures for representatives exclude vacancies. The counts exclude nonvoting delegates and commissioners from American Samoa, Guam, Puerto Rico, the Virgin Islands, and Washington, D.C.

[a] Single, widowed, or divorced.
[b] Includes Sen. John Durkin, D-N.H., seated September 1975.

Sources: Hispanic (1971–1985): Congressional Quarterly, *American Leaders, 1789–1987* (Washington, D.C.: Congressional Quarterly, 1987), 55; female and black (1971–2009) and Hispanic (1987–2009): *Congressional Quarterly Weekly Report (CQ Weekly)* (1970), 2756; (1972), 2991; (1974), 3104; (1976), 3155; (1978), 3252; (1980), 3318; (1982), 2805; (1984), 2921; (1986), 2863; (1988), 3294; (1990), 3835–3836; (January 16, 1993, Supplement), 12; (November 12, 1994, Supplement), 10; (1997), 28; (1999), 62; (2001), 178; (2003), 192; (2005), 243; (2006), 3008, 3064; (2008), 2998, 3374; not married and age (1971–1989): U.S. Bureau of the Census, *Statistical Abstract of the United States, 1988* (Washington, D.C.: Government Printing Office, 1987), 244; 1990, 257; age (1991–2009): calculated by the editors from *Congressional Quarterly Weekly Report (CQ Weekly)* (1991), 118–127; (January 16, 1993, Supplement), 12, 160–168; (1995), 541–549; (1997), 497–505; Congressional Quarterly, unpublished data.

Table 5-3   Black Members of Congress, 1869–2011

Congress		Black members of U.S. House of Representatives[a]	Black members of U.S. Senate	Total black members
41st	(1869–1871)	2	1	3
42nd	(1871–1873)	5	0	5
43rd	(1873–1875)	7	0	7
44th	(1875–1877)	7	1	8
45th	(1877–1879)	3	1	4
46th	(1879–1881)	0	1	1
47th	(1881–1883)	2	0	2
48th	(1883–1885)	2	0	2
49th	(1885–1887)	2	0	2
50th	(1887–1889)	0	0	0
51st	(1889–1891)	3	0	3
52nd	(1891–1893)	1	0	1
53rd	(1893–1895)	1	0	1
54th	(1895–1897)	1	0	1
55th	(1897–1899)	1	0	1
56th	(1899–1901)	1	0	1
57th	(1901–1903)	0	0	0
58th	(1903–1905)	0	0	0
59th	(1905–1907)	0	0	0
60th	(1907–1909)	0	0	0
61st	(1909–1911)	0	0	0
62nd	(1911–1913)	0	0	0
63rd	(1913–1915)	0	0	0
64th	(1915–1917)	0	0	0
65th	(1917–1919)	0	0	0
66th	(1919–1921)	0	0	0
67th	(1921–1923)	0	0	0
68th	(1923–1925)	0	0	0
69th	(1925–1927)	0	0	0
70th	(1927–1929)	0	0	0
71st	(1929–1931)	1	0	1
72nd	(1931–1933)	1	0	1
73rd	(1933–1935)	1	0	1
74th	(1935–1937)	1	0	1
75th	(1937–1939)	1	0	1
76th	(1939–1941)	1	0	1
77th	(1941–1943)	1	0	1
78th	(1943–1945)	1	0	1
79th	(1945–1947)	2	0	2
80th	(1947–1949)	2	0	2
81st	(1949–1951)	2	0	2
82nd	(1951–1953)	2	0	2
83rd	(1953–1955)	2	0	2
84th	(1955–1957)	3	0	3
85th	(1957–1959)	4	0	4

(Table continues)

Table 5-3   *(Continued)*

Congress		*Black members of U.S. House of Representatives*	*Black members of U.S. Senate*	*Total black members*
86th	(1959–1961)	4	0	4
87th	(1961–1963)	4	0	4
88th	(1963–1965)	5	0	5
89th	(1965–1967)	6	0	6
90th	(1967–1969)	5	1	6
91st	(1969–1971)	10	1	11
92nd	(1971–1973)	13	1	14
93rd	(1973–1975)	16	1	17
94th	(1975–1977)	17	1	18
95th	(1977–1979)	17	1	18
96th	(1979–1981)	17	0	17
97th	(1981–1983)	19	0	19
98th	(1983–1985)	21	0	21
99th	(1985–1987)	21	0	21
100th	(1987–1989)	23	0	23
101st	(1989–1991)	24	0	24
102nd	(1991–1993)	27	0	27
103rd	(1993–1995)	39	1	40
104th	(1995–1997)	40	1	41
105th	(1997–1999)	39	1	40
106th	(1999–2001)	39	0	39
107th	(2001–2003)	39	0	39
108th	(2003–2005)	39	0	39
109th	(2005–2007)	42	1	43
110th	(2007–2009)	42	1	43
111th	(2009–2011)	41	1	42

Note: The numbers reflect the highest number of black members to serve in the House of Representatives at any one time during a Congress. For example, a record forty-six black members were elected to the 110th Congress, but only forty-three served at any one time during the Congress.

Sources: 41st–110th Congresses: Mildred L. Amer, "African American Members of the United States Congress: 1870–2008," RL30378, Congressional Research Service, Washington, D.C., July 23, 2008; 111th Congress: *CQ Weekly* (2008) 2998; (2009), 132.

Table 5-4 Women Nominated, by Party, 1956–2008, and Women Elected to U.S. House of Representatives, by Party, 1916–2008

Election year	Congress	Major-party nominees			Elected			Success rate			Serving		
		Democratic	Republican	Total	Democratic	Republican	Total	Democratic	Republican	Total	Democratic	Republican	Total
1916	65th	—	—	—	0	1	1	—	—	—	0	1	1
1918	66th	—	—	—	0	0	0	—	—	—	0	0	0
1920	67th	—	—	—	0	1	1	—	—	—	0	3	3
1922	68th	—	—	—	0	1	1	—	—	—	0	1	1
1924	69th	—	—	—	1	0	1	—	—	—	1	2	3
1926	70th	—	—	—	1	3	4	—	—	—	2	3	5
1928	71st	—	—	—	4	4	8	—	—	—	5	4	9
1930	72nd	—	—	—	3	3	6	—	—	—	4	3	7
1932	73rd	—	—	—	3	2	5	—	—	—	4	3	7
1934	74th	—	—	—	4	2	6	—	—	—	4	2	6
1936	75th	—	—	—	4	1	5	—	—	—	5	1	6
1938	76th	—	—	—	2	2	4	—	—	—	4	4	8
1940	77th	—	—	—	3	4	7	—	—	—	5	4	9
1942	78th	—	—	—	1	6	7	—	—	—	2	6	8
1944	79th	—	—	—	4	5	9	—	—	—	6	5	11
1946	80th	—	—	—	3	4	7	—	—	—	3	4	7
1948	81st	—	—	—	4	4	8	—	—	—	5	4	9
1950	82nd	—	—	—	2	6	8	—	—	—	4	6	10
1952	83rd	—	—	—	5	6	11	—	—	—	5	6	11
1954	84th	—	—	—	9	6	15	—	—	—	10	6	16
1956	85th	15	14	29	9	6	15	60.0%	42.9%	51.7%	9	6	15
1958	86th	13	14	27	8	8	16	61.5	57.1	59.3	9	8	17
1960	87th	15	8	23	9	6	15	60.0	75.0	65.2	11	7	18
1962	88th	12	11	23	6	5	11	50.0	45.5	47.8	6	6	12
1964	89th	11	7	18	6	4	10	54.5	57.1	55.6	7	4	11
1966	90th	10	13	23	6	5	11	60.0	38.5	47.8	6	5	11
1968	91st	13	6	19	6	4	10	46.2	66.7	52.6	6	4	10

(Table continues)

Table 5-4 (Continued)

Election year	Congress	Major-party nominees			Elected			Success rate			Serving		
		Democratic	Republican	Total	Democratic	Republican	Total	Democratic	Republican	Total	Democratic	Republican	Total
1970	92nd	14	10	24	9	3	12	64.3	30.0	50.0	10	3	13
1972	93rd	23	10	33	12	2	14	52.2	20.0	42.4	14	2	16
1974	94th	27	16	43	14	4	18	51.9	25.0	41.9	14	5	19
1976	95th	34	20	54	13	5	18	38.2	25.0	33.3	13	5	18
1978	96th	26	18	44	10	5	15	38.5	27.8	34.1	11	5	16
1980	97th	27	26	53	10	9	19	37.0	34.6	35.8	11	10	21
1982	98th	27	27	54	12	9	21	44.4	33.3	38.9	13	9	22
1984	99th	28	36	64	11	11	22	39.3	30.6	34.4	12	11	23
1986	100th	30	34	64	12	11	23	40.0	32.4	35.9	13	11	24
1988	101st	33	25	58	14	11	25	42.4	44.0	43.1	16	13	29
1990	102nd	38	29	67	19	9	28	50.0	31.0	41.8	20	9	29
1992	103rd	69	35	104	35	12	47	50.7	34.3	45.2	35	12	47
1994	104st	72	42	114	31	16	47	43.1	38.1	41.2	32	17	49
1996	105th	78	42	120	35	16	51	44.9	38.1	42.5	37	18	55
1998	106th	73	45	118	39	17	56	53.4	37.8	47.5	39	17	56
2000	107th	81	43	124	41	18	59	50.6	41.9	47.6	42	18	60
2002	108th	77	44	121	38	21	59	49.4	47.7	48.8	39	21	60
2004	109th	85	52	137	42	23	65	49.4	44.2	47.4	43	25	68
2006	110th	94	42	136	50	21	71	53.2	50.0	52.2	55	21	76
2008	111th	95	38	133	58	17	75	61.1	44.7	56.4	58	17	75

Note: "—" indicates data not available. "Major-party nominees," "elected," and "success rate" refer to women candidates in regularly scheduled elections for the election year indicated. "Serving" includes women elected in regularly scheduled elections in the election year indicated as well as those elected in special elections over the course of the congressional session. One woman was elected as an independent: Jo Ann Emerson was elected simultaneously as a Republican to the 104th Congress and as an independent to the 105th Congress by special election to fill the vacancy caused by the death of her husband, U.S. Representative Bill Emerson. She changed from an independent to a Republican on January 8, 1997, and was elected as a Republican to the 106th and subsequent Congresses. In the counts, Emerson is considered a Republican.

Source: Barbara Palmer and Dennis Simon, *Breaking the Political Glass Ceiling: Women and Congressional Elections*, 2nd ed. (New York: Routledge, 2008). Data and update for 2008 provided by Palmer and Simon.

Table 5-5 Members of Congress: Seniority and Occupation, 1999–2009

	Representatives					111th (2009)			Senators					111th (2009)		
	106th (1999)	107th (2001)	108th (2003)	109th (2005)	110th (2007)	Dem.	Rep.	Total	106th (1999)	107th (2001)	108th (2003)	109th (2005)	110th (2007)	Dem.	Rep.	Total
Seniority[a]																
Under 2 years	48	44	62	44	59	40	26	66	8	13	11	9	11[b]	11	4	15
2–9 years	247	242	190	185	159	87	78	165	41	41	41	41	32	17[b]	14	31
10–19 years	95	96	126[c]	147[c]	161	88	54	142	31	24	28	28[d]	30	14	14	28
20–29 years	41	44	49	45	37	26	16	42	14	16	13	15	18	10[e]	6	16
30 years or more	3	7	8	13	17	14	4	18	6	6	7	7	9	6	3	9[f]
Total	434[f]	433[f]	435[c]	434[c,f]	433[f]	255	178	433[f]	100	100	100	100[d]	100	58	41	99[f]
Occupation																
Agriculture	22	25	26	29	23	—	—	26	6	6	5	5	6	—	—	5
Business or banking	159	159	165	205	166	—	—	175	24	24	25	30	27	—	—	26
Education	84	92	88	91	88	—	—	78	13	16	12	13	14[b]	—	—	16
Journalism	9	9	11	11	7	—	—	7	8	7	6	7	8[b]	—	—	5
Law	163	156	161	178	162	—	—	152	55	53	60	64[d]	59	—	—	54
Public service/ politics	106	126	145	209	174	—	—	182	18	28	30	45	32	—	—	32

Note: "—" indicates not available. Members of Congress may state more than one occupation; therefore, sum may be greater than total. Not all occupations reported are listed. Data for earlier years can be found in previous editions of *Vital Statistics on American Politics*.

[a] Represents consecutive years of service.
[b] Includes Sen. Bernard Sanders, I-Vt.
[c] Includes Rep. Bernard Sanders, I-Vt.
[d] Includes Sen. James M. Jeffords, I-Vt.
[e] Includes Sen. Joseph I. Lieberman, I-Conn.
[f] Includes one or more vacancies.

Sources: Congressional Quarterly Weekly Report (CQ Weekly) (1999), 63; (2001), 181; (2003), 193; (2005), 241; (2007), 605; *CQ Today,* November 26, 2008, 72; seniority: *1999 Congressional Staff Directory* (Washington, D.C.: CQ Press, 1999), 5, 190–193; *2001,* 5, 194–197; *2003,* 5, 208–211; *2005,* 5, 230–233; *2007,* 5, 240–243; *2009,* 5, 242–245 (revised by the editors).

Table 5-6 Congressional Committees and Majority Party Chairmanships, 1975–2009

Congress		Number of committees[a]	Party in majority	Number of majority party members	Number of majority party members chairing standing committees and subcommittees	Percentage of majority party members chairing standing committees and subcommittees	Number of majority party members chairing all committees and subcommittees	Percentage of majority party members chairing all committees and subcommittees
House								
94th	(1975–1977)	204	D	289	142	49.1	150	51.9
96th	(1979–1981)	193	D	276	144	52.2	149	54.0
97th	(1981–1983)	174	D	243	121	49.8	125	51.4
98th	(1983–1985)	172	D	267	124	46.4	127	47.6
99th	(1985–1987)	191	D	253	129	51.0	131	51.8
100th	(1987–1989)	192	D	258	128	49.6	132	51.2
101st	(1989–1991)	189	D	260	134	51.5	137	52.7
102nd	(1991–1993)	185	D	267	130	48.7	135	50.6
103rd	(1993–1995)	146	D	258	113	43.8	116	45.0
104th	(1995–1997)	110	R	230	86	37.4	86	37.4
105th	(1997–1999)	112	R	225	100	44.4	100	44.4
106th	(1999–2001)	108	R	222	100	45.0	100	45.0
107th	(2001–2003)	116	R	221	109	49.3	109	49.3
108th	(2003–2005)	122	R	228	89	39.0	97	42.5
109th	(2005–2007)	121	R	230	107	46.5	112	48.7
110th	(2007–2009)	131	D	232	114	49.1	119	51.3
111th	(2009–2011)	131	D	254	109	42.9	117	46.1
Senate								
94th	(1975–1977)	205	D	62[b]	57	91.9	57	91.9
96th	(1979–1981)	130	D	59[b]	58	98.3	58	98.3
97th	(1981–1983)	136	R	53	51	96.2	52	98.1
98th	(1983–1985)	137	R	54	52	96.3	52	96.3

99th	(1985–1987)	120	R	53	92.4	49	92.4	49	92.4
100th	(1987–1989)	118	D	54	87.0	47	87.0	47	87.0
101st	(1989–1991)	118	D	55	83.6	46	83.6	46	83.6
102nd	(1991–1993)	119	D	56	89.3	50	89.3	50	89.3
103rd	(1993–1995)	111	D	57	80.7	46	80.7	46	80.7
104th	(1995–1997)	92	R	54	81.5	44	81.5	44	81.5
105th	(1997–1999)	92	R	54	90.7	49	90.7	49	90.7
106th	(1999–2001)	94	R	55	94.5	52	94.5	52	94.5
107th	(2001–2003)	92	R[c]	50	98.0	49	98.0	49	98.0
108th	(2003–2005)	92	R	51	98.0	50	98.0	50	98.0
109th	(2005–2007)	96	R	55	94.5	52	94.5	53	96.4
110th	(2007–2009)	96	D	50[d]	80.0	40	80.0	40	80.0
111th	(2009–2011)	89	D	58[d]	79.3	46	79.3	46	79.3

Note: "D" indicates Democratic; "R" indicates Republican.

[a] Includes standing committees, subcommittees of standing committees, select and special committees, subcommittees of select and special committees, joint committees, and subcommittees of joint committees. Data for additional years can be found in previous editions of *Vital Statistics on American Politics.*

[b] Includes Harry Byrd Jr., Va., elected as independent.

[c] Split 50–50 at the start of the session, the Senate was controlled by Republicans by virtue of Vice President Dick Cheney's vote. On May 24, 2001, Sen. James M. Jeffords, Vt., announced that he would switch from Republican to independent and that he would caucus with the Democrats. This changed shifted control of the Senate to the Democratic Party.

[d] Includes Joseph I. Lieberman, Conn., elected in 2006 under the label "Connecticut for Lieberman," and Bernard Sanders, Vt., elected as an independent, both of whom caucus with the Democrats.

Sources: 94th–103rd: Norman J. Ornstein, Thomas E. Mann, and Michael J. Malbin, eds., *Vital Statistics on Congress, 1993–1994* (Washington, D.C.: Congressional Quarterly, 1994), 113, 117–118; 104th–109th: calculated by the editors from *Congressional Quarterly Weekly Report (CQ Weekly)*, supplement to vol. 53, no. 12 (March 25, 1995); vol. 55, no. 12 (March 22, 1997); vol. 57, no. 11 (March 13, 1999); vol. 59 (April 28, 2001); vol. 61 (April 12, 2003); vol. 63 (April 11, 2005); vol. 65 (April 16, 2007); vol. 67 (April 13, 2009), supplemented by House committee list (*www.house.gov*) and Senate committee list (*www.senate.gov*).

Table 5-7   Congressional Measures Introduced and Enacted, 1947–2009

Congress		Measures introduced			Measures enacted		
		Bills	Joint resolutions	Total	Public	Private	Total
80th	(1947–1949)	10,108	689	10,797	906	457	1,363
81st	(1949–1951)	14,219	769	14,988	921	1,103	2,024
82nd	(1951–1953)	12,062	668	12,730	594	1,023	1,617
83rd	(1953–1955)	14,181	771	14,952	781	1,002	1,783
84th	(1955–1957)	16,782	905	17,687	1,028	893	1,921
85th	(1957–1959)	18,205	907	19,112	936	784	1,720
86th	(1959–1961)	17,230	1,031	18,261	800	492	1,292
87th	(1961–1963)	17,230	1,146	18,376	885	684	1,569
88th	(1963–1965)	16,079	1,401	17,480	666	360	1,026
89th	(1965–1967)	22,483	1,520	24,003	810	473	1,283
90th	(1967–1969)	24,786	1,674	26,460	640	362	1,002
91st	(1969–1971)	24,631	1,672	26,303	695	246	941
92nd	(1971–1973)	21,363	1,606	22,969	607	161	768
93rd	(1973–1975)	21,950	1,446	23,396	651	123	774
94th	(1975–1977)	19,762	1,334	21,096	588	141	729
95th	(1977–1979)	18,045	1,342	19,387	633	170	803
96th	(1979–1981)	11,722	861	12,583	613	123	736
97th	(1981–1983)	10,582	908	11,490	473	56	529
98th	(1983–1985)	10,134	1,022	11,156	623	54	677
99th	(1985–1987)	8,697	1,188	9,885	664	24	688
100th	(1987–1989)	8,515	1,073	9,588	713	48	761
101st	(1989–1991)	9,257	1,095	10,352	404	7	411
102nd	(1991–1993)	9,601	909	10,510	589	14	603
103rd	(1993–1995)	7,883	661	8,544	465	8	473
104th	(1995–1997)	6,545	263	6,808	234	2	236
105th	(1997–1999)	7,532	200	7,732	394	10	404
106th	(1999–2001)	8,968	190	9,158	580	24	604
107th	(2001–2003)	8,956	178	9,134	377	6	383
108th	(2003–2005)	8,468	157	8,625	498	6	504
109th	(2005–2007)	10,560	143	10,703	395	1	396
110th	(2007–2009)	11,081	147	11,228	416	0	416

Note: Measures exclude simple and concurrent resolutions.

Sources: 80th–99th: United States Congress, *Calendars of the U.S. House of Representatives and History of Legislation,* 99th Cong., final ed., 19–57 through 19–68; 100th–106th: successive issues of *Congressional Quarterly Almanac* (Washington, D.C.: CQ Press); 107th: *Congressional Record—Daily Digest,* May 6, 2003, D456–D457; 108th: *Congressional Record—Daily Digest,* February 15, 2005, D96–D97; 109th: *Congressional Record—Daily Digest,* December 30, 2005, D1341, and December 27, 2006, D1173; 110th: *Congressional Record—Daily Digest,* February 4, 2008, D80, and January 2, 2009, D1336.

Figure 5-2   Measures Introduced in Congress That Were Passed, 1789–2009 (percent)

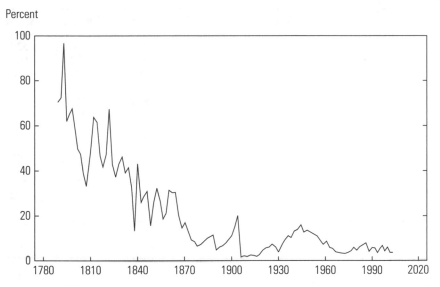

Note: Measures include bills and joint resolutions. Before 1824, only bills are included. Figures are for each Congress.

Sources: 1789–1968: U.S. Bureau of the Census, *Historical Statistics of the United States*, Series Y189-198 (Washington, D.C.: Government Printing Office, 1975), 1081–1082; 1969–2009: Table 5-7, this volume.

Table 5-8   Record Votes in the House and the Senate, 1947–2008

Year	House	Senate	Year	House	Senate
1947	84	138	1978	834	520
1948	79	110	1979	672	509
1949	121	226	1980	604	546
1950	154	229	1981	353	497
1951	109	202	1982	459	469
1952	72	129	1983	498	381
1953	71	89	1984	408	292
1954	76	181	1985	439	381
1955	73	88	1986	451	359
1956	74	136	1987	488	420
1957	100	111	1988	451	379
1958	93	202	1989	368	312
1959	87	215	1990	510	326
1960	93	207	1991	428	280
1961	116	207	1992	473	270
1962	124	227	1993	597	395
1963	119	229	1994	497	329
1964	113	312	1995	867	613
1965	201	259	1996	454	306
1966	193	238	1997	633	298
1967	245	315	1998	533	314
1968	233	280[a]	1999	609	374
1969	177	245	2000	600	298
1970	266	422	2001	507	380
1971	320	423	2002	483	253
1972	329	532	2003	675	459
1973	541	594	2004	543	216
1974	537	544	2005	669	366
1975	612	611	2006	539	279
1976	661	700	2007	1177	442
1977	706	636	2008	688	215

Note: In the House, *record votes* are defined as yea-and-nay (roll call) votes plus so-called recorded votes, which refers to votes cast electronically using the system introduced in the House after the Legislative Reorganization Act of 1970. In the Senate, there is no electronic system, so record votes are simply yea-and-nay (roll call) votes. Quorum votes are excluded for both the House and the Senate.

[a] The Senate record vote total does not include one "yea-and-nay" vote that was ruled invalid for lack of a quorum.

Source: "Résumé of Congressional Activity," *Congressional Record—Daily Digest*, various issues, 80th Congress (1947) through 110th Congress (2008).

Figure 5-3   Party Votes in the House, 1878–2008

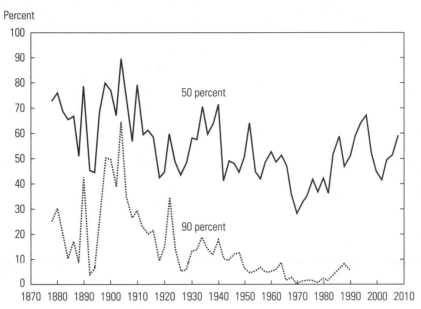

Note: Figures shown by Congress. A party vote occurs when the specified percentage (or more) of one party votes against the specified percentage (or more) of the other party.

Sources: 1878–1886 and 90 percent vote for 1972–1990: Brinck Kerr, "Structural Determinants of Party Voting in the U.S. Congress, 1877–1990," PhD diss., Texas A&M University, 1993; 1887–1969: Joseph Cooper, David William Brady, and Patricia A. Hurley, "The Electoral Basis of Party Voting: Patterns and Trends in the U.S. House of Representatives, 1887–1969," in *The Impact of the Electoral Process,* ed. Louis Maisel and Joseph Cooper (Beverly Hills, Calif.: Sage Publications, 1977), 139; 1970–1990: *Congressional Quarterly Almanac* (Washington, D.C.: Congressional Quarterly, annual volumes); 1991–2008: *Congressional Quarterly Weekly Report* (*CQ Weekly*) (1992), 3906; (1993), 3480; (1994), 3658; (1996), 199, 3432; (1998), 18; (1999), 79; (2000), 2975; (2001), 56; (2002), 114, 3240; (2004), 11, 2907; (2006), 93; (2007), 33; (2008), 144, 3333.

Table 5-9   Party Unity and Polarization in Congressional Voting, 1953–2008 (percent)

Year	House	Senate	Year	House	Senate
1953	52	52	1981	37	48
1954	38	48	1982	36	43
1955	41	30	1983	56	44
1956	44	53	1984	47	40
1957	59	36	1985	61	50
1958	40	44	1986	57	52
1959	55	48	1987	64	41
1960	53	37	1988	47	43
1961	50	62	1989	56	35
1962	46	41	1990	49	54
1963	49	47	1991	55	49
1964	55	36	1992	65	53
1965	52	42	1993	66	67
1966	42	50	1994	62	52
1967	36	35	1995	73	69
1968	35	32	1996	56	62
1969	31	36	1997	50	50
1970	27	35	1998	56	56
1971	38	42	1999	47	63
1972	27	37	2000	43	49
1973	42	40	2001	40	55
1974	29	44	2002	43	46
1975	48	48	2003	52	67
1976	36	37	2004	47	52
1977	42	42	2005	49	63
1978	33	45	2006	55	57
1979	47	47	2007	62	60
1980	38	46	2008	53	52

Note: Data indicate the percentage of all record votes on which a majority of voting Democrats opposed a majority of voting Republicans.

Source: CQ Weekly (2008), 3338.

Table 5-10   Party Unity in Congressional Voting, 1954–2008 (percent)

| | House | | | Senate | | |
| | All | Southern | | All | Southern | |
Year	Democrats	Democrats	Republicans	Democrats	Democrats	Republicans
1954	80	—	84	77	—	89
1955	84	68	78	82	78	82
1956	80	79	78	80	75	80
1957	79	71	75	79	81	81
1958	77	67	73	82	76	74
1959	85	77	85	76	63	80
1960	75	62	77	73	60	74
1961	—	—	—	—	—	—
1962	81	—	80	80	—	81
1963	85	—	84	79	—	79
1964	82	—	81	73	—	75
1965	80	55	81	75	55	78
1966	78	55	82	73	52	78
1967	77	53	82	75	59	73
1968	73	48	76	71	57	74
1969	71	47	71	74	53	72
1970	71	52	72	71	49	71
1971	72	48	76	74	56	75
1972	70	44	76	72	43	73
1973	75	55	74	79	52	74
1974	72	51	71	72	41	68
1975	75	53	78	76	48	71
1976	75	52	75	74	46	72
1977	74	55	77	72	48	75
1978	71	53	77	75	54	66
1979	75	60	79	76	62	73
1980	78	64	79	76	64	74
1981	75	57	80	77	64	85
1982	77	62	76	76	62	80
1983	82	67	80	76	70	79
1984	81	68	77	75	61	83
1985	86	76	80	79	68	81
1986	86	76	76	74	59	80
1987	88	78	79	85	80	78
1988	88	81	80	85	78	74
1989	86	77	76	79	69	79
1990	86	78	78	82	75	77
1991	86	78	81	83	73	83
1992	86	79	84	82	70	83
1993	89	83	87	87	78	86
1994	88	83	87	86	77	81
1995	84	75	93	84	76	91
1996	84	76	90	86	75	91

(Table continues)

Table 5-10   *(Continued)*

	House			Senate		
Year	All Democrats	Southern Democrats	Republicans	All Democrats	Southern Democrats	Republicans
1997	85	78	91	86	75	88
1998	86	79	89	90	85	88
1999	86	77	88	91	86	90
2000	86	80	90	90	80	91
2001	86	77	94	90	79	90
2002	90	82	93	85	69	88
2003	91	85	95	90	76	95
2004	91	83	93	88	76	93
2005	91	84	93	90	81	90
2006	90	82	92	89	77	87
2007	95	85	90	92	93	84
2008	97	—	92	92	—	87

Note: "—" indicates not available. Data show percentage of members voting with a majority of their party on party unity votes. Party unity votes are those roll calls on which a majority of Democrats vote against a majority of Republicans. Percentages are calculated to eliminate the impact of absences as follows: unity = (unity)/(unity + opposition).

Sources: 1954–1992: Norman J. Ornstein, Thomas E. Mann, and Michael J. Malbin, eds., *Vital Statistics on Congress, 1993–1994* (Washington, D.C.: Congressional Quarterly, 1994), 201–202; 1993–2004: *Congressional Quarterly Weekly Report* (*CQ Weekly*) (1993), 3479; (1994), 3659; (1996), 245, 3461; (1998), 33; (1999), 92, 2993; (2001), 67; (2002), 142, 3281; (2004), 48, 2952; (2006), 97; (2007), 38; (2008), 147, 3337.

Table 5-11 The 111th Congress: House of Representatives

State/district/representative	Party	Year born	Year first elected	% vote in 2008 Primary	% vote in 2008 General	Campaign expenditures (2007–2008)	VP	PS	PU	AFL-CIO	ADA	CCUS	ACU
Alabama													
1 Bonner	R	1959	2002	U	98	$736,705	95	76	97	13	15	94	83
2 Bright	D	1952	2008	67	50	1,193,166	—	—	—	—	—	—	—
3 Rogers	R	1958	2002	U	53	2,056,912	97	53	88	40	50	89	50
4 Aderholt	R	1965	1996	U	75	688,864	95	67	96	21	25	82	92
5 Griffith	D	1942	2008	90	51	1,786,989	—	—	—	—	—	—	—
6 Bachus	R	1947	1992	U	98	1,414,799	92	68	94	20	20	94	84
7 Davis	D	1967	2002	U	99	820,467	98	24	96	93	85	67	12
Alaska													
AL Young	R	1933	1973	45	50	3,213,532	84	54	88	77	55	73	71
Arizona													
1 Kirkpatrick	D	1950	2008	47	56	1,997,089	—	—	—	0	0	—	—
2 Franks	R	1957	2002	U	59	442,232	98	87	99	0	0	76	100
3 Shadegg	R	1949	1994	U	54	2,911,880	98	83	99	0	0	83	96
4 Pastor	D	1943	1991	U	72	815,864	99	13	99	100	100	50	4
5 Mitchell	D	1940	2006	U	53	2,324,598	97	25	80	87	75	67	32
6 Flake	R	1962	2000	U	62	845,005	96	85	99	0	0	61	100
7 Grijalva	D	1948	2002	U	63	720,896	91	10	99	100	100	44	8
8 Giffords	D	1970	2006	U	55	2,775,313	98	19	86	87	80	67	20
Arkansas													
1 Berry	D	1942	1996	U	U	848,986	95	21	96	86	75	56	13
2 Snyder	D	1947	1996	U	77	307,060	95	20	97	100	90	67	5
3 Boozman	R	1950	2001	U	79	325,926	99	71	95	13	25	94	84
4 Ross	D	1961	2000	U	86	1,722,151	99	24	95	93	85	67	12

(Table continues)

Table 5-11 *(Continued)*

State/district/ representative	Party	Year born	Year first elected	% vote in 2008 Primary	% vote in 2008 General	Campaign expenditures (2007–2008)	VP	PS	PU	AFL-CIO	ADA	CCUS	ACU
California													
1 Thompson	D	1951	1998	88	68	1,391,605	99	15	95	100	90	56	8
2 Herger	R	1945	1986	U	58	1,256,602	97	78	97	0	10	89	88
3 Lungren	R	1946	2004	U	49	1,325,036	97	86	95	7	5	94	88
4 McClintock	R	1956	2008	53	50	3,532,595	—	—	—	—	—	—	0
5 Matsui	D	1944	2005	U	74	889,113	99	13	99	100	100	56	0
6 Woolsey	D	1937	1992	U	72	686,383	85	16	98	100	80	56	4
7 Miller	D	1945	1974	U	73	948,684	93	13	99	100	95	50	0
8 Pelosi	D	1940	1987	89	72	2,727,177	9	25	98	100	50	38	0
9 Lee	D	1946	1998	U	86	1,048,228	95	14	99	100	100	41	4
10 Tauscher[b]	D	1951	1996	U	65	1,049,777	98	16	98	100	95	61	0
11 McNerney	D	1951	2006	U	55	2,957,100	98	17	93	100	85	61	13
12 Speier	D	1950	2008	90	75	893,615	83	10	99	100	60	43	0
13 Stark	D	1931	1972	U	76	659,570	87	13	94	93	90	47	13
14 Eshoo	D	1942	1992	U	70	1,476,279	99	14	99	100	90	61	0
15 Honda	D	1941	2000	U	72	833,894	91	15	100	100	95	50	0
16 Lofgren	D	1947	1994	U	71	592,974	98	14	99	100	100	56	0
17 Farr	D	1941	1993	U	74	775,793	96	13	99	100	100	61	0
18 Cardoza	D	1959	2002	U	U	962,057	95	16	97	93	85	65	8
19 Radanovich	R	1955	1994	U	98	712,277	89	77	97	7	20	94	87
20 Costa	D	1952	2004	U	74	922,364	93	26	94	100	80	67	9
21 Nunes	R	1973	2002	U	68	734,226	96	83	97	7	0	94	100
22 McCarthy	R	1965	2006	U	U	709,687	98	73	97	13	10	94	100
23 Capps	D	1938	1998	U	68	957,695	99	14	99	100	100	61	0

Voting ratings[a]

24 Gallegly	R	1944	1986	77	58	737,060	95	63	96	13	15	89	92
25 McKeon	R	1939	1992	U	58	903,400	98	78	97	7	5	100	88
26 Dreier	R	1952	1980	74	53	2,919,351	96	78	96	13	10	100	86
27 Sherman	D	1954	1996	U	69	565,838	97	14	98	100	85	61	9
28 Berman	D	1941	1982	U	U	1,287,898	94	20	98	100	85	69	4
29 Schiff	D	1960	2000	U	69	909,396	99	14	98	100	90	61	4
30 Waxman	D	1939	1974	U	U	745,084	94	16	99	100	95	61	4
31 Becerra	D	1958	1992	U	U	1,396,520	97	10	99	100	100	50	8
32 Solis^c	D	1957	2000	U	U	659,981	95	12	99	100	95	50	4
33 Watson	D	1933	2001	88	88	229,692	96	10	99	100	100	53	4
34 Roybal-Allard	D	1941	1992	U	77	594,045	98	11	99	100	95	44	8
35 Waters	D	1938	1990	U	83	829,614	92	18	98	100	95	47	0
36 Harman	D	1945	1992	74	69	687,693	93	18	98	100	95	65	0
37 Richardson	D	1962	2007	U	75	1,075,767	91	16	99	100	100	59	0
38 Napolitano	D	1936	1998	U	82	385,568	98	10	99	100	95	44	8
39 Sánchez	D	1969	2002	U	70	439,587	98	10	99	100	100	50	8
40 Royce	R	1951	1992	82	63	1,172,942	98	82	99	0	0	83	100
41 Lewis	R	1934	1978	U	62	1,192,618	98	82	94	20	20	100	84
42 Miller	R	1948	1998	66	60	325,244	91	79	97	27	5	100	81
43 Baca	D	1947	1999	U	69	885,963	94	19	98	100	90	67	8
44 Calvert	R	1953	1992	89	51	1,150,432	97	76	96	13	15	100	83
45 Bono Mack	R	1961	1998	87	58	1,622,511	95	64	90	29	40	88	74
46 Rohrabacher	R	1947	1988	U	53	741,821	90	74	95	14	10	82	96
47 Sanchez	D	1960	1996	U	69	1,258,594	94	9	96	93	80	41	8
48 Campbell	R	1955	2005	U	56	776,452	84	89	97	0	5	76	86
49 Issa	R	1953	2000	U	58	950,631	96	79	99	7	10	94	100
50 Bilbray	R	1951	2006	76	50	1,456,454	97	67	94	20	15	88	92
51 Filner	D	1942	1992	72	73	927,615	95	13	95	93	100	47	12
52 Hunter	R	1976	2008	88	56	1,280,755	—	—	—	—	—	—	—
53 Davis	D	1944	2000	88	68	455,081	99	15	99	100	95	56	0

(Table continues)

207

Table 5-11 *(Continued)*

State/ district/ representative	Party	Year born	Year first elected	% vote in 2008 — Primary	% vote in 2008 — General	Campaign expenditures (2007–2008)	VP	PS	PU	AFL-CIO	ADA	CCUS	ACU
Colorado													
1 DeGette	D	1957	1996	U	72	925,776	96	13	99	100	80	59	0
2 Polis	D	1975	2008	42	63	7,323,502	—	—	—	—	—	—	12
3 Salazar	D	1953	2004	U	62	901,272	99	19	96	93	85	61	12
4 Markey	D	1956	2008	U	56	2,897,153	—	—	—	—	—	—	—
5 Lamborn	R	1954	2006	44	60	606,051	99	83	99	0	0	83	100
6 Coffman	R	1955	2008	40	61	1,325,282	—	—	—	—	—	—	—
7 Perlmutter	D	1953	2006	U	63	1,276,238	98	16	97	93	95	59	0
Connecticut													
1 Larson	D	1948	1998	P	72	1,381,640	95	13	99	100	95	65	0
2 Courtney	D	1953	2006	P	66	1,792,920	99	10	99	100	95	50	8
3 DeLauro	D	1943	1990	P	77	1,098,930	98	13	99	100	100	56	0
4 Himes	D	1966	2008	87	51	3,909,937	—	—	—	—	—	—	—
5 Murphy	D	1973	2006	P	59	3,056,641	99	17	98	100	95	61	0
Delaware													
AL Castle	R	1939	1992	U	61	1,808,076	99	41	70	73	65	78	28
Florida													
1 Miller	R	1959	2001	U	70	458,359	96	85	99	7	5	89	100
2 Boyd	D	1945	1996	U	62	962,421	99	23	92	71	75	67	12
3 Brown	D	1946	1992	U	U	562,421	87	17	98	100	95	69	0
4 Crenshaw	R	1944	2000	U	65	613,594	90	74	97	7	10	100	90
5 Brown-Waite	R	1943	2002	80	61	563,685	79	60	87	31	35	79	77
6 Stearns	R	1941	1988	U	61	789,774	99	76	97	13	15	89	100
7 Mica	R	1943	1992	U	62	1,031,911	99	77	93	0	10	94	100
8 Grayson	D	1958	2008	48	52	3,062,686	—	—	—	—	—	—	—
9 Bilirakis	R	1963	2006	U	62	1,542,342	99	63	89	13	30	83	88

[a] Voting ratings

Member	Party	Born	Elected			Population							
10 Young	R	1930	1970	U	61	969,224	94	64	92	33	25	83	88
11 Castor	D	1966	2006	U	72	662,366	94	14	99	100	95	63	9
12 Putnam	R	1974	2000	U	57	2,054,571	94	75	95	7	15	94	83
13 Buchanan	R	1951	2006	U	56	4,345,554	99	44	80	40	50	83	60
14 Mack	R	1967	2004	77	59	1,008,108	92	77	98	7	10	88	100
15 Posey	R	1947	2008	37	53	909,257	—	—	—	—	—	—	—
16 Rooney	R	1970	2008	U	60	1,819,259	—	—	—	—	—	—	—
17 Meek	D	1966	2002	U	58	1,311,327	93	18	99	100	95	61	4
18 Ros-Lehtinen	R	1952	1989	U	66	2,838,976	95	33	67	67	65	78	32
19 Wexler	D	1961	1996	U	77	2,372,548	85	15	99	100	90	54	5
20 Wasserman Schultz	D	1966	2004	85	58	1,475,436	97	13	99	100	100	59	0
21 Diaz-Balart	R	1954	1992	89	55	3,390,478	93	41	80	60	55	82	52
22 Klein	D	1957	2006	72	82	2,372,293	99	17	98	100	95	67	4
23 Hastings	D	1936	1992	U	57	671,962	95	13	99	100	95	65	0
24 Kosmas	D	1944	2008	76	53	2,083,810	—	—	—	—	—	—	—
25 Diaz-Balart	R	1961	2002	64	53	2,583,098	94	41	80	60	55	83	52
Georgia													
1 Kingston	R	1955	1992	U	67	873,385	93	68	93	15	10	61	96
2 Bishop	D	1947	1992	U	69	1,034,540	95	21	98	100	90	67	4
3 Westmoreland	R	1950	2004	U	66	920,966	97	76	98	80	0	67	100
4 Johnson	D	1954	2006	69	U	381,100	97	12	99	100	100	47	8
5 Lewis	D	1940	1986	U	U	1,195,110	95	15	99	100	95	50	4
6 Price	R	1954	2004	U	68	1,607,716	98	76	99	7	10	72	100
7 Linder	R	1942	1992	86	62	375,540	94	77	97	0	0	72	100
8 Marshall	D	1948	2002	U	57	1,736,540	95	33	83	0	70	72	28
9 Deal	R	1942	1992	71	76	898,875	95	74	99	7	5	83	100
10 Broun	R	1946	2007	U	61	1,800,502	97	83	100	0	0	67	100
11 Gingrey	R	1942	2002	76	68	1,242,887	95	72	99	7	10	78	96
12 Barrow	D	1955	2004	64	66	2,502,783	97	27	83	87	75	67	24
13 Scott	D	1946	2002	U	69	1,433,435	98	18	98	100	95	67	4

(Table continues)

Table 5-11 *(Continued)*

State/ district/ representative	Party	Year born	Year first elected	% vote in 2008 Primary	% vote in 2008 General	Campaign expenditures (2007–2008)	Voting ratings[a] VP	PS	PU	AFL-CIO	ADA	CCUS	ACU
Hawaii													
1 Abercrombie	D	1938	1990	U	77	1,005,218	94	16	96	100	95	50	8
2 Hirono	D	1947	2006	U	76	970,819	98	13	99	100	100	56	4
Idaho													
1 Minnick	D	1942	2008	U	51	2,649,953	—	—	—	—	—	—	—
2 Simpson	R	1950	1998	85	71	649,431	96	62	92	27	35	94	80
Illinois													
1 Rush	D	1946	1992	88	86	435,961	25	29	99	100	30	67	13
2 Jackson	D	1965	1995	U	89	1,673,968	100	14	99	100	100	61	4
3 Lipinski	D	1966	2004	54	73	553,030	96	16	97	100	90	59	8
4 Gutierrez	D	1953	1992	U	81	188,438	84	16	99	100	90	56	0
5 Emanuel[d]	D	1959	2002	U	74	2,105,109	97	16	99	100	95	67	0
6 Roskam	R	1961	2006	U	58	2,708,859	98	71	95	13	10	94	96
7 Davis	D	1941	1996	91	85	413,001	93	16	99	100	80	56	0
8 Bean	D	1962	2004	83	61	2,985,976	96	33	88	80	65	83	20
9 Schakowsky	D	1944	1998	88	75	1,227,724	99	16	99	100	100	61	0
10 Kirk	R	1959	2000	U	53	5,450,659	97	53	73	47	55	83	48
11 Halvorson	D	1958	2008	U	58	2,266,615	—	—	—	—	—	—	—
12 Costello	D	1949	1988	U	71	830,944	94	15	96	100	85	50	13
13 Biggert	R	1937	1998	77	54	1,585,536	98	69	89	20	35	94	84
14 Foster	D	1955	2008	50	58	5,047,815	99	21	92	92	65	56	13
15 Johnson	R	1946	2000	U	64	295,919	92	43	72	36	50	67	68
16 Manzullo	R	1944	1992	U	61	1,346,244	97	73	92	13	20	83	92
17 Hare	D	1949	2006	U	U	556,136	97	12	99	100	100	56	0
18 Schock	R	1981	2008	71	59	2,619,861	—	—	—	—	—	—	—
19 Shimkus	R	1958	1996	U	64	1,209,093	93	71	94	8	20	88	91

Indiana													
1 Visclosky	D	1949	1984	U	71	1,664,250	97	12	99	100	80	53	8
2 Donnelly	D	1955	2006	U	67	1,599,268	99	25	79	87	70	72	28
3 Souder	R	1950	1994	77	55	1,064,302	95	64	92	29	20	94	72
4 Buyer	R	1958	1992	72	60	969,469	91	66	93	29	25	81	84
5 Burton	R	1938	1982	52	66	1,810,296	92	77	99	7	10	89	100
6 Pence	R	1959	2000	U	64	1,575,412	91	88	99	0	5	81	100
7 Carson	D	1974	2008	47	65	1,600,840	95	12	99	100	75	53	4
8 Ellsworth	D	1958	2006	U	65	1,366,664	99	25	85	87	75	72	16
9 Hill	D	1953	1998	68	58	2,185,740	97	18	72	86	75	61	20
Iowa													
1 Braley	D	1957	2006	U	65	979,333	92	13	98	100	90	56	4
2 Loebsack	D	1952	2006	U	57	805,024	93	13	97	100	90	56	0
3 Boswell	D	1934	1996	61	56	1,547,567	88	17	98	100	95	61	4
4 Latham	R	1948	1994	U	61	1,627,654	99	63	90	20	30	89	88
5 King	R	1949	2002	U	60	873,230	98	77	97	0	5	83	96
Kansas													
1 Moran	R	1954	1996	U	82	2,769,946	97	69	90	14	15	89	92
2 Jenkins	R	1963	2008	51	51	1,666,239	—	—	—	—	—	—	—
3 Moore	D	1945	1998	U	56	1,868,504	99	22	97	100	80	71	4
4 Tiahrt	R	1951	1994	U	63	964,059	93	69	92	14	15	94	91
Kentucky													
1 Whitfield	R	1943	1994	U	64	1,052,635	96	56	89	29	35	72	78
2 Guthrie	R	1964	2008	U	53	1,257,624	—	—	—	—	—	—	—
3 Yarmuth	D	1947	2006	U	59	2,138,457	99	13	98	100	95	61	4
4 Davis	R	1958	2004	85	63	1,811,169	98	73	95	13	15	89	96
5 Rogers	R	1937	1980	U	84	796,760	99	69	96	13	20	94	84
6 Chandler	D	1959	2004	U	65	481,994	99	19	93	100	85	61	12

(Table continues)

Table 5-11 *(Continued)*

State/ district/ representative	Party	Year born	Year first elected	% vote in 2008 Primary	% vote in 2008 General	Campaign expenditures (2007–2008)	Voting ratings[a] VP	PS	PU	AFL-CIO	ADA	CCUS	ACU
Louisiana													
1 Scalise	R	1965	2008	U	66	1,628,134	99	79	99	0	5	94	100
2 Cao	R	1967	2008	U	50[e]	234,559	—	—	—	—	—	—	12
3 Melancon	D	1947	2004	U	U	904,878	95	27	93	93	80	71	—
4 Fleming	R	1951	2008	35[f]	48[e]	1,828,695	—	—	—	—	—	—	84
5 Alexander	R	1946	2002	90	U	1,021,984	94	70	95	20	25	94	—
6 Cassidy	R	1957	2008	U	48	1,252,457	—	—	—	—	—	—	83
7 Boustany	R	1956	2004	U	62	1,606,461	96	68	94	8	20	94	—
Maine													
1 Pingree	D	1955	2008	44	55	2,213,642	—	—	—	—	—	—	12
2 Michaud	D	1955	2002	U	67	569,114	99	13	94	100	90	50	—
Maryland													
1 Kratovil	D	1968	2008	40	49	1,994,553	—	—	—	—	—	—	4
2 Ruppersberger	D	1946	2002	U	72	636,162	91	21	97	100	90	67	0
3 Sarbanes	D	1962	2006	89	70	799,506	99	16	99	100	100	61	7
4 Edwards	D	1958	2008	59	86	1,443,942	98	17	99	100	—	58	0
5 Hoyer	D	1939	1981	83	74	3,435,232	99	18	99	100	90	67	96
6 Bartlett	R	1926	1992	78	58	204,443	99	65	94	0	15	78	5
7 Cummings	D	1951	1996	93	80	684,420	95	12	99	100	100	50	0
8 Van Hollen	D	1959	2002	88	75	1,279,456	99	14	99	100	100	61	0
Massachusetts													
1 Olver	D	1936	1991	79	73	857,631	99	14	100	100	100	56	0
2 Neal	D	1949	1988	U	98	766,166	92	14	100	100	100	61	0
3 McGovern	D	1959	1996	U	98	848,694	99	13	99	100	100	50	0
4 Frank	D	1940	1980	U	68	2,953,741	96	14	99	100	100	61	4
5 Tsongas	D	1946	2007	U	99	3,287,403	99	15	99	100	100	56	0
6 Tierney	D	1951	1996	U	70	498,041	94	12	98	100	95	59	4

Member	Party	Born	Elected										
7 Markey	D	1946	1976	U	76	1,021,890	97	14	99	100	100	56	0
8 Capuano	D	1952	1998	U	99	554,013	97	22	99	100	95	67	4
9 Lynch	D	1955	2001	U	99	739,421	98	10	98	100	95	53	8
10 Delahunt	D	1941	1996	U	99	1,217,875	90	10	99	100	95	56	10
Michigan													
1 Stupak	D	1952	1992	U	65	1,281,683	99	15	94	100	90	56	12
2 Hoekstra	R	1953	1992	U	62	828,852	97	76	96	27	20	83	88
3 Ehlers	R	1934	1993	U	61	319,953	96	64	81	33	40	100	61
4 Camp	R	1953	1990	U	62	2,568,143	99	72	95	20	20	94	83
5 Kildee	D	1929	1976	U	70	559,948	99	15	99	100	100	61	0
6 Upton	R	1953	1986	U	59	1,527,587	99	47	84	73	60	89	44
7 Schauer	D	1961	2008	66	49	2,331,667	—	—	—	—	—	—	—
8 Rogers	R	1963	2000	U	57	1,565,888	97	68	91	33	25	89	84
9 Peters	D	1958	2008	U	52	2,528,897	—	—	—	—	—	—	—
10 Miller	R	1954	2002	U	66	756,978	99	44	83	67	50	78	63
11 McCotter	R	1965	2002	U	51	1,058,502	98	58	86	60	40	82	72
12 Levin	D	1931	1982	U	72	660,710	94	16	99	100	95	59	0
13 Kilpatrick	D	1945	1996	39	74	1,066,838	93	13	99	100	95	53	4
14 Conyers	D	1929	1964	U	92	1,196,772	91	12	98	100	100	50	9
15 Dingell	D	1926	1955	U	71	2,522,180	94	15	99	100	90	56	4
Minnesota													
1 Walz	D	1964	2006	U	63	2,707,385	99	14	96	93	85	50	20
2 Kline	R	1947	2002	U	57	1,484,962	99	77	97	13	15	94	88
3 Paulsen	R	1965	2008	U	48	2,744,927	—	—	—	—	—	—	—
4 McCollum	D	1954	2000	84	68	719,710	98	13	99	100	100	56	0
5 Ellison	D	1963	2006	86	71	1,476,449	93	13	99	100	100	56	0
6 Bachmann	R	1956	2006	U	46	3,565,248	98	75	96	7	0	94	100
7 Peterson	D	1944	1990	U	72	1,036,463	94	21	91	80	80	50	20
8 Oberstar	D	1934	1974	U	68	1,409,685	89	15	99	100	80	56	4
Mississippi													
1 Childers	D	1958	2008[g]	57[f]	54	1,822,307	99	26	68	83	—	64	41
2 Thompson	D	1948	1993	86	69	1,081,785	93	13	99	100	90	50	8

(Table continues)

Table 5-11 (Continued)

State/district/representative	Party	Year born	Year first elected	% vote in 2008 Primary	% vote in 2008 General	Campaign expenditures (2007–2008)	Voting ratings[a] VP	PS	PU	AFL-CIO	ADA	CCUS	ACU
3 Harper	R	1956	2008	57[f]	63	1,143,197	—	—	—	—	—	—	—
4 Taylor	D	1953	1989	U	75	513,266	96	17	88	93	75	56	24
Missouri													
1 Clay	D	1956	2000	U	87	622,529	97	11	97	100	100	47	8
2 Akin	R	1947	2000	U	62	838,986	98	81	99	0	10	89	96
3 Carnahan	D	1958	2004	U	66	883,674	95	16	99	100	90	61	0
4 Skelton	D	1931	1976	U	66	1,203,525	99	20	97	100	85	61	4
5 Cleaver	D	1944	2004	U	64	554,037	98	13	99	100	90	61	4
6 Graves	R	1963	2000	U	59	2,633,443	95	54	89	47	40	83	88
7 Blunt	R	1950	1996	U	68	2,597,311	93	80	97	7	15	83	88
8 Emerson	R	1950	1996	U	71	1,285,597	97	53	86	60	65	83	56
9 Luetkemeyer	R	1952	2008	40	50	2,778,724	—	—	—	—	—	—	—
Montana													
AL Rehberg	R	1955	2000	U	64	897,187	99	65	93	33	40	89	84
Nebraska													
1 Fortenberry	R	1960	2004	U	70	341,030	95	56	82	27	40	72	84
2 Terry	R	1962	1998	84	52	1,838,836	97	68	90	13	15	100	92
3 Smith	R	1970	2006	87	77	623,810	99	74	98	7	15	89	96
Nevada													
1 Berkley	D	1951	1998	90	68	1,985,063	95	18	97	100	85	67	4
2 Heller	R	1960	2006	86	52	1,605,810	98	68	92	36	25	89	80
3 Titus	D	1950	2008	85	47	1,777,641	—	—	—	—	—	—	—
New Hampshire													
1 Shea-Porter	D	1952	2006	98	52	1,576,897	98	14	97	100	90	50	12
2 Hodes	D	1951	2006	99	56	2,022,042	96	15	97	100	90	56	12

New Jersey													
1 Andrews	D	1957	1990	h	72	3,502,678	76	17	100	100	85	63	0
2 LoBiondo	R	1946	1994	89	59	1,520,178	99	39	73	67	60	72	52
3 Adler	D	1959	2008	U	52	2,863,993	—	—	—	—	—	—	—
4 Smith	R	1953	1980	U	66	1,076,919	97	32	68	80	65	67	28
5 Garrett	R	1959	2002	U	56	1,726,631	98	77	97	0	5	78	100
6 Pallone	D	1951	1988	U	67	1,542,502	98	17	99	100	100	67	0
7 Lance	R	1952	2008	39	50	1,419,698	—	—	—	—	—	—	—
8 Pascrell	D	1937	1996	U	71	1,137,316	93	13	99	100	95	56	4
9 Rothman	D	1952	1996	U	68	1,288,656	95	14	98	100	100	56	8
10 Payne	D	1934	1988	U	99	502,611	91	13	99	100	95	47	8
11 Frelinghuysen	R	1946	1994	87	62	1,206,615	98	73	87	13	15	100	80
12 Holt	D	1948	1998	U	63	1,268,760	98	15	98	100	100	61	0
13 Sires	D	1951	2006	U	75	802,335	94	16	99	100	90	71	0
New Mexico													
1 Heinrich	D	1971	2008	44	56	2,481,040	—	—	—	—	—	—	—
2 Teague	D	1949	2008	52	56	3,458,821	—	—	—	—	—	—	—
3 Luján	D	1972	2008	42	57	1,520,908	—	—	—	—	—	—	—
New York													
1 Bishop	D	1950	2002	U	58	1,478,623	95	16	99	100	85	71	0
2 Israel	D	1958	2000	U	67	1,436,880	97	15	99	100	95	61	0
3 King	R	1944	1992	88	64	875,084	97	67	87	53	45	94	50
4 McCarthy	D	1944	1996	U	64	1,520,492	98	16	99	100	95	65	0
5 Ackerman	D	1942	1983	U	71	988,775	96	15	99	100	100	67	0
6 Meeks	D	1953	1998	U	U	1,343,648	90	19	99	100	90	65	0
7 Crowley	D	1962	1998	U	85	1,729,732	98	19	98	100	95	67	0
8 Nadler	D	1947	1992	U	80	1,044,454	94	14	99	100	100	53	0
9 Weiner	D	1964	1998	U	93	524,607	90	15	99	100	95	59	0
10 Towns	D	1934	1982	68	94	1,568,247	91	13	99	100	100	56	0
11 Clarke	D	1964	2006	U	93	545,983	99	16	99	100	100	56	0

(Table continues)

Table 5-11 *(Continued)*

State/ district/ representative	Party	Year born	Year first elected	% vote in 2008 Primary	% vote in 2008 General	Campaign expenditures (2007–2008)	VP	PS	PU	AFL-CIO	ADA	CCUS	ACU
12 Velázquez	D	1953	1992	U	90	816,108	96	14	100	100	100	50	0
13 McMahon	D	1957	2008	U	61	1,272,811	—	—	—	—	—	—	—
14 Maloney	D	1948	1992	U	80	1,257,989	93	17	99	100	95	65	0
15 Rangel	D	1930	1970	U	89	4,209,400	84	16	100	100	85	61	0
16 Serrano	D	1943	1990	U	97	386,734	99	13	99	100	100	39	8
17 Engel	D	1947	1988	U	80	776,808	90	17	98	100	95	65	0
18 Lowey	D	1937	1988	U	68	1,489,302	94	14	99	100	100	67	0
19 Hall	D	1948	2006	U	59	2,136,773	98	14	99	100	95	56	0
20 Gillibrand[i]	D	1966	2008	U	62	4,488,475	87	22	91	100	70	69	23
21 Tonko	D	1949	2008	40	62	753,520	—	—	—	—	—	—	—
22 Hinchey	D	1938	1992	U	66	735,253	94	15	98	100	95	50	12
23 McHugh[j]	R	1948	1992	U	65	645,795	99	51	81	73	60	83	40
24 Arcuri	D	1959	2006	U	52	1,616,138	99	20	96	100	90	67	4
25 Maffei	D	1968	2008	U	55	2,410,865	—	—	—	—	—	—	—
26 Lee	R	1964	2008	U	55	2,220,960	—	—	—	—	—	—	—
27 Higgins	D	1959	2004	U	74	844,699	95	20	99	100	80	65	4
28 Slaughter	D	1929	1986	U	78	756,579	94	12	100	100	95	47	0
29 Massa	D	1959	2008	U	51	2,159,314	—	—	—	—	—	—	—
North Carolina													
1 Butterfield	D	1947	2004	U	70	703,692	93	11	98	93	100	56	12
2 Etheridge	D	1941	1996	U	67	984,575	99	20	98	100	85	67	0
3 Jones	R	1943	1994	59	66	915,298	94	37	77	53	50	59	58
4 Price	D	1940	1986	U	63	940,570	99	14	99	100	100	61	0
5 Foxx	R	1943	2004	U	58	852,649	99	84	97	7	5	78	100
6 Coble	R	1931	1984	U	67	688,818	97	65	96	13	20	89	88

District	Party					Population							
7 McIntyre	D	1956	1996	U	69	1,160,679	99	17	89	93	85	61	32
8 Kissell	D	1951	2008	U	55	1,509,753	—	—	—	—	—	—	—
9 Myrick	R	1941	1994	92	62	1,164,506	95	79	99	14	10	94	91
10 McHenry	R	1975	2004	67	58	1,587,880	94	78	98	13	10	78	100
11 Shuler	D	1971	2006	U	62	769,941	91	18	83	87	75	56	24
12 Watt	D	1945	1992	U	72	646,075	99	15	99	100	100	61	0
13 Miller	D	1953	2002	88	66	907,519	98	15	99	100	100	61	0
North Dakota													
AL Pomeroy	D	1952	1992	U	62	1,795,714	98	20	97	100	85	61	4
Ohio													
1 Driehaus	D	1966	2008	U	52	1,447,544	—	—	—	—	—	—	—
2 Schmidt	R	1951	2005	58	45	1,276,573	95	72	95	21	15	94	87
3 Turner	R	1960	2002	U	63	1,058,000	96	58	85	57	55	81	63
4 Jordan	R	1964	2006	U	65	436,919	99	85	95	0	0	83	100
5 Latta	R	1956	2007	75	64	2,051,669	99	73	99	7	15	89	96
6 Wilson	D	1943	2006	U	62	598,718	97	22	97	100	80	67	4
7 Austria	R	1958	2008	55	58	1,196,189	—	—	—	—	—	—	—
8 Boehner	R	1949	1990	U	68	5,342,022	92	85	99	0	0	94	92
9 Kaptur	D	1946	1982	U	74	501,404	95	9	95	100	100	47	13
10 Kucinich	D	1946	1996	50	57	2,430,560	99	20	91	93	95	39	8
11 Fudge	D	1952	2008	74	85	94,049	100	100	100	100	—	—	0
12 Tiberi	R	1962	2000	90	55	1,714,042	97	60	92	40	35	94	72
13 Sutton	D	1963	2006	U	65	719,608	96	13	99	100	100	61	4
14 LaTourette	R	1954	1994	U	58	1,425,133	95	46	82	73	60	76	52
15 Kilroy	D	1949	2008	U	46	2,611,122	—	—	—	—	—	—	—
16 Boccieri	D	1969	2008	64	55	1,722,377	95	20	98	100	90	61	4
17 Ryan	D	1973	2002	U	78	1,151,775	95	20	98	100	80	61	12
18 Space	D	1961	2006	85	60	2,041,891	96	23	94	100	80	61	12

(Table continues)

Table 5-11 *(Continued)*

State/ district/ representative	Party	Year born	Year first elected	% vote in 2008 Primary	% vote in 2008 General	Campaign expenditures (2007–2008)	VP	PS	PU	AFL-CIO	ADA	CCUS	ACU
										Voting ratings[a]			
Oklahoma													
1 Sullivan	R	1965	2002	92	66	1,171,990	95	69	97	13	20	100	92
2 Boren	D	1973	2004	85	70	960,350	99	36	91	73	65	78	24
3 Lucas	R	1960	1994	U	70	644,446	95	66	96	14	15	89	96
4 Cole	R	1949	2002	U	66	1,116,842	96	73	95	7	10	94	88
5 Fallin	R	1954	2006	U	66	1,081,684	98	67	95	13	15	94	92
Oregon													
1 Wu	D	1955	1998	78	72	1,214,535	97	13	97	100	90	50	4
2 Walden	R	1957	1998	U	70	1,646,853	95	63	93	20	30	89	75
3 Blumenauer	D	1948	1996	87	75	1,132,494	97	15	98	100	95	53	12
4 DeFazio	D	1947	1986	U	82	471,179	97	13	93	100	90	50	20
5 Schrader	D	1951	2008	54	54	1,389,044	—	—	—	—	—	—	—
Pennsylvania													
1 Brady	D	1945	1998	U	91	1,013,835	97	14	99	100	100	56	0
2 Fattah	D	1956	1994	U	89	699,411	94	13	99	100	95	53	0
3 Dahlkemper	D	1957	2008	45	51	1,301,838	—	—	—	—	—	—	—
4 Altmire	D	1968	2006	U	56	2,986,360	100	24	84	100	80	61	24
5 Thompson	R	1959	2008	19	57	442,425	—	—	—	—	—	—	—
6 Gerlach	R	1955	2002	U	52	2,310,342	94	44	75	64	60	81	48
7 Sestak	D	1951	2006	U	60	1,162,719	94	18	97	100	90	61	0
8 Murphy	D	1973	2006	U	57	3,834,971	98	20	95	93	85	67	12
9 Shuster	R	1961	2001	U	64	979,174	98	67	94	13	20	94	92
10 Carney	D	1959	2006	U	56	2,333,358	97	26	83	100	85	59	20
11 Kanjorski	D	1937	1984	U	52	3,153,006	99	23	96	93	80	67	12

	Party													
12 Murtha	D	1932	1974	U	58	3,656,397	93	23	97	100	85	65	4
13 Schwartz	D	1948	2004	U	63	1,745,577	97	15	99	100	90	56	0
14 Doyle	D	1953	1994	U	91	838,611	93	16	99	100	95	56	0
15 Dent	R	1960	2004	U	59	1,775,398	99	49	78	60	55	83	56
16 Pitts	R	1939	1996	U	56	621,729	90	76	98	0	5	88	100
17 Holden	D	1957	1992	U	64	1,096,079	98	20	95	100	85	61	16
18 Murphy	R	1952	2002	U	64	2,073,251	97	45	76	73	60	81	48
19 Platts	R	1962	2000	U	67	192,495	97	49	80	47	55	78	68
Rhode Island													
1 Kennedy	D	1967	1994	U	69	1,791,870	92	14	99	100	100	59	0
2 Langevin	D	1964	2000	U	70	679,026	96	15	99	100	100	61	0
South Carolina													
1 Brown	R	1935	2000	70	52	1,287,308	99	69	92	14	20	94	83
2 Wilson	R	1947	2001	85	54	1,266,821	97	82	98	7	10	100	92
3 Barrett	R	1961	2002	U	65	765,832	97	83	98	0	5	94	96
4 Inglis	R	1959	2004	67	60	495,289	98	79	93	7	5	89	84
5 Spratt	D	1942	1982	U	62	829,176	97	20	98	100	85	61	4
6 Clyburn	D	1940	1992	U	67	2,391,430	98	18	99	100	95	56	0
South Dakota													
AL Herseth Sandlin	D	1970	2004	U	68	1,568,455	98	22	91	80	70	56	28
Tennessee													
1 Roe	R	1945	2008	50	72	717,171	—	—	—	—	—	—	—
2 Duncan	R	1947	1988	U	78	511,959	99	67	94	0	15	72	84
3 Wamp	R	1957	1994	91	69	1,440,107	96	70	96	7	15	100	96
4 Davis	D	1943	2002	90	59	1,074,524	95	24	93	93	80	61	12
5 Cooper	D	1954	2002	U	66	429,556	96	28	92	79	60	72	20
6 Gordon	D	1949	1984	U	74	1,123,083	94	21	93	100	80	67	4
7 Blackburn	R	1952	2002	62	69	1,558,273	94	78	99	0	10	83	96
8 Tanner	D	1944	1988	U	U	923,816	94	22	95	100	80	71	13
9 Cohen	D	1949	2006	79	88	886,339	96	14	99	100	100	61	0

(Table continues)

Table 5-11   *(Continued)*

State/district/representative	Party	Year born	Year first elected	% vote in 2008 Primary	% vote in 2008 General	Campaign expenditures (2007–2008)	Voting ratings[a] VP	PS	PU	AFL-CIO	ADA	CCUS	ACU
Texas													
1 Gohmert	R	1953	2004	U	88	834,732	90	63	92	7	10	75	96
2 Poe	R	1948	2004	U	89	391,238	92	68	94	7	10	56	96
3 Johnson	R	1930	1991	87	60	1,569,813	96	81	99	0	0	83	96
4 Hall	R	1923	1980	73	69	939,674	97	65	96	33	30	83	84
5 Hensarling	R	1957	2002	U	84	1,005,714	99	87	99	0	5	78	100
6 Barton	R	1949	1984	U	62	1,934,766	95	82	98	14	10	94	96
7 Culberson	R	1956	2000	U	56	1,757,226	92	77	97	7	5	88	100
8 Brady	R	1955	1996	U	73	610,288	93	77	94	7	10	88	86
9 Green	D	1947	2004	U	94	384,442	95	14	99	100	100	67	4
10 McCaul	R	1962	2004	U	54	1,728,339	97	68	95	13	25	89	96
11 Conaway	R	1948	2004	U	88	951,802	92	76	97	0	5	89	92
12 Granger	R	1943	1996	U	68	1,452,977	90	80	96	7	5	100	92
13 Thornberry	R	1958	1994	U	78	789,264	99	82	98	0	5	89	92
14 Paul	R	1935	1996	70	U	2,735,129	83	70	89	8	10	47	90
15 Hinojosa	D	1940	1996	U	66	388,362	88	22	97	100	80	59	9
16 Reyes	D	1944	1996	80	82	1,034,725	92	24	97	100	70	67	8
17 Edwards	D	1951	1990	U	53	2,114,653	96	22	97	100	80	67	8
18 Jackson-Lee	D	1950	1994	U	77	562,704	90	14	98	100	100	59	4
19 Neugebauer	R	1949	2003	U	72	1,052,072	95	80	98	0	5	82	96
20 Gonzalez	D	1945	1998	U	72	821,805	94	23	98	100	90	61	8
21 Smith	R	1947	1986	U	80	1,069,346	97	70	95	20	15	100	88
22 Olson	R	1962	2008	69f	52	2,366,149	—	—	—	—	—	—	—
23 Rodriguez	D	1946	1997	U	56	2,356,020	98	23	95	93	80	61	24
24 Marchant	R	1951	2004	U	56	644,822	89	82	98	0	0	83	100

	Party	Born	Elected										
25 Doggett	D	1946	1994	U	66	401,449	93	11	97	100	90	50	8
26 Burgess	R	1950	2002	U	60	1,021,104	93	73	94	14	10	76	96
27 Ortiz	D	1937	1982	U	58	719,709	88	27	95	100	75	65	17
28 Cuellar	D	1955	2004	U	69	1,171,941	97	30	94	87	80	72	12
29 Green	D	1947	1992	U	75	860,643	94	26	94	100	80	59	26
30 Johnson	D	1935	1992	U	82	459,462	94	14	99	100	100	56	0
31 Carter	R	1941	2002	U	60	1,053,850	93	80	99	0	5	94	96
32 Sessions	R	1955	1996	U	57	1,629,824	96	85	99	0	5	100	92
Utah													
1 Bishop	R	1951	2002	P	65	325,769	89	78	96	8	0	81	100
2 Matheson	D	1960	2000	P	63	1,389,004	99	32	86	67	55	78	36
3 Chaffetz	R	1967	2008	60	66	409,628	—	—	—	—	—	—	—
Vermont													
AL Welch	D	1947	2006	88	83	654,436	98	15	98	100	90	56	8
Virginia													
1 Wittman	R	1959	2007	P	57	952,691	99	63	93	20	35	83	92
2 Nye	D	1974	2008	P	52	1,333,931	—	—	—	—	—	—	—
3 Scott	D	1947	1992	P	97	506,728	98	11	99	100	100	53	8
4 Forbes	R	1952	2001	P	60	942,026	92	60	95	25	25	78	91
5 Perriello	D	1974	2008	P	50	1,822,148	—	—	—	—	—	—	—
6 Goodlatte	R	1952	1992	P	62	1,996,993	99	64	94	14	15	83	96
7 Cantor	R	1963	2000	P	63	3,823,907	96	79	98	7	5	94	92
8 Moran	D	1945	1990	87	68	1,207,945	93	15	98	100	95	61	0
9 Boucher	D	1946	1982	P	97	1,153,918	89	23	96	100	80	61	8
10 Wolf	R	1939	1980	92	59	2,053,375	98	66	87	21	30	94	79
11 Connolly	D	1950	2008	58	55	1,974,640	—	—	—	—	—	—	—
Washington													
1 Inslee	D	1951	1998	66[k]	68	777,233	98	15	99	100	90	61	12
2 Larsen	D	1965	2000	54[k]	62	1,147,005	98	16	98	100	90	56	0
3 Baird	D	1956	1998	51[k]	64	926,288	96	16	94	100	80	50	4

(Table continues)

Table 5-11 *(Continued)*

State/ district/ representative	Party	Year born	Year first elected	% vote in 2008 Primary	General	Campaign expenditures (2007–2008)	Voting ratings[a] VP	PS	PU	AFL-CIO	ADA	CCUS	ACU
4 Hastings	R	1941	1994	62^k	63	682,931	95	70	98	13	15	88	96
5 McMorris Rodgers	R	1969	2004	56^k	65	1,139,376	96	64	95	20	20	89	92
6 Dicks	D	1940	1976	57^k	67	1,159,160	93	19	98	100	90	67	0
7 McDermott	D	1936	1988	74^k	84	1,033,233	97	17	98	100	95	50	8
8 Reichert	R	1950	2004	49^k	53	2,852,514	99	53	75	60	60	78	56
9 Smith	D	1965	1996	65^k	65	612,066	94	20	97	100	85	67	4
West Virginia													
1 Mollohan	D	1943	1982	U	U	793,612	94	20	98	100	85	59	4
2 Capito	R	1953	2000	U	57	2,283,316	97	46	82	73	60	78	48
3 Rahall	D	1949	1976	U	67	592,264	99	18	97	93	85	67	8
Wisconsin													
1 Ryan	R	1970	1998	U	64	2,251,389	97	86	97	20	15	83	84
2 Baldwin	D	1962	1998	U	69	1,159,239	99	14	99	100	100	56	0
3 Kind	D	1963	1996	U	63	916,105	95	28	95	100	80	72	8
4 Moore	D	1951	2004	96	88	559,761	97	19	99	100	95	50	4
5 Sensenbrenner	R	1943	1978	78	80	567,709	96	82	98	0	10	67	96
6 Petri	R	1940	1979	U	64	635,888	99	62	91	33	40	72	80
7 Obey	D	1938	1969	U	61	1,560,229	98	13	99	100	95	56	0
8 Kagen	D	1949	2006	U	54	2,218,166	97	11	96	93	90	50	16
Wyoming													
AL Lummis	R	1954	2008	46	53	1,517,018	—	—	—	—	—	—	—

Note: "—" indicates no basis for voting ratings); "AL" indicates "at large"; "D" indicates Democrat; "R" indicates Republican; "U" indicates the candidate received more than 99 percent of the vote or was unopposed and did not appear on the ballot; "p" indicates the candidate was nominated by party convention; "I" indicates independent. Information as of July 16, 2009. Table entries reflect those initially elected to serve in the 111th Congress.

[a] Voting ratings based on recorded votes in 2008. "VP" indicates voting participation score (percentage of recorded votes on which a representative voted "yea" or "nay"). "PS" indicates presidential support score (percentage of votes on which the president took a position that the representative supported). "PU" indicates party unity score (percentage of votes on which a representative supported his or her party when a majority of voting Democrats opposed a majority of voting Republicans). Congressional Quarterly calculates "VP," "PS," and "PU" scores. Group ratings indicate the percentage of time a representative supported the group-preferred position on votes the group selects. "AFL–CIO" (American Federation of Labor–Congress of Industrial Organizations) is a labor group; "ADA" (Americans for Democratic Action) is a liberal group; "CCUS" (Chamber of Commerce of the United States) is a business group; and "ACU" (American Conservative Union) is a conservative group. Voting participation and "ADA" scores are lowered by a member's failure to vote. Failure to vote does not lower the other scores.

[b] Ellen O. Tauscher (D) resigned on June 26, 2009, to become undersecretary of state for arms control and international security. A special election to fill her seat has been scheduled for September 1, 2009.

[c] Hilda L. Solis (D) resigned on February 24, 2009, to become secretary of labor. An all-party primary for special elections was held on May 19, 2009. No one secured a majority, so a special general election was held on July 14, 2009, and was won by Judy Chu (D).

[d] Rep. Rahm Emanuel (D) resigned on January 3, 2009, to become White House chief of staff. Mike Quigley (D) won a special election for the seat on April 7, 2009.

[e] Due to Hurricane Gustav, Louisiana's congressional first round party primaries, originally scheduled for September 6, were postponed to October 4. If no candidate won 50 percent of the vote, a runoff was held on November 4 (the day of the general election in the rest of the state and nation) and the general election on December 6, 2008. Contested congressional primaries in the second and fourth districts led to December general elections there.

[f] Runoffs for nomination by majority vote occurred in 2008 in Louisiana CD-4, Mississippi CD-1 and CD-3, as well as in Texas CD-22. In these cases, the vote percentage shown in the primary column is for the runoff.

[g] Travis Childers (D) was initially elected in a special election on May 13, 2008.

[h] Robert E. Andrews (D) lost the Democratic primary for U.S. Senate and so did not appear on the Democratic ballot for New Jersey's first congressional district. He was then appointed to the general election ballot and ran for reelection to the House.

[i] Kirsten Gillibrand (D) resigned on January 26, 2009, after her appointment to the U.S. Senate. Scott Murphy (D) won a special election for the seat on March 31, 2009. (The contest was close, and the results were not declared until late April.)

[j] John M. McHugh (R) of New York announced his intention to resign to become secretary of the army, but the timing of his resignation is unknown.

[k] In Washington's "top two" primary system in 2008 voters were able to vote for one candidate among all candidates running for each office. The two candidates who received the most votes then qualified for the general election.

Sources: Congressional Quarterly, unpublished data; "Biographical Directory of the United States Congress" (*http://bioguide.congress.gov*).

Table 5-12 The 111th Congress: Senate

State/senator	Party	Year born	Year first elected	% vote in last election		Last campaign expenditures[a]	Voting ratings[b]						
				Primary	General		VP	PS	PU	AFL-CIO	ADA	CCUS	ACU
Alabama													
Shelby	R	1934	1986	U	68	$1,922,646	99	74	95	20	15	75	84
Sessions	R	1946	1996	92	63	3,240,151	99	74	98	10	20	50	84
Alaska													
Murkowski	R	1957	2002[c]	58	49	5,429,904	97	72	72	40	25	86	58
Begich	D	1962	2008	91	48	4,453,292	—	—	—	—	—	—	—
Arizona													
McCain	R	1936	1986	U	77	2,140,807	20	89	93	0	5	100	63
Kyl	R	1942	1994	U	53	15,571,727	99	83	100	0	0	63	96
Arkansas													
Lincoln	D	1960	1998	83	56	5,816,913	99	41	81	90	80	75	8
Pryor	D	1963	2002	U	80	3,284,632	99	46	79	100	85	75	4
California													
Feinstein	D	1933	1992	87	59	8,030,489	99	38	91	100	100	63	4
Boxer	D	1940	1992	U	58	14,886,426	94	30	99	100	95	57	4
Colorado													
Udall	D	1950	2008	U	53	12,987,562	78[d]	21[d]	94[d]	93[d]	80[d]	61[d]	13[d]
Salazar[e]	D	1955	2004	73	51	9,886,551	99	43	87	100	95	63	4
Connecticut													
Dodd	D	1944	1980	P	66	3,938,132	98	31	96	100	100	50	4
Lieberman	I	1942	1988	f	50	17,210,710	95	52	81	100	85	75	8
Delaware													
Carper	D	1947	2000	U	67	2,632,478	99	45	80	100	85	63	0
Biden[g]	D	1942	1972	U	65	4,907,245	83	33	97	100	80	71	0

State / Senator	Party												
Florida													
Nelson	D	1942	2000	U	60	16,116,224	99	42	89	100	95	50	8
Martinez	R	1946	2004	45	49	12,837,220	98	67	78	30	30	88	60
Georgia													
Chambliss	R	1943	2002	U	57	15,692,294	98	72	95	30	25	100	76
Isakson	R	1944	2004	53	58	8,038,200	99	72	94	20	25	88	76
Hawaii													
Inouye	D	1924	1962	94	76	1,768,886	90	46	83	100	85	71	0
Akaka	D	1924	1990[h]	55	61	2,651,026	100	30	99	100	100	50	0
Idaho													
Crapo	R	1951	1998	U	U	1,031,912	99	76	94	20	15	75	88
Risch	R	1943	2008	65	58	3,573,256	—	—	—	—	—	—	—
Illinois													
Durbin	D	1944	1996	U	68	8,016,455	100	31	98	100	100	63	4
Obama[i]	D	1961	2004	53	70	14,532,493	36	28	95	100	45	67	17
Indiana													
Lugar	R	1932	1976	U	87	3,133,830	98	87	81	20	25	100	63
Bayh	D	1955	1998	U	62	2,250,428	97	47	65	80	70	63	29
Iowa													
Grassley	R	1933	1980	U	70	6,403,445	100	72	93	30	25	100	76
Harkin	D	1939	1984	U	63	5,022,490	96	25	97	100	95	50	4
Kansas													
Brownback	R	1956	1996	87	69	2,476,585	98	78	94	20	20	88	76
Roberts	R	1936	1996	U	60	6,297,288	99	65	87	30	20	88	72
Kentucky													
McConnell	R	1942	1984	86	53	21,306,296	100	76	97	20	20	100	80
Bunning	R	1931	1998	84	51	6,075,399	95	79	95	10	5	75	88

(Table continues)

Table 5-12 *(Continued)*

| State/senator | Party | Year born | Year first elected | % vote in last election | | Last campaign expenditures[a] | Voting ratings[b] | | | | | | |
				Primary	General		VP	PS	PU	AFL-CIO	ADA	CCUS	ACU
Louisiana													
Landrieu	D	1955	1996	U	52[j]	10,146,669	94	53	69	100	65	75	32
Vitter	R	1961	2004	[j]	51[j]	7,206,714	97	76	98	20	5	88	84
Maine													
Snowe	R	1947	1994	99	74	2,773,431	99	48	39	100	80	71	12
Collins	R	1952	1996	U	61	7,765,295	100	59	46	100	75	75	20
Maryland													
Mikulski	D	1936	1986	90	65	5,997,093	97	42	88	100	90	63	0
Cardin	D	1943	2006	44	54	8,676,056	99	31	97	100	100	63	8
Massachusetts													
Kennedy	D	1932	1962	U	69	7,043,877	59	18	99	100	60	50	0
Kerry	D	1943	1984	69	66	12,279,425	97	30	98	100	95	63	4
Michigan													
Levin	D	1934	1978	U	63	5,784,520	99	31	97	100	100	63	0
Stabenow	D	1950	2000	U	57	11,220,506	98	31	98	100	100	50	4
Minnesota													
Franken[k]	D	1951	2008	65	42	21,066,834	—	—	—	—	—	—	—
Klobuchar	D	1960	2006	93	58	9,155,313	98	31	94	100	100	57	16
Mississippi													
Cochran	R	1937	1978	U	61	2,063,627	99	74	85	10	15	88	68
Wicker	R	1951	2007[l]	[l]	55	6,160,116	96	70	94	20	10	88	80
Missouri													
Bond	R	1939	1986	88	56	7,848,506	94	78	92	33	20	100	75
McCaskill	D	1953	2006	81	50	11,705,967	94	45	81	90	80	75	20

State / Senator	Party												
Montana													
Baucus	D	1941	1978	U	73	8,164,703	99	35	89	90	80	75	8
Tester	D	1956	2006	61	49	5,588,292	98	30	92	90	85	63	16
Nebraska													
Nelson	D	1941	2000	U	64	7,492,134	97	48	72	100	75	71	16
Johanns	R	1950	2008	78	58	3,781,316	—	—	—	—	—	—	—
Nevada													
Reid	D	1939	1986	U	61	7,040,588	99	43	84	50	70	75	16
Ensign	R	1958	2000	90	55	4,456,881	95	83	100	10	0	88	92
New Hampshire													
Gregg	R	1947	1992	92	66	1,897,466	94	82	95	20	15	86	83
Shaheen	D	1947	2008	88	52	8,225,580	—	—	—	—	—	—	—
New Jersey													
Lautenberg	D	1924	1982	59	56	8,135,752	96	30	99	100	100	63	4
Menendez	D	1954	2006[m]	84	53	13,328,665	98	28	98	100	100	63	4
New Mexico													
Bingaman	D	1943	1982	U	71	2,628,276	99	28	99	100	100	50	0
Udall	D	1948	2008	U	61	7,841,887	92[d]	14[d]	96[d]	100[d]	90[d]	47[d]	12[d]
New York													
Schumer	D	1950	1998	U	71	15,467,530	100	30	98	100	100	63	4
Clinton[n]	D	1947	2000	84	67	34,358,255	51	38	99	100	70	67	11
North Carolina													
Burr	R	1955	2004	88	52	12,853,110	96	81	99	10	5	100	79
Hagan	D	1953	2008	60	53	8,953,274	—	—	—	—	—	—	—
North Dakota													
Conrad	D	1948	1986	U	69	3,532,732	97	40	91	100	90	57	0
Dorgan	D	1942	1992	U	68	2,676,756	97	30	92	100	90	50	8
Ohio													
Voinovich	R	1936	1998	77	64	8,956,380	100	74	67	30	25	88	52
Brown	D	1952	2006	78	56	10,751,765	99	30	97	100	95	63	8

(Table continues)

Table 5-12 *(Continued)*

State/senator	Party	Year born	Year first elected	% vote in last election Primary	General	Last campaign expenditures[a]	VP	PS	PU	AFL-CIO	ADA	CCUS	ACU
Oklahoma													
Inhofe	R	1934	1994	84	57	5,477,730	92	75	99	22	5	63	96
Coburn	R	1948	2004	61	53	5,078,647	94	85	99	0	0	75	96
Oregon													
Wyden	D	1949	1996	U	63	2,817,706	99	28	97	100	95	50	8
Merkley	D	1956	2008	45	49	6,501,315	—	—	—	—	—	—	—
Pennsylvania													
Specter	Dº	1930	1980	51	53	20,307,099	99	58	62	70	45	86	42
Casey	D	1960	2006	85	59	17,592,212	100	35	93	100	90	63	8
Rhode Island													
Reed	D	1949	1996	87	73	2,258,706	99	35	99	100	95	50	4
Whitehouse	D	1955	2006	82	54	6,426,874	100	41	95	100	90	50	8
South Carolina													
Graham	R	1955	2002	67	58	4,463,619	86	72	97	14	15	100	82
DeMint	R	1951	2004	59	54	9,036,086	94	84	100	0	0	57	100
South Dakota													
Johnson	D	1946	1996	U	62	4,550,590	100	44	80	100	80	75	12
Thune	R	1961	2004	U	51	14,666,225	99	76	95	30	10	100	84
Tennessee													
Alexander	R	1940	2002	U	65	4,571,728	91	77	92	11	25	75	72
Corker	R	1952	2006	48	51	18,565,935	96	72	90	10	20	75	83
Texas													
Hutchison	R	1943	1993	U	62	5,734,146	97	67	94	20	20	100	76
Cornyn	R	1952	2002	81	55	16,454,518	92	73	97	11	20	100	79

State / Senator	Party					Expenditures							
Utah													
Hatch	R	1934	1976	P	62	3,340,902	99	80	93	20	10	100	80
Bennett	R	1933	1992	P	69	2,649,234	99	85	85	10	15	100	64
Vermont													
Leahy	D	1940	1974	94	71	1,531,833	99	30	98	100	100	50	4
Sanders	I	1941	2006	p	65	6,004,222	99	30	98	100	100	38	8
Virginia													
Webb	D	1946	2006	53	50	8,558,861	98	42	89	100	95	63	8
Warner	D	1954	2008	P	65	12,515,479	—	—	—	—	—	—	—
Washington													
Murray	D	1950	1992	92	55	11,556,148	96	28	99	100	95	63	0
Cantwell	D	1958	2000	91	57	14,013,932	99	28	97	100	100	50	12
West Virginia													
Byrd	D	1917	1958	86	64	4,944,546	75	31	95	100	55	57	0
Rockefeller	D	1937	1984	77	64	4,820,379	97	45	84	100	85	63	0
Wisconsin													
Kohl	D	1935	1988	86	67	6,347,126	100	37	94	100	95	63	4
Feingold	D	1953	1992	U	55	9,239,908	100	30	93	100	100	38	24
Wyoming													
Enzi	R	1944	1996	U	76	1,247,841	99	78	99	10	5	75	96
Barrasso	R	1952	2007[d]	U	73	1,981,441	100	76	99	10	5	75	96

Note: "—" indicates a newly elected senator (no basis for voting ratings); "D" indicates Democrat; "R" indicates Republican; "U" indicates the candidate received more than 99 percent of the vote or was unopposed and did not appear on the ballot; "P" indicates the candidate was nominated by party convention; "I" indicates independent. Information as of June 22, 2009. Table entries reflect those elected to or continuing service in the 111th Congress.

[a] Figures for campaign expenditures cover from January 1 of the year preceding the last campaign (or whenever the campaign registered with the Federal Election Commission during the election cycle) through December 31 of the election year.

[b] For a description of the voting ratings, see note a, Table 5–11, this volume.

[c] Lisa Murkowski (R) was appointed to the Senate on December 20, 2002, to fill the vacancy caused by the resignation of her father, Frank H. Murkowski; elected to a six-year term in 2004.

[d] The vote study and interest group scores for Mark Udall of Colorado and Tom Udall of New Mexico pertain to their prior House service.

(Notes continued)

Table 5-12 *(Continued)*

e Ken Salazar (D) resigned on January 21, 2009, to become secretary of the interior. Michael Bennett (D) was sworn in on January 22, 2009.

f Joseph I. Lieberman (D) lost the Democratic primary race in 2006; elected as an independent in the general election.

g Joseph R. Biden Jr. (D) resigned on January 15, 2009, prior to his inauguration as vice president. Ted Kaufman (D) was sworn in on January 16, 2009.

h Daniel K. Akaka (D) was appointed to the Senate on April 30, 1990, to fill the vacancy caused by the death of Spark Masayuki Matsunaga and began his term on May 16, 1990; elected to a four-year term by special election on November 6, 1990.

i Barack Obama (D) resigned on November 16, 2008, after his election on November 4, 2008, as president of the United States. Roland W. Burris (D) was sworn in on January 15, 2009.

j In 2004 David Vitter was elected in an "open" primary. Louisiana election law for federal office called for a primary open to candidates of all parties and held on the same day as the general election in the rest of the nation. If a candidate won 50 percent or more of the vote in that primary, that candidate was declared elected and no runoff, normally held about a month later, occurred. Vitter won with a majority of the vote in the first round and the voter percentage from that is shown in the general election column. In 2008 the law changed so that party primaries select nominees for the general election, and Landrieu won the general election.

k Incumbent Norm Coleman lost the November 2008 Senate election in Minnesota by 225 votes to Democrat Al Franken, filed suit challenging the final tally, and conceded June 30, 2009, after an adverse Minnesota State Supreme Court decision.

l Roger Wicker (R) was appointed to the Senate on December 31, 2007, to fill the vacancy caused by the resignation of Trent Lott (R); elected to a four-year term in November 2008 in a nonpartisan special election without a primary.

m Robert Menendez (D) was appointed to the Senate on January 18, 2006, to fill the vacancy caused by the resignation of Jon S. Corzine (D); elected to the Senate in November 2006 for a six-year term.

n Hillary Clinton (D) resigned on January 21, 2009, to become secretary of state. Kirsten Gillibrand (D) was sworn in on January 27, 2009.

o Arlen Specter (R) announced on April 28, 2009, that he was changing his party affiliation from Republican to Democrat.

p Bernard Sanders (I) won the Democratic primary race in 2006, but did not run on that party's ballot line in the general election. He ran and won as an independent in November.

q John Barrasso (R) was appointed to the Senate on June 25, 2007, to fill the vacancy caused by the death of Craig Thomas (R) on June 4, 2007; elected to a four-year term in a special election in November 2008.

Sources: Congressional Quarterly, unpublished data; U.S. Senate (*www.senate.gov*); "Biographical Directory of the United States Congress" (*http://bioguide congress.gov*).

6

The Presidency and Executive Branch

- **Presidents**
- **Ratings**
- **Backgrounds**
- **Cabinet and Staff**
- **Congressional Relations**
- **Civil Service Employment**
- **Regulations**

The presidency poses a special problem for those interested in collecting statistical data. The scope and variety of data available on the presidency are limited by the singularity of the office and how individual presidents change the office's organization and operation. The modern presidency has evolved since Franklin D. Roosevelt took office in the 1930s. Since then, the end of the Cold War and the rise of the war on terror, the rapid developments in modes of communication, the growth of government power, and the shift in emphasis from conventions to primaries as a way of nominating presidential candidates have further changed the nature of the presidency and the characteristics of incumbent presidents. Indeed, analysts wishing to collect data on many points have found that there have simply been too few modern-day occupants of the Oval Office to sustain statistical analysis.

   In spite of this seemingly insurmountable problem, the visibility of the president provides a considerable amount of relevant data. Of all elected officials, for example, only for presidents are public judgments about how well they are doing displayed prominently and repeatedly: the twists and turns in the public approval ratings of a president's job performance are themselves news items. Consequently, elsewhere in this book a graph is devoted to this subject alone—Figure 3-6 shows the overall presidential approval scores for Presidents Bill Clinton and George W. Bush as well as President Barack Obama in his first days in office. But presidents are not judged only by the public or only while they are in office. At various times and in various ways, historians and political scientists have rated all the U.S. presidents (Table 6-2).

Apart from approval ratings (and, of course, presidential elections), the presidency has not been subjected to extensive statistical scrutiny. However, perhaps because the number of presidents has now reached forty-three (Table 6-1), some additional areas are beginning to receive systematic study.[1] The president's relationship with Congress is one such area. Information about presidential "victories" on votes in Congress (Table 6-7), the extent to which the president is supported by his own party and by the other party (Table 6-8), the number of vetoes presidents from Washington to George W. Bush have exercised (Table 6-9), and presidents' success in securing approval of their nominations (Tables 6-10 and 6-11) are all regularly tabulated and increasingly analyzed.

As discussed in Chapter 4, analysts are beginning to study media coverage of the president more systematically. In part, this study results from the extreme visibility of the president and of the federal government in general (Figure 4-1 and Table 4-16); it also stems from the changing relationships between the president and the press, as indicated, for example, by the considerable decline in press conferences since the 1930s (Table 4-3).

Compilations of various presidential characteristics and activities also have become more numerous or more meaningful as the number of presidents has grown. How individuals get to be president, for example, has been a subject of considerable interest (Tables 6-3 and 6-4). As shown in Chapter 7, presidential appointments have been assessed for their partisan characteristics (Table 7-6) and increasingly for their racial and sex distributions (Table 7-5).

The executive branch, apart from the president, has received little statistical analysis. Yet here too there is ample opportunity for meaningful tabulations, if not for t-tests and correlations. The tremendous size of the federal government (Tables 6-5 and 6-12) necessitates such an interest. The expanded involvement of the government in regulation (Table 6-13 and Figure 6-1) also compels attention. But these data also contain other more subtle and more significant messages. For example, the changing priorities of the nation and of particular presidents are reflected in such mundane listings as the size and composition of the White House staff over time (Table 6-6).

Thus, although the presidency is a source of data for conventional statistical analyses in only a few areas, the increasing numerical data available provide considerable insight into what traditionally has been viewed as an office of impressive singularity.

Note

1. Only forty-three persons have served as president, but President Barack Obama is known as the forty-fourth president because President Grover Cleveland is counted twice—his nonconsecutive terms make him the twenty-second and twenty-fourth president (*www.whitehouse.gov/about/presidents*).

Table 6-1 Presidents and Vice Presidents of the United States

President (political party)	Born	Died	Age at inauguration	Native of . . .	Elected from . . .	Term of service	Vice president
George Washington (F)	1732	1799	57	Va.	Va.	April 30, 1789–March 4, 1793	John Adams
George Washington (F)			61			March 4, 1793–March 4, 1797	John Adams
John Adams (F)	1735	1826	61	Mass.	Mass.	March 4, 1797–March 4, 1801	Thomas Jefferson
Thomas Jefferson (D-R)	1743	1826	57	Va.	Va.	March 4, 1801–March 4, 1805	Aaron Burr
Thomas Jefferson (D-R)			61			March 4, 1805–March 4, 1809	George Clinton
James Madison (D-R)	1751	1836	57	Va.	Va.	March 4, 1809–March 4, 1813	George Clinton
James Madison (D-R)			61			March 4, 1813–March 4, 1817	Elbridge Gerry
James Monroe (D-R)	1758	1831	58	Va.	Va.	March 4, 1817–March 4, 1821	Daniel D. Tompkins
James Monroe (D-R)			62			March 4, 1821–March 4, 1825	Daniel D. Tompkins
John Q. Adams (NR)	1767	1848	57	Mass.	Mass.	March 4, 1825–March 4, 1829	John C. Calhoun
Andrew Jackson (D)	1767	1845	61	S.C.	Tenn.	March 4, 1829–March 4, 1833	John C. Calhoun
Andrew Jackson (D)			65			March 4, 1833–March 4, 1837	Martin Van Buren
Martin Van Buren (D)	1782	1862	54	N.Y.	N.Y.	March 4, 1837–March 4, 1841	Richard M. Johnson
W. H. Harrison (W)	1773	1841	68	Va.	Ohio	March 4, 1841–April 4, 1841	John Tyler
John Tyler (W)	1790	1862	51	Va.	Va.	April 6, 1841–March 4, 1845	
James K. Polk (D)	1795	1849	49	N.C.	Tenn.	March 4, 1845–March 4, 1849	George M. Dallas
Zachary Taylor (W)	1784	1850	64	Va.	La.	March 4, 1849–July 9, 1850	Millard Fillmore
Millard Fillmore (W)	1800	1874	50	N.Y.	N.Y.	July 10, 1850–March 4, 1853	
Franklin Pierce (D)	1804	1869	48	N.H.	N.H.	March 4, 1853–March 4, 1857	William R. King
James Buchanan (D)	1791	1868	65	Pa.	Pa.	March 4, 1857–March 4, 1861	John C. Breckinridge
Abraham Lincoln (R)	1809	1865	52	Ky.	Ill.	March 4, 1861–March 4, 1865	Hannibal Hamlin
Abraham Lincoln (R)			56			March 4, 1865–April 15, 1865	Andrew Johnson
Andrew Johnson (R)	1808	1875	56	N.C.	Tenn.	April 15, 1865–March 4, 1869	
Ulysses S. Grant (R)	1822	1885	46	Ohio	Ill.	March 4, 1869–March 4, 1873	Schuyler Colfax
Ulysses S. Grant (R)			50			March 4, 1873–March 4, 1877	Henry Wilson

(Table continues)

Table 6-1 *(Continued)*

President (political party)	Born	Died	Age at inauguration	Native of . . .	Elected from . . .	Term of service	Vice president
Rutherford B. Hayes (R)	1822	1893	54	Ohio	Ohio	March 4, 1877–March 4, 1881	William A. Wheeler
James A. Garfield (R)	1831	1881	49	Ohio	Ohio	March 4, 1881–Sept. 19, 1881	Chester A. Arthur
Chester A. Arthur (R)	1830	1886	50	Vt.	N.Y.	Sept. 20, 1881–March 4, 1885	
Grover Cleveland (D)	1837	1908	47	N.J.	N.Y.	March 4, 1885–March 4, 1889	Thomas A. Hendricks
Benjamin Harrison (R)	1833	1901	55	Ohio	Ind.	March 4, 1889–March 4, 1893	Levi P. Morton
Grover Cleveland (D)	1837	1908	55		Ohio	March 4, 1893–March 4, 1897	Adlai E. Stevenson
William McKinley (R)	1843	1901	54	Ohio		March 4, 1897–March 4, 1901	Garret A. Hobart
William McKinley (R)			58			March 4, 1901–Sept. 14, 1901	Theodore Roosevelt
Theodore Roosevelt (R)	1858	1919	42	N.Y.	N.Y.	Sept. 14, 1901–March 4, 1905	
Theodore Roosevelt (R)			46			March 4, 1905–March 4, 1909	Charles W. Fairbanks
William H. Taft (R)	1857	1930	51	Ohio	Ohio	March 4, 1909–March 4, 1913	James S. Sherman
Woodrow Wilson (D)	1856	1924	56	Va.	N.J.	March 4, 1913–March 4, 1917	Thomas R. Marshall
Woodrow Wilson (D)			60			March 4, 1917–March 4, 1921	Thomas R. Marshall
Warren G. Harding (R)	1865	1923	55	Ohio	Ohio	March 4, 1921–Aug. 2, 1923	Calvin Coolidge
Calvin Coolidge (R)	1872	1933	51	Vt.	Mass.	Aug. 3, 1923–March 4, 1925	
Calvin Coolidge (R)			52			March 4, 1925–March 4, 1929	Charles G. Dawes
Herbert C. Hoover (R)	1874	1964	54	Iowa	Calif.	March 4, 1929–March 4, 1933	Charles Curtis
Franklin D. Roosevelt (D)	1882	1945	51	N.Y.	N.Y.	March 4, 1933–Jan. 20, 1937	John N. Garner
Franklin D. Roosevelt (D)			55			Jan. 20, 1937–Jan. 20, 1941	John N. Garner
Franklin D. Roosevelt (D)			59			Jan. 20, 1941–Jan. 20, 1945	Henry A. Wallace
Franklin D. Roosevelt (D)			63			Jan. 20, 1945–April 12, 1945	Harry S. Truman
Harry S. Truman (D)	1884	1972	60	Mo.	Mo.	April 12, 1945–Jan. 20, 1949	
Harry S. Truman (D)			64			Jan. 20, 1949–Jan. 20, 1953	Alben W. Barkley
Dwight D. Eisenhower (R)	1890	1969	62	Texas	N.Y.	Jan. 20, 1953–Jan. 20, 1957	Richard Nixon
Dwight D. Eisenhower (R)			66		Pa.	Jan. 20, 1957–Jan. 20, 1961	Richard Nixon

President	Born	Died	Age	Birthplace	State	Term	Vice President
John F. Kennedy (D)	1917		43	Mass.	Mass.	Jan. 20, 1961–Nov. 22, 1963	Lyndon B. Johnson
Lyndon B. Johnson (D)	1906	1973	55	Texas	Texas	Nov. 22, 1963–Jan. 20, 1965	Hubert H. Humphrey
Lyndon B. Johnson (D)			56			Jan. 20, 1965–Jan. 20, 1969	Spiro T. Agnew
Richard Nixon (R)	1913	1994	56	Calif.	N.Y.	Jan. 20, 1969–Jan. 20, 1973	Spiro T. Agnew
Richard Nixon (R)			60			Jan. 20, 1973–Aug. 9, 1974	Gerald R. Ford
Gerald R. Ford (R)	1913	2006	61	Neb.	Mich.	Aug. 9, 1974–Jan. 20, 1977	Nelson A. Rockefeller
Jimmy Carter (D)	1924		52	Ga.	Ga.	Jan. 20, 1977–Jan. 20, 1981	Walter F. Mondale
Ronald Reagan (R)	1911	2004	69	Ill.	Calif.	Jan. 20, 1981–Jan. 20, 1985	George H. W. Bush
Ronald Reagan (R)			73			Jan. 20, 1985–Jan. 20, 1989	George H. W. Bush
George H. W. Bush (R)	1924		64	Mass.	Texas	Jan. 20, 1989–Jan. 20, 1993	Dan Quayle
Bill Clinton (D)	1946		46	Ark.	Ark.	Jan. 20, 1993–Jan. 20, 1997	Al Gore
Bill Clinton (D)			50			Jan. 20, 1997–Jan. 20, 2001	Al Gore
George W. Bush (R)	1946		54	Conn.	Texas	Jan. 20, 2001–Jan. 20, 2005	Dick Cheney
George W. Bush (R)			58			Jan. 20, 2005–Jan. 20, 2009	Dick Cheney
Barack Obama (D)	1961		47	Hawaii	Ill.	Jan. 20, 2009–	Joseph R. Biden, Jr.

Note: "D" indicates Democrat; "D-R" indicates Democratic-Republican; "F" indicates Federalist; "NR" indicates National Republican; "R" indicates Republican; "W" indicates Whig.

Source: Congressional Quarterly, *Presidential Elections, 1789–2004* (Washington, D.C.: Congressional Quarterly, 2005), 3; updated by the editors.

Table 6-2 Ratings of U.S. Presidents

Schlesinger (1948)	Schlesinger (1962)	Maranell-Dodder (1970)	Tribune (1982)	Murray-Blessing (1982)[a]	Ridings-McIver (1989,1996)	Schlesinger (1997)	Federalist Society–Wall Street Journal (2005)[b]	C-SPAN (2009)[b]
Great	Great	Accomplishments of administration	Ten best presidents	Great	Overall ranking	Great	Great	Overall ranking
1. Lincoln	1. Lincoln	1. Lincoln	1. Lincoln (best)	1. Lincoln	1. Lincoln	1. Lincoln	1. Washington	1. Lincoln
2. Washington	2. Washington	2. F. Roosevelt	2. Washington	2. F. Roosevelt	2. F. Roosevelt	2. Washington	2. Lincoln	2. Washington
3. F. Roosevelt	3. F. Roosevelt	3. Washington	3. F. Roosevelt	3. Washington	3. Washington	3. F. Roosevelt	3. F. Roosevelt	3. F. Roosevelt
4. Wilson	4. Wilson	4. Jefferson	4. T. Roosevelt	4. Jefferson	4. Jefferson	Near great	Near great	4. T. Roosevelt
5. Jefferson	5. Jefferson	5. T. Roosevelt	5. Jefferson	Near great	5. T. Roosevelt	4. Jefferson	4. Jefferson	5. Truman
6. Jackson	Near great	6. Truman	6. Wilson	5. T. Roosevelt	6. Wilson	5. Jackson	5. T. Roosevelt	6. Kennedy
Near great	6. Jackson	7. Wilson	7. Jackson	6. Wilson	7. Truman	6. T. Roosevelt	6. Reagan	7. Jefferson
7. T. Roosevelt	7. T. Roosevelt	8. Jackson	8. Truman	7. Jackson	8. Jackson	7. Wilson	7. Truman	8. Eisenhower
8. Cleveland	8. Polk/Truman (tie)	9. L. Johnson	9. Eisenhower	8. Truman	9. Eisenhower	8. Truman	8. Eisenhower	9. Wilson
9. J. Adams	9. J. Adams	10. Polk	10. Polk (10th best)	Above average	10. Madison	9. Polk	9. Polk	10. Reagan
10. Polk	10. Cleveland	11. J. Adams	Ten worst presidents	9. J. Adams	11. Polk	High average	10. Jackson	11. L. Johnson
Average	Average	12. Kennedy	1. Harding (worst)	10. L. Johnson	12. L. Johnson	10. Eisenhower	Above average	12. Polk
11. J. Q. Adams	11. Madison	13. Monroe	2. Nixon	11. Eisenhower	13. Monroe	11. J. Adams	11. Wilson	13. Jackson
12. Monroe	12. J. Q. Adams	14. Cleveland	3. Buchanan	12. Polk	14. J. Adams	12. Kennedy	12. Cleveland	14. Monroe
13. Hayes	13. Hayes	15. Madison	4. Pierce	13. Kennedy	15. Kennedy	13. Cleveland	13. J. Adams	15. Clinton
14. Madison	14. McKinley	16. Taft	5. Grant	14. Madison	16. Cleveland	14. L. Johnson	14. McKinley	16. McKinley
15. Van Buren	15. Taft	17. McKinley	6. Fillmore	15. Monroe	17. McKinley	15. Monroe	15. Kennedy	17. J. Adams
16. Taft	16. Van Buren	18. J. Q. Adams	7. A. Johnson	16. J. Q. Adams	18. J. Q. Adams	16. McKinley	16. Monroe	18. G. H. W. Bush
17. Arthur	17. Monroe	19. Hoover	8. Coolidge	17. Cleveland	19. Carter	Average	Average	19. J. Q. Adams
18. McKinley	18. Hoover	20. Eisenhower	9. Tyler	Average	20. Taft	17. Madison	17. Madison	20. Madison
19. A. Johnson	19. B. Harrison	21. A. Johnson	10. Carter (10th worst)	18. McKinley	21. Van Buren	18. J. Q. Adams	18. L. Johnson	21. Cleveland
20. Hoover	20. Eisenhower/ Arthur (tie)	22. Van Buren		19. Taft	22. G. H. W. Bush	19. B. Harrison	19. G. W. Bush	22. Ford
21. B. Harrison	21. A. Johnson	23. Arthur		20. Van Buren	23. Clinton	20. Clinton	20. Taft	23. Grant
		24. Hayes			24. Hoover			24. Taft
		25. Tyler			25. Hayes			25. Carter
		26. B. Harrison			26. Reagan			26. Coolidge

Below average
22. Tyler
23. Coolidge
24. Fillmore
25. Taylor
26. Buchanan
27. Pierce

Failure
28. Grant
29. Harding

Below average
22. Taylor
23. Tyler
24. Fillmore
25. Coolidge
26. Pierce
27. Buchanan

Failure
28. Grant
29. Harding

---

27. Taylor
28. Buchanan
29. Fillmore
30. Coolidge
31. Pierce
32. Grant
33. Harding

---

21. Hoover
22. Hayes
23. Arthur
24. Ford
25. Carter
26. B. Harrison

Below average
27. Taylor
28. Reagan
29. Tyler
30. Fillmore
31. Coolidge
32. Pierce

Failure
33. A. Johnson
34. Buchanan
35. Nixon
36. Grant
37. Harding

---

27. Ford
28. Arthur
29. Taylor
30. Garfield
31. B. Harrison
32. Nixon
33. Coolidge
34. Tyler
35. W. H. Harrison
36. Fillmore
37. Pierce
38. Grant
39. A. Johnson
40. Buchanan
41. Harding

---

21. Taft
22. Van Buren
23. Hayes
24. G. H. W. Bush
25. Reagan
26. Arthur
27. Carter
28. Ford

Below average
29. Taylor
30. Coolidge
31. Fillmore
32. Tyler

Failure
33. Pierce
34. Grant
35. Hoover
36. Nixon
37. A. Johnson
38. Buchanan
39. Harding

---

21. G. H. W. Bush
22. Clinton
23. Coolidge
24. Hayes
25. J. Q. Adams
26. Arthur
27. Van Buren
28. Ford
29. Grant
30. B. Harrison
31. Hoover
32. Nixon
33. Taylor
34. Carter
35. Tyler

Failure
36. Fillmore
37. A. Johnson
38. Pierce
39. Harding
40. Buchanan

---

27. Nixon
28. Garfield
29. Taylor
30. B. Harrison
31. Van Buren
32. Arthur
33. Hayes
34. Hoover
35. Tyler
36. G. W. Bush
37. Fillmore
38. Harding
39. W. H. Harrison
40. Pierce
41. A. Johnson
42. Buchanan

Note: These ratings are derived from surveys of scholars. The sample sizes range from 49 to 846. In addition to these ratings, the Siena College Research Institute developed an alternative rating system based on scores given across twenty different categories. Using this method, it rated presidents in 1982, 1990, 1994, and 2002. See Douglas A. Lonnstrom and Thomas O. Kelly II, "The Contemporary Presidency: Rating the Presidents: A Tracking Study," *Presidential Studies Quarterly* 33 (2003), 625–634. An additional rating of the ten greatest presidents can be found in previous editions of *Vital Statistics on American Politics.*

[a] The rating of President Ronald Reagan was obtained in a separate poll conducted in 1989.

[b] An earlier rating by the same organization, with slightly different results, was conducted in 1999 (C-SPAN) or 2000 (Federalist Society). See previous editions of *Vital Statistics on American Politics.*

Sources: Henry J. Abraham, *Justices and Presidents: Appointments to the Supreme Court,* 2nd ed. (New York: Oxford University Press, 1985), 380–383 (copyright © Henry J. Abraham, 1974, 1985, reprinted by permission of Oxford University Press, Inc.); Robert K. Murray and Tim H. Blessing, *Greatness in the White House,* 2nd updated ed. (University Park: Pennsylvania State University Press, 1994), 16–17, 81; Arthur M. Schlesinger Jr., "Rating the Presidents: Washington to Clinton," *Political Science Quarterly* (Summer 1997); "C-Span 2009 Historians Presidential Leadership Survey" (*www.c-span.org/PresidentialSurvey/Overall-Ranking.aspx*); "Presidential Leadership: The Rankings," Federalist Society—*Wall Street Journal,* September 12, 2005 (*www.opinionjournal.com*); William J. Ridings Jr. and Stuart B. McIver, *Rating the Presidents* (Secaucus, N.J.: Carol Publishing, 1997), xi.

Table 6-3   Previous Public Positions Held by Presidents, 1788–2009

Position	*Number of presidents holding position prior to presidency*	
	Pre-1900 (24)	Post-1900 (19)
Vice president	7	7
Cabinet member	7	3
U.S. representative	13	5
U.S. senator	9	6
U.S. Supreme Court justice	0	0
Federal judge	0	1
Governor	11	8
State legislator	16	5
State judge	1	2
Mayor	2	1
Diplomat, ambassador	7	2
Military general	11	1

Position	*Last public position held prior to presidency*	
	Pre-1900 (24)	Post-1900 (19)
Vice president		
Succeeded to presidency	4	5
Won presidency in own right	3	2
Congress		
House	1	0
Senate	3	3
Appointive federal office		
Military general	3	1
Cabinet secretary	3	2
Ambassador	2	0
Other civilian	1	0
Governor	4	6

Note: Included in the list of generals are Andrew Johnson, who held the rank of general when serving as military governor of Tennessee, and Chester A. Arthur, who held the rank of general when serving as quartermaster general. President Cleveland is counted only at his first term.

Source: Compiled by the editors from Robert G. Ferris, *The Presidents,* rev. ed. (Washington, D.C.: National Park Service, 1977); updated by the editors through President Barack Obama.

Table 6-4 Latest Public Office Held by Candidates for Democratic and Republican Presidential Nominations, 1936–2008

Public office[a]	Percentage of all persons polling at least 1 percent in Gallup Poll	Percentage of all presidential nominees
President[b]	1	32
Vice president	1	13
U.S. senator	40	18
Governor	20	28
Cabinet officer	13	0
U.S. representative	10	0
Mayor	2	0
U.S. Supreme Court justice	1	0
All others	2	0
No public office	10	8
Total	100	99
	(N = 187)	(N = 38)

[a] Last or current office at time person first polled at least 1 percent support for presidential nomination among fellow partisans or was first nominated.
[b] Presidents Harry S. Truman and Gerald R. Ford received poll support for the presidential nomination only after they actually served in the office.

Source: William R. Keech and Donald R. Matthews, *The Party's Choice: With an Epilogue on the 1976 Nominations* (Washington, D.C.: Brookings, 1976), 18; updated by the editors.

Table 6-5 The President's Cabinet, 2009

Cabinet office	Year established[a]	Current secretary[b]	Date confirmed	Number of paid civilian employees		Number of non–civil service positions[c]	Percentage of all positions
				1980[c]	2008[c]		
State	1789	Hillary R. Clinton	1/21/2009	23,644	35,651	27,316	77
Treasury	1789	Timothy F. Geithner	1/26/2009	123,754	107,872	6,354	6
War	1789[d]						
Navy	1798[d]						
Interior	1849	Ken Salazar	1/20/2009	79,505	65,099	8,799	14
Justice	1870	Eric H. Holder Jr.	2/2/2009	56,426	107,405	44,938	42
Post Office	1872[e]						
Agriculture	1889	Tom Vilsack	1/20/2009	122,839	98,523	11,164	11
Commerce and Labor	1903[f]						
Commerce	1913	Gary Locke	3/24/2009	46,189	40,380	9,766	24
Labor	1913	Hilda L. Solis	2/24/2009	23,717	12,244	1,695	14
Defense	1947	Robert M. Gates	12/6/2006	972,999	673,654	142,337	21
Health, Education and Welfare	1953[g]						
Health and Human Services	1979	Kathleen Sebelius	4/28/2009	158,644	61,403	12,677	21
Housing and Urban Development	1965	Shaun Donovan	1/22/2009	16,890	9,498	958	10

Department	Year	Secretary	Date				
Transportation	1966	Ray LaHood	1/21/2009	72,066	54,144	46,297	86
Energy	1977	Steven Chu	1/20/2009	21,729	14,601	2,082	14
Education	1979	Arne Duncan	1/20/2009	7,370	4,173	960	23
Veterans Affairs	1989	Eric K. Shinseki	1/20/2009	235,501[h]	260,261	136,395	52
Homeland Security	2003[i]	Janet Napolitano	1/20/2009		162,120	83,504	52

Note: Also included in the cabinet are the vice president, the director of the Office of Management and Budget, the White House chief of staff, the administrator of the Environmental Protection Agency, the U.S. trade representative, the U.S. ambassador to the United Nations, and the chair of the Council of Economic Advisers.

[a] The year is that in which a department achieved cabinet status. The Offices of Attorney General and Postmaster General were created in 1789, but the executive departments were not created until later. A Department of Agriculture was established in 1862, but the commissioner did not achieve cabinet status until 1889.

[b] As of May 1, 2009.

[c] December 1980; January 2008. Non–civil service positions include excepted and senior executive service and are as of January 2008.

[d] Incorporated into Defense Department in 1947.

[e] Independent agency as of 1971.

[f] Split into separate departments in 1913.

[g] Split into Health and Human Services and Education in 1979.

[h] Figures are for the Veterans Administration, the agency that was upgraded on March 15, 1989, to the Department of Veterans Affairs.

[i] In January 2003, the Department of Homeland Security was organized with more than 180,000 employees drawn from other agencies.

Sources: "President Obama's Cabinet" (*www.whitehouse.gov*); year established: Ronald C. Moe, "The Federal Executive Establishment: Evolution and Trends," prepared for the U.S. Senate Committee on Governmental Affairs by the Congressional Research Service (Washington, D.C.: Government Printing Office, 1980), 26–27; *Congressional Quarterly Weekly Report* (1988), 3059; U.S. Office of Personnel Management, *Federal Civilian Workforce Statistics, Employment and Trends,* January 1981, 8–9, 11; January 2008, table 11 (*www.opm.gov*).

Table 6-6 White House Staff and Executive Office of the President, 1943–2007

Year	White House	Bureau of Budget/OMB[a]	Council of Economic Advisers	National Security Council	Office of Economic Opportunity	Office of Science and Technology	Office of Administration	Special Representative for Trade Negotiations	Domestic Policy Staff/Office of Policy Development	Total, executive office[b]
1943[c]	51	543								703
1944[c]	58	542								683
1945[c]	64	705								820
1946[c]	216	692	26							1,034
1947[c]	228	549	26							1,077
1948[c]	209	521	38	20						1,205
1949	243	517	36	17						1,240
1950	313	509	38	17						1,408
1955	366	422	33	27						1,221
1960	423	441	31	64						2,779
1961	439	456	45	43						1,586
1962	338	465	65	39		63				1,492
1963	376	485	57	43		48		30		1,572
1964	328	493	46	41		57		29		1,478
1965	292	506	45	39	1,768	75		24		3,307
1970	491	636	57	82	2,633	77		26	26	4,808
1971	580	717	62	80	2,304	75		33	44	4,809
1972	583	703	58	80	2,066	76		38	53	5,721
1973	528	642	49	85	1,148			39	24	3,877
1974	560	646	46	87	1,090			45	32	2,868
1975	525	664	48	85				56	55	1,801
1976	534	694	39	79		19		55	43	1,796
1977	387	721	36	68		44		52	41	1,637
1978	381	617	35	76		46	197	58	55	1,679
1979	418	638	36	73		44	180	70	60	1,918
1980	426	631	38	74		50	182	131	68	2,013
1981	378	679	38	65		13	190	139	48	1,674
1982	374	617	35	59		20	196	138	46	1,608
1983	376	619	34	61		23	213	139	39	1,622

Year									
1984	371	605	28	63	21	196	147	40	1,593
1985	362	569	32	61	17	193	152	38	1,549
1986	365	537	36	69	11	200	144	40	1,526
1987	375	573	31	56	11	199	155	37	1,604
1988	357	573	35	63	10	232	162	32	1,594
1989	370	536	32	62	20	213	164	37	1,640
1990	391	568	35	60	22	215	172	37	1,729
1991	358	608	36	61	39	241	181	33	1,797
1992	392	553	34	62	47	247	185	42	1,869
1993	392	522	31	52	35	185	177	42	1,570
1994	381	544	29	49	36	182	166	38	1,577
1995	387	522	28	44	34	182	165	30	1,555
1996	387	527	30	43	33	185	161	28	1,582
1997	389	507	28	43	34	178	154	29	1,591
1998	391	509	27	42	34	170	169	30	1,604
1999	393	525	28	40	33	180	180	28	1,651
2000	398	510	29	45	30	194	174	31	1,665
2001	382	509	32	49	19	198	201	33	1,652
2002	408	506	30	64	28	205	193	30	1,712
2003	401	502	29	57	31	216	198	31	1,717
2004	409	509	29	61	31	216	217	30	1,784
2005	411	473	24	61	30	221	210	27	1,697
2006	414	472	24	64	30	225	233	25	1,739
2007	419	476	23	59	32	224	226	22	1,707

Note: In almost all instances, when no figures are shown the office did not exist as a separate entity. Data as of December of the year indicated, except 1947 (January) and 1960 (October). Data for additional years can be found in previous editions of *Vital Statistics on American Politics*.

[a] The Bureau of the Budget became the Office of Management and Budget (OMB) in 1970.
[b] Includes offices not shown separately.
[c] Total, executive office, excludes personnel in war establishments or emergency war agencies.

Source: U.S. Office of Personnel Management, *Federal Manpower Statistics, Federal Civilian Workforce Statistics*, bimonthly release (*www.opm.gov*).

Table 6-7   Presidential Victories on Votes in Congress, 1953–2008

President (political party)/year	House and Senate victories (percent)	House		Senate	
		Victories (percent)	Number of votes	Victories (percent)	Number of votes
Eisenhower (R)					
1953	89.2	91.2	34	87.8	49
1954	82.8	78.9	38	77.9	77
1955	75.3	63.4	41	84.6	52
1956	69.2	73.5	34	67.7	65
1957	68.4	58.3	60	78.9	57
1958	75.7	74.0	50	76.5	98
1959	52.9	55.6	54	50.4	121
1960	65.1	65.1	43	65.1	86
Average	69.9	68.4		70.7	
Total			354		605
Kennedy (D)					
1961	81.5	83.1	65	80.6	124
1962	85.4	85.0	60	85.6	125
1963	87.1	83.1	71	89.6	115
Average	84.6	83.7		85.2	
Total			196		364
L. Johnson (D)					
1964	87.9	88.5	52	87.6	97
1965	93.1	93.8	112	92.6	162
1966	78.9	91.3	103	68.8	125
1967	78.8	75.6	127	81.2	165
1968	74.5	83.5	103	68.9	164
Average	82.2	85.9		79.7	
Total			497		713
Nixon (R)					
1969	74.8	72.3	47	76.4	72
1970	76.9	84.6	65	71.4	91
1971	74.8	82.5	57	69.5	82
1972	66.3	81.1	37	54.3	46
1973	50.6	48.0	125	52.4	185
1974	59.6	67.9	53	54.2	83
Average	64.3	68.2		61.5	
Total			384		559
Ford (R)					
1974	58.2	59.3	54	57.4	68
1975	61.0	50.6	89	71.0	93
1976	53.8	43.1	51	64.2	53
Average	58.3	51.0		65.0	
Total			194		214
Carter (D)					
1977	75.4	74.7	79	76.1	88
1978	78.3	69.6	112	84.8	151
1979	76.8	71.7	145	81.4	161
1980	75.1	76.9	117	73.3	116
Average	76.6	73.1		79.7	
Total			453		516

Table 6-7   *(Continued)*

President (political party)/year	House and Senate victories (percent)	House		Senate	
		Victories (percent)	Number of votes	Victories (percent)	Number of votes
Reagan (R)					
1981	82.4	72.4	76	88.3	128
1982	72.4	55.8	77	83.2	119
1983	67.1	47.6	82	85.9	85
1984	65.8	52.2	113	85.7	77
1985	59.9	45.0	80	71.6	102
1986	56.5	33.3	90	80.7	83
1987	43.5	33.3	99	56.4	78
1988	47.4	32.7	104	64.8	88
Average	62.2	45.6		77.9	
Total			721		760
G. H. W. Bush (R)					
1989	62.6	50.0	86	73.3	101
1990	46.8	32.4	108	63.4	93
1991	54.2	43.2	111	67.5	83
1992	43.0	37.1	105	53.3	60
Average	51.8	40.2		65.6	
Total			410		337
Clinton (D)					
1993	86.4	87.3	102	85.4	89
1994	86.4	87.2	78	85.5	62
1995	36.2	26.3	133	49.0	102
1996	55.1	53.2	79	57.6	59
1997	53.6	38.7	75	71.4	63
1998	50.6	36.6	82	66.7	72
1999	37.8	35.4	82	42.2	45
2000	55.0	49.3	69	65.0	40
Average	57.4	50.9		66.0	
Total			700		532
G. W. Bush (R)					
2001	87.0	83.7	43	88.3	77
2002	88.0	82.5	40	91.4	58
2003	78.7	87.3	55	74.8	119
2004	72.6	70.6	34	74.0	50
2005	78.0	78.3	46	77.8	45
2006	80.9	85.0	40	78.6	70
2007	38.3	15.4	117	66.0	97
2008	47.8	33.8	80	68.5	54
Average	64.1	56.3		76.9	
Total			455		570

Note: "R" indicates Republican; "D" indicates Democrat. Percentages based on the number of congressional votes supporting the president divided by the total number of votes on which the president had taken a position. The percentages differ slightly from those found in *Congressional Quarterly Almanac, Congressional Quarterly Weekly Report (CQ Weekly)*, and Norman J. Ornstein et al.'s *Vital Statistics on Congress* because of corrections and consistent rounding of percentages to one decimal place. Averages are weighted by number of roll calls in each year.

Sources: Congressional Quarterly Almanac (Washington, D.C.: Congressional Quarterly, various years); *Congressional Quarterly Weekly Report (CQ Weekly)* (1992), 3894; (1993), 3473; (1994), 3620; (1996), 3428; (1998), 14; (1999), 76, 2972; (2001), 54; (2002), 142, 3237; (2004), 54–55, 2947–2948; (2006), 87; (2007), 50; (2008), 138–139, 3328.

Table 6-8   Congressional Voting in Support of the President's Position, 1954–2008 (percent)

President (political party)/year	House		Senate	
	Democrats	Republicans	Democrats	Republicans
Eisenhower (R)				
1954	44	71	38	73
1955	53	60	56	72
1956	52	72	39	72
1957	49	54	57	69
1958	44	67	44	67
1959	40	68	38	72
1960	44	59	43	66
Average	46.3	63.8	43.6	70.0
Kennedy (D)				
1961	73	37	65	36
1962	72	42	63	39
1963	72	32	63	44
Average	72.3	36.7	63.7	39.6
L. Johnson (D)				
1964	74	38	61	45
1965	74	41	64	48
1966	63	37	57	43
1967	69	46	61	53
1968	64	51	48	47
Average	68.4	43.2	58.0	47.6
Nixon (R)				
1969	48	57	47	66
1970	53	66	45	60
1971	47	72	40	64
1972	47	64	44	66
1973	35	62	37	61
1974	46	65	39	57
Average	44.1	64.2	40.9	61.7
Ford (R)				
1974	41	51	39	55
1975	38	63	47	68
1976	32	63	39	62
Average	37.3	59.7	42.5	62.4
Carter (D)				
1977	63	42	70	52
1978	60	36	66	41
1979	64	34	68	47
1980	63	40	62	45
Average	62.6	37.4	66.4	45.6

Table 6-8   *(Continued)*

President (political party)/year	House		Senate	
	Democrats	Republicans	Democrats	Republicans
Reagan (R)				
1981	42	68	49	80
1982	39	64	43	74
1983	28	70	42	73
1984	34	60	41	76
1985	30	67	35	75
1986	25	65	37	78
1987	24	62	36	64
1988	25	57	47	68
Average	30.5	63.7	41.7	74.0
G. H. W. Bush (R)				
1989	36	69	55	82
1990	25	63	38	70
1991	34	72	41	83
1992	25	71	32	73
Average	29.7	68.7	42.8	77.3
Clinton (D)				
1993	77	39	87	29
1994	75	47	86	42
1995	75	22	81	29
1996	74	38	83	37
1997	71	30	85	60
1998	74	26	82	41
1999	73	23	84	34
2000	73	27	89	46
Average	74.2	31.0	84.3	38.4
G. W. Bush (R)				
2001	31	86	66	94
2002	32	82	71	89
2003	26	89	48	94
2004	30	80	60	91
2005	24	81	38	86
2006	31	85	51	85
2007	7	72	37	78
2008	16	64	34	70
Average	20.9	77.5	50.2	86.5

Note: "R" indicates Republican; "D" indicates Democrat. Entries indicate the percentage of roll calls on which members voted in agreement with the president's position (based on a set of roll calls on which the president took a clear position). Averages are weighted by the number of such roll calls in each year, as shown in Table 6-7, this volume. Congressional Quarterly no longer provides information on absences, so "nonsupport" may include not voting on the roll call. Also, CQ no longer provides separate scores for southern Democrats. For results reflecting absences and for scores for southern Democrats in earlier years, see previous editions of *Vital Statistics on American Politics*.

Source: CQ Weekly (2008), 3327.

Table 6-9   Presidential Vetoes, 1789–2008, and Signing Statements, 1929–2008

Years	President	Regular vetoes	Vetoes overridden	Pocket vetoes	Total vetoes	Signing statements[a] Those raising constitutional concerns	Total
1789–1797	Washington	2	0	0	2	—	—
1797–1801	J. Adams	0	0	0	0	—	—
1801–1809	Jefferson	0	0	0	0	—	—
1809–1817	Madison	5	0	2	7	—	—
1817–1825	Monroe	1	0	0	1	—	—
1825–1829	J. Q. Adams	0	0	0	0	—	—
1829–1837	Jackson	5	0	7	12	—	—
1837–1841	Van Buren	0	0	1	1	—	—
1841–1841	W. H. Harrison	0	0	0	0	—	—
1841–1845	Tyler	6	1	4	10	—	—
1845–1849	Polk	2	0	1	3	—	—
1849–1850	Taylor	0	0	0	0	—	—
1850–1853	Fillmore	0	0	0	0	—	—
1853–1857	Pierce	9	5	0	9	—	—
1857–1861	Buchanan	4	0	3	7	—	—
1861–1865	Lincoln	2	0	5	7	—	—
1865–1869	A. Johnson	21	15	8	29	—	—
1869–1877	Grant	45	4	48	93	—	—
1877–1881	Hayes	12	1	1	13	—	—
1881–1881	Garfield	0	0	0	0	—	—
1881–1885	Arthur	4	1	8	12	—	—
1885–1889	Cleveland	304	2	110	414	—	—
1889–1893	B. Harrison	19	1	25	44	—	—
1893–1897	Cleveland	42	5	128	170	—	—
1897–1901	McKinley	6	0	36	42	—	—
1901–1909	T. Roosevelt	42	1	40	82	—	—
1909–1913	Taft	30	1	9	39	—	—
1913–1921	Wilson	33	6	11	44	—	—
1921–1923	Harding	5	0	1	6	—	—
1923–1929	Coolidge	20	4	30	50	—	—
1929–1933	Hoover	21	3	16	37	—	16
1933–1945	F. Roosevelt	372	9	263	635	—	42
1945–1953	Truman	180	12	70	250	—	107
1953–1961	Eisenhower	73	2	108	181	—	145
1961–1963	Kennedy	12	0	9	21	—	36
1963–1969	L. Johnson	16	0	14	30	—	175
1969–1974	Nixon	26[b]	7	17	43	—	117
1974–1977	Ford	48	12	18	66	—	137
1977–1981	Carter	13	2	18	31	—	225
1981–1989	Reagan	39	9	39	78	86	250[c]

Table 6-9   *(Continued)*

Years	President	Regular vetoes	Vetoes overridden	Pocket vetoes	Total vetoes	Signing statements[a] Those raising constitutional concerns	Total
1989–1992	G. H. W. Bush	29	1	15[d]	46	107	228
1993–2000	Clinton	36	2	1	37	70	381
2001–2008	G. W. Bush	12	4	0[e]	12	118[f]	162
Total		1,496	110	1,066	2,562	—	—

Note: "—" indicates not available.

[a] Presidents issue "signing statements" in writing when signing legislation. Often these statements merely comment on the bill signed. Some statements involve more controversial claims by the president that some part of the legislation is unconstitutional and that he intends to disregard it or to implement it in ways he thinks is constitutional.
[b] Two pocket vetoes, overruled in the courts, are counted here as regular vetoes.
[c] The American Presidency Project lists 249 signing statements for Reagan.
[d] President George H. W. Bush attempted to pocket veto two bills during intrasession recesses. These two disputed vetoes are not incuded here.
[e] President George W. Bush characterized his veto of H.R. 1585 as a pocket veto; however, the 110th Congress treated it as a normal veto. It is counted as a normal veto here.
[f] Through September 17, 2007.

Sources: Vetoes: Kevin R. Kosar, "Regular Vetoes and Pocket Vetoes: An Overview," RS22188, Congressional Research Service, Washington, D.C., July 18, 2008; signing statements (total), Hoover to Carter and G. W. Bush (2008): John Woolley and Gerhard Peters, "Signing Statements," American Presidency Project (*www.presidency.ucsb.edu*); signing statements (those raising constitutional concerns and total), Reagan to G. W. Bush (through 2007): T. J. Halstead, "Presidential Signing Statements: Constitutional and Institutional Implications," RL33667, Congressional Research Service, Washington, D.C., September 17, 2007.

Table 6-10   Senate Action on Nominations, 1937–2009

Congress		Received[a]	Confirmed	Withdrawn	Rejected[b]	Unconfirmed[c]
75th	(1937–1939)	15,330	15,193	20	27	90
80th	(1947–1949)	66,641	54,796	153	0	11,692
81st	(1949–1951)	87,266	86,562	45	6	653
82nd	(1951–1953)	46,920	46,504	45	2	369
83rd	(1953–1955)	69,458	68,563	43	0	852
84th	(1955–1957)	84,173	82,694	38	3	1,438
85th	(1957–1959)	104,193	103,311	54	0	828
86th	(1959–1961)	91,476	89,900	30	1	1,545
87th	(1961–1963)	102,849	100,741	1,279	0	829
88th	(1963–1965)	122,190	120,201	36	0	1,953
89th	(1965–1967)	123,019	120,865	173	0	1,981
90th	(1967–1969)	120,231	118,231	34	0	1,966
91st	(1969–1971)	134,464	133,797	487	2	178
92nd	(1971–1973)	117,053	114,909	11	0	2,133
93rd	(1973–1975)	134,384	131,254	15	0	3,115
94th	(1975–1977)	135,302	131,378	21	0	3,903
95th	(1977–1979)	137,509	124,730	66	0	12,713
96th	(1979–1981)	156,141	154,665	18	0	1,458
97th	(1981–1983)	186,264	184,856	55	0	1,353
98th	(1983–1985)	97,893	97,262	4	0	627
99th	(1985–1987)	99,614	95,811	16	0	3,787
100th	(1987–1989)	94,687	88,721	23	1	5,942
101st	(1989–1991)	96,130	88,078	48	1	8,003
102nd	(1991–1993)	76,628	75,802	24	0	802
103rd	(1993–1995)	79,956	76,122	1,080	0	2,754
104th	(1995–1997)	82,214	73,711	22	0	8,481
105th	(1997–1999)	46,290	45,878	40	0	372
106th	(1999–2001)	46,952	44,980	25	0	1,947
107th	(2001–2003)	50,406	48,724	79	0	1,603
108th	(2003–2005)	59,655	48,627	39	0	10,989
109th	(2005–2007)	57,514	55,545	40	0	1,929
110th	(2007–2009)	45,453	44,677	74	0	702

Note: Data for earlier years can be found in previous editions of *Vital Statistics on American Politics.*

[a] Count includes those in the second session carried over from the first session.

[b] Category includes only those nominations rejected outright by a vote of the Senate. Most nominations that fail to win approval of the Senate are unfavorably reported by committees and never reach the Senate floor, having been withdrawn. In some cases, the full Senate may vote to recommit a nomination to committee, in effect killing it.

[c] Includes "returned" nominations. Nominations must be returned to the president unless confirmed or rejected during the session in which they are made. If the Senate adjourns or recesses for more than thirty days within a session, all pending nominations must be returned (Senate Rule XXI).

Sources: 1929–1999: *Congressional Quarterly's Guide to Congress,* 5th ed. (Washington, D.C.: CQ Press, 2000), 1: 295; 1999–2001: *Congressional Record—Daily Digest,* D45; 2001–2003: D456–D457; 2003–2005: D96–D97; 2005–2007: D158, D1173; 2007–2009: D80, D1336–D1337.

Table 6-11   Senate Rejections of Cabinet Nominations

Nominee	Position	President	Date	Vote
Roger B. Taney	secretary of Treasury	Jackson	6/23/1834	18–28
Caleb Cushing	secretary of Treasury	Tyler	3/3/1843	19–27
Caleb Cushing	secretary of Treasury	Tyler	3/3/1843	10–27
Caleb Cushing	secretary of Treasury	Tyler	3/3/1843	2–29
David Henshaw	secretary of navy	Tyler	1/15/1844	6–34
James M. Porter	secretary of war	Tyler	1/30/1844	3–38
James S. Green	secretary of Treasury	Tyler	6/15/1844	[a]
Henry Stanbery	attorney general	A. Johnson	6/2/1868	11–29
Charles B. Warren	attorney general	Coolidge	3/10/1925	39–41
Charles B. Warren	attorney general	Coolidge	3/16/1925	39–46
Lewis L. Strauss	secretary of commerce	Eisenhower	6/19/1959	46–49
John Tower	secretary of defense	G. H. W. Bush	3/9/1989	47–53

[a] Not recorded.

Source: Congressional Quarterly's Guide to Congress, 5th ed. (Washington, D.C.: CQ Press, 2000), 1:292.

Table 6-12   Number of Civilian Federal Government Employees and
Percentage under Merit Civil Service, 1816–2007

Year	Total number of employees[a]	Percentage under merit	Year	Total number of employees[a]	Percentage under merit
1816	4,837	—	1946	2,696,529	—
1821	6,914	—	1947	2,111,001	80.2
1831	11,491	—	1948	2,071,009	82.4
1841	18,038	—	1949	2,102,109	84.3
1851	26,274	—	1950	1,960,708	84.5
1861	36,672	—	1951	2,482,666	86.4
1871	51,020	—	1952	2,600,612	86.4
1881	100,020	—	1953	2,558,416	83.6
1891	157,442	21.5	1954	2,407,676	82.7
1901	239,476	44.3	1955	2,397,309	83.6
1910	388,708	57.2	1956	2,398,736	85.1
1911	395,905	57.5	1957	2,417,565	85.5
1912	400,150	54.3	1958	2,382,491	85.3
1913	396,494	71.3	1959	2,382,807	85.7
1914	401,887	72.8	1960	2,398,704	85.5
1915	395,429	73.9	1961	2,435,804	86.1
1916	399,381	74.3	1962	2,514,197	85.9
1917	438,500	74.5	1963	2,527,960	85.6
1918	854,500	75.2	1964	2,500,503	86.1
1919[b]	794,271	86.6	1965	2,527,915	85.2
1920[c]	655,265	75.9	1966	2,759,019	85.8
1921[c]	561,142	79.9	1967	3,002,461	82.8
1922	543,507	77.4	1968	3,055,212	84.1
1923	536,900	76.6	1969	3,076,414	82.9
1924	543,484	76.5	1970	2,981,574	82.3
1925	553,045	76.6	1971	2,862,894	84.1
1926	548,713	77.0	1972[d]	2,779,261	61.6
1927	547,127	77.3	1973	2,732,377	62.0
1928	560,772	77.0	1974[e]	2,893,118	57.0
1929	579,559	88.2	1975[e]	2,896,944	57.4
1930	601,319	87.9	1976[e]	2,883,134	57.6
1931	609,746	76.8	1977[e]	2,893,334	57.1
1932	605,496	77.2	1978[e]	2,929,100	57.3
1933	603,587	75.6	1979[e]	2,949,630	56.6
1934	698,649	64.5	1980	3,121,769	56.1
1935	780,582	58.3	1981	2,947,428	58.7
1936	867,432	57.5	1982	2,917,095	59.2
1937	895,993	59.4	1983	2,920,514	59.2
1938	882,226	63.8	1984	2,959,317	58.7
1939	953,891	69.5	1985	3,059,987	57.2
1940	1,042,420	69.7	1986	3,061,210	56.6
1941	1,437,682	68.9	1987	3,125,635	56.2
1942	2,296,384	—	1988	3,126,171	56.0
1943	3,299,414	—	1989[f]	3,151,334	56.2
1944	3,332,356	—	1990	3,503,550	50.5
1945	3,816,310	—	1991	3,138,180	56.4

Table 6-12   *(Continued)*

Year	Total number of employees[a]	Percentage under merit	Year	Total number of employees[a]	Percentage under merit
1992	3,134,915	56.7	2000	3,206,791	42.7
1993	3,050,711	56.7	2001	2,719,529	50.4
1994	2,992,840	55.4	2002	2,700,876	50.4
1995	2,958,447	54.8	2003	2,758,463	50.4
1996	2,888,623	53.7	2004	2,735,359	49.9
1997	2,825,370	51.1	2005	2,728,432	48.8
1998	2,798,992	50.4	2006	2,718,917	48.8
1999	2,783,281	49.8	2007	2,715,395	48.6

Note: "—" indicates not available. As of June, except where indicated.

[a] Excludes employees of the Central Intelligence Agency and National Security Agency.
[b] As of November.
[c] As of July.
[d] Under the Postal Reorganization Act of 1970, U.S. Postal Service employees were changed from competitive (merit) service to excepted service.
[e] Excludes those employees in temporary and indefinite competitive status. In June 1973, 3.6 percent of federal civilian employees were in such service. In June 1980, 2.9 percent were.
[f] As of May.

Sources: 1816–1970: U.S. Bureau of the Census, *Historical Statistics of the United States* (Washington, D.C.: Government Printing Office, 1975), 1102–1103; 1971–2007: U.S. Office of Personnel Management, *Federal Civilian Workforce Statistics, Employment and Trends* (*www.opm.gov*).

Table 6-13   Major Regulatory Agencies

Agency	Year established	Agency head		Number of employees[a]
		Number	Title	
Consumer Product Safety Commission	1972	3	commissioner	386
Environmental Protection Agency	1970	1	administrator	17,964
Equal Employment Opportunity Commission	1965	5	commissioner	2,184
Federal Communications Commission	1934	5	commissioner	1,789
Federal Deposit Insurance Corporation	1933	5	board of directors	4,686
Federal Election Commission	1971	6	commissioner	350
Federal Energy Regulatory Commission	1977	5	commissioner	1,349
Federal Reserve System	1913	7	governor	1,873
Federal Trade Commission	1914	5	commissioner	1,131
Food and Drug Administration	1906	1	commissioner	10,070
National Labor Relations Board	1935	5	board of directors	1,686
Occupational Safety and Health Administration	1970	1	assistant secretary	2,186
Securities and Exchange Commission	1934	5	commissioner	3,513

Note: The Interstate Commerce Commission, established in 1887, was terminated on December 30, 1995. It was succeeded by the Surface Transportation Board.

[a] As of January 2008, except for Food and Drug Administration (FY 2008), Occupational Safety and Health Administration (FY 2008), and Federal Energy Regulatory Commission (October 2008).

Sources: Year established, agency head: *Federal Regulatory Directory,* 9th ed. (Washington, D.C.: Congressional Quarterly, 1999); number of employees: U.S. Office of Personnel Management, *Federal Civilian Workforce Statistics, Employment and Trends*, January 2008 (*www.opm.gov*); agency Web sites.

Figure 6-1   Number of Pages in *Federal Register*, 1940–2008

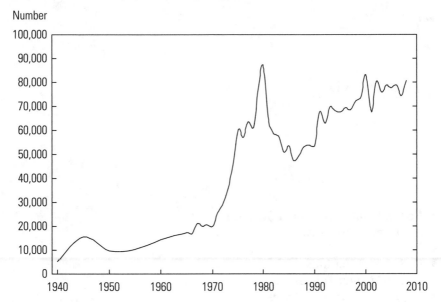

Number

Source: Compiled from successive volumes of the *Federal Register* (Washington, D.C.: Government Printing Office).

7

The Judiciary

- **Federal and State Court Structures**
- **Supreme Court Justices**
- **Ratings**
- **Failed Nominations**
- **Federal Court Judges**
- **Supreme Court Caseloads**
- **Federal Court Caseloads**
- **Laws Overturned**

The judiciary, although one of the three "separate but equal" branches of government, is often considered beyond the political push and pull that characterizes the executive and legislative branches. Preoccupied with process, precedent, and the meaning of the law, the courts present a strikingly different appearance. Nevertheless, because they must grapple with the constitutionality of abortion or the death penalty and because they must pour practical meaning into ambiguous, generally worded statutes enacted by legislatures, the courts are squarely in the middle of the political process.

Even if the courts are considered political, are statistics essential to understanding the judiciary? They are for two reasons. First, the courts themselves have to deal with statistics. One line of cases, for example, has dealt with the question of racially disparate patterns in the imposition of the death penalty. It has been noted that proportionately more African Americans are on death row; in addition, defendants who kill whites are more likely to be sentenced to die than are those who kill blacks. Courts have had to decide whether the numbers they are given are accurate and meaningful as well as whether the defendant being tried is a victim of racial discrimination.

Other cases also often turn on conclusions drawn from numerical data—voting rights (Table 1-30), reapportionment and redistricting (Tables 1-20, 1-29, and 5-1), and school desegregation (Table 10-13) are three examples.

And although the courts do not explicitly take public opinion into account, they cannot help but be aware that cases often involve issues about which public opinion is strong and divided (for example, on abortion, Table 3-13).

Statistics also provide useful insight into the operation of the judicial system. A single case does not lend itself to statistical analysis, but the large number, the hierarchy (Figure 7-1), and the geographical spread (Figure 7-2) of the federal courts, as well as the even greater variety of state courts and appointment methods (Table 7-1), suggest that numerical summarization aids comprehension.

Although the nature of the courts might suggest that appointments are merely a matter of judicial qualifications, the record indicates otherwise. Federal judicial appointments have always been subject to partisan considerations (Tables 7-2 and 7-6), and other characteristics of federal judges vary with the appointing president (Table 7-5). Partisan and ideological differences also explain part of the frustration presidents have encountered in making nominations to the Supreme Court (Table 7-4). As for more subjective judgments of court appointees, just as historians have judged presidents, legal scholars have evaluated Supreme Court justices (Table 7-3).

As they climbed dramatically, the growing caseloads of the courts became a major concern in recent decades (Tables 7-7 through 7-10 and Figure 7-3). The Supreme Court has managed to handle a crushing workload by deciding fewer cases by signed opinions (Table 7-7). In the lower federal courts, the workload per judge has risen sharply. The number of cases filed in district courts almost doubled between 1980 and 2004 (although it has backed off slightly since then), but the number of judges increased by only one-third (Table 7-9). The number of appeals filed in the courts of appeals almost tripled over the same period (again, backing off slightly over the past few years), but the number of judgeships rose by less than one-third (Table 7-8).

Considerable information is also available on the nature of judicial work. For example, civil rather than criminal cases have accounted for much of the increased workload (Table 7-10), and they have dealt with a wide range of topics (Table 7-11). Dramatic changes also have occurred in the kinds of cases courts must deal with and in the ways they have responded. The Supreme Court, for one, struck down more federal, state, and local laws on constitutional grounds in the twentieth century than in the nineteenth (Table 7-12). Over the years, however, doctrinal trends changed. For example, beginning in the 1930s the Court rejected far fewer economic regulatory laws and increasingly struck down laws restricting civil liberties (Figure 7-4). All these examples demonstrate that statistics not only play an important role in how the executive and legislative branches undertake their responsibilities, but also are a necessary component of any understanding of the courts and their decisions.

258

Figure 7-1 The U.S. Court System

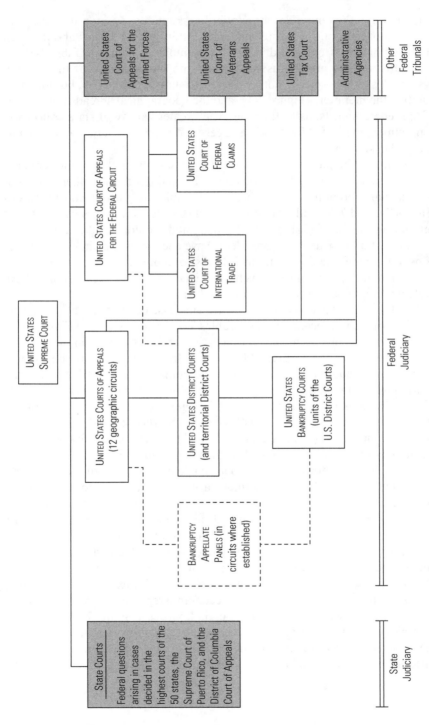

Source: Judicial Conference of the United States, *Long Range Plan for the Federal Courts* (*www.uscourts.gov/lrp/CH05CHRT.PDF*).

Figure 7-2 The Thirteen Federal Judicial Circuits and Ninety-four District Courts

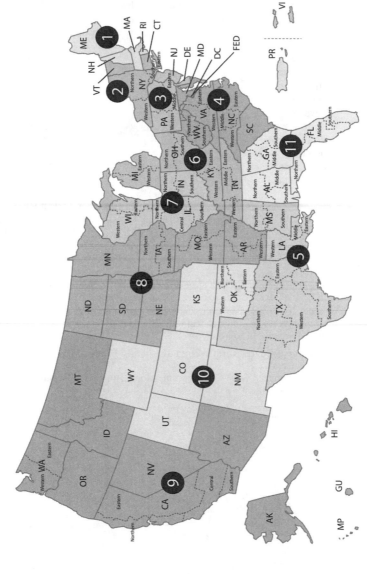

Source: Administrative Office of the United States Courts (*www.uscourts.gov*).

Note: The D.C. Circuit, not shown here, is also a geographic circuit. In addition, there is a Federal Circuit (see Figure 7-1, this volume).

Table 7-1   Principal Methods of Judicial Selection for State Appellate Courts

Partisan election	Nonpartisan election	Legislative appointment	Gubernatorial appointment	Merit plan
Alabama	Arkansas	South Carolina	California	Alaska
Illinois	Georgia	Virginia	Maine	Arizona
Louisiana	Idaho		New Hampshire	Colorado
New Mexico	Kentucky		New Jersey	Connecticut
Ohio	Michigan			Delaware
Pennsylvania	Minnesota			Florida
Texas	Mississippi			Hawaii
West Virginia	Montana			Indiana
	Nevada			Iowa
	North Carolina			Kansas
	North Dakota[a]			Maryland
	Oregon			Massachusetts
	Washington			Missouri
	Wisconsin			Nebraska
				New York[b]
				Oklahoma
				Rhode Island
				South Dakota
				Tennessee
				Utah
				Vermont
				Wyoming

Note: "Merit plan" typically involves appointment by the governor from a list of candidates submitted by an independent or quasi-independent judiciary council or commission. For details on all selection methods, see notes in source.

[a] For North Dakota Supreme Court. North Dakota Temporary Court of Appeals judges are appointed by the Supreme Court.
[b] For New York Court of Appeals. New York Supreme Court Appellate Division judges are selected by gubernatorial appointment.

Source: Council of State Governments, *The Book of the States,* vol. 40 (Lexington, Ky.: Council of State Governments, 2008), 286–288.

Table 7-2 Supreme Court Justices of the United States

Seat number and justice	Party	Home state	Years on Court	Age at nomination	Years of previous judicial experience
Washington appointees					
1 John Jay	Federalist	New York	1789–1795	44	2
2 John Rutledge	Federalist	South Carolina	1789–1791	50	6
3 William Cushing	Federalist	Massachusetts	1789–1810[a]	57	29
4 James Wilson	Federalist	Pennsylvania	1789–1798[a]	47	0
5 John Blair Jr.	Federalist	Virginia	1789–1795	57	11
6 James Iredell	Federalist	North Carolina	1790–1799[a]	38	0.5
2 Thomas Johnson	Federalist	Maryland	1791–1793	59	1.5
2 William Paterson	Federalist	New Jersey	1793–1806[a]	47	0
1 John Rutledge	Federalist	South Carolina	1795	55	6[b]
5 Samuel Chase	Federalist	Maryland	1796–1811[a]	55	8
1 Oliver Ellsworth	Federalist	Connecticut	1796–1800	51	5
J. Adams appointees					
4 Bushrod Washington	Federalist	Virginia	1798–1829[a]	36	0
6 Alfred Moore	Federalist	North Carolina	1799–1804	44	1
1 John Marshall	Federalist	Virginia	1801–1835[a]	45	3
Jefferson appointees					
6 William Johnson	Jeffersonian	South Carolina	1804–1834[a]	32	6
2 H. Brockholst Livingston	Jeffersonian	New York	1806–1823[a]	49	0
7 Thomas Todd	Jeffersonian	Kentucky	1807–1826[a]	42	6
Madison appointees					
5 Gabriel Duvall	Jeffersonian	Maryland	1811–1835	58	6
3 Joseph Story	Jeffersonian	Massachusetts	1811–1845[a]	32	0
Monroe appointee					
2 Smith Thompson	Jeffersonian	New York	1823–1843[a]	55	16
J. Q. Adams appointee					
7 Robert Trimble	Jeffersonian	Kentucky	1826–1828[a]	49	11

(Table continues)

Table 7-2 *(Continued)*

Seat number and justice	Party	Home state	Years on Court	Age at nomination	Years of previous judicial experience
Jackson appointees					
7 John McLean	Democrat	Ohio	1829–1861[a]	44	6
4 Henry Baldwin	Democrat	Pennsylvania	1830–1844[a]	50	0
6 James Wayne	Democrat	Georgia	1835–1867[a]	45	5
1 Roger B. Taney	Democrat	Maryland	1836–1864[a]	59	0
5 Philip P. Barbour	Democrat	Virginia	1836–1841[a]	52	8
Van Buren appointees					
8 John Catron	Democrat	Tennessee	1837–1865[a]	51	10
9 John McKinley	Democrat	Alabama	1837–1852[a]	57	0
5 Peter V. Daniel	Democrat	Virginia	1841–1860[a]	57	0
Tyler appointee					
2 Samuel Nelson	Democrat	New York	1845–1872	52	22
Polk appointees					
3 Levi Woodbury	Democrat	New Hampshire	1845–1851[a]	55	6
4 Robert C. Grier	Democrat	Pennsylvania	1846–1870	52	13
Fillmore appointee					
3 Benjamin R. Curtis	Whig	Massachusetts	1851–1857	41	0
Pierce appointee					
9 John A. Campbell	Democrat	Alabama	1853–1861	41	0
Buchanan appointee					
3 Nathan Clifford	Democrat	Maine	1858–1881[a]	54	0
Lincoln appointees					
7 Noah H. Swayne	Republican	Ohio	1862–1881	57	0
5 Samuel F. Miller	Republican	Iowa	1862–1890[a]	46	0
9 David Davis	Republican	Illinois	1862–1877	47	14
10 Stephen J. Field	Democrat	California	1863–1897	46	6
1 Salmon P. Chase	Republican	Ohio	1864–1873[a]	56	0

Grant appointees					
4 William Strong	Republican	Pennsylvania	1870–1880	61	11
6 Joseph P. Bradley	Republican	New Jersey	1870–1892[a]	56	0
2 Ward Hunt	Republican	New York	1873–1882	62	8
1 Morrison R. Waite	Republican	Ohio	1874–1888[a]	57	0
Hayes appointees					
9 John M. Harlan	Republican	Kentucky	1877–1911[a]	44	1
4 William B. Woods	Republican	Georgia	1880–1887[a]	56	12
Garfield appointee					
7 Stanley Matthews	Republican	Ohio	1881–1889[a]	56	4
Arthur appointees					
3 Horace Gray	Republican	Massachusetts	1881–1902	53	18
2 Samuel Blatchford	Republican	New York	1882–1893[a]	62	15
Cleveland appointees (first term)					
4 Lucius Q. C. Lamar	Democrat	Mississippi	1888–1893[a]	62	0
1 Melville W. Fuller	Democrat	Illinois	1888–1910[a]	55	0
Harrison appointees					
7 David J. Brewer	Republican	Kansas	1889–1910[a]	52	19
5 Henry B. Brown	Republican	Michigan	1891–1906	54	16
6 George Shiras Jr.	Republican	Pennsylvania	1892–1903	60	0
4 Howell E. Jackson	Democrat	Tennessee	1893–1895[a]	60	7
Cleveland appointees (second term)					
2 Edward D. White	Democrat	Louisiana	1894–1910[a]	48	1.5
4 Rufus W. Peckham	Democrat	New York	1895–1909[a]	57	9
McKinley appointee					
8 Joseph McKenna	Republican	California	1898–1925	54	5
T. Roosevelt appointees					
3 Oliver W. Holmes	Republican	Massachusetts	1902–1932	61	20

(Table continues)

Table 7-2 *(Continued)*

Seat number and justice	Party	Home state	Years on Court	Age at nomination	Years of previous judicial experience
6 William R. Day	Republican	Ohio	1903–1922	53	7
5 William H. Moody	Republican	Massachusetts	1906–1910	52	0
Taft appointees					
4 Horace H. Lurton	Democrat	Tennessee	1909–1914[a]	65	26
7 Charles E. Hughes	Republican	New York	1910–1916	48	0
1 Edward D. White	Democrat	Louisiana	1910–1921[a]	65	1.5[b]
2 Willis Van Devanter	Republican	Wyoming	1910–1937	51	8
5 Joseph R. Lamar	Democrat	Georgia	1910–1916[a]	53	2
9 Mahlon Pitney	Republican	New Jersey	1912–1922	54	11
Wilson appointees					
4 James C. McReynolds	Democrat	Tennessee	1914–1941	52	0
5 Louis D. Brandeis	Republican	Massachusetts	1916–1939	59	0
7 John H. Clarke	Democrat	Ohio	1916–1922	59	2
Harding appointees					
1 William H. Taft	Republican	Ohio	1921–1930	63	13
7 George Sutherland	Republican	Utah	1922–1938	60	0
6 Pierce Butler	Democrat	Minnesota	1923–1939[a]	56	0
9 Edward T. Sanford	Republican	Tennessee	1923–1930[a]	57	14
Coolidge appointee					
8 Harlan Fiske Stone	Republican	New York	1925–1941	52	0
Hoover appointees					
1 Charles E. Hughes	Republican	New York	1930–1941	67	0
9 Owens J. Roberts	Republican	Pennsylvania	1930–1945	55	0
3 Benjamin N. Cardozo	Democrat	New York	1932–1938[a]	61	18
F. Roosevelt appointees					
2 Hugo L. Black	Democrat	Alabama	1937–1971[a]	51	1.5
7 Stanley F. Reed	Democrat	Kentucky	1938–1957	53	0

3 Felix Frankfurter	Independent	Massachusetts	1939–1962	56	0
5 William O. Douglas	Democrat	Connecticut	1939–1975	40	0
6 Frank Murphy	Democrat	Michigan	1940–1949[a]	49	7
4 James F. Byrnes	Democrat	South Carolina	1941–1942	62	0
1 Harlan Fiske Stone	Republican	New York	1941–1946[a]	68	0[b]
8 Robert H. Jackson	Democrat	New York	1941–1954[a]	49	0
4 Wiley B. Rutledge	Democrat	Iowa	1943–1949[a]	48	4
Truman appointees					
9 Harold H. Burton	Republican	Ohio	1945–1958	57	0
1 Fred M. Vinson	Democrat	Kentucky	1946–1953[a]	56	5
6 Tom C. Clark	Democrat	Texas	1949–1967	49	0
4 Sherman Minton	Democrat	Indiana	1949–1956	58	8
Eisenhower appointees					
1 Earl Warren	Republican	California	1953–1969	62	0
8 John M. Harlan	Republican	New York	1955–1971	55	1
4 William J. Brennan	Democrat	New Jersey	1956–1990	50	7
7 Charles E. Whittaker	Republican	Missouri	1957–1962	56	3
9 Potter Stewart	Republican	Ohio	1958–1981	43	4
Kennedy appointees					
7 Byron R. White	Democrat	Colorado	1962–1993	44	0
3 Arthur J. Goldberg	Democrat	Illinois	1962–1965	54	0
L. Johnson appointees					
3 Abe Fortas	Democrat	Tennessee	1965–1969	55	0
6 Thurgood Marshall	Democrat	New York	1967–1991	59	4
Nixon appointees					
1 Warren E. Burger	Republican	Minnesota	1969–1986	61	13
3 Harry A. Blackmun	Republican	Minnesota	1970–1994	61	11
2 Lewis F. Powell Jr.	Democrat	Virginia	1971–1987	64	0
8 William H. Rehnquist	Republican	Arizona	1971–1986	47	0

(Table continues)

Table 7-2 *(Continued)*

Seat number and justice	Party	Home state	Years on Court	Age at nomination	Years of previous judicial experience
Ford appointee					
5 John Paul Stevens	Republican	Illinois	1976–	55	5
Reagan appointees					
9 Sandra Day O'Connor	Republican	Arizona	1981–2006	51	6.5
1 William H. Rehnquist	Republican	Arizona	1986–2005[a]	61	0[b]
8 Antonin Scalia	Republican	Illinois	1986–	50	4
2 Anthony M. Kennedy	Republican	California	1988–	51	12
G. H. W. Bush appointees					
4 David H. Souter	Republican	New Hampshire	1990–2009	50	13
6 Clarence Thomas	Republican	Georgia	1991–	43	1
Clinton appointees					
7 Ruth Bader Ginsburg	Democrat	New York	1993–	60	13
3 Stephen G. Breyer	Democrat	Massachusetts	1994–	55	15
G. W. Bush appointees					
1 John G. Roberts Jr.	Republican	Maryland	2005–	50	2
9 Samuel A. Alito Jr.	Republican	New Jersey	2006–	55	15
Obama appointee					
4 Sonia Sotomayor[c]	Democrat	New York	2009–	54	18

Note: Seat number 1 is always held by the chief justice of the United States.

[a] Died in office.

[b] Prior to appointment to associate justice.

[c] Nominated to the position on May 26, 2009.

Sources: Sheldon Goldman, *Constitutional Law: Cases and Essays* (New York: Harper and Row, 1987); previous judicial experience: Henry J. Abraham, *Justices and Presidents: Appointments to the Supreme Court,* 2nd ed. (New York: Oxford University Press, 1985), 56–58 (copyright © Henry J. Abraham, 1974, 1985, reprinted by permission of Oxford University Press Inc.); *Congressional Quarterly's Guide to Congress,* 2nd ed. (Washington, D.C.: Congressional Quarterly, 1982), 786–788; updated by the editors.

Table 7-3 Ratings of Supreme Court Justices

Great dissenters		Lists of "great" justices									Blaustein and Mersky (1978) ratings of all justices					
Zobell (1959)	CQ (1990)	Frankfurter (1957)	Hughes (1928)	Pound (1938)	Frank (1958)	Nagel (1970)	Currie (1964)	Schwartz (1979)	Asch (1971)	Bradley (1993)	*Great*	*Near great*	*Average*		*Below average*	*Failure*
W. Johnson	W. Johnson	J. Marshall	J. Marshall	J. Marshall	J. Marshall	J. Marshall	J. Marshall	J. Marshall	Jay	J. Marshall	J. Marshall	W. Johnson	McKinley	Shiras	T. Johnson	Van Devanter
Curtis	Curtis	W. Johnson	Story	Story	W. Johnson	W. Johnson	W. Johnson	Story	J. Marshall		Story	Curtis	Daniel	Peckham	Moore	McReynolds
Harlan I	Harlan I	Story	Curtis	Holmes	Story	Story	Story	Holmes	Taney		Taney	Miller	Nelson	McKenna	Trimble	Butler
Holmes	Holmes	Taney	Miller	Cardozo	McLean	Holmes	Taney	Cardozo	Miller		Harlan I	Field	Woodbury	Day	Barbour	Byrnes
	Brandeis	Curtis	Field		Taney	Cardozo	Miller	Black	Harlan I		Holmes	Bradley	Grier	Moody	Woods	Burton
	Cardozo	Campbell			Curtis		Bradley	Warren	Holmes		Hughes	Waite	Campbell	Lurton	H. E. Jackson	Vinson
	Stone	Miller			Campbell		Harlan I		Brandeis		Brandeis	E. D. White	Clifford	J. R. Lamar		Minton
	Frankfurter	Field			Gray		Brewer		Hughes		Stone	Taft	Swayne	Pitney		Whittaker
	Brennan	Bradley			Brewer		Holmes		Stone		Cardozo	Sutherland	Davis	J. H. Clarke		
	T. Marshall	Matthews			Holmes		Moody		Cardozo		Black	Douglas	S. P. Chase	Sanford		
							Hughes		Frankfurter		Frankfurter	R. H. Jackson	Strong	Roberts		
							Brandeis		R. H. Jackson		Warren	W. B. Rutledge	Hunt	Reed		
									Black				Duvall	Matthews		
									Douglas				Thompson	Gray		
									Warren				McLean	Blatchford		
													Brewer	Baldwin		
													B. R. White	Wayne		
													Goldberg	Catron		
													T. Marshall	Brown		
													Jay	Livingston		
													J. Rutledge	Todd		
													Cushing	Murphy		
													Wilson	T. C. Clark		
													Blair	Stewart		
													Iredell	L. Q. C. Lamar		
													Paterson	Fuller		

(Table continues)

Table 7-3 (Continued)

Great dissenters	Lists of "great" justices		Blaustein and Mersky (1978) ratings of all justices	
E. White	Cardozo	Holmes	Harlan II	S. Chase
Holmes	Black	Warren	Brennan	Ellsworth
Moody	Frankfurter	Brandeis	Fortas	Washington
Hughes	Douglas	Brennan		
Brandeis	R. H. Jackson	Black		
Cardozo	Warren	Harlan I		
		Douglas		
		Frankfurter		
		Cardozo		

Note: Blaustein and Mersky's ratings reflect evaluations by sixty-five law school deans and professors of law, history, and political science with expertise in the judicial process. Bradley's ratings reflect evaluations by ninety-six scholars (mostly political scientists) with expertise in the judicial process. Other ratings reflect the views of the individual compiler. State judges, not shown above, were included in the lists by Pound (Kent, Gibson, Shaw, Ruffin, Cooley, and Doe) and Schwartz (Kent, Shaw, Vanderbilt, and Traynor). For more details, see the sources.

Sources: Albert P. Blaustein and Roy M. Mersky, *The First One Hundred Justices: Statistical Studies on the Supreme Court of the United States* (Hamden, Conn.: Shoe String Press, Archon Books, 1978), 37–40; Robert C. Bradley, "Who Are the Great Justices and What Criteria Did They Meet?" in *Great Justices of the U.S. Supreme Court,* ed. William D. Pederson and Normal W. Provizer (New York: Peter Lang, 1993), 1–32.

Table 7-4   Supreme Court Nominations That Failed

Nominee	Date nomination received in Senate[a]	President	Action
William Paterson[b]	1793	Washington	withdrawn
John Rutledge[c]	1795	Washington	rejected, 10–14
Alexander Wolcott	1811	Madison	rejected, 9–24
John J. Crittenden	1828	J. Q. Adams	postponed
Roger B. Taney[b]	1835	Jackson	postponed
John C. Spencer	1844	Tyler	rejected, 21–26
Reuben H. Walworth	1844	Tyler	withdrawn
Edward King	1844	Tyler	tabled, 29–18
John C. Spencer	1844	Tyler	withdrawn
Reuben H. Walworth	1844	Tyler	motion to consider objected to
Reuben H. Walworth	1844	Tyler	withdrawn
Edward King	1844	Tyler	withdrawn
John M. Read	1845	Tyler	motion to consider unsuccessful
George W. Woodward	1845	Polk	rejected, 20–29
Edward A. Bradford	1852	Fillmore	tabled
George E. Badger	1853	Fillmore	postponed, 26–25
William C. Micou	1853	Fillmore	discharged
Jeremiah S. Black	1861	Buchanan	motions to consider unsuccessful
Henry Stanbery	1866	A. Johnson	no record of action
Ebenezer R. Hoar	1869	Grant	rejected, 24–33
George H. Williams[c]	1873	Grant	withdrawn
Caleb Cushing[c]	1874	Grant	withdrawn
Stanley Matthews[b]	1881	Hayes	postponed
William B. Hornblower	1893	Cleveland	no record of action
William B. Hornblower	1893	Cleveland	rejected, 24–30
Wheeler H. Peckham	1894	Cleveland	rejected, 32–41
Pierce Butler[b]	1922	Harding	no record of action
John J. Parker	1930	Hoover	rejected, 39–41
John Marshall Harlan II[b]	1954	Eisenhower	no record of action
Abe Fortas[c]	1968	L. Johnson	withdrawn
Homer Thornberry	1968	L. Johnson	not acted on
Clement F. Haynsworth Jr.	1969	Nixon	rejected, 45–55
G. Harrold Carswell	1970	Nixon	rejected, 45–51
Robert H. Bork	1987	Reagan	rejected, 42–58
Harriet Miers	2005	G. W. Bush	withdrawn

Note: Seven individuals were confirmed but declined to serve: Robert H. Harrison, 1789; William Cushing, 1796; John Jay, 1800; Levi Lincoln, 1811; John Quincy Adams, 1811; William Smith, 1837; Roscoe Conkling, 1882. One person, Edwin Stanton (1869), was confirmed but died before he could take his seat. In 1987 the nomination of Douglas Ginsburg was publicly announced by President Ronald Reagan but was withdrawn before the president formally submitted his nomination to the Senate.

[a] The date of the president's nomination and the date the nomination is received in the Senate are often, but not always, the same.

[b] Later nominated and confirmed (Taney as chief justice). See Table 7-2, this volume.

[c] For chief justice.

Sources: Henry B. Hogue, "Supreme Court Nominations Not Confirmed, 1789–2004," Congressional Research Service Report for Congress *(www.fas.org/sgp/crs/misc/RL31171.pdf)*; Richard S. Beth and Betsy Palmer, "Supreme Court Nominations: Senate Floor Procedure and Practice, 1789–2005" *(www.opencrs .com/rpts/RL33247_20060124.pdf)*.

Table 7-5 Characteristics of Federal District and Appellate Court Appointees, Presidents Lyndon B. Johnson to George W. Bush (percent)

	L. Johnson appointees	Nixon appointees	Ford appointees	Carter appointees	Reagan appointees	G. H. W. Bush appointees	Clinton appointees	G. W. Bush appointees
District courts								
Occupation								
Politics/government	21.3	10.6	21.2	5.0	13.4	10.8	11.5	13.4
Judiciary	31.1	28.5	34.6	44.6	36.9	41.9	48.2	48.3
Large law firm[a]	2.5	11.2	9.6	13.9	17.9	25.7	16.1	18.8
Moderate law firm[a]	18.9	27.9	25.0	19.3	19.0	14.9	13.4	10.0
Small/solo law firm[a]	23.0	19.0	9.6	13.9	10.0	4.7	8.2	6.2
Other	3.3	2.8	0.0	3.5	2.8	2.0	2.6	3.4
Experience								
Judicial	34.4	35.2	42.3	54.0	46.2	46.6	52.1	52.1
Prosecutorial	45.9	41.9	50.0	38.1	44.1	39.2	41.3	47.1
Neither	33.6	36.3	30.8	31.2	28.6	31.8	28.9	24.9
Political affiliation								
Democrat	94.3	7.3	21.2	91.1	4.8	6.1	87.5	8.0
Republican	5.7	92.7	78.8	4.5	91.7	88.5	6.2	83.1
Independent or other	0.0	0.0	0.0	4.5	3.4	5.4	5.9	8.8
Past party activism	49.2	48.6	50.0	61.4	60.3	64.2	50.2	52.5
Religion								
Protestant	58.2	73.2	73.1	60.4	60.3	64.2	—	—
Catholic	31.1	18.4	17.3	27.7	30.0	28.4	—	—
Jewish	10.7	8.4	9.6	11.9	9.3	7.4	—	—
Race/ethnicity								
White	93.4	95.5	88.5	78.2	92.4	89.2	75.1	81.6
Black	4.1	3.4	5.8	13.9	2.1	6.8	17.4	6.9
Asian American	0.0	0.0	3.9	0.5	0.7	0.0	1.3	1.5

Hispanic	2.5	1.1	1.9	6.9	4.8	4.0	5.9	10.0
Native American	—	—	—	0.5	—	—	0.3	0.0
Sex								
Women	1.6	0.6	1.9	14.4	19.6	19.6	28.5	20.7
Number of appointees	122	179	52	202	290	148	305	261
Courts of appeals								
Occupation								
Politics/government	10.0	4.4	8.3	5.4	6.4	10.8	6.6	18.6
Judiciary	57.5	53.3	75.0	46.4	55.1	59.5	52.5	49.1
Large law firm[a]	5.0	4.4	8.3	10.7	14.1	16.2	18.0	11.9
Moderate law firm[a]	17.5	22.2	8.3	16.1	9.0	10.8	13.1	6.8
Small/solo law firm[a]	7.5	6.7	0.0	5.4	1.3	0.0	1.6	3.4
Other	2.5	8.9	0.0	16.1	14.1	2.7	8.2	10.2
Experience								
Judicial	65.0	57.8	75.0	53.6	60.3	62.2	59.0	61.0
Prosecutorial	47.5	46.7	25.0	30.4	28.2	29.7	37.7	33.9
Neither	20.0	17.8	25.0	39.3	34.6	32.4	29.5	25.4
Political affiliation								
Democrat	95.0	6.7	8.3	82.1	0.0	2.7	85.2	6.8
Republican	5.0	93.3	91.7	7.1	96.2	89.2	6.6	91.5
Independent or other	0.0	0.0	0.0	10.7	3.8	8.1	2.9	1.7
Past party activism	57.5	60.0	58.3	73.2	66.7	70.3	54.1	67.8
Religion								
Protestant	60.0	75.6	58.3	60.7	55.1	59.4	—	—
Catholic	25.0	15.6	33.3	23.2	30.8	24.3	—	—
Jewish	15.0	8.9	8.3	16.1	14.1	16.3	—	—

(Table continues)

Table 7-5 (Continued)

	L. Johnson appointees	Nixon appointees	Ford appointees	Carter appointees	Reagan appointees	G. H. W. Bush appointees	Clinton appointees	G. W. Bush appointees
Race/ethnicity								
White	95.0	97.8	100.0	78.6	97.4	89.2	73.8	84.7
Black	5.0	0.0	0.0	16.1	1.3	5.4	13.1	10.2
Asian American	0.0	2.2	0.0	1.8	0.0	0.0	1.6	0.0
Hispanic	0.0	0.0	0.0	3.6	1.3	5.4	11.5	5.1
Sex								
Women	2.5	0.0	0.0	19.6	5.1	18.9	32.8	25.4
Number of appointees	40	45	12	56	78	37	61	59

Note: "—" indicates not available.

[a] Large law firm: twenty-five or more partners and associates; moderate: five to twenty-four; small: two to four.

Sources: Sheldon Goldman, "Bush's Judicial Legacy: The Final Imprint," *Judicature 76* (April–May 1993): 287, 293; Sheldon Goldman, *Picking Federal Judges: Lower Court Selection from Roosevelt through Reagan* (New Haven, Conn.: Yale University Press, 1997); Sheldon Goldman, Elliot Slotnick, Gerard Gryski, and Sara Schiavoni, "W. Bush's Judiciary: The First Term Record," *Judicature 88* (May–June 2005); Sheldon Goldman, Elliot Slotnick, Gerard Gryski, and Sara Schiavoni, "Picking Judges in a Time of Turmoil: W. Bush's Judiciary During the 109th Congress," *Judicature 90* (May–June 2007); Sheldon Goldman, Sara Schiavoni, and Elliot Slotnick, "W. Bush's Judicial Legacy: Mission Accomplished," *Judicature 92* (May–June 2009).

Table 7-6   Federal Judicial Appointments of Same Party as President,
Presidents Grover Cleveland to George W. Bush

President	Party	Percentage
Cleveland	Democratic	97.3
Harrison	Republican	87.9
McKinley	Republican	95.7
T. Roosevelt	Republican	95.8
Taft	Republican	82.2
Wilson	Democratic	98.6
Harding	Republican	97.7
Coolidge	Republican	94.1
Hoover	Republican	85.7
F. Roosevelt	Democratic	96.4
Truman	Democratic	93.1
Eisenhower	Republican	95.1
Kennedy	Democratic	90.9
L. Johnson	Democratic	94.5
Nixon	Republican	92.8
Ford	Republican	81.2
Carter	Democratic	89.1
Reagan	Republican	92.7
G. H. W. Bush	Republican	88.6
Clinton	Democratic	87.2
G. W. Bush	Republican	86.0

Sources: Cleveland–Kennedy: Henry J. Abraham, *Justices and Presidents: Appointments to the Supreme Court,* 3rd ed. (New York: Oxford University Press, 1991), 68 (copyright © Henry J. Abraham, 1974, 1985, 1991, reprinted by permission of Oxford University Press, Inc.); L. Johnson–G. W. Bush: calculated from Table 7-5, this volume.

Figure 7-3   Cases Filed in U.S. Supreme Court, 1880–2007 Terms

Number of cases

Note: Number of cases filed in term starting in year indicated.

Sources: 1880–2004: Lee Epstein, Jeffrey A. Segal, Harold J. Spaeth, and Thomas G. Walker, *The Supreme Court Compendium: Data, Decisions, and Developments*, 4th ed. (Washington, D.C.: CQ Press, 2007), 62–67; 2005–2007: "2006 Year-End Report on the Federal Judiciary," January 1, 2007; "2008," December 31, 2008 (*www.supremecourtus.gov*).

Table 7-7 Caseload of the U.S. Supreme Court, 1970–2007 Terms

Action	1970	1975	1980	1985	1990	1995	2000	2001	2002	2003	2004	2005	2006	2007
Appellate cases on docket	1,903	2,352	2,749	2,571	2,351	2,456	2,305	2,210	2,190	2,058	2,041	2,025	2,069	1,969
From prior term	325	431	527	400	365	361	351	324	321	336	300	354	346	385
Docketed during present term	1,578	1,921	2,222	2,171	1,986	2,095	1,954	1,886	1,869	1,722	1,741	1,671	1,723	1,614
Cases acted upon[a]	1,613	1,900	2,324	2,185	2,042	2,130	2,024	1,932	1,899	1,798	1,727	1,703	1,736	—
Granted review	214	244	167	166	114	92	85	82	83	74	69	63	62	85
Denied, dismissed, or withdrawn	1,285	1,538	1,999	1,863	1,802	1,945	1,842	1,751	1,727	1,641	1,529	1,554	1,611	—
Summarily decided	114	118	90	78	81	62	63	57	46	37	89	46	39	—
Cases not acted upon	290	452	425	386	309	326	281	278	291	260	314	322	333	—
Pauper cases on docket	2,289	2,395	2,371	2,577	3,951	5,098	6,651	6,958	7,209	6,818	6,543	7,575	8,181	7,628
Cases acted upon[a]	1,802	1,997	2,027	2,189	3,436	4,514	5,736	6,139	6,488	6,036	5,815	6,533	7,186	—
Granted review	41	28	17	20	27	13	14	6	8	13	11	15	15	10
Denied, dismissed, or withdrawn	1,683	1,903	1,968	2,136	3,369	4,439	5,658	6,114	6,459	6,005	5,061	6,459	6,925	—
Summarily decided	78	66	32	24	28	55	61	13	17	13	737	58	239	—
Cases not acted upon	487	398	344	388	515	584	915	819	721	782	728	1,042	995	—
Original cases on docket	20	14	24	10	14	11	9	8	7	6	4	8	6	5
Cases disposed of during term	7	7	7	2	3	5	1	1	1	2	0	4	1	1
Total cases available for argument	267	280	264	276	201	145	138	137	139	140	128	122	108	—
Cases disposed of	160	181	162	175	131	93	89	90	87	93	87	88	80	—
Cases argued	151	179	154	171	125	90	86	88	84	91	87	90	78	75
Cases dismissed or remanded without argument	9	2	8	4	6	3	3	2	3	2	0	1	2	3
Cases remaining	107	99	102	101	70	52	49	47	40	47	41	31	28	47

(Table continues)

Table 7-7 *(Continued)*

Action	1970	1975	1980	1985	1990	1995	2000	2001	2002	2003	2004	2005	2006	2007
Cases decided by signed opinion	126	160	144	161	121	87	83	85	79	89	85	82	74	72
Cases decided per curiam opinion	22	16	8	10	4	3	4	3	5	2	2	5	4	2
Number of signed opinions	109	138	123	146	112	75	77	76	71	73	74	69	67	67
Total cases on docket	4,212	4,761	5,144	5,158	6,316	7,565	8,965	9,176	9,406	8,882	8,588	9,608	10,256	9,602

Note: "—" indicates not available. The Supreme Court begins its regular annual session on the first Monday in October. This session, known as the October term, lasts about nine months. The year shown indicates when the term began. These data were previously provided by the Supreme Court in its unpublished statistical sheets. Beginning with the 2007 term, the Court no longer provides these statistical sheets to the public. Data for additional years can be found in previous editions of *Vital Statistics on American Politics*.

[a] For 1980 and later, includes cases granted review and carried over to next term, not shown separately.

Sources: 1970–1980: U.S. Bureau of the Census, *Statistical Abstract of the United States, 1977* (Washington, D.C.: Government Printing Office, 1976), 184; 1987, 168; 1985–2006: reprinted with permission from *The United States Law Week* (Washington, D.C.: Bureau of National Affairs), vol. 56, 3102; vol. 61, 3098; vol. 65, 3100; vol. 69, 3134; vol. 71, 3080; vol. 73, 3044; vol. 74, 3076; vol. 75, 3016; vol. 76, 3016 (copyright © Bureau of National Affairs); U.S. Supreme Court, "Statistics as of June 27, 2008," J. Sup. Ct. U.S. October Term 2007, ii (*www.supremecourtus.gov/orders/journal.html*).

Table 7-8 Caseload of U.S. Courts of Appeals, 1980–2008

	1980	1985	1990	1995	2000	2005	2006	2007	2008
Number of judgeships	132	156	156	167	167	167	167	167	166
Number of sitting senior judges	42	45	60	80	81	90	89	86	89
Number of vacant judgeship months	217.1	275.0	153.3	185.5	278.9	165.6	178.7	179.9	146.9
Appeals filed									
Prisoner	3,704	6,532	10,019	14,985	17,252	17,034	16,776	15,472	16,853
All other civil	12,141	18,660	18,631	21,630	23,501	21,666	21,494	19,389	19,001
Criminal	4,405	4,989	9,655	10,162	10,707	16,060	15,246	13,167	13,667
Administrative	2,950	3,179	2,553	3,295	3,237	13,713	13,102	10,382	11,583
Total	23,200	33,360	40,858	50,072	54,697	68,473	66,618	58,410	61,104
Appeals terminated									
Consolidations and cross appeals	2,704	2,669	3,839	3,177	2,740	2,317	2,356	2,374	2,327
Procedural	6,170	12,349	14,008	18,856	26,256	29,745	30,646	28,755	27,161
On the merits									
Prisoner	2,267	2,835	4,988	7,242	5,328	4,435	4,277	4,068	4,025
All other civil	5,861	9,208	9,563	11,293	13,497	12,443	12,881	11,190	10,485
Criminal	2,718	3,070	5,223	7,652	7,236	8,614	10,990	10,393	9,731
Administrative	1,167	1,256	1,169	1,585	1,455	4,421	6,432	6,066	5,367
Total on the merits	12,013	16,369	20,943	27,772	27,516	29,913	34,580	31,717	29,608
Total	20,887	31,387	38,790	49,805	56,512	61,975	67,582	62,846	59,096
Pending appeals	20,252	24,758	32,299	37,536	40,410	57,724	56,486	51,742	53,071
Per active judge[a]									
Termination on the merits	227	308	367	449	458	457	539	481	448
Procedural terminations	—	103	99	109	168	170	172	168	156

Note: "—" indicates not available. Data for additional years can be found in previous editions of *Vital Statistics on American Politics.*

[a] Includes only judges active during the entire twelve-month period.

Sources: 1980, 1985: Director of the Administrative Office of the United States Courts, *Federal Court Management Statistics 1985* (Washington, D.C.: Government Printing Office, 1985), 29–30; 1990: *1991,* 27–31; 1995: *1996;* 2000: *2001,* 31; 2005–2008: Administrative Office of the United States Courts (*www.uscourts.gov*).

Table 7-9 Caseload of U.S. District Courts, 1980–2008

	1980	1985	1990	1995	2000	2005	2006	2007	2008
Overall									
Filings	188,487	299,164	251,166	281,681	310,346	330,721	335,868	335,655	349,969
Terminations	180,245	293,545	245,014	259,336	306,211	347,196	350,807	317,277	317,056
Pending	199,019	272,636	273,301	268,197	290,167	323,914	309,006	324,673	358,303
Number (and percentage) of civil cases over three years old	20,592	16,726	25,672	13,538	30,434	39,600	27,574	17,446	21,820
	11.7	6.6	10.6	5.6	12.2	14.9	11.1	6.6	7.3
Number of judgeships	516	575	575	649	655	678	678	678	678
Vacant judgeship months	956.2	895.8	540.1	642.0	597.5	309.2	399.3	424.7	397.9
Per judgeship									
Civil filings	327	476	381	383	396	374	383	380	394
Criminal felony filings	38	44	56	51	78	87	84	85	91
Total filings	365	520	437	434	474	488[a]	495[a]	495[a]	516[a]
Pending cases	386	474	475	413	443	478	456	479	528
Terminations	349	511	426	400	467	512	517	468	468
Trials completed	38	36	35	27	22	19	19	20	20
Median time from filing to disposition (months)									
Criminal felony	3.7	3.7	5.4	6.6	6.5	7.3	7.6	7.6	7.3
Civil	8.0	7.0	9.0	8.0	8.2	9.5	8.3	8.6	8.1
Median time from filing to trial (months)									
Civil only[b]	15	14	14	18	20	23	23	25	25

Note: Data for additional years can be found in previous editions of *Vital Statistics on American Politics*.

[a] Includes a number of "supervised release hearings."

[b] Time is computed from the date that the answer or response is filed to the date trial begins.

Sources: 1980, 1985: Director of the Administrative Office of the United States Courts, *Federal Court Management Statistics 1985* (Washington, D.C.: Government Printing Office, 1985); 1990: *1993*; 1995: *1996*; 2000: *2001*; 2005–2008: Administrative Office of the United States Courts (*www.uscourts.gov*).

Table 7-10 Civil and Criminal Cases Filed in U.S. District Courts, 1950–2008

Year	Civil cases		Criminal cases	
	Commenced	Terminated	Commenced	Terminated
1950	44,454	42,482	36,383	37,675
1955	48,308	47,959	35,310	38,990
1960	49,852	48,847	28,137	30,512
1965	67,678	63,137	31,569	33,718
1970	87,321	79,466	38,102	36,356
1975	117,320	103,787	41,108	49,212
1980	168,789	160,481	28,932	29,297
1981	180,576	177,975	31,328	30,221
1982	206,193	189,473	32,682	31,889
1983	241,842	215,356	35,913	33,985
1984	261,485	243,113	36,845	35,494
1985	273,670	269,848	39,500	37,139
1986	254,828	266,765	41,490	39,328
1987	239,185	238,001	43,292	42,287
1988	239,634	238,753	44,585	42,115
1989	233,529	235,219	45,995	42,810
1990	217,879	213,922	48,904	44,295
1991	207,742	211,713	47,035	41,569
1992	230,509	231,304	48,356	44,147
1993	230,597	227,316	46,098	45,280
1994	238,590	227,015	45,269	44,924
1995	248,335	229,820	45,788	41,527
1996	269,132	250,387	47,889	45,499
1997	272,027	249,641	50,363	46,887
1998	256,787	262,301	57,691	51,428
1999	260,271	272,526	59,923	56,511
2000	259,517	259,637	62,745	58,102
2001	250,907	248,174	62,708	58,718
2002	274,841	259,537	67,000	60,991
2003	252,962	253,015	70,642	65,628
2004	281,338	252,761	71,022	64,621
2005	253,273	271,753	69,575	66,561
2006	259,541	273,193	66,860	67,499
2007	257,507	239,678	68,413	67,851
2008	267,257	234,571	70,896	70,629

Note: Data are for the twelve-month period ending on September 30 of the year shown.

Sources: 1950–1975: U.S. Bureau of the Census, *Statistical Abstract of the United States, 1971* (Washington, D.C.: Government Printing Office, 1971), 152; *1976,* 168; 1980–2006: Director of the Administrative Office of the United States Courts, *Annual Report of the Director of the Administrative Office of the United States Courts, Judicial Business of the United States Courts 1987* (Washington, D.C.: Government Printing Office, 1987), 7, 13; 1989, 7, 12; 1991, 7, 10; 1992, 4, 6; 1994; 1996; 1998, 16; 1999, 16; 2001–2008, tables C, D (*www.uscourts.gov*).

Table 7-11   Types of Civil and Criminal Cases in U.S. District Courts, 2008

Civil cases	Percentage	Criminal cases	Percentage
Contract actions	12.8	Drug offenses	22.4
Recovery of overpayments and	(1.3)	Immigration	30.3
enforcements of judgments		Fraud	11.0
Insurance	(4.8)	Traffic offenses	5.7
Other contract actions	(6.7)	Firearms and explosives	11.4
Tort actions	26.9[a]	Larceny and theft	3.9
Personal injury, not	(6.0)	Homicide, robbery, assault,	2.6
product liability		and burglary	
Product liability,	(19.5)	Embezzlement	0.9
personal injury		Forgery and counterfeiting	1.0
Personal property damage	(1.5)	Escape, aiding and abetting,	1.0
Statutory actions	58.3	and failure to appear	
Prisoner petitions	(20.5)	All other	9.8
Civil rights	(12.0)		
Labor laws	(6.3)	Total number of	
Social Security	(4.9)	criminal cases	70,429
Protected property rights	(3.6)		
Bankruptcy	(0.9)		
Tax suits	(0.5)		
Other statutory	(9.6)		
Real property actions	1.9		
Total number of	267,257		
civil cases			

Note: Data are for the twelve-month period ending on September 30, 2008. Data for earlier years can be found in previous editions of *Vital Statistics on American Politics*. Categories have changed slightly over the years.

[a] Due to rounding, the categories shown do not sum to 26.9.

Source: Director of the Administrative Office of the United States Courts, *Annual Report of the Director of the Administrative Office of the United States Courts, Judicial Business of the United States Courts 2008* (Washington, D.C.: Government Printing Office, 2009), tables C-2 A, D-2 (*www.uscourts.gov*).

Table 7-12 Federal, State, and Local Laws Declared Unconstitutional by
U.S. Supreme Court, by Decade, 1789–2008

Years	Federal	State and local
1789–1799	0	0
1800–1809	1	1
1810–1819	0	7
1820–1829	0	8
1830–1839	0	3
1840–1849	0	10
1850–1859	1	7
1860–1869	4	24
1870–1879	7	36
1880–1889	4	46
1890–1899	5	36
1900–1909	9	40
1910–1919	6	119
1920–1929	15	139
1930–1939	13	92
1940–1949	2	61
1950–1959	5	66
1960–1969	16	151
1970–1979	20	195
1980–1989	16	164
1990–1999	23	62
2000–2008	14	34
Total	161	1,301

Note: Counts have changed since the previous edition of this volume because the Congressional Research Service reevaluated the cases. For details, see the source and the sources cited therein.

Source: Lawrence Baum, *The Supreme Court,* 10th ed. (Washington, D.C.: CQ Press, 2010); Lawrence Baum, Department of Political Science, Ohio State University, personal communication.

Figure 7-4   Economic and Civil Liberties Laws Overturned by U.S. Supreme Court, by Decade, 1900–2008

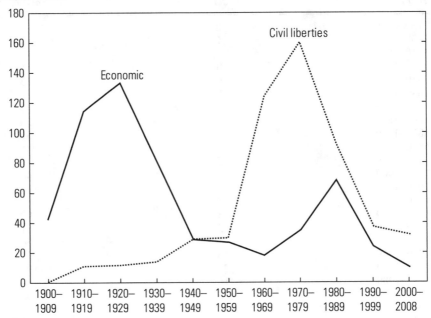

Note: Civil liberties category does not include laws supportive of civil liberties. Laws include federal, state, and local. State and local cases include those in which the Court held that a state law was preempted by federal law.

Source: Lawrence Baum, Department of Political Science, Ohio State University, personal communication.

8
Federalism

- **Historical Data**
- **State Constitutional Provisions**
- **States and the Federal Constitution**
- **State and Local Governments and Employees**
- **Revenues and Spending**
- **Personal Income**
- **Intergovernmental Revenue Flows**
- **State Government Performance**

From a statistical point of view, a major problem in studying American government below the federal level is the fifty state governments and thousands of local government units that operate there (Table 8-7). Among other things, this large number of governments often makes it difficult for researchers to procure accurate, up-to-date information about all the relevant jurisdictions. Even for state-level data, a researcher often must turn to each of the fifty state capitals, or to fifty-one units if data about the District of Columbia are needed, or even more if Puerto Rico and areas such as the Northern Mariana Islands are included, which might be necessary to study delegates to the national party conventions. If a researcher's interest is in counties, cities, school districts, and the like, the data collection task can be enormous—well beyond the capacity of one person.

Fortunately, organizations and publications devoted to data collection have stepped up to the challenge. Some organizations, such as the Council of State Governments and the International City Management Association, are well established. The Council of State Governments has published *The Book of the States* since 1935, and the International City Management Association has issued *The Municipal Year Book* since 1934. Other sources are newer, such as Congressional Quarterly's magazine *GOVERNING*, which began publication in 1987. The U.S. Census Bureau also offers systematic collections of data covering increasingly longer spans. Two examples are the *State and Metropolitan*

Area Data Book, published periodically since 1980, and the *County and City Data Book,* published with varying frequency since 1952. Such groups and publications make data collection far easier and more systematic, and they ensure higher quality than in the past.

Even when data are available, a researcher can still be frustrated by the inevitable variety that occurs across units. Simple tables or one-sentence summaries are often inadequate. As revealed in Table 2-2 on financing state election campaigns, there is enormous variation among states. Similarly, state provisions for the initiative and referendum (Table 8-4) vary in important ways—in who proposes initiatives, whether they apply to statutes or the state constitution or both, and whether the state also provides for a legislative referendum.

In studying state and local governments, their interrelationships, and their relations with the federal government, a researcher must pay attention to details. Even more than usual, it is essential to read notes and check several sources. Differences in data collection procedures, the timing of data collection, and variations in the detail of reports all become important. The user also must keep in mind the purpose of examining the data. It takes a careful researcher to know when variations can be ignored and when they become so frequent or so large that they must be an explicit part of the analysis.

Despite improvements in data collection, states and localities must be approached directly for some information. Fortunately, this approach too has become easier, because the many searchable Web site directories now available provide the names of specific individuals and offices, typically with addresses, phone numbers, and e-mail addresses. Although the availability of such sources will still not make a project involving twenty-five or fifty states easy, at least one can gather missing information or exact details about specific states and localities.

Because of the surge in the availability of information over the last decade or so, it is now possible to take a serious look at cities, counties, states, and regions, and the relationships among all these governments. The tables in this chapter and others deal mainly with three kinds of information. The first is about specific states, often with an eye toward how states rank relative to one another. This information covers historical data and population, state constitutions, elected officials, provisions for direct democracy, economic provisions and resources (Tables 8-1 through 8-6, 8-8, 8-10, and Figures 8-1 and 10-4), and government performance in various domains (Table 8-16). The second is data on states and localities as a whole and how they differ from the federal government and from each other (Tables 8-7 and 8-9 and Figures 8-2 and 8-3). The third reflects the considerable emphasis placed on intergovernmental relationships because of the growing fiscal interdependence between federal and state governments, state and local units, and even directly between federal and local governments (Figure 8-4 and Tables 8-11 through 8-15).

As these tables amply demonstrate, students as well as professionals now have access to systematic information about all fifty states and increasingly about localities. Although users may have to make an extra effort to absorb all the details provided by these tables, they are rewarded by the new possibilities for research and understanding.

Table 8-1   The States: Historical Data

State	Date organized as territory	Date admitted to Union	Chronological order of admissions to Union
Alabama	March 3, 1817	December 14, 1819	22
Alaska	August 24, 1912	January 3, 1959	49
Arizona	February 24, 1863	February 14, 1912	48
Arkansas	March 2, 1819	June 15, 1836	25
California	a	September 9, 1850	31
Colorado	February 28, 1861	August 1, 1876	38
Connecticut	—	January 9, 1788[b]	5
Delaware	—	December 7, 1787[b]	1
Florida	March 30, 1822	March 3, 1845	27
Georgia	—	January 2, 1788[b]	4
Hawaii	June 14, 1900	August 21, 1959	50
Idaho	March 4, 1863	July 3, 1890	43
Illinois	February 3, 1809	December 3, 1818	21
Indiana	May 7, 1800	December 11, 1816	19
Iowa	June 12, 1838	December 28, 1846	29
Kansas	May 30, 1854	January 29, 1861	34
Kentucky	a	June 1, 1792	15
Louisiana	March 26, 1804	April 30, 1812	18
Maine	a	March 15, 1820	23
Maryland	—	April 28, 1788[b]	7
Massachusetts	—	February 6, 1788[b]	6
Michigan	January 11, 1805	January 26, 1837	26
Minnesota	March 3, 1849	May 11, 1858	32
Mississippi	April 7, 1798	December 10, 1817	20
Missouri	June 4, 1812	August 10, 1821	24
Montana	May 26, 1864	November 8, 1889	41
Nebraska	May 30, 1854	March 1, 1867	37
Nevada	March 2, 1861	October 31, 1864	36
New Hampshire	—	June 21, 1788[b]	9
New Jersey	—	December 18, 1787[b]	3
New Mexico	September 9, 1850	January 6, 1912	47
New York	—	July 26, 1788[b]	11
North Carolina	—	November 21, 1789[b]	12
North Dakota	March 2, 1861	November 2, 1889	39
Ohio	May 7, 1800	March 1, 1803	17
Oklahoma	May 2, 1890	November 16, 1907	46
Oregon	August 14, 1848	February 14, 1859	33
Pennsylvania	—	December 12, 1787[b]	2
Rhode Island	—	May 29, 1790[b]	13
South Carolina	—	May 23, 1788[b]	8
South Dakota	March 2, 1861	November 2, 1889	40
Tennessee	June 8, 1790[c]	June 1, 1796	16
Texas	a	December 29, 1845	28
Utah	September 9, 1850	January 4, 1896	45
Vermont	a	March 4, 1791	14

Table 8-1   *(Continued)*

State	Date organized as territory	Date admitted to Union	Chronological order of admissions to Union
Virginia	—	June 25, 1788[b]	10
Washington	March 2, 1853	November 11, 1889	42
West Virginia	[a]	June 20, 1863	35
Wisconsin	April 20, 1836	May 29, 1848	30
Wyoming	July 25, 1868	July 10, 1890	44

Note: "—" indicates one of the original thirteen states.

[a] No territorial status before admission to Union.
[b] Date of ratification of U.S. Constitution.
[c] Date Southwest Territory (boundaries identical to Tennessee's) was created.

Source: Council of State Governments, *The Book of the States, 2008* (Lexington, Ky.: Council of State Governments, 2008), 554–555.

Table 8-2 State Constitutions

State	Number of constitutions[a]	Dates of adoption	Present constitution Effective date	Estimated length (number of words)	Number of amendments Submitted to voters	Adopted
Alabama	6	1819, 1861, 1865, 1868, 1875, 1901	November 28, 1901	350,000	1,093	799
Alaska	1	1956	January 3, 1959	15,988	41	29
Arizona	1	1911	February 14, 1912	45,783	254	141
Arkansas	5	1836, 1861, 1864, 1868, 1874	October 30, 1874	59,500	190	92
California	2	1849, 1879	July 4, 1879	54,645	870	514
Colorado	1	1876	August 1, 1876	74,522	315	150
Connecticut	4	1818, 1965	December 30, 1965	17,256	30	29
Delaware	4	1776, 1792, 1831, 1897	June 10, 1897	19,000	b	140
Florida	6	1839, 1861, 1865, 1868, 1886, 1968	January 7, 1969	51,456	141	110
Georgia	10	1777, 1789, 1798, 1861, 1865, 1868, 1877, 1945, 1976, 1982	July 1, 1983	39,526	86	66
Hawaii	1	1950	August 21, 1959	20,774	128	108
Idaho	1	1889	July 3, 1890	24,232	206	119
Illinois	4	1818, 1848, 1870, 1970	July 1, 1971	16,510	17	11
Indiana	2	1816, 1851	November 1, 1851	10,379	78	46
Iowa	2	1846, 1857	September 3, 1857	11,500	57	52
Kansas	1	1859	January 29, 1861	12,296	123	93
Kentucky	4	1792, 1799, 1850, 1891	September 28, 1891	23,911	75	41

Louisiana	11	1812, 1845, 1852, 1861, 1864, 1868, 1879, 1898, 1913, 1921, 1974	January 1, 1975	54,112	214	151
Maine	1	1819	March 15, 1820	16,276	203	171
Maryland	4	1776, 1851, 1864, 1867	October 5, 1867	44,000	257	221
Massachusetts	1	1780	October 25, 1780	36,700	148	120
Michigan	4	1835, 1850, 1908, 1963	January 1, 1964	34,659	66	28
Minnesota	1	1857	May 11, 1858	11,547	214	119
Mississippi	4	1817, 1832, 1869, 1890	November 1, 1890	24,323	158	123
Missouri	4	1820, 1865, 1875, 1945	March 30, 1945	42,600	170	109
Montana	2	1889, 1972	July 1, 1973	13,145	54	30
Nebraska	2	1866, 1875	October 12, 1875	34,220	344	224
Nevada	1	1864	October 31, 1864	31,377	226	134
New Hampshire	2	1776, 1784	June 2, 1784	9,200	287	145
New Jersey	3	1776, 1844, 1947	January 1, 1948	22,956	76	42
New Mexico	1	1911	January 6, 1912	27,200	284	155
New York	4	1777, 1822, 1846, 1894	January 1, 1895	51,700	292	217
North Carolina	3	1776, 1868, 1970	July 1, 1971	16,532	42	34
North Dakota	1	1889	November 2, 1889	19,130	262	149
Ohio	2	1802, 1851	September 1, 1851	48,521	275	163
Oklahoma	1	1907	November 16, 1907	74,075	340	175
Oregon	1	1857	February 14, 1859	54,083	478	238
Pennsylvania	5	1776, 1790, 1838, 1873, 1968	1968c	27,711	36	30
Rhode Island	3	1842, 1986	December 4, 1986	10,908	11	10
South Carolina	7	1776, 1778, 1790, 1861, 1865, 1868, 1895	January 1, 1896	32,541	679	492
South Dakota	1	1889	November 2, 1889	27,675	223	213
Tennessee	3	1796, 1835, 1870	February 23, 1870	13,300	61	38
Texas	5	1845, 1861, 1866, 1869, 1876	February 15, 1876	90,000	631	456

(Table continues)

Table 8-2 *(Continued)*

State	Number of constitutions[a]	Dates of adoption	Present constitution			
			Effective date	Estimated length (number of words)	Number of amendments	
					Submitted to voters	Adopted
Utah	1	1895	January 4, 1896	18,037	158	107
Vermont	3	1777, 1786, 1793	July 9, 1793	10,286	211	53
Virginia	6	1776, 1830, 1851, 1869, 1902, 1970	July 1, 1971	21,601	51	43
Washington	1	1889	November 11, 1889	33,564	174	101
West Virginia	2	1863, 1872	April 9, 1872	26,000	121	71
Wisconsin	1	1848	May 29, 1848	14,749	193	144
Wyoming	1	1889	July 10, 1890	31,800	123	97

Note: Constitutions as of January 1, 2008. For more details on the constitutions, see source.

[a] The constitutions include those Civil War documents customarily listed by the individual states. In Connecticut and Rhode Island, colonial charters served as the first constitutions.

[b] Proposed amendments are not submitted to the voters in Delaware.

[c] Certain sections of the constitution were revised in 1967–1968. Amendments proposed and adopted are since 1968.

Source: Council of State Governments, *The Book of the States, 2008* (Lexington, Ky.: Council of State Governments, 2008), 10–11.

Table 8-3   Governors' Terms, Term Limits, and Item Veto

State	Length of term in 1900	Length of term in 2008	Year of change	Maximum number of consecutive terms	Item veto[a]
Alabama	2	4	1902	2	yes
Alaska	b	4		2	yes[c]
Arizona	b	4	1970	2	yes[c]
Arkansas	2	4	1986	2	yes[c]
California	4	4		2	yes[c]
Colorado	2	4	1958	2	yes[c]
Connecticut	2	4	1950	no limit	yes[c]
Delaware	4	4		2	yes
Florida	4	4		2	yes
Georgia	2	4	1942	2	yes[c]
Hawaii	b	4		2	yes
Idaho	2	4	1946	no limit	yes
Illinois	4	4		no limit	yes
Indiana	4	4		2	no
Iowa	2	4	1974	no limit	yes[c]
Kansas	2	4	1974	2	yes[c]
Kentucky	4	4		2	yes
Louisiana	4	4		2	yes[c]
Maine	2	4	1958	2	yes[c]
Maryland	4	4		2	yes
Massachusetts	1	4	1920, 1966[d]	no limit	yes
Michigan	2	4	1966	2	yes[c]
Minnesota	2	4	1962	no limit	yes[c]
Mississippi	4	4		2	yes
Missouri	4	4		2	yes[c]
Montana	4	4		2[e]	yes[c]
Nebraska	2	4	1966	2[f]	yes[c]
Nevada	4	4		2	no
New Hampshire	2	2		no limit	no
New Jersey	3	4	1949	2	yes
New Mexico	b	4	1916, 1970	2	yes[c]
New York	2	4	1938	no limit	yes
North Carolina	4	4		2	no
North Dakota	2	4	1964	no limit	yes[c]
Ohio	2	4	1958	2	yes[c]
Oklahoma	b	4		2	yes[c]
Oregon	4	4		2	yes[c]
Pennsylvania	4	4		2	yes[c]
Rhode Island	1	4	1912, 1994[d]	2	no
South Carolina	2	4	1926	2	yes[c]
South Dakota	2	4	1974	2	yes[c]
Tennessee	1	4	1954	2	yes[c]
Texas	2	4	1974	no limit	yes[c]
Utah	4	4		3	yes[c]

(Table continues)

Table 8-3   *(Continued)*

State	Length of term in 1900	Length of term in 2008	Year of change	Maximum number of consecutive terms	Item veto[a]
Vermont	2	2		no limit	no
Virginia	4	4		1	yes[c]
Washington	4	4		no limit	yes
West Virginia	4	4		2	yes[c]
Wisconsin	2	4	1970	no limit	yes[c]
Wyoming	4	4		2[e]	yes

[a] In all states except North Carolina the governor has the power to veto bills passed by the state legislature. Item veto refers to the power to veto items within a bill. Provisions to override vary, requiring as many as two-thirds of the legislators elected. For details, see *The Book of the States* in source.

[b] Oklahoma was admitted to the Union in 1907, Arizona and New Mexico in 1912, and Alaska and Hawaii in 1959. Oklahoma, Alaska, and Hawaii have always had four-year gubernatorial terms. Arizona started with two years. New Mexico started with four years, went to two years in 1916 and back to four years in 1970.

[c] Over appropriations only. In Wisconsin, the governor has a broader veto on appropriations bills.

[d] Massachusetts went from one year to two years in 1920 and from two years to four years in 1966. Rhode Island went from one year to two years in 1912 and from two years to four years in 1994.

[e] Governor cannot serve more than eight years in any sixteen-year period.

[f] After two consecutive terms, governor must wait four years before being eligible again.

Sources: Length of term in 1900 and year of change: Congressional Quarterly, *Gubernatorial Elections, 1787–1997* (Washington, D.C.: Congressional Quarterly, 1998), 2–3; all other: Council of State Governments, *The Book of the States, 2008* (Lexington, Ky.: Council of State Governments, 2008), 180–181, 185–186.

Table 8-4 State Provisions for Initiative and Referendum

State	Initiative for statutes	Citizen petition referendum for statutes	Legislative referendum for statutes	Constitutional initiative
Alaska	D/I	yes	no	none
Arizona	D	yes	yes	D
Arkansas	D	yes	yes	D
California	D	yes	yes	D
Colorado	D	yes	no	D
Florida	none	no	no	D
Idaho	D	yes	yes	none
Illinois	none	no	yes	D
Kentucky	none	yes	yes	none
Maine	I	yes	yes	none
Maryland	none	yes	yes	none
Massachusetts	I	yes	yes	I
Michigan	I	yes	yes	D
Mississippi	none	no	no	I
Missouri	D	yes	yes	D
Montana	D	yes	yes	D
Nebraska	D	yes	yes	D
Nevada	I	yes	yes	D
New Mexico	none	yes	yes	none
North Dakota	D	yes	yes	D
Ohio	I	yes	yes	D
Oklahoma	D	yes	yes	D
Oregon	D	yes	yes	D
South Dakota	D	yes	yes	D
Utah	D and I	yes	yes	none
Washington	D and I	yes	yes	none
Wyoming	D/I	yes	no	none

Note: An initiative is a law or constitutional amendment introduced by the citizens either to the legislature or directly to the voters. A referendum is a process by which voters may express their judgments on statutes or constitutional amendments enacted by the legislature. Every state but Delaware requires state constitutional amendments to be placed on the ballot for voter approval or rejection. "D" indicates direct initiative—proposals that qualify go directly on the ballot. "I" indicates indirect initiative; proposals are submitted to the legislature, which has an opportunity to act on the proposed legislation. Depending on the state, the initiative question may go on the ballot if the legislature rejects it, submits a different proposal, or takes no action. "D/I" indicates that Alaska and Wyoming's initiative processes exhibit characteristics of both the direct and indirect initiative. For details, see sources.

Sources: National Conference of State Legislatures, "The Initiative and Referendum States" (*www.ncsl.org*); Initiative and Referendum Institute, "States with Legislative Referendum for Statutes and Constitutional Amendments" (*www.iandrinstitute.org*).

Figure 8-1   Initiatives in the States, 1904–2008

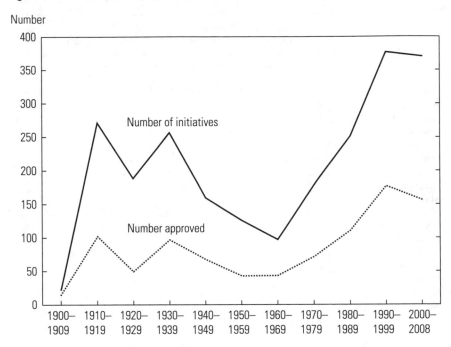

Note: Only initiatives—new laws placed on the ballot by petition—are included. The numbers do not include popular referendums or measures placed on the ballot by the legislature.

Source: Initiative and Referendum Institute, "Overview of Initiative Use, 1904–2008," February 2009 (*www.iandrinstitute.org*).

Table 8-5   Incorporation of Bill of Rights to Apply to State Governments

Year	Issue (amendment)	Supreme Court case	Vote
[1868 Fourteenth Amendment to Constitution passed][a]			
1897	Eminent domain (V)	Chicago, Burlington & Quincy RR v. Chicago, 166 U.S. 266	9–0
1927	Freedom of speech (I)	Fiske v. Kansas, 274 U.S. 380	9–0
1931	Freedom of press (I)	Near v. Minnesota, 283 U.S. 697	5–4
1932	Counsel in capital criminal cases (VI)	Powell v. Alabama, 287 U.S. 45	7–2
1934	Free exercise of religion (I)	Hamilton v. Regents of the U. of California, 293 U.S. 245	9–0
1937	Freedom of assembly and petition (I)	De Jonge v. Oregon, 299 U.S. 353	8–0
1947	Separation of church and state (I)	Everson v. Board of Education of Ewing Township, 330 U.S. 1	5–4
1948	Public trial (VI)	In re Oliver, 333 U.S. 257	7–2
1961	Unreasonable searches and seizures (IV)	Mapp v. Ohio, 367 U.S. 643	6–3
1962	Cruel and unusual punishment (VIII)	Robinson v. California, 370 U.S. 660	6–2
1963	Counsel in all criminal cases (VI)	Gideon v. Wainwright, 372 U.S. 335	9–0
1964	Self-incrimination (V)	Malloy v. Hogan, 378 U.S. 1	5–4
		Murphy v. Waterfront Commission, 378 U.S. 52	9–0
1965	Right to confront adverse witnesses (VI)	Pointer v. Texas, 380 U.S. 400	7–2
1966	Impartial jury (VI)	Parker v. Gladden, 385 U.S. 363	8–1
1967	Obtaining and confronting favorable witnesses (VI)	Washington v. Texas, 388 U.S. 14	9–0
1967	Speedy trial (VI)	Klopfer v. North Carolina, 386 U.S. 213	9–0
1968	Jury trial in non-petty criminal cases (VI)	Duncan v. Louisiana, 391 U.S. 145	7–2
1969	Double jeopardy (V)	Benton v. Maryland, 395 U.S. 784	7–2

Note: Enumerated rights not incorporated: grand jury indictment, trial by jury in civil cases, excessive fines and bail, right to bear arms, and safeguards on quartering troops in private homes.

[a] The Fourteenth Amendment's due process clause is the basis for applying the Bill of Rights to the states.

Sources: Henry J. Abraham, The Judiciary: The Supreme Court in the Governmental Process, 9th ed. (Dubuque, Iowa: William C. Brown, 1994); votes: United States Reports (Washington, D.C.: Government Printing Office, various years).

Table 8-6 Length of Time between Congressional Approval and Actual Ratification of the Twenty-seven Amendments to the U.S. Constitution

Amendment		Time required for ratification	Year ratified
I–X	Bill of Rights	2 years, 2.5 months	1791
XI	Lawsuits against states	11 months	1795
XII	Presidential elections	6.5 months	1804
XIII	Abolition of slavery	10 months	1865
XIV	Civil rights	2 years, 1 month	1868
XV	Suffrage for all races	11 months	1870
XVI	Income tax	3 years, 6.5 months	1913
XVII	Senatorial elections	11 months	1913
XVIII	Prohibition	1 year, 1 month	1919
XIX	Women's suffrage	1 year, 2 months	1920
XX	Terms of office	11 months	1933
XXI	Repeal of prohibition	9.5 months	1933
XXII	Limit on presidential terms	3 years, 11 months	1951
XXIII	Washington, D.C., vote	9 months	1961
XXIV	Abolition of poll taxes	1 year, 4 months	1964
XXV	Presidential succession	1 year, 10 months	1967
XXVI	Eighteen-year-old suffrage	3 months	1971
XXVII	Congressional salaries	203 years	1992

Sources: Congressional Research Service, *The Constitution of the United States: Analysis and Interpretation* (Washington, D.C.: Government Printing Office, 1973), 23–44 (92nd Cong., 2nd sess., S. Doc. 92-82); *Congressional Quarterly Weekly Report* (1992), 1423.

Figure 8-2   Government Employees: Federal, State, and Local, 1929–2007

Number of employees (millions)

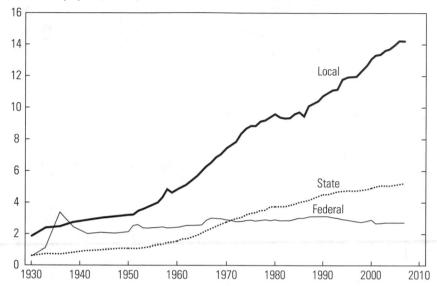

Note: No annual survey of government employment and payroll was conducted in 1996.

Sources: 1929–1944, 1949, 1952, 1954, 1959, 1964, 1969–1992: U.S. Advisory Commission on Intergovernmental Relations, *Significant Features of Fiscal Federalism, 1994*, vol. 2 (Washington, D.C.: U.S. Advisory Commission on Intergovernmental Relations, 1994), 151; 1993–1994: (1995), 159; 1995–2007: U.S. Census Bureau (*www.census.gov/govs/www/apes .html*); other years: U.S. Bureau of the Census, *Historical Statistics of the United States,* Series Y189-198 (Washington, D.C.: Government Printing Office, 1975), 1100.

Table 8-7 Federal, State, and Local Governments: Number of Units and Employees, 1942–2007

| Year | Federal government | State government | Local government | | | | | | | Total |
			County	Municipal	School district	Township and town	Special district[a]	Total	
1942										
Number	1	48	3,050	16,220	108,579	18,919	8,299	155,067	155,116
Employees (thousands)[b]	2,664	503[c]	333[c]	872[c]	—	223[c,d]	[d]	1,428[c]	5,915
1952[d]										
Number	1	50	3,052	16,807	67,355	17,202	12,340	116,756	116,807
Employees (thousands)	2,583	1,060	573	1,341	1,234	312[c]	[c]	3,461	7,105
1962										
Number	1	50	3,043	18,000	34,678	17,142	18,323	91,186	91,237
Employees (thousands)	2,539	1,680	862	1,696	2,161	449[c]	[c]	5,169	9,388
1972										
Number	1	50	3,044	18,517	15,781	16,991	23,885	78,218	78,269
Employees (thousands)	2,832	2,957	1,369	2,376	3,587	348	327	8,007	13,759
1982										
Number	1	50	3,041	19,076	14,851	16,734	28,078	81,780	81,831
Employees (thousands)	2,862	3,744	1,824	2,397	4,194	356	478	9,249	15,841
1992										
Number	1	50	3,043	19,279	14,422	16,656	31,555	84,955	85,006
Employees (thousands)	3,047	4,595	2,253	2,665	5,134	424	627	11,103	18,745
1997										
Number	1	50	3,043	19,372	13,726	16,629	34,683	87,453	87,504
Employees (thousands)	2,807	4,733	2,425	2,755	5,675	455	691	12,000	19,540

	Number	Number	Number	Number	Number	Number	Number	Number	Number
2002									
Number	1	50	3,034	19,429	13,506	16,504	35,052	87,525	87,576
Employees (thousands)	2,690	5,072	2,729	2,972	6,367	488	721	13,277	21,039
2007									
Number	1	50	3,033	19,492	13,051	16,519	37,381	89,476	89,527
Employees (thousands)	2,730	5,200	—	—	—	—	—	14,186	22,116

Note: "—" indicates not available. A census of governmental units is conducted every five years. Data for additional years can be found in previous editions of *Vital Statistics on American Politics*.

a Special districts include independent public housing authorities, local irrigation units, power authorities, and other such bodies.
b Month for employee counts varies across years. For details, see sources. Numbers include full- and part-time employees.
c Employees in other than education.
d Townships and special districts are combined.

Sources: 1942–1962: U.S. Bureau of the Census, *Historical Statistics of the United States* (Washington, D.C.: Government Printing Office, 1975), 1086, 1100; 1972–1992 governmental units: U.S. Bureau of the Census, *Census of Governments, 1987* (Washington, D.C.: Government Printing Office, 1988), vi; *1993*, 3; 1972–1992 employees: U.S. Office of Personnel Management, *Federal Manpower Statistics, Federal Civilian Workforce Statistics* (Washington, D.C.: Government Printing Office, various years); U.S. Bureau of the Census, *Public Employment in 1985* (Washington, D.C.: Government Printing Office, 1986), 2; *1989*, vi; *1992*, vi, ix; 1997 governmental units: U.S. Bureau of the Census, *Statistical Abstract of the United States* (Washington, D.C.: Government Printing Office, 1998), 305; 1997 employees: "1997 State and Local Government Employment and Payroll Estimates" (*www.census.gov*); 2002 governmental units and employees: U.S. Census Bureau, 2002 Census of Governments, vol. 3, no. 2, "Compendium of Public Employment: 2002" (Washington, D.C.: Government Printing Office, 2002), ix, 2, 34; 2007 governmental units: "Local Governments and Public School Systems by Type and State: 2007" (*www.census.gov*); 2007 employees: U.S. Census Bureau, "Federal, State, and Local Governments," 2007 Census of Governments (*www.census.gov/govs/www/cog2007.html*).

Table 8-8   State Lottery Revenues and Usages (millions)

State	Year established	FY '08 sales	FY '08 profit	Program(s)[a]	Cumulative contributions since year established[b]
Arizona	1982	$472.9	$144.6	Total	$1,960.5
				Local Transportation Assistance Fund	558.0
				General fund (education)	445.6
				Heritage Fund	298.5
California	1985	3,049.6	1,069.4	Education	18,457.6
Colorado	1983	505.8	122.3	Total	1,739.4
				Conservation Trust Fund	646.3
				Great Outdoors Colorado Trust Fund	461.6
				Capital Construction Fund	439.8
Connecticut	1972	998.1	285.1	General fund	5,847.7
Delaware	1975	736.4	252.5	Total	2,334.7
				General fund	2,321.5
				Health and social services	13.2
District of Columbia	1982	252.3	70.4	General fund	1,340.0
Florida	1987	4,170.0	1,280.0	Education Enhancement Trust Fund	15,203.0
Georgia	1993	3,520.0	867.7	Total	8,076.3
				HOPE Scholarships	3,580.4
				Pre-kindergarten program	2,695.9
				Capital outlay and technology for schools	1,800.0
Idaho	1989	136.8	36.2	Total	300.6
				Public schools (K–12)	150.3
				Public buildings	150.3
Illinois	1974	2,078.2	657.0	Illinois Common School Fund (K–12)	12,896.0
Indiana	1989	822.8	217.1	Total	2,661.1
				Build Indiana Fund	1,920.4
				Teachers' Retirement Fund	462.6
				Police and Fire Pension Relief Fund	276.3
Iowa	1985	249.0	57.0	Total	1,015.3
				General fund	647.2
				Iowa Plan (economic development)	170.3
				Sales tax	136.0

Table 8-8   *(Continued)*

State	Year established	FY '08 sales	FY '08 profit	Program(s)[a]	Cumulative contributions since year established[b]
Kansas	1987	236.7	71.0	Total	888.1
				Economic Development Initiatives Fund	647.0
				State general fund (FY 1995–2004)	122.0
				Correctional Institutions Building Fund	76.3
Kentucky	1989	778.2	192.1	Total	2,282.0
				General fund	1,387.6
				Postsecondary and college scholarships	609.6
				Education	214.0
Louisiana	1991	373.7	131.8	Total	1,734.3
				Minimum Foundation Program–schools	1,512.3
				Various state agencies	147.3
				State general fund	69.2
Maine	1974	228.5	49.5	Total	743.9
				General fund	732.0
				Outdoor Heritage Fund	11.9
Maryland	1973	1,673.0	529.4	Total	9,744.8
				General fund	9,270.9
				Stadium Authority	442.7
				Subdivisions (FY 1984–FY 1985 only)	31.3
Massachusetts	1972	4,709.0	913.0	Total	15,219.9
				Cities and towns	12,028.1
				General fund	2,991.4
				Arts Council	189.9
Michigan	1972	2,330.2	740.7	Education (K–12)	12,916.6
Minnesota	1989	461.5	116.3	Total	1,428.0
				General fund	866.5
				Environment and Natural Resources Trust Fund	381.4
				Game and Fish Fund	61.5
				Natural Resources Fund	61.5
Missouri	1986	995.5	266.6	Total	2,457.9
				Public education	1,915.3
				General revenue fund (1986–1993)	542.5

(Table continues)

Table 8-8   *(Continued)*

State	Year established	FY '08 sales	FY '08 profit	Program(s)[a]	Cumulative contributions since year established[b]
Montana	1987	43.8	11.0	Total	130.3
				General fund	78.2
				Elementary and secondary schools	34.1
				Property tax relief	15.3
Nebraska	1993	121.9	31.0	Total	258.8
				Education Innovation Fund	106.4
				Environmental Trust Fund	103.8
				Solid Waste Landfill Closure Assistance Fund	18.5
New Hampshire	1964	261.1	75.7	Education	1,080.1
New Jersey	1970	2,538.5	882.1	Education and institutions	15,571.2
New Mexico	1996	147.1	40.8	Total	283.8
				Lottery Tuition Fund	217.2
				Public school capital outlay	66.6
New York	1967	7,548.4	2,556.1	Education	30,000.0
North Carolina	2006	1,078.1	350.0	—	—
North Dakota	2004	22.1	6.1	Total	7.7
				State general fund	7.3
				Compulsive Gambling Fund	0.4
Ohio	1974	2,325.1	672.2	Education	14,300.0
Oklahoma	2005	203.8	71.6	Education	69.0
Oregon	1985	1,245.5	678.7	Total	4,652.0
				Public education	2,715.0
				Economic development	1,570.0
				Natural resource programs	367.0
Pennsylvania	1972	3,089.2	928.1	Older Pennsylvanians	15,500.0
Rhode Island	1974	2,398.9	355.6	General fund	2,600.0
South Carolina	2002	992.5	263.9	Education Lottery Fund	1,190.4
South Dakota	1989	704.3	122.6	Total	1,444.2
				Property Tax Reduction Fund	1,045.0
				General fund	376.4
				Capital Construction Fund	21.0

Table 8-8   *(Continued)*

State	Year established	FY '08 sales	FY '08 profit	Program(s)[a]	Cumulative contributions since year established[b]
Tennessee	2004	1,065.0	283.1	Total	636.9
				Lottery for Education Account	620.6
				After School Program	16.3
Texas	1992	3,671.2	1,038.0	Total	12,898.2
				Foundation School Fund	7,629.3
				General fund	4,997.8
				Tertiary Care Facility Account	131.1
Vermont	1978	102.0	22.6	Total	341.2
				General fund	212.5
				Education fund	128.7
Virginia	1988	1,386.4	455.3	Total	5,961.0
				Public education (K–12) (FY 1999–present)	3,003.9
				General fund (FY 1989–FY 1998)	2,788.4
				Literary Fund (school construction/renovation)	155.6
Washington	1982	521.1	130.3	Total	2,399.9
				General fund	1,836.1
				Education fund	476.2
				King County Stadium and Exhibition Center	42.4
				Seattle Mariners Stadium	42.4
West Virginia	1986	1,523.0	579.0	Total	3,231.2
				Other	1,079.4
				Education	903.1
				General fund	535.6
Wisconsin	1988	494.7	140.0	Public benefit such as property tax relief	2,368.0

Note: "—" indicates not available. Amounts in current dollars. Due to rounding, numbers for individual categories may not sum to the state total. Data for additional years can be found in previous editions of *Vital Statistics on American Politics*.

[a] If only one beneficiary, no separate total is shown. If more than three, only the top three are shown (or four if tied).
[b] Contributions to beneficiaries from start-up to June 30, 2006.

Source: North American Association of State and Provincial Lotteries (*www.naspl.org*).

Table 8-9 State and Local Government Expenditures, by Function, 1902–2006 (percent)

Function	1902	1952	1962	1972	1977	1982	1987	1992	1997	2002	2005	2006
Education	23.3	27.0	31.5	34.6	31.7	29.4	29.3	28.5	28.8	29.1	29.1	29.1
Highways	16.0	15.1	14.7	10.0	7.1	6.6	6.8	5.8	5.6	5.7	5.3	5.4
Public welfare	3.4	9.0	7.2	11.1	11.1	11.1	10.5	13.5	13.7	13.7	15.3	14.8
Health	1.6	1.4	0.9	1.4	1.7	2.0	2.2	2.6	2.9	2.9	2.8	2.8
Hospitals	3.9	5.7	5.2	5.5	5.4	5.8	5.2	5.1	4.7	4.3	4.4	4.4
Police	4.6	3.0	3.0	3.2	3.2	3.2	3.2	3.0	3.3	3.2	3.2	3.2
Fire protection	3.7	1.9	1.6	1.4	1.4	1.3	1.4	1.3	1.3	1.3	1.3	1.4
Natural resources	0.8	2.5	1.9	1.6	1.3	1.3	1.3	1.1	1.1	1.1	1.1	1.0
Corrections	—	1.1	1.1	1.1	1.3	1.6	2.2	2.5	2.7	2.7	2.5	2.5
Sanitation and sewerage	4.7	3.2	2.8	2.5	2.9	2.9	2.8	2.8	2.9	2.5	2.5	2.5
Housing and community development	—	2.0	1.6	1.4	1.0	1.6	1.5	1.5	1.6	1.6	1.7	1.7
Parks and recreation	2.6	1.0	1.3	1.2	1.5	1.4	1.4	1.4	1.4	1.5	1.3	1.4
Financial administration	12.9	3.9	1.5	1.3	1.4	1.5	1.7	1.6	1.7	1.6	1.5	1.5
Other government administration	—	—	1.8	1.8	1.9	2.7	2.9	2.8	2.9	2.9	1.5	1.5
Employment security administration[a]	—	0.6	0.6	0.6	0.5	0.4	0.4	0.3	0.3	0.3	0.2	0.2
Interest on general debt	6.2	1.8	2.9	3.2	3.5	3.8	5.4	4.8	4.3	3.7	3.4	3.4

Utilities	7.5	9.9	7.7	6.0	7.5	9.2	8.5	7.1	6.6	6.8	6.6	6.8
Liquor store expenditure	—	—	—	—	—	—	0.4	0.3	0.2	0.2	0.2	0.2
Insurance trust expenditure	—	5.5	6.9	5.5	8.1	7.5	6.6	7.9	7.6	8.3	8.3	8.2
Other	8.9	4.2	4.8	6.7	7.7	6.7	6.8	6.1	6.4	6.6	7.8	8.0
Total direct expenditure (millions)	$1,095	$30,863	$70,547	$190,496	$324,554	$524,817	$772,864	$1,147,075	$1,456,885	$2,044,331	$2,368,692	$2,500,583

Note: "—" indicates not available. Amounts in current dollars. For 1902–1952, financial administration includes other government administration. For 1902–1982, the category utilities includes liquor store expenditures. Data for additional years can be found in previous editions of *Vital Statistics on American Politics.*

[a] Formerly Social Insurance administration.

Sources: 1902–1982: U.S. Bureau of the Census, *Census of Government, 1982* (Washington, D.C.: Government Printing Office, 1985), 32–33; 1987: U.S. Bureau of the Census, *Governmental Finances in 1987–88* (Washington, D.C.: Government Printing Office, 1990), 13; 1992–2006: U.S. Census Bureau, "United States State and Local Government Finances by Level of Government" (*www.census.gov*).

Table 8-10   Disposable Personal Income Per Capita, by State, 1950–2007

State	1950	1960	1970	1980	1990	2000	2005	2006	2007
Alabama	$855	$1,418	$2,670	$6,996	$14,091	$20,905	$26,666	$27,684	$28,960
Alaska	—	2,543	4,534	12,738	19,931	26,149	32,843	34,713	36,031
Arizona	1,259	1,833	3,385	8,493	15,226	21,866	27,332	28,701	29,063
Arkansas	803	1,293	2,548	6,741	12,975	19,402	24,443	25,625	27,041
California	1,703	2,489	4,272	10,497	19,021	26,391	32,398	34,402	35,666
Colorado	1,388	2,060	3,559	9,347	17,232	27,690	33,142	34,525	35,545
Connecticut	1,700	2,562	4,414	10,655	23,259	33,083	40,096	42,770	45,217
Delaware	1,709	2,340	3,814	8,984	18,598	26,628	31,943	33,919	34,917
District of Columbia	2,016	2,499	4,313	10,480	22,864	31,562	47,436	49,733	52,526
Florida	1,205	1,826	3,560	8,857	17,711	24,375	30,777	32,848	33,831
Georgia	1,002	1,534	3,000	7,442	15,523	24,121	27,721	28,392	29,288
Hawaii	—	2,002	4,382	10,054	19,415	24,570	30,771	32,653	34,365
Idaho	1,244	1,697	3,194	7,779	14,064	20,797	25,657	26,899	27,948
Illinois	1,661	2,378	3,930	9,519	18,032	27,286	32,164	33,630	35,697
Indiana	1,411	1,970	3,333	8,246	15,390	23,557	27,345	28,494	29,394
Iowa	1,430	1,849	3,419	8,366	15,288	23,206	28,450	29,233	31,020
Kansas	1,353	1,941	3,363	8,674	16,005	23,694	28,707	30,590	32,067
Kentucky	922	1,474	2,812	7,267	13,617	20,972	25,035	26,352	27,357
Louisiana	1,040	1,539	2,796	7,709	13,673	20,539	21,962	29,539	32,074
Maine	1,119	1,739	3,075	7,502	15,408	22,014	27,472	28,681	30,097
Maryland	1,478	2,097	3,866	9,530	19,702	28,291	36,064	37,799	39,750
Massachusetts	1,505	2,191	3,866	9,121	19,902	30,406	37,129	39,466	41,491
Michigan	1,568	2,172	3,641	9,009	16,587	25,226	28,837	29,422	30,611
Minnesota	1,323	1,918	3,557	8,867	17,318	27,120	32,535	33,775	35,454
Mississippi	733	1,141	2,385	6,347	11,920	18,810	23,361	24,765	26,008
Missouri	1,312	1,912	3,364	8,195	15,603	23,745	27,900	28,855	30,042
Montana	1,533	1,866	3,221	8,009	13,778	20,023	26,463	27,666	29,433
Nebraska	1,455	1,910	3,358	8,099	16,061	23,980	29,481	30,168	32,066
Nevada	1,779	2,536	4,360	10,348	18,081	25,428	33,012	34,206	34,753
New Hampshire	1,251	1,960	3,424	8,757	18,441	28,645	33,512	35,448	36,775
New Jersey	1,649	2,450	4,233	10,137	21,487	31,104	37,652	40,241	42,081
New Mexico	1,114	1,706	2,850	7,520	13,381	19,097	25,254	26,305	27,389
New York	1,668	2,416	4,188	9,480	19,879	28,772	34,783	36,907	38,800
North Carolina	1,013	1,478	2,891	7,208	15,241	23,236	27,455	28,312	29,423
North Dakota	1,285	1,672	2,892	7,085	14,313	22,315	28,877	29,109	32,487
Ohio	1,474	2,119	3,591	8,797	16,439	24,112	27,943	28,981	30,260
Oklahoma	1,057	1,728	3,095	8,329	14,256	20,984	27,140	29,132	31,118
Oregon	1,502	1,997	3,431	8,788	15,992	23,399	27,559	29,167	30,385
Pennsylvania	1,422	2,042	3,568	8,817	17,422	25,406	30,708	32,272	33,870
Rhode Island	1,407	1,983	3,661	8,520	17,771	24,982	31,436	33,115	34,894
South Carolina	866	1,314	2,745	6,880	14,190	21,198	25,340	26,756	27,580
South Dakota	1,215	1,729	2,982	7,362	14,837	23,130	29,676	29,342	32,451
Tennessee	963	1,469	2,840	7,449	15,181	23,525	28,188	29,275	30,248
Texas	1,246	1,751	3,227	8,616	15,589	24,516	30,199	31,670	33,181
Utah	1,263	1,827	3,026	7,515	13,207	20,191	24,794	25,815	26,203
Vermont	1,086	1,724	3,161	7,663	15,831	23,513	29,194	31,214	33,156
Virginia	1,165	1,719	3,264	8,784	17,890	26,308	32,981	34,758	35,721

Table 8-10   *(Continued)*

State	1950	1960	1970	1980	1990	2000	2005	2006	2007
Washington	1,588	2,179	3,754	9,544	17,753	26,958	32,617	34,558	36,557
West Virginia	987	1,455	2,757	7,162	12,997	19,314	23,901	25,249	26,408
Wisconsin	1,382	1,989	3,457	8,811	15,809	24,293	28,904	30,266	31,719
Wyoming	1,594	2,063	3,476	10,166	16,067	23,621	34,648	37,999	40,921
United States	1,382	2,018	3,584	8,848	17,135	25,214	30,573	32,219	33,619

Note: "—" indicates not available. Amounts in current dollars. Data for additional years can be found in previous editions of *Vital Statistics on American Politics.*

Source: U.S. Department of Commerce, Bureau of Economic Analysis, Regional Economic Data, "Annual State Personal Income" (*www.bea.gov*).

Figure 8-3   Surpluses and Deficits in Federal, State, and Local Government Finances, 1948–2007

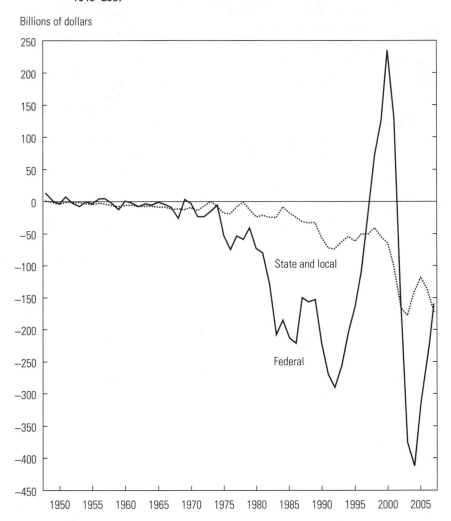

Billions of dollars

Note: Amounts in current dollars. State and local receipts and expenditures were subject to major revisions in 2003. The revisions made National Income and Product Accounts (NIPA) state and local government receipts and expenditures more comparable to the federal unified budget receipts and outlays. For details, see source and Brent R. Moulton and Eugene P. Seskin, "Preview of the 2003 Comprehensive Revision of the National Income and Product Accounts," *Survey of Current Business* (June 2003): 17–34.

Source: U.S. Office of Management and Budget, *Budget of the U.S. Government, Fiscal Year 2009, Historical Tables* (Washington, D.C.: Government Printing Office, 2008), 326–327.

Figure 8-4   State and Local Government Deficits Compared with Federal Grants-in-Aid, 1948–2007

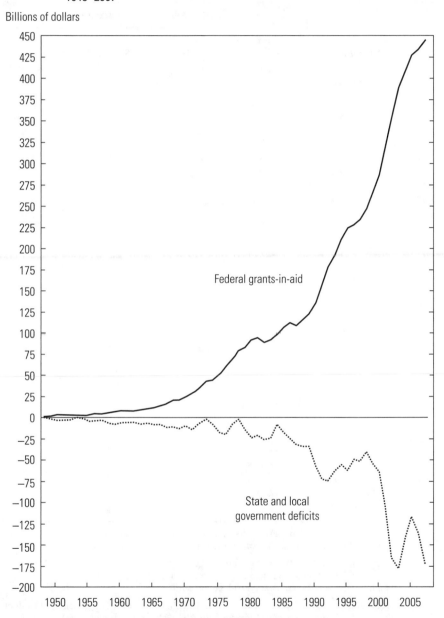

Note: Amounts in current dollars. See note to Figure 8-3, this volume.

Source: U.S. Office of Management and Budget, *Budget of the U.S. Government, Fiscal Year 2009, Historical Tables* (Washington, D.C.: Government Printing Office, 2008), 232–233, 326–327.

Table 8-11   Federal Grants-in-Aid Outlays, 1940–2014

		Federal grants as a percentage of			
		Federal outlays[a]		State and	Gross
	Total grants-in-aid		Domestic	local	domestic
Year	(billions)	Total	programs[b]	expenditures[c]	product
1940	$0.9	9.2	—	—	0.9
1945	0.9	0.9	—	—	0.4
1950	2.3	5.3	—	—	0.8
1955	3.2	4.7	—	—	0.8
1960	7.0	7.6	18.0	14.8	1.4
1965	10.9	9.2	18.3	15.5	1.6
1970	24.1	12.3	23.2	20.1	2.4
1975	49.8	15.0	21.7	24.0	3.2
1980	91.4	15.5	22.2	27.4	3.4
1985	105.9	11.2	18.2	22.0	2.6
1990	135.3	10.8	17.1	18.9	2.4
1995	225.0	14.8	21.6	22.8	3.1
1996	227.8	14.6	21.0	24.0	3.0
1997	234.2	14.6	21.0	24.0	2.9
1998	246.1	14.9	21.0	25.0	2.9
1999	267.9	15.7	22.0	25.0	2.9
2000	285.9	16.0	22.0	22.2	2.9
2001	318.5	17.1	22.9	25.2	3.2
2002	352.9	17.5	23.2	26.3	3.4
2003	388.5	18.0	23.7	26.1	3.6
2004	407.5	17.8	23.9	25.0	3.5
2005	428.0	17.3	23.5	24.7	3.5
2006	434.1	16.3	22.4	23.3	3.3
2007	443.8	16.3	—	—	3.3
2008	461.3	15.5	21.2	22.0	3.2
2009 est.	567.8	14.2	17.6	—	4.0
2010 est.	652.2	18.2	23.5	—	4.4
2011 est.	619.5	17.1	—	—	4.0
2012 est.	610.0	16.8	—	—	3.7
2013 est.	620.1	16.2	—	—	3.5
2014 est.	637.7	15.9	—	—	3.5

Note: "—" indicates not available. Amounts in current dollars. Fiscal years. Data for additional years can be found in previous editions of *Vital Statistics on American Politics.*

[a] Includes off-budget outlays; all grants are on-budget.
[b] Excludes outlays for national defense, international affairs, and net interest.
[c] As defined in the National Income and Product Accounts.

Sources: Total grants, total federal outlays, and GDP: U.S. Office of Management and Budget, *Budget of the United States Government, Fiscal Year 2010, Historical Tables* (Washington, D.C.: Government Printing Office, 2009), 238–239; domestic programs and state and local expenditures: U.S. Office of Management and Budget, *Budget of the United States Government, Analytical Perspectives* (Washington, D.C.: Government Printing Office, various years), Trends in Federal Grants to State and Local Governments (table).

Table 8-12 Federal Grants-in-Aid to State and Local Governments, by Function, 1940–2010 (percent)

Function	1940	1945	1950	1955	1960	1965	1970	1975	1980	1985	1990	1995	2000	2005	2008	2010 est.
Health	3	11	5	4	3	6	16	18	17	23	32	42	44	46	47	48
Income security	39	52	59	54	38	32	24	19	20	26	27	24	22	21	21	17
Education, training, employment, and social services	3	14	7	10	8	10	27	24	24	17	17	15	15	13	13	16
Transportation	19	4	21	19	43	38	19	12	14	16	14	11	11	10	11	11
Natural resources and environment	—	1	1	1	2	2	2	5	6	4	3	2	2	1	1	2
Community and regional development	32	14	—	2	2	6	7	6	7	5	4	3	3	5	4	3
General-purpose fiscal assistance	1	1	2	3	2	2	2	14	9	7	2	1	1	1	1	1
Agriculture	3	3	5	7	4	5	3	1	1	2	1	1	—	—	—	—
Other	—	—	—	—	—	—	—	1	2	1	1	1	2	1	1	2
Total	100	100	100	100	102	101	100	100	100	101	101	99	100	98	99	100

Note: "___" indicates 0.5 percent or less. Due to rounding, percentages may not sum to 100 percent. Data for additional years can be found in previous editions of *Vital Statistics on American Politics*.

Sources: 1940–1990: U.S. Office of Management and Budget, *Budget Baselines, Historical Data, and Alternatives for the Future* (Washington, D.C.: Government Printing Office, 1993), 429–432; 1995: U.S. Office of Management and Budget, *Budget of the U.S. Government, Fiscal Year 1997, Analytical Perspectives* (Washington, D.C.: Government Printing Office, 1996), 172–177; 2000: *2002*, 204–211; 2005: *2007*, 111–118; 2008, 2010: *2010*, 95–104.

Table 8-13 Flow of Federal Funds to and from the States, 1982–2005

State	1982–1984	1986–1988	1989–1991	1992–1994	1995–1997	1998–2000	2001–2003	2005[a]
Alabama	$1.29	$1.37	$1.41	$1.38	$1.35	$1.47	$1.62	$1.63
Alaska	1.01	1.16	1.19	1.26	1.28	1.56	1.81	1.83
Arizona	1.14	1.20	1.21	1.19	1.14	1.16	1.19	1.19
Arkansas	1.27	1.33	1.27	1.26	1.28	1.38	1.49	1.40
California	1.09	0.98	0.89	0.94	0.94	0.88	0.79	0.80
Colorado	0.91	1.10	1.18	1.05	0.95	0.89	0.80	0.83
Connecticut	1.02	0.84	0.77	0.69	0.77	0.65	0.66	0.73
Delaware	0.83	0.76	0.68	0.70	0.81	0.83	0.84	0.80
District of Columbia	—	5.07	5.38	5.42	5.61	6.49	6.25	—
Florida	1.09	1.02	1.00	1.05	1.05	1.01	1.02	0.95
Georgia	1.09	1.02	0.96	1.04	1.02	0.99	0.99	1.03
Hawaii	1.38	1.40	1.24	1.17	1.41	1.52	1.56	1.43
Idaho	1.13	1.31	1.36	1.19	1.18	1.23	1.29	1.19
Illinois	0.70	0.72	0.72	0.75	0.72	0.74	0.76	0.78
Indiana	0.83	0.89	0.89	0.89	0.89	0.92	0.98	1.07
Iowa	0.80	1.09	1.05	1.05	1.00	1.10	1.15	1.09
Kansas	1.02	1.10	1.03	1.03	1.02	1.04	1.13	1.13
Kentucky	1.10	1.23	1.27	1.21	1.23	1.41	1.47	1.51
Louisiana	0.90	1.08	1.26	1.30	1.21	1.35	1.46	1.85
Maine	1.30	1.21	1.22	1.38	1.34	1.34	1.34	1.41
Maryland	1.27	1.25	1.19	1.25	1.27	1.31	1.27	1.30
Massachusetts	1.10	1.02	0.99	0.99	0.97	0.86	0.79	0.85
Michigan	0.78	0.74	0.77	0.82	0.77	0.81	0.87	0.94
Minnesota	0.85	0.92	0.87	0.81	0.80	0.77	0.76	0.73
Mississippi	1.61	1.72	1.70	1.72	1.56	1.69	1.83	2.02
Missouri	1.43	1.31	1.32	1.28	1.36	1.24	1.31	1.32

Montana	1.07	1.37	1.43	1.38	1.38	1.63	1.65	1.43
Nebraska	0.95	1.16	1.10	1.05	0.99	1.06	1.14	1.09
Nevada	0.92	0.99	0.86	0.81	0.84	0.71	0.73	0.67
New Hampshire	0.98	0.76	0.70	0.74	0.80	0.71	0.67	0.75
New Jersey	0.70	0.64	0.63	0.68	0.69	0.66	0.62	0.65
New Mexico	1.80	2.07	2.02	1.95	1.84	1.98	2.15	2.00
New York	0.92	0.84	0.80	0.83	0.87	0.85	0.83	0.82
North Carolina	0.95	0.94	0.94	0.98	0.98	1.03	1.07	1.08
North Dakota	1.06	1.56	1.55	1.50	1.43	1.69	1.92	1.65
Ohio	0.85	0.93	0.94	0.92	0.90	0.94	1.02	1.06
Oklahoma	0.88	1.10	1.21	1.24	1.21	1.43	1.49	1.35
Oregon	0.89	0.97	0.95	0.94	0.93	0.92	0.99	0.93
Pennsylvania	0.96	0.97	0.95	1.00	1.00	1.05	1.08	1.08
Rhode Island	1.05	0.99	1.00	1.07	1.07	1.15	1.08	1.01
South Carolina	1.25	1.25	1.31	1.26	1.23	1.27	1.33	1.35
South Dakota	1.24	1.51	1.42	1.30	1.30	1.44	1.53	1.48
Tennessee	1.20	1.18	1.15	1.15	1.12	1.19	1.25	1.29
Texas	0.78	0.89	0.98	0.96	0.92	0.96	0.94	0.97
Utah	1.27	1.45	1.40	1.17	1.11	1.04	1.15	1.08
Vermont	1.10	0.94	0.88	0.94	1.03	1.06	1.13	1.09
Virginia	1.52	1.56	1.40	1.39	1.45	1.51	1.51	1.51
Washington	1.09	1.16	1.03	0.93	1.04	0.91	0.87	0.89

(Table continues)

Table 8-13 *(Continued)*

State	1982–1984	1986–1988	1989–1991	1992–1994	1995–1997	1998–2000	2001–2003	2005[a]
West Virginia	1.07	1.27	1.40	1.47	1.42	1.72	1.79	1.75
Wisconsin	0.82	0.84	0.85	0.83	0.80	0.84	0.87	0.88
Wyoming	0.75	1.04	1.13	1.04	1.04	1.06	1.11	1.09

Note: "——" indicates not available. Numbers are the estimated amount of federal expenditures in each state for each $1.00 of federal taxes paid by the residents of each state. Includes all federal expenditures that can be allocated by state. All figures are adjusted proportionally so that, overall, there is $1.00 of revenue for each $1.00 of expenditure (but see qualification about further adjustment due to borrowing for 1995–1997). Three-year averages for expenditures and revenue were used to ensure that unusually high or low figures in a particular state in any single year would not unduly influence the flow-of-fund ratios. Calculations do not take into account the precise location of taxes and expenditures—for example, where procurement spending actually occurred as indicated by subcontracts, not just the major contract (Michael Lawson, formerly with the U.S. Advisory Commission on Intergovernmental Relations, personal communication). To account for the larger use of borrowed funds to finance federal spending in the states, the fiscal year 1995–1997 total expenditure figures were lowered and set equal to total fiscal year tax collections. This total was then reallocated among the states using the actual fiscal year federal expenditure per state proportions. The ratios were then calculated by dividing the adjusted expenditures by the taxes paid. Data for earlier years can be found in previous editions of *Vital Statistics on American Politics*.

[a] Note source change for 2005. Numbers may not be fully comparable with previous years. See sources for details.

Sources: 1982–1984: U.S. Advisory Commission on Intergovernmental Relations, *Significant Features of Fiscal Federalism, 1985–86* (Washington, D.C.: U.S. Advisory Commission on Intergovernmental Relations, 1986), 178; 1986–1994: calculated by the editors from U.S. Bureau of the Census, *Federal Expenditures by State for Fiscal Year 1987* (Washington, D.C.: Government Printing Office, 1988), 1; *1988*, 1; *1989*, 1; *1991*, 1; *1992*, 1; *1993*, 1; *1994*, 1; Paul G. Merski, "The 1992 Federal Tax Burden by State," *Tax Foundation Special Report*, May 1992, 6; *Facts and Figures on Government Finance* (Washington, D.C.: Tax Foundation, 1994), 83–84; Tax Foundation, "1996 Federal Tax Burden by State, 1995"; 1995–2000: Tax Foundation, "Total Fiscal Tax Burden by State," Special Report, July 1996, 7; 1997, 7; 1998, 7; 1999, 7; 2000, 2–3; 2001, 2–3; 2002, 10; 2003, 2; 2004, 2; 2005: Northeast Midwest Institute, "Per Capita Tax Burden and Return on Federal Tax Dollar: Fiscal Year 2005" (*www.nemw.org*).

Table 8-14   Fiscal Dependency of Lower Levels on Higher Levels of
Government, 1927–2006

Year	Intergovernmental revenue as a percentage of total revenue		
	State from federal	Local from federal	Local from state[a]
1927	5.0	b	9.4
1934	27.3	1.3	20.7
1940	11.6	3.6	21.4
1946	9.4	0.1	21.9
1952	13.9	1.2	26.0
1957	14.2	1.2	25.2
1962	18.9	1.8	25.2
1965	20.2	2.2	32.5
1967	22.3	2.7	28.5
1970	21.6	2.9	30.2
1973	24.2	6.1	31.0
1977	22.4	8.4	30.7
1980	22.3	8.2	31.5
1981	21.8	7.8	30.9
1982	20.0	6.7	30.2
1983	19.3	6.2	29.1
1984	19.2	5.7	28.9
1985	19.2	5.4	28.9
1986	19.3	4.7	29.2
1987	18.5	4.2	29.1
1988	18.5	3.5	29.4
1989	18.4	3.3	29.6
1990	18.7	3.2	29.7
1991	20.4	3.1	29.8
1992	21.4	3.1	30.3
1993	22.0	3.1	30.3
1994	22.7	3.3	30.2
1995	22.3	3.5	30.7
1996	21.5	3.3	30.3
1997	20.7	3.4	30.5
1998	20.3	3.4	30.3
1999	20.7	3.3	31.1
2000	20.6	3.2	31.3
2001	24.4	3.3	31.9
2002	28.9	4.0	32.8
2003	26.5	4.0	32.5
2004	23.6	4.0	30.4
2005	23.5	4.0	30.5
2006	22.4	3.9	30.0

Note: Data for additional years can be found in previous editions of *Vital Statistics on American Politics*.

[a] Includes indirect federal aid passed through the states.

[b] Less than 0.1 percent.

Sources: 1927–1992: Calculated by the editors from U.S. Advisory Commission on Intergovernmental Relations, *Significant Features of Fiscal Federalism, 1994*, vol. 2 (Washington, D.C.: U.S. Advisory Commission on Intergovernmental Relations, 1994), 44; 1993–2006: U.S. Census Bureau (*www.census.gov/govs/estimate*).

Table 8-15   Variations in Local Dependency on State Aid, 2005–2006

Rank	State	Percentage	Rank	State	Percentage
1	Vermont	66.7	27	Virginia	33.7
2	Arkansas	52.0	28	Kansas	33.5
3	New Mexico	50.7	29	Indiana	33.3
4	Delaware	47.8	30	Iowa	33.3
5	Minnesota	46.1	31	New York	33.0
6	California	44.4	32	Utah	33.0
7	West Virginia	44.0	33	Alaska	32.4
8	Michigan	43.0	34	Rhode Island	31.5
9	Wisconsin	42.8	35	New Hampshire	31.1
10	Mississippi	42.0	36	South Carolina	30.4
11	Kentucky	39.4	37	Connecticut	30.2
12	North Carolina	38.9	38	Maine	29.9
13	Arizona	37.7	39	New Jersey	29.8
14	Massachusetts	37.6	40	Tennessee	29.7
15	Oklahoma	37.0	41	Georgia	29.6
16	Nevada	36.9	42	Missouri	29.2
17	Ohio	36.7	43	Illinois	28.1
18	Montana	35.9	44	Maryland	27.5
19	Idaho	35.8	45	Nebraska	26.3
20	Alabama	35.5	46	South Dakota	26.0
21	Oregon	35.2	47	Texas	25.0
22	Pennsylvania	35.2	48	Florida	24.6
23	Wyoming	34.6	49	Colorado	24.5
24	Louisiana	34.4	50	Hawaii	10.9
25	North Dakota	34.3			
26	Washington	34.1		Total	34.5

Note: Percentages reflect state transfers (including "pull-through" monies from the federal government) as a percentage of total local general revenues. Where ties occur, the rank order was determined by the second decimal. Data for earlier years can be found in previous editions of *Vital Statistics on American Politics.*

Source: U.S. Census Bureau, "State and Local Government Finances, by Level of Government and by State: 2005–2006" (*www.census.gov*).

Table 8-16   State Government Performance, 2008

State	Overall	Money[a]	People[b]	Infrastructure[c]	Information[d]
Alabama	C+	C–	B–	C+	C
Alaska	C–	C–	C–	C–	B–
Arizona	B–	C+	B–	B–	B–
Arkansas	C	B–	C–	C+	C–
California	C	D+	C–	B–	C+
Colorado	C+	C+	C	C+	C
Connecticut	B–	B–	B–	C+	B–
Delaware	B+	A–	B	B+	B–
Florida	B–	B–	C–	A–	B–
Georgia	B+	B+	A–	B	B+
Hawaii	C+	C+	B–	C	C–
Idaho	B–	B+	C+	B–	C+
Illinois	C	C–	C–	C	C+
Indiana	B	B+	B	B+	B–
Iowa	B	B+	B+	C+	B+
Kansas	B–	B–	C+	C+	B
Kentucky	B–	C+	C+	A–	B
Louisiana	B	B	B	C+	B+
Maine	C	C	C–	C+	C
Maryland	B	B+	C+	B+	B–
Massachusetts	C	C+	C	D+	C
Michigan	B+	C+	B+	A–	A
Minnesota	B–	B+	B–	C+	B
Mississippi	C+	C+	C	C+	C
Missouri	B+	B+	B–	B+	A
Montana	C+	C+	B–	C+	C+
Nebraska	B	A–	B–	B+	B–
Nevada	C+	C+	C–	B–	B–
New Hampshire	D+	C–	D	D+	D+
New Jersey	C	C–	B–	C+	C–
New Mexico	B–	B–	C	C+	B
New York	B–	C+	B–	B–	C+
North Carolina	B–	B–	B	B–	B–
North Dakota	B–	B	C	B–	C+
Ohio	B–	B	C+	B–	B–
Oklahoma	C+	B–	C+	C–	C
Oregon	C+	C+	C+	C+	B–
Pennsylvania	B–	B	C+	B–	B
Rhode Island	C–	D+	D	C+	C
South Carolina	B–	B–	A–	C–	B–
South Dakota	C+	B+	C+	B	D+
Tennessee	B–	B–	C	B	B
Texas	B+	B	B	B	A–
Utah	A–	A	B+	A	A
Vermont	B–	B–	C+	B+	C–
Virginia	A–	A–	A	B+	A
Washington	A–	A–	A–	B+	A

(Table continues)

Table 8-16   *(Continued)*

State	Overall	Money[a]	People[b]	Infrastructure[c]	Information[d]
West Virginia	C+	B	C	C−	C
Wisconsin	B−	C+	B−	B−	C+
Wyoming	B−	B	C−	B	C+
Fifty-state average	B−	B−	C+	B−	B−
Grade distribution (percent)					
A	0	2	2	2	10
A−	6	8	6	6	2
B+	10	16	6	16	6
B	10	14	10	10	12
B−	36	20	22	20	26
C+	20	24	20	30	16
C	14	2	14	4	16
C−	2	10	16	8	8
D+	2	4	0	4	4
D	0	0	4	0	0

Note: Grades result from a collaboration between staffers and editors at *GOVERNING* magazine and the Pew Center on the States Government Performance Project. They are based on a variety of sources, including public documents and data, interviews, and surveys. For details on the sources, grading criteria, and meaning of the assessment categories, see *http://results.gppon line.org*. For other measures of state government performance, see previous editions of *Vital Statistics on American Politics.*

[a] How states manage fiscal resources, including budgeting, forecasting, accounting and financial reporting, procurement, contracting, investments, and debt.
[b] What states are doing to recruit and retain strong professionals and are offering in development and recognition for top-level service.
[c] How states maintain, improve, and plan for future physical infrastructure needs, including roads, bridges, and buildings.
[d] How effectively states apply data and technology to measure the effectiveness of services, make decisions, and communicate with the public.

Sources: *GOVERNING*, March 2008 (*www.governing.com*); Pew Center on the States, Government Performance Project (*http://results.gpponline.org*).

9

Foreign and Military Policy

- **Treaties and Agreements**
- **Military Engagements**
- **Military Personnel**
- **Expenditures**
- **Military Sales and Assistance**
- **Foreign Aid**
- **Investment and Trade**

Even researchers seeking to understand only U.S. domestic politics would find data on international relations essential. In the 1960 presidential campaign, for example, John F. Kennedy made the "missile gap" a major issue: the United States was falling behind the Soviet Union in its missile arsenal, which imperiled the defense of the free world. The actual existence of that missile gap has been disputed, but the charge fit in with Kennedy's pledge to get the country moving again and played well to the public in the aftermath of *Sputnik* and the U-2 incident. More recently, the events of September 11, 2001, the wars in Iraq and Afghanistan, and continuing acts of terrorism have made once "foreign" concerns very immediate.

Statistics related to foreign policy, especially its military aspects, may be difficult or impossible to find. After all, secrecy prevents publication of important information about U.S. defense capabilities. For example, the performance capabilities of spy satellites and the ability to fight computer hackers are understandably kept secret. Secret diplomatic and military initiatives also are undertaken by the Central Intelligence Agency and other organizations, and the public learns about these only later, if at all. One example is the sale of weapons to Iran in the 1980s while the United States was publicly declaring that it would have nothing to do with that country and the use of profits from these sales to support the Nicaraguan contras. Another example is the Central Intelligence Agency's pre-Iraq War assessments of weapons of mass destruction.

And yet despite these examples and the obvious need for secrecy in defense-related areas, a surprisingly wide array of data are available, in part because details about military hardware are not the only kinds of relevant information. As was especially evident during the 1960s, for example, public opinion on foreign policy is extraordinarily relevant and powerful information. But public opinion on U.S. involvement in world affairs has had its ups and downs (Table 3-16), and the public's judgment about whether foreign or domestic problems are "most important" has shifted sharply over time (Figures 3-11 and 3-12). Evaluations of U.S. involvement in Iraq (Figure 3-18) and the fight against terrorism (Table 3-18) have also fluctuated over time.

Diplomatic efforts, both current and historical, as well as international arms control and other agreements (Tables 9-1 and 9-2) are also relevant inasmuch as they are affected by and, in turn, affect domestic politics. The historical record of U.S. involvement abroad in both the distant and recent past (Tables 9-3 through 9-5) serves as a reminder that the end of the "new world order" has not signaled a withdrawal from foreign engagements. Likewise, the number and placement of U.S. troops abroad remain important issues (Table 9-6). More obviously, data on military personnel are sometimes directly related to domestic concerns, as, for example, in the table on military personnel categorized by sex, race, and Hispanic origin (Table 9-7).

A variety of other information is closely related to both defense and domestic policy, and this kind of data is emphasized here. Defense spending, for example, involves more than whether the United States has spent enough to defend itself. Elementary economics courses express the trade-off between defense and nondefense spending in terms of "guns or butter." Every dollar spent on weaponry means that a dollar less can be spent on social programs, tax reductions, and other politically worthy causes. Therefore, information on defense spending (Table 9-8 and Figure 9-1) is doubly relevant.

In information on defense spending, two elements arise. The first is the concept of "constant" versus "current" dollars. Current dollars are what people deal with every day. The price asked for goods is the price paid; whether the price has gone up more or less than other prices is not especially relevant. People may be aware that the prices of some goods have gone up (such as oil and gasoline in the 1970s and again in the 2000s) or down (such as many electronic products) more than others, but the price quoted is what is most significant. Constant dollars, by contrast, take into account what has happened to prices more generally (see Table 11-2 for the Consumer Price Index). Thus, for example, most food clearly costs more in current dollars than it did years ago—in the 1960s one never heard of a loaf of bread that cost $3.00. Yet relative to other prices the cost of bread has fallen. Its price may have only doubled over a given period of time while other prices have tripled. In a meaningful sense, then, bread and other foods are cheaper than they used to be; the "real" cost of bread has been reduced.

Another, perhaps simpler way to express this concept is to say that constant dollar calculations take inflation into account. For defense spending, then, the question is whether, after inflation is taken into account, spending has increased. If spending has risen only as fast as inflation, the new budget will buy only as much as the previous budget, even though nominally—that is, in current dollars—it is larger. Because this issue of real versus current dollars is so significant, Table 9-8 and many of the tables in Chapter 11 express expenditures both ways.

The second element in presenting information on defense spending is the relevance of what other countries are doing (Table 9-9). Whether the United States is spending a lot or a little is a relative question. If foreign adversaries raise their spending, then perhaps the United States must do the same.

Economic and social dimensions are also relevant to U.S. foreign and military policy, and data about these are widely available. The slippage of the U.S. trade balance (Table 9-13) and the increasing foreign investment in the United States and U.S. investment abroad (Table 9-12) are two aspects of the economic context of recent foreign policy discussions. Foreign aid, whether in the form of military (Table 9-10) or nonmilitary (Table 9-11) assistance, is another part of economic foreign policy. Finally, immigration policy has social and economic implications, and changes in the flow of immigrants, along with future prospects, make it a most significant aspect of U.S. foreign relations (Tables 10-2 through 10-4 and Figure 10-2).

Despite the end to the Cold War, public opinion about wars, international agreements, previous conflicts, levels of defense spending, foreign aid, the balance of trade, and so on—and the data about them—remain as relevant as ever. The emergence of the United States as a world power in the twentieth century elevated the political significance of international relations, so that no overview of American politics would be complete without a look at foreign and military policy. Foreign policy has often proved critical in domestic politics, and that accounts for the numbers presented here.

Table 9-1   Treaties and Executive Agreements Concluded by the United States, 1789–2008

Years	Number of treaties	Number of executive agreements
1789–1839	60	27
1839–1889	215	238
1889–1929	382	763
1930–1932	49	41
1933–1944 (F. Roosevelt)	131	369
1945–1952 (Truman)	132	1,324
1953–1960 (Eisenhower)	89	1,834
1961–1963 (Kennedy)	36	813
1964–1968 (L. Johnson)	67	1,083
1969–1974 (Nixon)	93	1,317
1975–1976 (Ford)	26	666
1977–1980 (Carter)	79	1,476
1981–1988 (Reagan)	125	2,840
1989–1992 (G. H. W. Bush)	67	1,350
1993–2000 (Clinton)	209	2,048
2001–2008 (G. W. Bush)	133	1,984

Note: Number of treaties includes those concluded during the indicated span of years. Some of these treaties did not receive the consent of the U.S. Senate. Because of varying definitions of what comprises an executive agreement and their entry-into-force date, the numbers in the table are approximate.

Sources: 1789–1992: *Congressional Quarterly's Guide to Congress*, 5th ed. (Washington, D.C.: CQ Press, 2000), 219; 1993–2008: Office of the Assistant Legal Adviser for Treaty Affairs, U.S. Department of State.

Table 9-2   Major Arms Control and Disarmament Agreements

Issue	Participants
Nuclear weapons	
To prevent the spread of nuclear weapons	
Antarctic Treaty, 1959	37 nations
Outer Space Treaty, 1967	127 nations
Latin American Nuclear-Free Zone Treaty, 1967	29 nations
Nuclear Non-proliferation Treaty, 1968	190 nations[a]
Seabed Treaty, 1971	117 nations
To reduce the risk of nuclear war	
Hot Line and Modernization Agreements, 1963	United States and Soviet Union
Accidents Measures Agreement, 1971	United States and Soviet Union
Prevention of Nuclear War Agreement, 1973	United States and Soviet Union
To limit nuclear testing	
Limited Test Ban Treaty, 1963	131 nations
Threshold Test Ban Treaty, 1974	United States and Soviet Union
Peaceful Nuclear Explosions Treaty, 1976[b]	United States and Soviet Union
Comprehensive Test Ban Treaty, 1996	177 nations[c]
To limit nuclear weapons	
ABM Treaty (SALT I) and Protocol, 1972	United States and Soviet Union
SALT I Interim Agreement, 1972[d]	United States and Soviet Union
SALT II, 1979[e]	United States and Soviet Union
Intermediate Range Nuclear Forces (INF) Treaty, 1987	United States and Soviet Union
Strategic Arms Reduction Treaty (START), 1991	United States, Russia, Belarus, Kazakstan, Ukraine[f]
Strategic Arms Reduction Treaty, II (START II), 1993	United States and Russia[g]
Moscow Treaty on Strategic Offensive Reductions, 2002	United States and Russia
Other weapons	
To prohibit use of gas	
Geneva Protocol, 1925	131 nations
To prohibit biological weapons	
Biological Weapons Convention, 1972	171 nations[h]
To prohibit techniques changing the environment	
Environmental Modification Convention, 1977	85 nations

(Table continues)

Table 9-2 *(Continued)*

Issue	Participants
To control use of inhumane weapons Convention on Conventional Weapons, 1981	100 nations[i]
To limit conventional weapons Conventional Forces in Europe Treaty, 1990	30 nations[j]
To ban use, development, production, stockpiling of chemical weapons Chemical Weapons Convention, 1993	180 nations[k]

Note: "Participation" does not necessarily imply signing without reservations or ratification. In some instances, an agreement is no longer in force. For details, see sources.

[a] Number of parties and signatories as of February 2007.

[b] Ratified by the United States and entered into force December 1990.

[c] Number of parties and signatories as of February 2007. Not entered into force as of February 2007.

[d] Expired by its terms October 3, 1977.

[e] Never ratified. If the treaty had entered into force, it would have expired by its terms December 31, 1985.

[f] Ratified by the United States October 1992; entered into force December 1994. President Obama and President Dmitri A. Medvedev of Russia signed an agreement on July 6, 2009, to cut deployed nuclear warheads and to reduce delivery systems, setting the stage for negotiations to replace the 1991 Strategic Arms Reduction Treaty that expires in December 2009.

[g] Ratified by the United States as of January 1996. Ratified by Russia in April: 2000, but with amendments not approved by the U.S. Senate.

[h] Number of parties and signatories as of June 2005.

[i] Entered into force December 1983. Number of parties and signatories as of February 2006. Full title of treaty is Convention on Prohibitions or Restrictions on the Use of Certain Conventional Weapons Which May Be Deemed to Be Excessively Injurious or to Have Indiscriminate Effects (and Protocols).

[j] Ratified by the United States December 1991; entered into force November 1992.

[k] Ratified by the United States April 25, 1997; took effect April 29, 1997. Number of parties and signatories as of October 2006.

Sources: U.S. Department of State, Bureau of Arms Control (*www.state.gov*); archive site for State Department information prior to January 20, 2001 (*www.state.gov*); note "a": United Nations Office for Disarmament Affairs, "Treaty on the Non-Proliferation of Nuclear Weapons (NPT)" (*http://disarmament.un.org*); note "c": CTBTO Preparatory Commission (*www.ctbto.org*); notes "h" and "k": Biological and Toxic Weapons Convention Web site (*www.opbw.org*); note "i": Defense Treaty Inspection Readiness Program, "Convention on Conventional Weapons" (*http://dtirp.dtra.mil*).

Table 9-3   Use of U.S. Armed Forces Abroad, 1798–2008

Decade	Number of instances	Example of use of armed forces
1798–1800	1	Undeclared naval war with France
1801–1810	4	Tripoli—First Barbary War
1811–1820	13	Caribbean—engagements with pirates, onshore and offshore
1821–1830	8	Cuba—fight, capture pirates
1831–1840	7	Fiji Islands—punish natives who attacked American explorers
1841–1850	8	China—after a clash at a trading post in Canton
1851–1860	22	Nicaragua—oppose William Walker's attempt to control country
1861–1870	13	Japan—several times, to protect American interests
1871–1880	5	Colombia—protect American interests in fighting over Panama
1881–1890	7	Hawaii—protect American interests
1891–1900	18	Philippine Islands—protect American interests; conquer islands
1901–1910	16	Colombia, Panama, Dominican Republic, Honduras, Nicaragua—protect American interests during civil turmoil
1911–1920	29	Honduras, China, Turkey, Mexico—protect American interests
1921–1930	15	Panama, Costa Rica—to prevent war over boundary dispute
1931–1940	7	Haiti—part of long-term stay to prevent chronic insurrection
1941–1950	13	Trieste—reinforce air forces after Yugoslav downing of plane
1951–1960	6	Korean War; Lebanon—protect against threatened insurrection
1961–1970	8	Vietnam War; Congo—airlift Congolese troops during rebellion
1971–1980	11	Lebanon—evacuate citizens fighting; Iran—rescue attempt
1981–1990	23	Libya—shoot down jets; Grenada—restore law and order
1991–2000	29	Persian Gulf War; Somalia—food aid; Haiti—oust military; Bosnia—keep peace; Yugoslavia—aid Kosovo
2001–2008	9	Afghanistan, Haiti, Iraq, Kosovo, Macedonia, Pakistan, Philippines, Somalia (pirates), and Yemen

Note: The count of instances is necessarily approximate; for example, numerous engagements with pirates in the Caribbean between 1814 and 1825 are counted as only one instance. Five of the instances were declared wars: War of 1812 (1812–1815); Mexican War (1846–1848); Spanish-American War (1898); World War I (1917–1918); World War II (1941–1945). Others might be considered undeclared wars: undeclared naval war with France (1798–1800); First Barbary War (1801–1805); Second Barbary War (1815); Korean War (1950–1953); Vietnam War (1964–1973); Persian Gulf War (1991); Iraq War (2003). (Actions that covered more than one decade are counted as occurring in each decade.) A detailed list of over five hundred incidents abroad appears in Benjamin O. Fordham and Christopher C. Sarver, "Militarized Interstate Disputes and United States Uses of Force," *International Studies Quarterly* (September 2001).

Sources: Ellen C. Collier, *Instances of Use of United States Armed Forces Abroad, 1798–1993* (Washington, D.C.: Congressional Research Service, 1993); updated by the editors based on reports in the *New York Times*.

Table 9-4 U.S. Personnel in Major Military Conflicts

Item	Civil War[a]	Spanish-American War	World War I	World War II	Korean conflict	Vietnam War	Persian Gulf War	Iraq War	Afghan conflict
Personnel serving (thousands)	2,213	307[b]	4,735	16,113[c]	5,720[d]	8,744[e]	2,233[f]	—	—
Average duration of service (months)	20	8	12	33	19	23	7	—	—
Casualties (thousands)									
Battle deaths	140	g	53	292	34	47[h]	g	3.4[i]	0.5[i]
Wounds not mortal	282	2	204	671	103	153[h]	g	31.2[i]	2.8[i]
Draftees: classified (thousands)	777	0	24,234	36,677	9,123	75,717[e]	0	0	0
Examined	522	0	3,764	17,955	3,685	8,611	0	0	0
Rejected	160	0	803	6,420	1,189	3,880	0	0	0
Inducted	46	0	2,820	10,022	1,560	1,759	0	0	0
Cost (millions)[j]									
Current	$2,300	$270	$32,700	$360,000	$50,000	$140,600	$7,300[k]	$664,963[l]	$187,034[l]
Constant (1967)	8,500	1,100	100,000	816,300	69,300	148,800	1,790	—	—

Note: "—" indicates not available. For Revolutionary War, the number of personnel serving is not known, but estimates range from 184,000 to 250,000; for War of 1812, 286,730 served; for Mexican-American War, 78,718 served.

a Union forces only. Estimates of the number serving in Confederate forces range from 600,000 to 1.5 million; cost for the Confederacy estimated at $1 million (current dollars) and $3.7 million (constant dollars).
b Covers April 21, 1898, to August 13, 1898.
c Covers December 1, 1941, to December 31, 1946.
d Covers June 25, 1950, to July 27, 1953.
e Covers August 4, 1964, to January 27, 1973.
f Covers August 1, 1990, to April 30, 1992.
g Fewer than 500.
h Covers January 1, 1961, to January 27, 1973.
i As of April 23, 2009. For the Afghan conflict, includes a small number of casualties in other locations in and around Afghanistan.
j Original direct costs only. Excludes service-connected veterans' benefits and interest payments on war loans.
k Total costs estimated at $61.6 billion (in current dollars). Shown is the portion of that amount estimated to have been paid by the United States.
l Estimate of cost through April 21, 2009. Costs are approximations because these wars are ongoing.

Sources: U.S. Bureau of the Census, *Statistical Abstract of the United States, 1994* (Washington, D.C.: Government Printing Office, 1994), 357, 362; *2004–2005* (2004), 333; cost (through Vietnam), *1994*, 357; Iraq War and Afghan conflict: U.S. Department of Defense (*www.defenselink.mil/news/casualty.pdf*); National Priorities Project (*http://costofwar.com*).

Table 9-5 U.S. Military Forces and Casualties in Vietnam, 1957–1993

Year	Military forces (thousands)	Battle deaths				Wounded, nonfatal[a]	
		Total[a]	Killed	Died of wounds	Died while missing[b]	Hospital care (thousands)	No hospital care (thousands)
1957–1964	23.3[c]	279	197	10	72	0.8	0.8
1965	184.3	1,432	1,124	111	197	3.3	2.8
1966	385.3	5,047	4,142	579	326	16.5	13.6
1967	485.6	9,463	7,525	1,598	401	32.4	29.7
1968	536.1	14,623	12,624	979	959	46.8	46.0
1969	475.2	9,426	8,117	1,168	141	32.9	37.3
1970	234.6	4,230	3,486	555	189	15.2	15.4
1971	156.8	1,376	1,082	160	134	4.8	4.2
1972	24.2	361	205	28	128	0.6	0.6
1973–1993	0.0	1,118	0	22	1,068	[d]	[d]
Total	[e]	47,355	38,502	5,210	3,615	153.3	150.4

Note: Military forces as of December 31. All U.S. forces withdrawn by January 27, 1973. Discrepancies in total battle deaths and sum of categories for 1967, 1968, and 1973–1993 are found in the source.

[a] Casualties from enemy action. Deaths exclude 10,803 servicemen who died in accidents or from disease.
[b] Includes 114 servicemen who died while captured.
[c] For 1964 only.
[d] Fewer than fifty.
[e] Not applicable.

Sources: Military forces, battle deaths: U.S. Bureau of the Census, *Statistical Abstract of the United States, 1995* (Washington, D.C.: Government Printing Office, 1995), 365; wounded, nonfatal: *Statistical Abstract of the United States, 1987*, 328.

Table 9-6 U.S. Military Personnel Abroad or Afloat, by Country, 1972–2008 (thousands)

Country	1972	1975	1980	1985	1990	1995	2000	2002	2003	2004	2005	2006	2007	2008
Outside United States[a]	628	517	502	515	609	238	258	230	253[b]	288[b]	291[b]	285[b]	295[b]	289[b]
Europe[a,c]	298	314	332	358	310	118	117	113	118	115	102	96	86	82
Germany	210	220	244	247	228	73	69	69	75	76	66	64	57	55
Greece	3	4	4	4	2	d	1	1	1	d	d	d	d	d
Iceland	3	3	3	4	3	2	2	2	2	1	1	d	d	d
Italy	10	12	12	15	14	12	11	12	13	13	12	10	10	10
Spain	9	9	9	9	7	3	2	3	2	2	2	2	1	1
Turkey	7	7	5	5	4	3	2	2	2	2	2	2	2	2
United Kingdom	22	21	24	30	25	12	11	10	12	11	11	10	10	9
Afloat	28	30	22	36	18	8	4	5	5	2	2	2	1	1
East Asia and Pacific[a]	275	156	115	125	119	89	101	96	100	90	79	75	73	69
Japan (includes Okinawa)	65	48	46	50	45	43	40	42	41	36	36	33	33	33
Korea, Rep. of	41	42	39	42	41	36	37	38	41	41	31	29	27	25
Philippines	17	15	13	15	14	d	d	d	d	d	d	d	d	d
Thailand	47	20	d	d	d	d	1	d	d	d	d	d	d	d
Vietnam	47	0	0	0	0	d	d	d	d	d	d	d	d	d
Afloat	51	28	16	20	16	13	23	16	17	12	12	11	12	10
U.S. outlying areas[e]	29	25	2	14	11	9	6	6	5	4	3	3	3	3
Troop and civilian employee dependents	342	365	369	385	400	223	200	165	171	213	166	—	—	—

Note: "—" indicates troops in countries not shown.

[a] Includes troops in countries not shown.

[b] In addition, as of September 30 each year, the following numbers of troops were in and around Iraq: 183,002 in 2003; 170,647 in 2004; 192,600 in 2005; 185,500 in 2006; 218,500 in 2007; and 190,400 in 2008. Also in and around Afghanistan: 19,500 in 2005; 21,500 in 2006; 25,240 in 2007; and 32,300 in 2008.

[c] Western Europe and related areas.

[d] Fewer than five hundred.

[e] Primarily Guam and Puerto Rico.

Sources: 1972–1985: U.S. Bureau of the Census, *Statistical Abstract of the United States, 1977* (Washington, D.C.: Government Printing Office, 1977), 370; *1986*, 343; 1990–1995: U.S. Department of Defense, *Selected Manpower Statistics, Fiscal Year 1990* (Washington, D.C.: Government Printing Office, 1991), 44–47, 51, 176; *1995*, 1–6; 2000–2005: U.S. Department of Defense, *Worldwide Manpower Distribution by Geographical Area* (Washington, D.C.: Government Printing Office, 2000), 8–12, 32; (2002), 8–12, 40; (2003), 8–11, 38; (2004), 12–16, 35; (2005), 8–11, 38; (2006), 1–4; (2007), 1–4; (2008), 1–4.

Table 9-7 U.S. Active Duty Forces, by Sex, Race, and Hispanic Origin, 1965–2007

Year	Female			Black			Hispanic[a]			Total[b]	
	Officers	Enlisted	Total	Officers	Enlisted	Total	Officers	Enlisted	Total	Officers (thousands)	Enlisted (thousands)
1965	3.1%	0.9%	1.2%	1.9%	10.5%	9.5%	—	—	—	339	2,317
1966	3.2	0.8	1.1	—	—	—	—	—	—	349	2,745
1967	3.3	0.8	1.0	2.1	9.9	8.9	—	—	—	385	2,992
1968	3.2	0.8	1.1	2.1	10.2	9.2	—	—	—	416	2,132
1969	3.1	0.9	1.1	2.1	9.6	8.7	—	—	—	419	3,041
1970	3.3	1.1	1.4	2.2	11.0	9.8	—	—	—	402	2,664
1971	3.5	1.3	1.6	2.3	12.1	10.7	1.3%	3.4%	3.1%	371	2,329
1972	3.8	1.6	1.9	2.4	13.5	11.9	1.2	4.0	3.6	336	1,987
1973	4.0	2.2	2.5	2.7	14.9	13.2	1.2	4.5	4.0	321	1,932
1974	4.3	3.3	3.5	3.0	16.2	14.4	1.3	4.5	3.9	303	1,860
1975	4.6	4.5	4.6	3.2	16.2	14.4	1.4	4.6	4.2	292	1,836
1976	5.0	5.3	5.2	3.6	17.1	15.2	1.3	4.6	4.2	281	1,801
1977	5.4	5.8	5.7	3.9	17.4	15.6	1.5	4.5	4.1	276	1,798
1978	6.2	6.5	6.5	4.3	19.3	17.3	1.6	4.5	4.1	274	1,788
1979	6.9	7.5	7.4	4.7	21.2	19.0	1.6	4.4	3.8	274	1,753
1980	7.7	8.5	8.4	5.0	21.9	19.6	1.2	4.0	3.6	278	1,759
1981	8.1	9.0	8.9	5.3	22.1	19.8	1.2	4.1	3.7	285	1,783
1982	8.6	9.0	9.0	5.3	22.0	19.7	1.2	4.1	3.7	292	1,804
1983	9.0	9.3	9.3	5.8	21.6	19.4	1.4	4.1	3.7	301	1,811
1984	9.4	9.5	9.5	6.2	21.1	19.0	1.4	3.9	3.6	304	1,820
1985	9.8	9.8	9.8	6.4	21.1	18.9	1.5	3.9	3.6	309	1,828
1986	10.1	10.0	10.1	6.5	21.2	19.1	1.7	4.1	3.7	311	1,845
1987	10.4	10.2	10.2	6.5	21.5	19.4	1.7	4.3	3.9	308	1,856
1988	10.7	10.4	10.4	6.7	22.0	19.8	1.8	4.5	4.1	305	1,819
1989	11.1	11.0	11.0	6.9	22.8	20.3	2.0	4.8	4.4	303	1,814
1990	11.4	10.9	10.9	6.9	22.9	20.5	2.1	5.0	4.6	304	1,762
1991	11.7	10.8	10.9	7.1	22.6	20.3	2.2	5.2	4.8	298	1,711

(Table continues)

Table 9-7 *(Continued)*

Year	Female			Black			Hispanic[a]			Total[b]	
	Officers	Enlisted	Total	Officers	Enlisted	Total	Officers	Enlisted	Total	Officers (thousands)	Enlisted (thousands)
1992	12.0	11.3	11.4	7.2	22.0	19.8	2.3	5.5	5.0	281	1,551
1993	12.4	11.5	11.7	7.1	21.6	19.4	2.4	5.8	5.3	264	1,466
1994	12.8	12.0	12.1	7.3	21.4	19.2	2.6	6.0	5.4	253	1,380
1995	13.0	12.5	12.6	7.5	21.5	19.3	2.8	6.4	5.8	245	1,295
1996	13.4	13.2	13.2	7.8	21.8	19.6	3.0	6.9	6.3	233	1,225
1997	13.6	13.7	13.7	8.0	22.1	19.8	3.2	7.5	6.8	228	1,198
1998	13.9	14.1	14.0	8.2	22.2	20.0	3.4	8.0	7.2	227	1,171
1999	14.0	14.2	14.2	8.3	22.0	19.8	3.7	8.5	7.7	224	1,179
2000	14.3	14.5	14.5	8.5	22.1	19.9	4.0	5.0	8.2	224	1,182
2001	14.6	14.8	14.8	8.8	22.1	20.0	3.9	9.4	8.6	223	1,181
2002	14.7	14.8	14.8	8.8	21.7	19.7	4.0	9.6	8.7	224	1,184
2003	15.2	14.9	14.9	8.9	20.6	18.8	4.5	9.8	9.0	235	1,227
2004	15.3	14.7	14.8	8.9	19.7	18.0	4.8	9.8	9.0	236	1,215
2005	15.3	14.3	14.5	8.9	19.1	17.4	4.9	9.8	9.0	234	1,179
2006	15.2	14.3	14.5	9.1	18.9	17.3	5.1	11.2	10.2	232	1,181
2007	15.1	14.1	14.3	9.1	18.5	17.0	5.2	11.4	10.4	230	1,177

Note: "___" indicates not available.

[a] Hispanics may be of any race. Data on percent Hispanic origin from 1971 to 1979 are based on male armed forces members only.
[b] Includes other races not shown separately.

Sources: 1965–1985: U.S. Bureau of the Census, *Statistical Abstract of the United States, 1976* (Washington, D.C.: Government Printing Office, 1976), 336; *1980, 375–376; 1984, 353; 1986, 341; 1987, 327; 1986–1988:* U.S. Department of Defense, unpublished data; 1989 (female, total officers, total enlisted): U.S. Department of Defense, *Selected Manpower Statistics, 1989* (Washington, D.C.: Government Printing Office, 1989), 78, 87, 101; 1989 (other): U.S. Department of Defense, *Defense 90 Almanac* (Washington, D.C.: Government Printing Office, 1990), 30; 1990–1998: *Defense Equal Opportunity Management Institute, Semi-Annual Race/Ethnic/Gender Profile of the Department of Defense Active Forces, Reserve Forces, and the United States Coast Guard* (Patrick Air Force Base, Fla.: Defense Equal Opportunity Management Institute—DEOMI, 1990), 24; (1991), 9; (1992)–(1998), 12; 1999–2002: Patrick Air Force Base (*www.patrick.af.mil*); 2003–2007: "Semiannual [now Annual] Demographic Profile of the Department of Defense and U.S. Coast Guard" (*www.deomi.org*).

Table 9-8   U.S. Defense Spending, 1940–2014

Year	Annual percentage change[a]		Defense outlays as a percentage of	
	Current dollars	Constant dollars	Federal outlays	Gross domestic product
1940	—	—	17.5	1.7
1941	287.7	225.1	47.1	5.6
1942	298.7	234.3	73.0	17.8
1943	160.0	143.2	84.9	37.0
1944	18.7	30.0	86.7	37.8
1945	4.8	13.2	89.5	37.5
1946	−48.6	−47.6	77.3	19.2
1947	−70.0	−72.2	37.1	5.5
1948	−28.9	−23.2	30.6	3.6
1949	44.4	43.1	33.9	4.9
1950	4.4	4.7	32.2	5.0
1951	71.7	63.3	51.8	7.4
1952	95.6	87.3	68.1	13.2
1953	14.6	4.9	69.4	14.2
1954	−6.7	−8.2	69.5	13.1
1955	−13.3	−16.2	62.4	10.8
1956	−0.5	−6.8	60.2	10.0
1957	6.8	1.7	59.3	10.1
1958	3.0	−1.3	56.8	10.2
1959	4.7	−0.7	53.2	10.0
1960	−1.8	0.9	52.2	9.3
1961	3.1	0.4	50.8	9.3
1962	5.5	4.8	49.0	9.2
1963	2.0	−2.1	48.0	8.9
1964	2.5	1.8	46.2	8.6
1965	−7.6	−7.3	42.8	7.4
1966	14.8	10.6	43.2	7.7
1967	22.9	18.7	45.4	8.8
1968	14.7	9.6	46.0	9.5
1969	0.7	−4.8	44.9	8.7
1970	−1.0	−6.2	41.8	8.1
1971	−3.5	−9.1	37.5	7.3
1972	0.4	−8.9	34.3	6.7
1973	−3.1	−10.2	31.2	5.9
1974	3.5	−4.0	29.5	5.5
1975	9.0	−1.8	26.0	5.5
1976	3.6	−3.8	24.1	5.2
TQ[b]	c	c	23.2	4.9
1977	8.5	−0.8	23.8	4.9
1978	7.5	0.2	22.8	4.7
1979	11.3	2.5	23.1	4.7
1980	15.2	3.8	22.7	4.9
1981	17.6	5.7	23.2	5.2
1982	17.6	8.8	24.8	5.7
1983	13.3	7.7	26.0	6.1

(Table continues)

Table 9-8   *(Continued)*

Year	Annual percentage change[a]		Defense outlays as a percentage of	
	Current dollars	Constant dollars	Federal outlays	Gross domestic product
1984	8.3	1.0	26.7	5.9
1985	11.1	6.7	26.7	6.1
1986	8.2	6.8	27.6	6.2
1987	3.2	1.7	28.1	6.1
1988	3.0	1.5	27.3	5.8
1989	4.5	1.5	26.5	5.6
1990	−1.4	−4.1	23.9	5.2
1991	−8.7	−12.8	20.6	4.6
1992	9.2	6.2	21.6	4.8
1993	−2.4	−4.0	20.7	4.4
1994	−3.2	−5.1	19.3	4.0
1995	−3.4	−5.2	17.9	3.7
1996	−2.3	−5.5	17.0	3.5
1997	1.8	−0.3	16.9	3.3
1998	−0.8	−2.1	16.2	3.1
1999	2.5	0.4	16.1	3.0
2000	7.1	3.8	16.5	3.0
2001	3.5	1.0	16.4	3.0
2002	14.3	10.8	17.3	3.4
2003	16.2	10.7	18.7	3.7
2004	12.6	8.2	19.9	4.0
2005	8.7	3.3	20.0	4.0
2006	5.4	1.1	19.7	4.0
2007	5.6	2.5	20.2	4.0
2008	11.8	9.3	20.7	4.3
2009 est.	12.0	11.0	17.3	4.8
2010 est.	3.3	2.0	19.9	4.8
2011 est.	−7.6	−8.8	18.2	4.2
2012 est.	−3.7	−5.3	17.5	3.8
2013 est.	0.3	−1.5	16.7	3.6
2014 est.	1.4	−0.4	16.1	3.5

Note: "—" indicates data not available.

[a] Change from prior year.
[b] Transition quarter, July–September.
[c] Not applicable.

Sources: Annual percentage change calculated from actual dollar amounts of defense spending in Table 11-3, this volume; percentage of federal outlays and GDP: U.S. Office of Management and Budget, *Budget of the U.S. Government, Fiscal Year 2010, Historical Tables* (Washington, D.C.: Government Printing Office, 2009), 119–126.

Figure 9-1   U.S. Defense Spending as a Percentage of Federal Outlays and of Gross
Domestic Product, 1940–2014

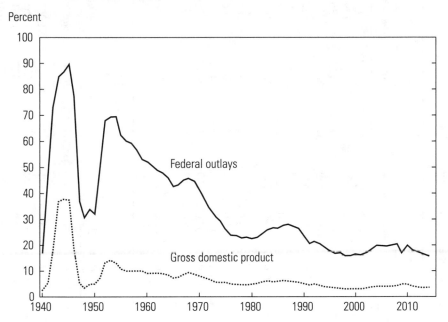

Note: Figures for 2009–2014 are estimates.

Source: Table 9-8, this volume.

Table 9-9 Military Expenditures: World, Regional, and Selected National Estimates, 1988–2008

Region[a]	Estimated expenditure (billions)										Percentage increase, 1988–2008
	1988	1990	1995	2000	2003	2004	2005	2006	2007	2008	
Africa	$12.1	$12.6	$10.9	$13.6	$15.1	$16.8	$17.3	$17.8	$18.6[b]	$20.4[b]	69
North	2.8	2.9	3.6	4.0	5.4	5.9	6.1	6.1	6.6[b]	7.8[b]	179
Sub-Saharan	9.3	9.7	7.3	9.5	9.7	10.9	11.2	11.7	11.9	12.6	35
Americas	525.0	493.0	396.0	383.0	482.0	523.0	549.0	559.0	576.0	603.0	15
North	499.0	473.0	370.0	354.0	453.0	493.0	516.0	525.0	539.0	564.0	13
Central	3.8	3.9	3.4	3.9	3.8	3.6	3.6	3.4	4.5	4.5	18
South	21.8	16.8	22.7	24.8	25.3	26.6	29.0	30.2	32.1	34.1	56
Asia and Oceania	103.0	110.0	124.0	139.0	160.0	169.0	177.0	186.0	196.0	206.0	100
Central Asia	c	c	0.5	c	c	c	c	c	c	c	c
East Asia	76.8	83.8	95.2	104.0	122.0	127.0	133.0	140.0	149.0	157.0	104
South Asia	15.0	15.8	17.5	22.8	24.2	27.5	28.9	29.2	29.9	30.9	106
Oceania	11.0	10.8	11.2	12.2	13.5	14.0	14.5	15.4	16.2	16.6	51
Europe	514.0	468.0	283.0	287.0	302.0	303.0	303.0	309.0	314.0	320.0	−38
Central and Eastern Europe	234.4	185.2	39.1	36.2	43.7	45.0	48.6	52.7	57.1	62.4	−73
Western	279.0	282.0	244.0	251.0	258.0	258.0	255.0	256.0	257.0	258.0	−8
Middle East	41.3	53.2	41.2	53.8	56.4	59.3	66.0	70.4	76.5	75.6	83

Top-spending nations in 2008 Country	Estimated expenditure (billions)										Spending per capita
	1988	1990	1995	2000	2003	2004	2005	2006	2007	2008	
United States	$484.0	$457.6	$357.4	$342.2	$440.8	$480.4	$503.4	$511.2	$524.6	$548.5	$1,967
China	—	13.1	15.0	23.8	36.4	40.6	44.9	52.2	57.9	63.6	63
France	56.9	57.3	52.8	50.2	52.6	54.1	52.9	53.2	53.4	52.6	1,061
United Kingdom	63.0	60.7	50.8	47.8	55.3	55.1	55.2	55.0	55.7	57.4	1,070

Russian Federation	218.4	171.3	21.7	19.1	25.1	26.1	28.5	31.2	33.8	38.2	413
Germany	55.6[d]	58.5[d]	43.2	41.1	40.0	38.8	38.1	37.1	37.2	37.2	568
Japan	37.1	39.5	42.5	43.8	44.8	44.5	44.2	43.7	43.5	42.8	361
Italy	30.1	29.2	25.8	34.1	34.7	34.9	33.5	32.4	33.0	32.1	689
Saudi Arabia	15.3	18.1	13.1	20.1	19.0	21.1	25.4	28.9	33.3	33.1	1,511
India	11.4	12.0	12.6	17.7	18.7	21.7	22.9	23.0	23.5	24.7	25
Korea, Rep. of	12.0	12.5	15.5	16.7	18.2	19.0	20.6	21.2	22.1	23.8	501
Brazil	11.8	8.0	11.7	12.9	12.1	12.4	13.4	12.7	14.8	15.5	120
Canada	15.1	15.0	12.7	11.4	12.0	12.4	13.0	13.6	14.8	15.9	581
Spain	12.2	11.8	10.8	11.1	11.4	11.7	11.8	13.8	14.3	14.7	430
Australia	9.4	9.4	10.0	11.0	12.3	12.8	13.3	14.1	14.9	15.3	876
World	1,195.0	1,137.0	856.0	877.0	1,015.0	1,071.0	1,113.0	1,142.0	1,182.0	1,226.0	217
Percentage change from previous year	—	-4.9	-24.7	2.5	15.7	5.5	3.9	2.6	3.5	3.7	—

Note: "—" indicates not available. Amounts in constant 2005 U.S. dollars, market exchange rates. Regional figures do not always add up to totals because of rounding. Figures are estimates for China and the Russian Federation in 1998–2008, for Brazil in 1988–1995, and for Saudi Arabia in 1990. Some countries are excluded because of lack of data or of consistent time series data. World totals exclude Cuba, Equatorial Guinea, Guyana, Haiti, Myanmar (Burma), North Korea, Qatar, Somalia, Trinidad and Tobago, and Vietnam. For details on the derivations of the estimates as well as differences among countries and over time in what counts as military expenditures, see source.

a For the country composition of the regions, see source (*www.sipri.org*).

b Because of missing data for some countries for some years, these regional or subregional totals are based on data accounting for less than 90 percent of what would presumably be the regional or subregional total if all countries could have been included.

c No subregional totals are presented when the estimate would be based on data accounting for less than 60 percent of what would presumably be the subregional total if all countries with missing data could have been included.

d Figures for Germany for 1988 and 1990 refer to the former Federal Republic of Germany (West Germany).

Sources: Adapted by the editors from Stockholm International Peace Research Institute, *SIPRI Yearbook 2009: Armaments, Disarmament and International Security* (Oxford: Oxford University Press, 2009), and from "World and Regional Military Expenditure Estimates, 1988–2008," "The Fifteen Major Spenders in 2008," and the SIPRI Military Expenditure Database (*www.sipri.org/contents/milap/milex/mex_data_index.html*). © SIPRI 2009. Reprinted by permission of SIPRI.

Table 9-10 U.S. Military Sales and Military Assistance to Foreign Governments, Principal Recipients, 1950–2007 (millions)

Country	Military sales								Military assistance[a]
	1950–2000	2001	2002	2003	2004	2005	2006	2007	1950–2007
Australia	$9,238.6	$303.0	$215.8	$208.0	$195.7	$349.6	$350.7	$789.4	$0.0
Belgium	3,385.7	169.0	68.3	70.6	42.1	49.6	52.6	48.9	1,203.8
Canada	3,952.5	113.3	85.2	154.8	144.4	150.7	183.0	281.0	0.0
France	1,636.8	141.7	206.1	276.0	98.9	69.2	42.7	47.0	4,047.8
Germany	12,799.7	329.6	221.2	241.4	263.6	208.4	149.2	206.0	884.8
Greece	5,791.9	447.8	469.1	1,324.3	1,224.8	468.3	180.5	222.4	1,673.2
Indochina	8.5	0.0	0.0	0.0	0.0	0.0	0.0	0.0	709.0
Iran	10,713.6	0.0	0.0	0.0	0.0	0.0	0.0	0.0	766.7
Israel	17,944.3	777.6	629.8	926.9	1,204.0	1,523.9	1,285.9	1,269.0	160.1
Italy	2,005.6	187.7	102.7	185.2	281.4	126.8	299.5	157.6	2,243.7
Korea, Rep. of	9,766.8	735.3	533.4	560.1	601.0	605.5	600.8	598.4	5,471.7
Netherlands	7,185.4	569.0	405.7	223.6	277.4	177.9	231.4	216.5	1,178.2
Saudi Arabia	56,605.9	1,876.2	1,307.8	1,010.7	1,223.2	994.3	994.6	1,083.7	23.9
Taiwan	17,160.4	1,162.4	1,393.1	709.9	917.4	1,415.0	1,074.2	789.4	2,554.6
Thailand	3,868.7	118.5	170.6	152.7	179.8	91.8	83.0	49.8	1,174.4
Turkey	10,857.9	465.5	280.8	276.6	290.0	189.5	247.2	196.2	3,165.3
United Kingdom	13,024.5	525.3	385.6	350.1	452.9	383.7	294.5	429.6	1,022.0
Vietnam	1.2	0.0	0.0	0.0	0.0	0.0	0.0	0.0	14,773.9
Total[b]	260,318.4	12,426.5	10,442.1	16,879.3	10,533.3	11,277.5	11,717.7	12,615.5	55,698.8

Note: Figures exclude training. Amounts in current dollars. Data for additional years can be found in previous editions of *Vital Statistics on American Politics.*

[a] Military assistance, especially to Europe, has been very low for a decade or more.
[b] Includes countries not shown.

Source: U.S. Defense Security Cooperation Agency, "Historical Facts Book as of September 30, 2007" (*www.dsca.mil*).

Table 9-11   U.S. Foreign Aid, Principal Recipients, 1962–2006 (millions)

Region/country	1962–2002	2003	2004	2005	2006
Asia[a]	$28,709	$1,333	$2,029	$2,864	$2,683
India	4,558	109	126	134	94
Indonesia	2,501	134	115	548	234
Korea, Rep. of	1,080	[b]	0	0	[b]
Pakistan	5,019	243	277	338	452
Philippines	3,393	92	115	100	97
Vietnam	4,528	13	11	9	9
Western Europe[a]	6,306	52	8	82	26
Eastern Europe[a]	5,313	507	493	371	374
Latin America and Caribbean[a]	25,398	593	630	719	654
Brazil	1,584	20	20	21	14
Costa Rica	1,395	2	1	2	2
Dominican Republic	1,066	28	33	27	26
El Salvador	3,644	44	41	41	38
Honduras	1,737	43	39	37	40
Jamaica	1035	21	24	40	20
Middle East and North Africa[a]	58,926	4,169	4,069	2,203	2,041
Egypt	22,249	403	653	269	487
Israel	30,271	597	479	411	295
Jordan	2,536	1032	385	350	324
Morocco	717	14	18	29	28
Sub-Saharan Africa[a]	20,414	1,278	1,643	1,524	1,559
Cameroon	327	[b]	1	1	1
Chad	184	[b]	[b]	5	5
Kenya	977	63	68	42	70
Niger	404	[b]	[b]	4	4
Senegal	685	39	40	37	46
Somalia	471	8	7	11	16
Sudan	983	63	185	354	316
Zaire/Dem. Rep. of Congo	739	71	81	79	93
Zambia	640	57	59	35	50
Zimbabwe	642	24	32	27	18
Eurasia[a]	8,040	861	734	699	627
Russia	2,310	161	119	107	107
Ukraine	1097	60	134	134	130
Oceania and other	224	[b]	1	[b]	0
Total[c]	194,238	10,534	11,414	10,273	9,827

Note: Amounts in current dollars. Shown are loans and grants made by the U.S. Agency for International Development and its predecessor agencies. Excluded are Food for Peace and "other" economic assistance. Data for individual years before 2002 can be found in previous editions of *Vital Statistics on American Politics.*

[a] Includes countries not shown separately.
[b] Less than $1 million.
[c] Includes interregional aid.

Source: U.S. Agency for International Development, *U.S. Overseas Loans and Grants and Assistance from International Organizations, July 1, 1945–September 30, 2006* (Washington, D.C.: Government Printing Office, 2008) (*www.usaid.gov*).

Table 9-12   Foreign Investment in the United States and U.S. Investment Abroad, 1950–2007 (millions)

Year	All areas	Canada	Europe	Japan
Foreign direct investment in the United States				
1950	$3,391	$1,029	$2,228	—
1960	6,910	1,934	4,707	$88
1970	13,270	3,117	9,554	229
1980	83,046	12,162	54,688	4,723
1985	184,615	17,131	121,413	19,313
1990	396,702	30,037	250,973	81,775
1995	535,553	45,618	332,374	104,997
2000	1,256,867	114,309	887,014	159,690
2001	1,343,987	92,420	999,069	149,859
2002	1,327,170	92,529	958,330	147,372
2003	1,395,159	95,707	1,001,237	157,176
2004	1,520,316	125,276	1,078,782	174,490
2005	1,634,121	165,667	1,154,048	189,851
2006	1,843,885	175,198	1,324,355	204,833
2007	2,093,049	213,224	1,482,978	233,148
U.S. investment abroad				
1950	11,788	3,579	1,733	19
1960	32,778	11,198	6,681	254
1970	78,178	22,790	24,516	1,483
1980	215,578	44,978	96,539	6,243
1985	230,250	46,909	105,171	9,235
1990	430,521	69,508	214,739	22,599
1995	699,015	83,498	344,596	37,309
2000	1,316,247	132,472	687,320	57,091
2001	1,460,352	152,601	771,936	55,651
2002	1,616,548	166,473	859,378	66,468
2003	1,769,613	187,953	976,889	57,794
2004	2,160,844	214,931	1,180,130	71,005
2005	2,241,656	231,836	1,210,679	81,175
2006	2,454,674	230,045	1,341,116	92,383
2007	2,791,269	257,058	1,551,165	101,607

Note: "—" indicates not available. Amounts are in current dollars. Data for additional years can be found in previous editions of *Vital Statistics on American Politics.*

Sources: 1950–1960: U.S. Department of Commerce, *Foreign Business Investments in the United States: A Supplement to Survey of Current Business* (Washington, D.C.: Government Printing Office, 1962), 34; 1970–2007: *Survey of Current Business*, August 1973, 50; September 1973, 24; August 1982, 21; August 1985, 63; August 1988, 65, 80; August 1992, 89; August 1994, 134; September 1998, 83; October 1998, 129; September 2003, 67, 119; September 2004, 76–78, 118–120; September 2005, 134; September 2006, 56–59, 104–106; September 2008, D-65, D-67.

Table 9-13   U.S. Balance of Trade, 1946–2008 (millions)

Year	Balance on goods[a]	Balance on current account[b]	Year	Balance on goods[a]	Balance on current account[b]
1946	$6,697	$4,885	1978	-$33,927	-$15,143
1947	10,124	8,992	1979	-27,568	-285
1948	5,708	2,417	1980	-25,500	2,317
1949	5,339	873	1981	-28,023	5,030
1950	1,122	-1,840	1982	-36,485	-5,536
1951	3,067	884	1983	-67,102	-38,691
1952	2,611	614	1984	-112,492	-94,344
1953	1,437	-1,286	1985	-122,173	-118,155
1954	2,576	219	1986	-145,081	-147,177
1955	2,897	430	1987	-159,557	-160,655
1956	4,753	2,730	1988	-126,959	-121,153
1957	6,271	4,762	1989	-117,749	-99,486
1958	3,462	784	1990	-111,037	-78,968
1959	1,148	-1,282	1991	-76,937	2,897
1960	4,892	2,824	1992	-96,897	-50,078
1961	5,571	3,822	1993	-132,451	-84,805
1962	4,521	3,387	1994	-165,831	-121,612
1963	5,224	4,414	1995	-174,170	-113,567
1964	6,801	6,823	1996	-191,000	-124,764
1965	4,951	5,431	1997	-198,428	-140,726
1966	3,817	3,031	1998	-248,221	-215,062
1967	3,800	2,583	1999	-347,819	-301,630
1968	635	611	2000	-454,690	-417,426
1969	607	399	2001	-429,519	-384,699
1970	2,603	2,331	2002	-484,955	-461,275
1971	-2,260	-1,433	2003	-550,892	-523,400
1972	-6,416	-5,795	2004	-669,578	-624,993
1973	911	7,140	2005	-787,149	-728,993
1974	-5,505	1,962	2006	-838,270	-788,116
1975	8,903	18,116	2007	-819,373	-731,214
1976	-9,483	4,295	2008	-820,825[c]	-673,266[c]
1977	-31,091	-14,335			

Note: Amounts in current dollars and seasonally adjusted.

[a] "Balance on goods" measures the difference between the value of goods the United States imports and the value of goods the United States exports.
[b] "Balance on current account" is the broadest trade gauge, measuring the difference in imports and exports of merchandise trade and trade in services; also includes certain one-way flows of money into the United States such as pension payments.
[c] Preliminary.

Sources: 1946–2007: *Economic Report of the President 2009* (Washington, D.C.: Government Printing Office, 2008), table B-103; 2008: U.S. Department of Commerce, Bureau of Economic Analysis, "U.S. International Transactions Accounts Data," table 1 (*www.bea.gov*).

10

Social Policy

- **Population**
- **Immigration**
- **Medicare and Social Security**
- **Income Levels**
- **Public Aid**
- **Health Insurance**
- **Integration in Schooling and Employment**
- **Abortion**
- **Crime and Punishment**

The study of social policy might fairly be described as controversies informed by, but not settled by, statistics. No matter what the area, those on all sides of an issue try to support their arguments with the relevant data.

The data thought to pertain to questions and controversies about social policy are of many kinds and can be characterized in a variety of ways. First, there is factual information on, for example, how many whites, blacks, and Hispanics are below the poverty line (Table 10-9); what types of health care coverage are available and how many people are covered by health insurance (Tables 10-10 and 10-11); the historical pattern of immigration into the United States (Table 10-3 and Figure 10-2); how many unauthorized migrants are in the United States (Table 10-4); and how many crimes are committed in a given year (Table 10-17). Second, data are available on public opinion (see Chapter 3) and social policy. For example, social policy concerns not only the actual crime rate, but also what people think about crime—such as whether the courts are too easy on criminals (Table 3-15) and whether the death penalty is acceptable and desirable (Table 3-12). In another area, it matters not only what abortion rates are (Table 10-16), but also what people think and say about abortion (Table 3-13). One might also distinguish between data about the past or present and projections about the future. Much of the concern about Social Security payments and about health care costs revolves not just around present payments, but also around what to expect in the future (Tables 10-5 and 10-6, Figure 10-3).

Social policies are inherently controversial, and so too are the data relevant to such policies. The debate over how the 2000 U.S. Census was to be conducted illustrates the contentiousness surrounding how to determine even the basic facts of population counts (such as those in Tables 10-1, 10-2, and 10-4 or Figure 10-1). These population counts are important because the distribution of some federal funds as well as legislative apportionment turn on them. Even if analysts agree on a set of facts, they may disagree on the relevance of the material and its interpretation. Information about numbers of people without insurance coverage (Table 10-11), about the proportion of women and minorities elected to political office (Table 1-22 and Table 5-4), about the extent of crime and the cost of prisons (Tables 10-17 and 10-19), and so on, does not automatically answer causal questions (why the situation is as it is) any more than it answers normative questions (whether the existing situation is good and what should be done). As for projections, they often lead to special problems of inference. Any projection must be based on assumptions about what the future will be like. A note to Table 10-5, for example, might underscore the fact that no one can be certain in 2009 what health or Social Security costs will be in 2075.

Numerical and other data relevant to every social concern are available, but they are highly varied in type and always difficult to interpret. Information is provided here for a wide range of policies, including Medicare (Table 10-5), Social Security (Table 10-6 and Figure 10-3), income and poverty in general (Tables 10-7 through 10-9) and social welfare in particular (Figures 10-4 and 10-5), affirmative action in both the schools and in employment (Table 10-7 and Tables 10-12 through 10-15), abortion (Table 10-16), and crime and punishment (Tables 10-17 through 10-19). Often, a given set of data is relevant to more than one question. Information about poverty rates, for example, is relevant to questions about both social welfare and affirmative action. Because most debates about social policy involve expenditures, spending on other kinds of programs such as defense (Table 9-8), as well as overall taxation policies (Table 11-7), are also relevant.

In the face of enormous problems of inference, controversy about almost every fact, and the need to deal with future unknowns, one might well ask whether all these numbers are useful or necessary when discussing social policies. There are at least two answers to this question. The first is highly pragmatic. Some analysts will surely have factual information at their disposal; those who do not or cannot understand data and are unable or unwilling to provide any of their own will be hostage to others' information and interpretations.

Second, from a more theoretical perspective, although data are always subject to some error and interpretation, people often do agree on the facts and on roughly how they should be interpreted. There is no disagreement, for example, that—barring major unforeseen catastrophes or extremely large and unlikely changes in immigration—there will be a considerably smaller ratio of young people to old people over the next few decades. Knowing this does not solve the problems implicit in this fact, but it tells analysts that there will be problems and that the country needs to be thinking of solutions. It also suggests possible solutions—raising the retirement age, lowering Social Security payments, raising Social Security taxes, encouraging private pension plans so that the elderly need less government support, and so on.

In the area of social policy, as in other areas, data do not speak for themselves. They must be analyzed and interpreted. The facts alone will settle few arguments about causality or about normative questions. Still, data and an ability to interpret them are essential weapons in the arsenal of any well-educated social analyst, commentator, or student.

Figure 10-1   U.S. Population: Total, Urban, and Rural, 1790–2050

Population (millions)

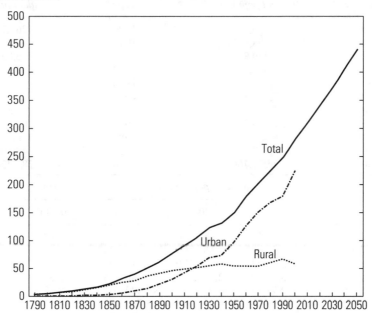

Sources: Population, total, 1790–2000: U.S. Census Bureau, "Resident Population of the United States," April 2, 2001; urban and rural, 1790–1990: U.S. Census Bureau, "Population: 1790 to 1990," March 31, 2001; urban and rural, 2000: U.S. Census Bureau, 2000 Census; population, total, 2010–2050: U.S. Census Bureau, "Projections of the Population and Components of Change for the United States: 2010 to 2050," August 14, 2008 (*www.census.gov*).

Table 10-1   U.S. Population, 1790–2000, and State Populations, 2000–2030

Year	Resident population[a]	Year	Resident population[a]
1790	3,929,214	1900	76,212,168
1800	5,308,483	1910	92,228,496
1810	7,239,881	1920	106,021,537
1820	9,638,453	1930	123,202,624
1830	12,860,702	1940	132,164,569
1840	17,063,353	1950	151,325,798
1850	23,191,876	1960	179,323,175
1860	31,443,321	1970	203,302,031
1870	38,558,371	1980	226,542,199
1880	50,189,209	1990	248,709,873
1890	62,979,766	2000	281,421,906

	Resident population[a]			Growth (percent)	
State	2000	2008	2030	2000–2008	2000–2030
Alabama	4,447,100	4,661,900	4,874,243	4.83	9.60
Alaska	626,932	686,293	867,674	9.47	38.40
Arizona	5,130,632	6,500,180	10,712,397	26.69	108.79
Arkansas	2,673,400	2,855,390	3,240,208	6.81	21.20
California	33,871,648	36,756,666	46,444,861	8.52	37.12
Colorado	4,301,261	4,939,456	5,792,357	14.84	34.67
Connecticut	3,405,565	3,501,252	3,688,630	2.81	8.31
Delaware	783,600	873,092	1,012,658	11.42	29.23
District of Columbia	572,059	591,833	433,414	3.46	−24.24
Florida	15,982,378	18,328,340	28,685,769	14.68	79.48
Georgia	8,186,453	9,685,744	12,017,838	18.31	46.80
Hawaii	1,211,537	1,288,198	1,466,046	6.33	21.01
Idaho	1,293,953	1,523,816	1,969,624	17.76	52.22
Illinois	12,419,293	12,901,563	13,432,892	3.88	8.16
Indiana	6,080,485	6,376,792	6,810,108	4.87	12.00
Iowa	2,926,324	3,002,555	2,955,172	2.61	0.99
Kansas	2,688,418	2,802,134	2,940,084	4.23	9.36
Kentucky	4,041,769	4,269,245	4,554,998	5.63	12.70
Louisiana	4,468,976	4,410,796	4,802,633	−1.30	7.47
Maine	1,274,923	1,316,456	1,411,097	3.26	10.68
Maryland	5,296,486	5,633,597	7,022,251	6.36	32.58
Massachusetts	6,349,097	6,497,967	7,012,009	2.34	10.44
Michigan	9,938,444	10,003,422	10,694,172	0.65	7.60
Minnesota	4,919,479	5,220,393	6,306,130	6.12	28.19
Mississippi	2,844,658	2,938,618	3,092,410	3.30	8.71
Missouri	5,595,211	5,911,605	6,430,173	5.65	14.92
Montana	902,195	967,440	1,044,898	7.23	15.82
Nebraska	1,711,263	1,783,432	1,820,247	4.22	6.37
Nevada	1,998,257	2,600,167	4,282,102	30.12	114.29
New Hampshire	1,235,786	1,315,809	1,646,471	6.48	33.23
New Jersey	8,414,350	8,682,661	9,802,440	3.19	16.50

Table 10-1   *(Continued)*

State	Resident population[a]			Growth (percent)	
	2000	2008	2030	2000–2008	2000–2030
New Mexico	1,819,046	1,984,356	2,099,708	9.09	15.43
New York	18,976,457	19,490,297	19,477,429	2.71	2.64
North Carolina	8,049,313	9,222,414	12,227,739	14.57	51.91
North Dakota	642,200	641,481	606,566	−0.11	−5.55
Ohio	11,353,140	11,485,910	11,550,528	1.17	1.74
Oklahoma	3,450,654	3,642,361	3,913,251	5.56	13.41
Oregon	3,421,399	3,790,060	4,833,918	10.78	41.28
Pennsylvania	12,281,054	12,448,279	12,768,184	1.36	3.97
Rhode Island	1,048,319	1,050,788	1,152,941	0.24	9.98
South Carolina	4,012,012	4,479,800	5,148,569	11.66	28.33
South Dakota	754,844	804,194	800,462	6.54	6.04
Tennessee	5,689,283	6,214,888	7,380,634	9.24	29.73
Texas	20,851,820	24,326,974	33,317,744	16.67	59.78
Utah	2,233,169	2,736,424	3,485,367	22.54	56.07
Vermont	608,827	621,270	711,867	2.04	16.92
Virginia	7,078,515	7,769,089	9,825,019	9.76	38.80
Washington	5,894,121	6,549,224	8,624,801	11.11	46.33
West Virginia	1,808,344	1,814,468	1,719,959	0.34	−4.89
Wisconsin	5,363,675	5,627,967	6,150,764	4.93	14.67
Wyoming	493,782	532,668	522,979	7.88	5.91
United States	281,421,906	304,059,724	363,584,435	8.04	29.20

Note: A counter with the U.S. Census Bureau's estimate of the current U.S. population can be found at *www.census.gov*. As of July 19, 2009 (12:33 p.m. CST), the count stood at 306,953,011. State projections shown are as of April 21, 2005. More recent population projections for the nation indicate that in 2030 the U.S. population will total 373,504,000 (U.S. Census Bureau, "National Population Projections Released 2008 [Based on Census 2000]," table 1, August 14, 2008).

[a] Resident population differs from apportionment population: "An area's resident population consists of those persons 'usually resident' in that particular area (where they live and sleep most of the time). A state's apportionment population, on the other hand, is the sum of its resident population and a count of overseas U.S. military and federal civilian employees (and their dependents living with them) allocated to the state, as reported by the employing federal agencies." United States Census 2000, "Resident Population" (*www.census.gov*).

Sources: U.S. Census Bureau, "Resident Population of the United States," December 28, 2000; "July 1, 2008, National, State, and Puerto Rico Population Estimates," December 22, 2008; and "Interim Projections of the Total Population for the United States and States: April 1, 2000 to July 1, 2030," table A1, April 21, 2005 (*www.census.gov*).

Table 10-2 Foreign- and Native-Born U.S. Population, Characteristics, 2007

Nativity	Population	Percent
Total	301,621,159	100.0
Total native born	263,572,703	87.4
Total foreign born	38,048,456	12.6
Mexico	11,739,560	30.9
South and East Asia	8,972,879	23.6
Caribbean	3,374,460	8.9
Central America	2,706,395	7.1
South America	2,576,530	6.8
Middle East[a]	1,315,115	3.5
All other	7,363,517	19.4

English ability by age and country or region of birth (percent)

	Under 18 years			18 years and over		
	English only	English very well	English less than very well	English only	English very well	English less than very well
Total native born	82.9	13.4	3.6	92.3	6.2	1.5
Total foreign born	16.4	49.9	33.6	15.9	30.7	53.8
Mexico	2.2	50.9	46.9	3.0	19.8	77.2
South and East Asia	24.0	46.5	29.4	10.5	41.6	47.9
Caribbean	25.7	46.6	27.6	33.2	23.7	43.1
Central America	12.0	47.6	40.3	5.7	25.8	68.5
South America	14.8	66.1	19.1	15.2	33.6	51.3
Middle East[a]	11.9	59.6	28.5	13.5	48.0	38.5
All other	36.7	45.7	17.6	37.2	35.2	27.7

Educational attainment by country or region of birth (percent)

	Less than 9th grade	9th to 12th grade	High school graduate	Some college	College graduate[b]	Advanced degree
Total native born	3.6	8.7	31.3	28.8	17.6	9.9
Total foreign born	20.4	11.5	24.0	17.1	16.1	10.9
Mexico	41.3	18.6	24.9	10.1	3.8	1.4
South and East Asia	9.1	6.5	17.8	17.3	29.3	20.0
Caribbean	14.6	12.9	30.4	22.4	13.2	6.4
Central America	32.2	15.9	26.0	15.5	7.8	2.6
South America	10.2	7.6	30.4	23.2	18.3	10.3
Middle East[a]	7.7	5.6	22.3	18.9	25.5	20.1
All other	8.2	7.1	24.8	23.0	19.6	17.2

Note: Table based on Pew Hispanic Center tabulations of the U.S. Census Bureau's 2007 American Community Survey, tables 2, 3, 20, and 22. The universe is the 2007 resident population for nativity and country or region of birth, the 2007 resident population ages five and over for language ability, and the 2007 resident population ages twenty-five and over for educational attainment.

[a] Middle East includes Afghanistan, Algeria, Egypt, Iran, Iraq, Israel/Palestine, Jordan, Kuwait, Lebanon, Morocco, Saudi Arabia, Sudan, Syria, Turkey, and Yemen.
[b] "College graduate" refers to a person who has attained a bachelor's degree.

Source: Pew Hispanic Center, "Statistical Portrait of the Foreign-Born Population in the United States," March 5, 2009 (*www.pewhispanic.org*).

Table 10-3 Immigrants to the United States, by Region of Origin, 1820–2007

Years	Europe				Asia[e]	Western Hemisphere			Africa and Oceania	Not specified	Total number (thousands)
	Northwestern[a]	Central[b]	Southern[c]	Eastern[d]		Canada	Mexico	Other[f]			
1820–1829	70.2%	4.5%	2.5%	0.1%	—	1.8%	3.0%	2.7%	—	15.2%	128.5
1830–1839	54.2	23.2	1.0	0.1	—	2.2	1.3	2.4	—	15.5	538.4
1840–1849	68.6	27.0	0.3	—	—	2.4	0.2	0.9	—	0.5	1,427.3
1850–1859	57.7	34.7	0.7	—	1.3%	2.3	0.1	0.6	—	2.6	2,814.6
1860–1869	54.2	35.0	0.9	0.1	2.6	5.7	0.1	0.5	—	0.9	2,081.3
1870–1879	48.4	30.0	2.4	1.3	4.9	11.8	0.2	0.6	0.4%	—	2,742.1
1880–1889	44.9	34.4	5.5	3.6	1.4	9.4	0.2	0.6	0.2	—	5,248.6
1890–1899	33.8	33.0	17.6	12.4	1.7	0.1	0.1	0.9	0.1	0.4	3,694.3
1900–1909	18.1	28.4	26.4	19.4	3.7	1.5	0.4	1.5	0.2	0.4	8,202.4
1910–1919	14.8	20.9	24.6	18.2	4.2	11.2	2.9	2.8	0.3	—	6,347.4
1920–1929	21.0	19.1	15.9	3.6	3.0	22.1	11.6	3.3	0.4	—	4,295.5
1930–1939	20.2	26.0	14.7	2.7	2.7	23.3	4.7	5.0	0.8	—	699.4
1940–1949	28.6	17.7	8.0	0.9	4.0	18.8	6.6	13.0	2.4	—	856.6
1950–1959	17.4	28.2	10.0	0.5	5.4	14.1	11.0	11.8	1.0	0.5	2,499.3
1960–1969	13.1	9.8	12.0	0.4	11.2	13.5	13.7	24.9	1.5	—	3,213.7
1970–1979	5.0	4.0	9.4	1.1	33.1	4.2	14.6	26.0	2.6	—	4,248.2
1980–1989	4.1	3.1	2.5	1.0	38.3	2.5	16.2	24.5	2.9	—	6,244.4
1990–1999	3.2	3.7	1.5	5.4	29.3	2.0	28.2	22.4	4.1	4.9	9,775.4
2000–2007	3.0	4.5	0.7	6.5	32.6	2.4	16.8	23.9	7.3	2.3	8,060.5

Note: "—" indicates less than 0.1 percent. Data for most years are for country of last permanent residence. See source for details.

[a] United Kingdom, Ireland, Finland, Norway, Sweden, Denmark, the Netherlands, Belgium, Switzerland, and France.
[b] Germany, Poland, Czechoslovakia (currently the Czech Republic and Slovak Republic), Yugoslavia (currently includes Bosnia-Herzegovina, Croatia, Macedonia, Slovenia, Serbia, and Montenegro), Hungary, and Austria.
[c] Italy, Spain, Portugal, and Greece.
[d] Russia, Bulgaria, Romania, and "other Europe." Russia and surrounding areas were reported differently in various historical periods. See source for details.
[e] Cambodia, China, Hong Kong (China), India, Iran, Israel, Japan, Jordan, Republic of Korea, Philippines, Syria, Taiwan, Thailand, Turkey, and "other Asia."
[f] Caribbean, and Central and South America.

Source: U.S. Department of Homeland Security, Office of Immigration Statistics, *Yearbook of Immigration Statistics, 2007* (Washington, D.C.: Government Printing Office, 2008), 6–11.

Figure 10-2 Immigrants to the United States, by Region of Origin, 1820–2007

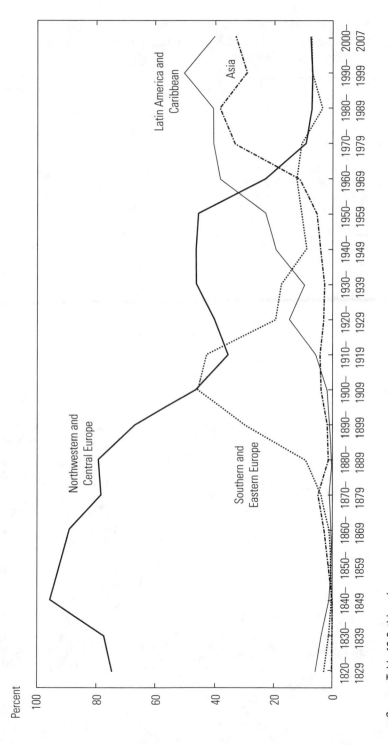

Source: Table 10-3, this volume.

Table 10-4   Legal Status of Immigrants, 2008; Origins of Unauthorized
Migrants, 2008; and State Populations of Unauthorized
Migrants, 1990–2008

	Number (millions)	Percentage of foreign born living in United States
Legal status of immigrants		
Legal permanent resident (LPR) aliens	12.3	31
Naturalized citizens (former LPRs)	14.2	36
Temporary legal residents (such as students or temporary workers)	1.4	4
Unauthorized migrants[a]	11.9	30
Total	39.9[b]	100[b]

	Number (millions)	Percentage of unauthorized migrants
Unauthorized migrants[a]: country/region of birth		
Mexico	7.0	60
Caribbean, Central America, South America	2.6	22
Asia	1.3	11
Europe or Canada	0.5	4
Africa or other	0.3	3
Total	11.9[b]	100

	Estimated population (millions)			Percentage of unauthorized migrants
	1990	2000	2008	2008
Unauthorized migrants[a]: state of residence				
California	1.5	2.3	2.7	23
Texas	0.5	1.1	1.5	12
Florida	0.2	0.6	1.1	9
New York	0.4	0.7	0.9	8
New Jersey	0.1	0.3	0.6	5
Arizona	0.1	0.3	0.5	4
Georgia	0.0	0.3	0.5	4
Illinois	0.2	0.5	0.5	4
North Carolina	0.0	0.2	0.4	3
Virginia	0.1	0.2	0.3	3
Subtotal	3.0[b]	6.4[b]	8.8[b]	74
Remaining 40 states and D.C.	0.5	2.0	3.2	26
Total, U.S.	3.5	8.4	11.9[b]	100

Table 10-4   *(Continued)*

Note: Demographic estimates based on U.S. Census Bureau, Current Population Surveys, March 2006–2008, with allowance for omissions. For details, see source. Percentages calculated before rounding. The ten states listed are those with the largest unauthorized migrant populations in 2008.

[a] "Unauthorized" includes those entering the United States clandestinely without inspection, with fraudulent documents, or overstaying visas. *Undocumented immigrants, illegals, illegal aliens,* and *illegal immigrants* are kindred terms, but *unauthorized migrants* more appropriately describes a group that includes those who enter the country with counterfeit documents and thus are not literally "undocumented." Moreover, the term *migrant* rather than *immigrant* highlights the fact that the unauthorized are more likely than other groups to leave the country.

[b] Due to rounding, the categories shown do not sum to the total or subtotal indicated.

Source: Jeffrey S. Passel and D'Vera Cohn, "A Portrait of Unauthorized Immigrants in the United States," Pew Hispanic Center, April 2009, 3, 21, 29 (*www.pewhispanic.org*).

Table 10-5   Hospital Insurance Trust Fund: Income, Expenditures, and
Balance, 1991–2018 (billions)

Year	Income	Disbursements	Net increase in fund	Fund at end of year
1991	$88.8	$72.6	$16.3	$115.2
1993	98.2	94.4	3.8	127.8
1996	124.6	129.9	−5.3	124.9
1997	130.2	139.5	−9.3	115.6
1998	140.5	135.8	4.8	120.4
1999	151.6	130.6	21.0	141.4
2000	167.2	131.1	36.1	177.5
2001	174.6	143.4	31.3	208.7
2002	178.6	152.5	26.1	234.8
2003	175.8	154.6	21.2	256.0
2004	183.9	170.6	13.3	269.3
2005	199.4	182.9	16.4	285.8
2006	211.5	191.9	19.6	305.4
2007	223.7	203.1	20.7	326.0
2008	230.8	235.6	−4.7	321.3
2009	225.1	245.6	−20.5	300.8
2010	237.1	254.2	−17.1	283.7
2011	249.4	268.8	−19.3	264.3
2012	261.8	289.1	−27.3	237.0
2013	274.8	312.9	−38.1	198.9
2014	287.4	341.9	−54.5	144.4
2015	299.9	352.7	−52.8	91.6
2016	312.0	376.5	−64.5	27.1
2017	324.6	403.1	−78.5	−51.4
2018	336.0	432.8	−96.7	−148.2

Note: The Hospital Insurance Program (Medicare Part A) pays for in-patient hospital care and other related care for those age sixty-five or older and for the long-term disabled. It represents more than half of all Medicare expenses. Income for the fund is derived from a 1.45 percent payroll tax on employees and employers. Figures for 1991–2008 represent actual experience. Figures for 2009 and beyond are "intermediate" projections; see sources for details. Amounts in current dollars.

Sources: 1991: U.S. Congress, House, "1992 Annual Report of the Board of Trustees of the Federal Hospital Insurance Trust Fund," 102nd Cong., 2nd sess., House Document 102–280, April 13, 1992, 14; 1993: 103rd Cong., 2nd sess., House Document 103–230, April 12, 1994, 14; 1996–2018: U.S. Department of Health and Human Services, "Annual Report of the Boards of Trustees of the Federal Hospital Insurance and Federal Supplementary Medical Insurance Trust Funds, Estimated Operations of the HI Trust Fund during Calendar Years, under Alternative Sets of Assumptions" (*www.cms.hhs.gov*).

Table 10-6 Social Security (OASDI)–Covered Workers and Beneficiaries, 1945–2085

Year	Covered workers[a] (thousands)	Beneficiaries[b] (thousands)			Covered workers per OASDI beneficiary	Beneficiaries per 100 covered workers
		OASI	DI	Total		
1945	46,390	1,106	—	1,106	41.9	2
1950	48,280	2,930	—	2,930	16.5	6
1955	64,975	7,564	—	7,564	8.6	12
1960	72,293	13,740	522	14,262	5.1	20
1965	80,437	18,509	1,648	20,157	4.0	25
1970	92,788	22,618	2,568	25,186	3.7	27
1975	100,198	26,998	4,125	31,123	3.2	31
1980	112,653	30,384	4,734	35,117	3.2	31
1985	120,245	32,763	3,874	36,636	3.3	30
1990	133,070	35,255	4,204	39,459	3.4	30
1995	140,878	37,364	5,731	43,096	3.3	31
2000	154,699	38,556	6,606	45,162	3.4	29
2005	158,814	39,961	8,172	48,133	3.3	30
2010	160,144	43,157	9,931	53,089	3.0	33
2015	171,132	49,673	10,983	60,656	2.8	35
2020	175,452	57,534	11,606	69,139	2.5	39
2025	179,250	65,121	12,349	77,470	2.3	43
2030	183,106	71,872	12,495	84,367	2.2	46
2035	187,414	76,555	12,613	89,168	2.1	48
2040	192,205	78,959	12,917	91,876	2.1	48
2045	197,188	80,387	13,500	93,887	2.1	48
2050	202,058	82,128	14,028	96,156	2.1	48
2055	206,843	84,536	14,534	99,070	2.1	48
2060	211,792	87,503	14,880	102,383	2.1	48
2065	216,705	90,492	15,312	105,804	2.0	49
2070	221,627	93,768	15,808	109,576	2.0	49
2075	226,528	97,221	16,274	113,495	2.0	50
2080	231,221	100,771	16,719	117,491	2.0	51
2085	235,851	104,471	17,123	121,594	1.9	52

Note: "—" indicates not available; "OASI" indicates Old-Age and Survivors' Insurance; "DI" indicates Disability Insurance. Projections (2010–2085) are the "intermediate" projections; see source for details. Data for additional years can be found in previous editions of *Vital Statistics on American Politics*.

[a] Workers who pay OASDI taxes at some time during the year.
[b] Beneficiaries with monthly benefits in current-payment status as of June 30.

Source: U.S. Social Security Administration, "2009 OASDI Trustees Report," table IV.B2 (*www.ssa.gov*).

Figure 10-3   Social Security Receipts, Spending, and Reserve Estimates, 2009–2037

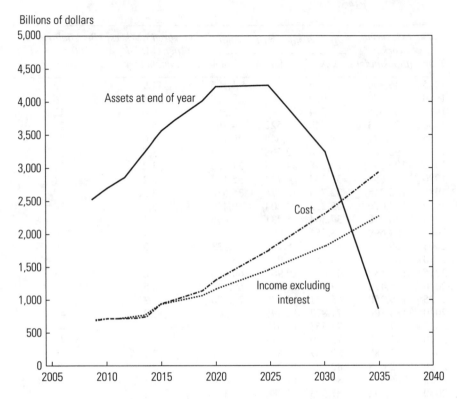

Billions of dollars

Note: Amounts in current dollars. Based on intermediate economic and demographic assumptions. Under these assumptions it is projected that the combined Old Age and Survivors Insurance (OASI) and Disability Insurance (DI) Trust Funds will be exhausted by 2037.

Source: U.S. Social Security Administration, "2009 OASDI Trustees Report," table VI.F8 (*www.ssa.gov*).

Table 10-7 Median Family Income, by Race and Hispanic Origin, 1950–2007

Year	Median income in current dollars				Median income in constant (2007) dollars				Annual percentage change in median income of all families	
	All families[a]	White alone[b]	Black alone[b]	Hispanic origin[c]	All families[a]	White alone[b]	Black alone[b]	Hispanic origin[c]	Current dollars	Constant dollars
1950	$3,319	—	—	—	$24,954	—	—	—	—	—
1955	4,418	—	—	—	29,895	—	—	—	6.8	5.5
1960	5,620	—	—	—	34,432	—	—	—	6.0	6.3
1965	6,957	—	—	—	40,045	—	—	—	5.9	4.3
1970	9,867	$10,236	$6,279	—	47,019	$48,777	$29,921	—	4.6	-0.2
1975	13,719	14,268	8,779	$9,551	48,072	49,995	30,762	$33,467	6.3	-1.8
1976	14,958	15,537	9,242	10,259	49,562	51,480	30,622	33,992	9.0	3.1
1977	16,009	16,740	9,563	11,421	49,895	52,173	29,805	35,596	7.0	0.7
1978	17,640	18,368	10,879	12,566	51,450	53,573	31,730	36,651	10.2	3.1
1979	19,587	20,439	11,574	14,169	52,135	54,403	30,807	37,714	11.0	1.3
1980	21,023	21,904	12,674	14,716	50,366	52,477	30,364	35,256	7.3	-3.4
1981	22,388	23,517	13,266	16,401	48,974	51,443	29,019	35,877	6.5	-2.8
1982	23,433	24,603	13,598	16,227	48,342	50,756	28,053	33,476	4.7	-1.3
1983	24,580	25,757	14,506	16,956	48,633	50,962	28,701	33,548	4.9	0.6
1984	26,433	27,686	15,431	18,832	50,243	52,624	29,330	35,795	7.5	3.3
1985	27,735	29,152	16,786	19,027	50,967	53,571	30,847	34,965	4.9	1.4
1986	29,458	30,809	17,604	19,995	53,171	55,610	31,775	36,091	6.2	4.3
1987	30,970	32,385	18,406	20,300	54,073	56,544	32,137	35,444	5.1	1.7
1988	32,191	33,915	19,329	21,769	54,215	57,119	32,554	36,663	3.9	0.3
1989	34,213	35,975	20,209	23,446	55,238	58,083	32,628	37,854	6.3	1.9
1990	35,353	36,915	21,423	23,431	54,369	56,771	32,946	36,034	3.3	-1.6
1991	35,939	37,783	21,548	23,895	53,357	56,094	31,991	35,476	1.7	-1.9

(Table continues)

Table 10-7 *(Continued)*

Year	Median income in current dollars				Median income in constant (2007) dollars				Annual percentage change in median income of all families	
	All families[a]	White alone[b]	Black alone[b]	Hispanic origin[c]	All families[a]	White alone[b]	Black alone[b]	Hispanic origin[c]	Current dollars	Constant dollars
1992	36,573	38,670	21,103	23,555	52,955	55,992	30,556	34,106	1.8	−0.8
1993	36,959	39,300	21,542	23,654	52,223	55,531	30,439	33,423	1.1	−1.4
1994	38,782	40,884	24,698	24,318	53,653	56,561	34,169	33,643	4.9	2.7
1995	40,611	42,646	25,970	24,570	54,863	57,612	35,084	33,192	4.7	2.3
1996	42,300	44,756	26,522	26,179	55,663	58,895	34,900	34,449	4.2	1.5
1997	44,568	46,754	28,602	28,142	57,407	60,222	36,841	36,249	5.4	3.1
1998	46,737	49,023	29,404	29,608	59,372	62,276	37,353	37,612	4.9	3.4
1999	48,831	51,079	31,850	31,523	60,764	63,562	39,634	39,227	4.5	2.3
2000	50,732	53,029	33,676	34,442	61,083	63,849	40,547	41,469	3.9	0.5
2001	51,407	54,067	33,598	34,490	60,206	63,321	39,348	40,393	1.3	−1.4
2002	51,680	54,633	33,525	34,185	59,563	62,966	38,639	39,399	0.5	−1.1
2003	52,680	55,768	34,369	34,272	59,389	62,871	38,746	38,637	1.9	−0.3
2004	54,061	56,723	35,148	35,440	59,342	62,264	38,582	38,902	2.6	−0.1
2005	56,194	59,317	35,464	37,867	59,683	63,000	37,666	40,218	3.9	0.6
2006	58,407	61,280	38,269	40,000	60,064	63,018	39,355	41,135	3.9	0.6
2007	61,355	64,427	40,143	40,566	61,355	64,427	40,143	40,566	5.0	2.1

Note: "—" indicates not available. Data for additional years can be found in previous editions of *Vital Statistics on American Politics.*

[a] Includes other races not shown separately.

[b] "White alone" and "black alone" refer to the fact that in the 2002 and later Current Population Surveys individuals could describe themselves as being of more than one race.

[c] Persons of Hispanic origin may be of any race.

Source: U.S. Census Bureau, "Current Population Reports, Historical Income Tables," table F-7 (*www.census.gov*).

Table 10-8   Persons below the Poverty Line, by Group, 2007

Group	Percentage of group that is poor	Group as a percentage of all poor people
Race/ethnicity		
White alone	10.6	67.4
White alone (not of Hispanic origin)	8.3	43.0
Black alone	24.5	24.8
Hispanic (of any race)	21.8	26.5
Family status		
Female householder, no husband present		
White alone	26.5	19.3
Black alone	39.7	14.6
Hispanic (of any race)	39.6	9.5
All other families		
White alone	5.9	26.7
Black alone	10.9	5.0
Hispanic (of any race)	15.1	12.7
Age		
Under 18 years	18.0	35.7
65 years and over	9.7	9.5
Residence		
Metropolitan residents	11.9	80.3
Nonmetropolitan residents	15.4	19.7
Region		
Northeast	11.4	16.5
Midwest	11.1	19.4
South	14.2	41.6
West	12.0	22.5
All persons	12.5	100.0

Note: The 2007 Current Population Survey asked respondents to choose one or more races. Shown are people who reported a single race of white or single race of black or African American. Hispanic origin may be of any race. Data for earlier years can be found in previous editions of *Vital Statistics on American Politics.*

Source: U.S. Census Bureau, *Income, Poverty, and Health Insurance Coverage in the United States: 2007* (Washington, D.C.: Government Printing Office, 2008), 13, 46–51.

Table 10-9 Persons below the Poverty Line, by Race and Hispanic Origin, 1959–2007 (percent)

Year	White	Black	Hispanic origin	Total
1959	18.1	55.1	—	22.4
1960	17.8	—	—	22.2
1965	13.3	—	—	17.3
1966	11.3	41.8	—	14.7
1967	11.0	39.3	—	14.2
1968	10.0	34.7	—	12.8
1969	9.5	32.2	—	12.1
1970	9.9	33.5	—	12.6
1971	9.9	32.5	—	12.5
1972	9.0	33.3	22.8	11.9
1973	8.4	31.4	21.9	11.1
1974	8.6	30.3	23.0	11.2
1975	9.7	31.3	26.9	12.3
1976	9.1	31.1	24.7	11.8
1977	8.9	31.3	22.4	11.6
1978	8.7	30.6	21.6	11.4
1979	9.0	31.0	21.8	11.7
1980	10.2	32.5	25.7	13.0
1981	11.1	34.2	26.5	14.0
1982	12.0	35.6	29.9	15.0
1983	12.1	35.7	28.0	15.2
1984	11.5	33.8	28.4	14.4
1985	11.4	31.3	29.0	14.0
1986	11.0	31.1	27.3	13.6
1987	10.4	32.4	28.0	13.4
1988	10.1	31.3	26.7	13.0
1989	10.0	30.7	26.2	12.8
1990	10.7	31.9	28.1	13.5
1991	11.3	32.7	28.7	14.2
1992	11.9	33.4	29.6	14.8
1993	12.2	33.1	30.6	15.1
1994	11.7	30.6	30.7	14.5
1995	11.2	29.3	30.3	13.8
1996	11.2	28.4	29.4	13.7
1997	11.0	26.5	27.1	13.3
1998	10.5	26.1	25.6	12.7
1999	9.8	23.6	22.7	11.9
2000	9.5	22.5	21.5	11.3
2001	9.9	22.7	21.4	11.7
2002	10.2	24.1	21.8	12.1
2003	10.5	24.4	22.5	12.5
2004	10.8	24.7	21.9	12.7
2005	10.6	24.9	21.8	12.6
2006	10.3	24.3	20.6	12.3
2007	10.5	24.5	21.5	12.5

Note: "—" indicates not available. Beginning in 2002, the Current Population Survey asked respondents to choose one or more races: for 2002–2007, white alone, black alone, Hispanic origin (of any race). The total includes other races not shown separately. Data for additional years can be found in previous editions of *Vital Statistics on American Politics.*

Source: U.S. Census Bureau, *Income, Poverty, and Health Insurance Coverage in the United States: 2007* (Washington, D.C.: Government Printing Office, 2008), 46–51.

Figure 10-4   Temporary Assistance for Needy Families (TANF) Benefit Levels as Percentage of Federal Poverty Line, 1996 and 2008

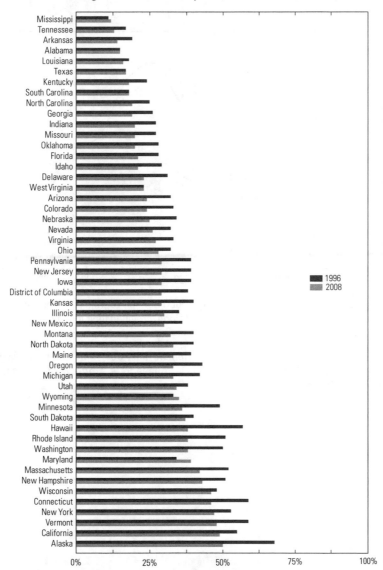

Note: The Temporary Assistance for Needy Families (TANF) program provides monthly cash benefits to eligible families with children. It is run directly by the states. Before 1996, this program was known as the Aid to Families with Dependent Children (AFDC) program. Figures are based on the 1996 and 2008 Poverty Guidelines of the Department of Health and Human Services for a family of three. In 1996 the poverty line was $12,980 ($16,220 in Alaska and $14,930 in Hawaii); in 2008 it was $17,600 ($22,000 in Alaska and $20,240 in Hawaii).

Source: Center on Budget and Policy Priorities, "TANF Benefits Are Low and Have Not Kept Pace with Inflation," November 24, 2008 (*www.cbpp.org*).

Figure 10-5   U.S. Population Receiving AFDC/TANF and Food Stamps, 1970–2006

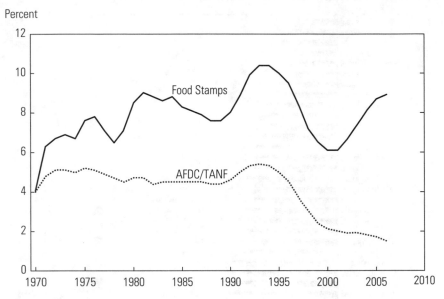

Note: See note to Figure 10-4, this volume. The Food Stamp Program provides monthly food stamp benefits to individuals living in families or alone, provided their income and assets are below the limits set by federal law.

Source: U.S. Department of Health and Human Services, "Indicators of Welfare Dependence: Annual Report to Congress 2008, Appendix A" (*http://aspe.hhs.gov/hsp/indicators08/index.shtml*).

Table 10-10   Health Insurance Coverage for the Noninstitutionalized U.S. Population under Sixty-five, 1987–2007

	Uninsured		Insured (percent)			
Year[a]	Number (millions)	Percent	Employment based[b]	Government[c]	Military[d]	Total population (millions)
1987	30.7	14.4	66.2	9.9	4.4	212.7
1988	32.4	15.1	66.0	10.0	4.2	214.7
1989	33.1	15.3	65.6	10.1	4.0	216.6
1990	34.4	15.7	64.1	11.5	4.0	218.8
1991	35.2	15.9	63.4	12.5	3.9	220.9
1992	38.3	16.9	61.3	13.4	3.7	226.4
1993	39.3	17.2	60.4	14.3	3.6	229.0
1994	39.4	17.1	64.4	14.1	4.2	230.8
1995	40.3	17.3	64.6	14.3	3.5	232.7
1996	41.4	17.6	64.8	14.0	3.3	234.9
1997	43.1	18.2	65.0	13.0	3.1	237.0
1998	43.9	18.4	65.8	12.4	3.2	239.3
1999	38.5	15.8	67.8	12.5	3.0	243.4
2000	38.2	15.5	68.3	12.9	3.1	246.0
2001	39.5	15.9	67.0	13.6	3.0	248.3
2002	41.8	16.6	65.7	14.2	3.1	251.7
2003	43.1	17.0	64.4	15.2	3.1	253.6
2004	43.0	16.8	63.9	16.0	3.2	255.9
2005	44.4	17.2	63.5	15.9	3.3	256.0
2006	46.5	17.6	62.9	15.9	3.0	260.8
2007	45.0	17.1	62.9	16.5	3.2	262.3

Note: Persons may have more than one type of coverage; percentages may total to more than 100.

[a] Because of questionnaire changes in the Current Population Survey in 1994 and 1999, numbers are not strictly comparable over time.
[b] Group health insurance through current or former employer or union.
[c] Medicare or Medicaid. For 1999 and after, this category also includes other state programs for low-income individuals.
[d] Includes CHAMPUS (Comprehensive Health and Medical Plan for Uniformed Services)/ Tricare, veterans, and military health care.

Sources: 1987–1998: U.S. Census Bureau, Health Insurance, "Historical Health Insurance Tables" (table HI-6); 1999–2007: Health Insurance, "Coverage Status and Type of Coverage by State—Persons under 65: 1999 to 2007" (table HIA-6) *(www.census.gov).*

Table 10-11 Persons without Health Insurance, by Demographic Characteristics, 2007

	Uninsured	
Group	Number (millions)	Percentage of U.S. population
Family status		
In families	34.6	14.1
Householder	10.3	13.2
Related children under 18 years	7.8	10.7
Related children under 6 years	2.6	10.4
In unrelated subfamilies	0.4	23.9
Unrelated individual	10.7	20.5
Race and Hispanic origin		
White	34.3	14.3
White, not Hispanic	20.5	10.4
Black	7.4	19.5
Asian	2.2	16.8
Hispanic origin (any race)	14.8	32.1
Age		
Under 18 years	8.1	11.0
18–24 years	8.0	28.1
25–34 years	10.3	25.7
35–44 years	7.7	18.3
45–64 years	10.8	14.0
65 years and older	0.7	1.9
Nativity		
Native born	33.3	12.7
Foreign born	12.4	33.2
Naturalized citizen	2.7	17.6
Not a citizen	9.7	43.8
Region		
Northeast	6.1	11.4
Midwest	7.5	11.4
South	20.2	18.4
West	11.8	16.9
Household income		
Less than $25,000	13.5	24.5
$25,000–49,999	14.5	21.1
$50,000–74,999	8.5	14.5
$75,000 or more	9.1	7.8

Note: For composition of regions, see Appendix, Table A-1, this volume.

Source: U.S. Census Bureau, *Income, Poverty, and Health Insurance Coverage in the United States: 2007* (Washington, D.C.: Government Printing Office, 2008), table 6 (*www.census.gov*).

Table 10-12 Persons Who Have Completed High School or College, by Race, Hispanic Origin, and Sex, 1940–2007 (percent)

	25 years and over						25–29 years					
	White[a]		Black[b]		Hispanic[c]		White[a]		Black[b]		Hispanic[c]	
Level/year	Male	Female	Male	Female	Male	Female	Male	Female	Male	Female	Male	Female
Completed four years of high school or more[d]												
1940	24.2	28.1	6.9	8.4	—	—	38.9	43.4	10.6	13.6	—	—
1947	33.2	36.7	12.7	14.5	—	—	52.9	56.8	19.6	24.7	—	—
1959	44.5	47.7	19.6	21.6	—	—	66.9	67.4	40.6	38.6	—	—
1970	57.2	57.6	32.4	34.8	—	—	79.2	76.4	54.5	57.9	—	—
1980	71.0	70.1	51.1	51.3	46.4	44.1	86.8	87.0	74.8	78.1	58.3	58.8
1990	79.1	79.0	65.8	66.5	50.3	51.3	84.6	88.1	81.5	81.8	56.6	59.9
2000	84.4	85.0	78.7	78.3	56.6	57.5	86.6	90.0	86.6	85.3	59.2	66.4
2003	84.5	85.7	79.6	80.3	56.3	57.8	83.8	87.6	86.4	88.4	59.7	64.2
2004	85.3	86.3	80.4	80.8	57.3	59.5	83.8	88.1	90.0	86.1	60.1	65.2
2005	85.2	86.2	81.0	81.2	57.9	59.1	84.3	87.1	86.4	86.5	63.2	63.4
2006	85.5	86.7	80.1	81.2	58.5	60.1	84.1	88.3	83.1	87.8	60.6	66.7
2007	85.3	87.1	81.9	82.5	58.2	60.6	84.2	89.0	86.9	87.7	60.6	70.6
Completed four years of college or more[e]												
1940	5.9	4.0	1.4	1.2	—	—	7.5	5.3	1.5	1.7	—	—
1947	6.6	4.9	2.4	2.6	—	—	6.2	5.7	2.6	2.9	—	—
1959	11.0	6.2	3.8	2.9	—	—	15.9	8.1	5.6	3.7	—	—
1970	15.0	8.6	4.6	4.4	—	—	21.3	13.3	6.7	8.0	—	—
1980	22.1	14.0	7.7	8.1	9.7	6.2	25.5	22.0	10.5	12.5	8.4	6.9
1990	25.3	19.0	11.9	10.8	9.8	8.7	24.2	24.3	15.1	11.9	7.3	9.1
2000	28.5	23.9	16.3	16.7	10.7	10.6	27.8	31.3	18.1	17.0	8.3	11.0
2003	29.4	25.9	16.7	17.8	11.2	11.6	25.3	31.5	17.4	16.9	8.5	11.9

(Table continues)

Table 10-12 *(Continued)*

Level/year	25 years and over						25–29 years					
	White[a]		Black[b]		Hispanic[c]		White[a]		Black[b]		Hispanic[c]	
	Male	Female	Male	Female	Male	Female	Male	Female	Male	Female	Male	Female
2004	30.0	26.4	16.6	18.5	11.8	12.3	25.8	32.1	13.5	19.7	9.6	12.4
2005	29.4	26.8	16.0	18.8	11.8	12.1	25.3	32.7	14.1	20.0	10.2	12.4
2006	29.7	27.1	17.2	19.4	11.9	12.9	25.0	31.7	14.9	21.6	6.9	12.8
2007	29.9	28.3	18.0	19.0	11.8	13.7	25.8	34.0	17.8	19.8	8.6	15.4

Note: "—" indicates not available. Data for additional years can be found in previous editions of *Vital Statistics on American Politics.*

[a] For 1940–2000, data are for white persons only; for 2003–2007, data are for people who reported a single race of white.
[b] For 1940–1960, data are for black and other races; for 1970–2000, data are for black persons only; for 2003–2007, data are for people who reported a single race of black or African American.
[c] Persons of Hispanic origin may be of any race.
[d] Beginning in 2000, high school graduate or more.
[e] Beginning in 2000, bachelor's degree or more.

Source: U.S. Census Bureau, "Current Population Reports, Educational Attainment in the United States: 2007," table 1 (*www.census.gov*).

Table 10-13   School Desegregation, by Region, 1968–2005 (percent)

Region/year	Percentage of black students in schools more than 50 percent minority	Percentage of Hispanic students in schools more than 50 percent minority	Percentage of black students in schools 90–100 percent minority	Percentage of Hispanic students in schools 90–100 percent minority
South				
1968	80.9	69.6	77.8	33.7
1972	55.3	69.9	24.7	31.4
1976	54.9	70.9	22.4	32.2
1980	57.1	76.0	23.0	37.3
1984	56.9	75.4	24.2	37.3
1988	56.5	80.2	24.0	37.9
1991	60.8	76.8	26.6	38.6
1994	63.4	75.6	—	38.0
1996	65.3	75.9	27.9	38.3
1998	67.2	76.1	29.7	39.1
2000	69.0	77.2	30.9	39.5
2001	69.8	77.7	31.0	39.9
2005	72.0	78.0	32.0	40.0
Border				
1968	71.6	—	60.2	—
1972	67.2	—	54.7	—
1976	60.1	—	42.5	—
1980	59.2	—	37.0	—
1984	62.5	—	37.4	—
1988	59.6	—	34.5	8.9
1991	59.3	37.4	33.2	10.8
1994	—	40.8	—	12.3
1996	63.2	43.5	37.3	12.6
1998	64.7	46.1	39.2	13.1
2000	67.0	49.2	39.6	13.4
2001	67.9	52.8	41.6	14.2
2005	70.0	57.0	42.0	17.0
Northeast				
1968	66.8	74.8	42.7	44.0
1972	69.9	74.4	46.9	44.1
1976	72.5	74.9	51.4	45.8
1980	79.9	76.3	48.7	45.8
1984	73.1	77.5	47.4	47.1
1988	77.3	79.7	48.0	44.2
1991	76.2	78.1	50.1	46.2
1994	—	77.6	—	45.1
1996	77.3	78.2	50.5	46.0
1998	77.5	78.5	50.9	45.7
2000	78.3	78.5	51.2	45.3
2001	78.4	78.2	51.2	44.8
2005	78.0	77.0	51.0	45.0

(Table continues)

Table 10-13 *(Continued)*

Region/year	Percentage of black students in schools more than 50 percent minority	Percentage of Hispanic students in schools more than 50 percent minority	Percentage of black students in schools 90–100 percent minority	Percentage of Hispanic students in schools 90–100 percent minority
Midwest				
1968	77.3	31.8	58.0	6.8
1972	75.3	34.4	57.4	9.5
1976	70.3	39.3	51.1	14.1
1980	69.5	46.6	43.6	19.6
1984	70.7	53.9	43.6	24.2
1988	70.1	52.3	41.8	24.9
1991	69.9	53.5	39.4	21.1
1994	—	53.1	—	21.8
1996	72.0	54.0	43.4	22.3
1998	72.8	55.6	45.5	24.1
2000	73.3	56.3	46.3	24.9
2001	72.9	56.6	46.8	24.6
2005	72.0	57.0	46.0	26.0
West				
1968	72.2	42.4	50.8	11.7
1972	68.1	44.7	42.7	11.5
1976	67.4	52.7	36.3	13.3
1980	66.8	63.5	33.7	18.5
1984	66.9	68.4	29.4	22.9
1988	67.1	71.3	28.6	27.5
1991	69.7	73.5	26.4	29.7
1994	—	75.9	—	32.1
1996	73.5	77.1	27.5	33.0
1998	74.0	78.3	28.8	35.2
2000	75.3	79.4	29.5	36.7
2001	75.8	80.1	30.0	37.4
2005	77.0	82.0	30.0	41.0
Total				
1968	76.6	54.8	64.3	23.1
1972	63.6	56.6	38.7	23.3
1976	62.4	60.8	35.9	24.8
1980	62.9	68.1	33.2	28.8
1984	63.5	70.6	33.2	31.0
1988	63.2	—	32.1	33.1
1991	66.0	73.4	33.9	34.0
1994	67.1	74.0	33.6	34.8
1996	68.8	74.8	35.0	35.4
1998	70.1	75.6	36.5	36.7
2000	71.6	76.4	37.4	37.4
2002	73.0	77.0	38.0	38.0
2005	73.0	77.0	38.0	39.0

Table 10-13   *(Continued)*

Note: "—" indicates not available. Data for 1968–1969 to 2005–2006 school years. "Total" data were not available for 2001; regional data were not available for 2002. For composition of regions, see Table A-4, this volume. Data for additional years can be found in previous editions of *Vital Statistics on American Politics.*

Sources: 1968–1980: Gary Orfield, testimony before the House Subcommittee on Civil and Constitutional Rights, *Civil Rights Implications of the Education Block Grant Program*, 97th Cong., 2nd sess., September 9, 1982, 67–72; 1984: Orfield, Franklin Monfort, and Melissa Aaron, "Status of School Desegregation 1968–1986," National School Boards Association, Alexandria, Va., 1989, 5, 7; 1988: Orfield and Monfort, "Status of School Desegregation: The Next Generation," National School Boards Association, Alexandria, Va., 1992, 3, 7–8; 1991: Orfield, "The Growth of Segregation in American Schools: Changing Patterns of Separation and Poverty Since 1968," National School Boards Association, Alexandria, Va., 1993, 9, © 1989, 1992, and 1993 National School Boards Association, all rights reserved; 1994: Orfield et al., "Deepening Segregation in American Public Schools," April 5, 1997, 11, 15; 1996: Orfield and John T. Yun, "Resegregation in American Schools," June 1999, tables 15, 19; 1998: Orfield, "Schools More Separate: Consequences of a Decade of Resegregation," July 2001, tables 9, 14, 18; 2000: Erica Frankenberg, Chungmei Lee, and Orfield, "A Multiracial Society with Segregated Schools: Are We Losing the Dream?" January 2003, tables 11, 29, 33, 37 (*www. civilrightsproject.harvard.edu*); 2001: Orfield and Lee, "Brown at 50: King's Dream or Plessy's Nightmare?" January 2004, tables 8, 9 (*www.civilrightsproject.harvard.edu*); 2002: Orfield and Lee, "Why Segregation Matters: Poverty and Educational Inequality," January 2005, table 4 (*www.civilrightsproject.harvard.edu*); 2005: Orfield and Lee, "Historic Reversals, Accelerating Resegregation, and the Need for New Integration Strategies," August 2007, tables 10, 14, 16, 17 (*www. civilrightsproject.ucla.edu*). Reprinted with permission of The Civil Rights Project/*Proyecto Derechos Civiles* at UCLA.

Table 10-14 Federal Employment, by Government Service Salary Level, Race, Hispanic Origin, and Sex, 2006

Government service (GS) salary level		Total number	Percentage black	Percentage Hispanic	Percentage female
GS-01	$16,352–20,450	2,962	25.8	10.2	58.5
GS-02	$18,385–23,134	4,507	25.3	10.5	61.1
GS-03	$20,060–26,081	17,525	22.1	9.4	63.9
GS-04	$22,519–29,278	51,636	24.3	8.6	65.1
GS-05	$25,195–32,755	99,673	26.7	9.1	64.8
GS-06	$28,085–36,509	79,163	26.3	8.0	67.8
GS-07	$31,209–40,569	138,208	22.5	8.9	59.8
GS-08	$34,563–44,931	56,953	26.7	10.7	62.4
GS-09	$38,175–49,632	133,615	19.5	7.9	52.6
GS-10	$42,040–54,649	16,482	18.1	5.8	48.5
GS-11	$46,189–60,049	198,470	14.7	10.6	45.5
GS-12	$55,360–71,965	228,461	14.8	6.3	42.7
GS-13	$65,832–85,578	206,476	12.7	5.2	36.2
GS-14	$77,793–101,130	100,523	11.4	4.3	34.6
GS-15	$91,507–118,957	64,318	7.1	3.8	29.8
Total, all pay plans		1,848,339	17.2	7.5	44.2
Total, GS and related		1,398,972	17.6	7.5	48.6

Note: Amounts in current dollars. Pay schedules effective January 2006. For 2007–2009 pay schedules, see *www.opm.gov.*

Source: U.S. Office of Personnel Management, "2006 Demographic Profile of the Federal Workforce" (*www.opm.gov*).

Table 10-15 State and Local Government Employment and Salary, by Sex, Race, and Hispanic Origin, 1973–2005 (thousands)

| | Employment | | | | | | | Median annual salary | | | | | | |
| | | | | | Minority | | | | | | | Minority | | |
Year	Male	Female	White[a]	Total	Black[a]	Hispanic	Total[b]	Male	Female	White[a]	Total	Black[a]	Hispanic	Total[b]
1973	2,486	1,322	3,115	3,809	523	125	693	$9.6	$7.0	$8.8	$8.6	$7.4	$7.4	$7.5
1975	2,436	1,464	3,102	3,899	602	147	797	11.3	8.2	10.2	9.8	8.6	8.9	8.8
1980	2,350	1,637	3,146	3,987	619	163	842	15.2	11.4	13.8	13.3	11.5	12.3	11.8
1981	2,740	1,925	3,591	4,665	780	205	1,074	17.7	13.1	16.1	15.6	13.3	14.7	13.5
1983	2,674	1,818	3,423	4,492	768	219	1,069	20.1	15.3	18.5	18.0	15.6	17.3	15.9
1984	2,700	1,880	3,458	4,580	799	233	1,121	21.4	16.2	19.6	19.1	16.5	18.4	17.4
1985	2,789	1,952	3,563	4,742	835	248	1,179	22.3	17.3	20.6	19.9	17.5	19.2	18.4
1986	2,797	1,982	3,549	4,779	865	259	1,230	23.4	18.1	21.5	—	18.7	20.2	19.6
1987	2,818	2,031	3,600	4,849	872	268	1,249	24.1	18.9	22.4	—	19.3	21.1	20.9
1989	3,030	2,227	3,863	5,257	961	308	1,394	26.1	20.6	24.1	—	20.7	22.7	22.1
1990	3,071	2,302	3,918	5,374	994	327	1,456	27.3	21.8	25.2	—	22.0	23.8	23.3
1991	3,110	2,349	3,965	5,459	1,011	340	1,494	28.4	22.7	26.4	25.5	22.7	24.5	—
1993[c]	2,820	2,204	3,588	5,024	948	341	1,436	30.6	24.3	28.5	27.7	24.2	26.8	—
1995	2,960	2,355	3,781	5,315	993	379	1,534	33.5	27.0	31.4	30.5	26.8	28.6	—
1997	2,898	2,307	3,676	5,204	973	392	1,529	34.6	27.9	32.2	31.2	27.4	29.5	—
1999	2,939	2,393	3,723	5,332	1,012	417	1,609	37.1	29.9	34.8	33.4	29.6	31.2	—
2001	3,080	2,554	3,888	5,634	1,077	471	1,746	39.8	32.1	37.5	36.2	31.5	33.8	—
2003	3,134	2,610	3,919	5,745	1,097	508	1,826	42.2	34.7	40.0	38.7	33.6	36.6	—
2005	3,185	2,644	3,973	5,829	1,100	532	1,856	44.1	36.4	41.5	40.3	35.3	38.9	—

Note: "—" indicates not available. Full-time employment as of June 30; excludes school systems and educational institutions. Amounts in current dollars. Data for additional years can be found in previous editions of *Vital Statistics on American Politics.*

[a] Non-Hispanic.
[b] Includes other minority groups, not shown separately.
[c] Reporting changes occurred in 1993 that affect comparability of 1993 and later numbers with earlier entries.

Sources: 1973–1991: U.S. Equal Employment Opportunity Commission, *State and Local Government Information Report* (Washington, D.C.: Government Printing Office, annual); 1993–2005: U.S. Equal Employment Opportunity Commission, *Job Patterns for Minorities and Women in State and Local Government,* annual, table 1 (full-time employment).

Table 10-16 Frequency of Legal Abortions, 1972–2005

	Total		White		Nonwhite	
Year	Number of abortions (thousands)	Percentage of pregnancies terminated by abortion	Number of abortions (thousands)	Percentage of pregnancies terminated by abortion	Number of abortions (thousands)	Percentage of pregnancies terminated by abortion
1972	587.0	15.5	455.0	14.9	132.0	18.2
1973	744.6	19.3	548.8	17.4	195.8	25.9
1974	898.6	22.0	629.3	19.6	269.3	31.6
1975	1,034.2	24.9	701.2	21.5	333.0	35.9
1976	1,179.3	26.5	784.9	23.0	394.4	38.9
1977	1,316.7	28.6	888.8	25.0	427.9	40.4
1978	1,409.6	29.2	969.4	26.1	440.2	39.6
1979	1,497.7	29.6	1,062.4	27.1	435.3	38.2
1980	1,553.9	30.0	1,093.6	27.4	460.3	39.2
1981	1,577.3	30.1	1,107.8	27.4	469.6	39.2
1982	1,573.9	30.0	1,095.3	27.1	478.7	39.2
1983	1,575.0	30.4	1,084.4	27.4	490.6	40.1
1984	1,577.2	29.7	1,086.6	26.8	490.6	39.2
1985	1,588.6	29.7	1,075.6	26.5	512.9	39.7
1986	1,574.0	29.4	1,044.7	25.9	529.3	39.8
1987	1,559.1	28.8	1,017.3	25.2	541.8	39.3
1988	1,590.8	28.6	1,025.7	25.0	565.1	38.9
1989	1,566.9	27.5	1,019.9	23.8	547.0	38.8
1990	1,608.6	28.0	1,038.7	24.1	569.9	39.6
1991	1,556.5	27.5	982.0	23.3	574.5	39.8
1992	1,528.9	27.5	943.5	22.9	585.4	40.5
1993	1,495.0	27.4	907.7	22.5	587.3	41.1
1994	1,423.0	26.6	855.8	21.6	567.2	41.0
1995	1,359.4	25.9	817.2	20.9	542.3	40.6
1996	1,360.2	25.9	796.9	20.5	563.3	41.1
1997	1,335.0	25.5	777.0	20.1	558.0	40.6
1998	1,319.0	25.1	761.9	19.6	557.1	40.4
1999	1,314.8	24.6	742.6	19.0	572.2	40.3
2000	1,313.0	24.5	732.7	18.7	580.3	40.3
2001	1,291.0	24.4	716.5	18.5	574.5	40.5
2002	1,269.0	23.8	705.8	18.1	563.2	39.8
2003	1,250.0	23.3	694.5	17.7	555.5	38.8
2004	1,222.1	22.9	673.8	17.3	548.3	37.8
2005	1,206.2	19.4	—	—	—	—

Note: "—" indicates not available. "Percentage of pregnancies terminated by abortion" indicates the percentage of pregnancies resulting in live birth or abortion that are terminated by abortion. The percentage is based on births occurring during the twelve-month period starting in July of that year (to match times of conception for pregnancies ending in births with those for pregnancies ending in abortion). Figures in 1983, 1986, 1989, 1990, 1993, 1994, 1997, 1998, 2001, 2002, and 2003 are estimated by interpolation of numbers of abortions.

Sources: 1973–1988: Stanley K. Henshaw and Jennifer Van Vort, eds., *Abortion Factbook, 1992 Edition: Readings, Trends, and State and Local Data to 1988* (New York: Alan Guttmacher Institute, 1992), 174–175; total, 1989–2005: Rachel K. Jones, Mia R. S. Zolna, Stanley K. Henshaw, and Lawrence B. Finer, "Abortion in the United States: Incidence and Access to Services, 2005," *Perspectives on Sexual Reproductive Health* 40 (2008): 9 (*www.guttmacher.org*); total, 1972, and white and nonwhite, 1972, 1989–2005: Guttmacher Institute, unpublished data. Reprinted with the permission of the Guttmacher Institute.

Table 10-17 Crime Rates, 1960–2007

Year	Violent crime					Property crime				Total
	Murder	Rape	Robbery	Aggravated assault	Total	Burglary	Larceny theft	Vehicle theft	Total	
1960	5.1	9.6	60	86	160.7	509	1,035	183	1,727	1,888
1965	5.1	12.1	72	111	200.2	663	1,329	257	2,249	2,449
1970	7.9	18.7	172	165	363.6	1,085	2,079	457	3,621	3,985
1975	9.6	26.3	218	227	480.9	1,526	2,805	469	4,800	5,281
1980	10.2	36.8	251	299	597.0	1,684	3,167	502	5,353	5,950
1985	7.9	36.7	209	303	556.6	1,287	2,901	462	4,650	5,207
1990	9.4	41.1	256	423	729.5	1,232	3,185	656	5,073	5,803
1995	8.2	37.1	221	418	684.3	987	3,043	560	4,590	5,274
2000	5.5	32.0	145	324	506.5	729	2,477	412	3,618	4,125
2001	5.6	31.8	149	319	505.4	742	2,486	431	3,659	4,164
2002	5.6	33.1	146	310	494.7	747	2,451	433	3,631	4,126
2003	5.7	32.3	143	295	476.0	741	2,417	434	3,592	4,068
2004	5.5	32.4	137	289	463.9	730	2,362	422	3,514	3,978
2005	5.6	31.8	141	291	469.4	727	2,288	417	3,432	3,901
2006	5.7	31.0	149	288	473.7	729	2,207	398	3,334	3,808
2007	5.6	30.0	148	284	467.6	723	2,178	363	3,264	3,732

Note: Figures are rates per 100,000 inhabitants. For definitions of crimes, see the sources. Data for additional years can be found in previous editions of *Vital Statistics on American Politics.*

Sources: 1960–1985: U.S. Bureau of the Census, *Statistical Abstract of the United States, 1976* (Washington, D.C.: Government Printing Office, 1976), 153; *1987*, 155; 1990–2007: U.S. Department of Justice, Federal Bureau of Investigation, "Uniform Crime Reports: Crime in the United States, 2007," table 1 (*www.fbi.gov*).

Table 10-18 Death Penalty in the States: Number of Executions, 1930–2009, and Number on Death Row, 2008

State	Method of execution[a]	Number executed								Number awaiting execution[c]
		1930s	1940s	1950s	1960s	1970s	1980s	1990s	2000s[b]	
Alabama	electrocution or lethal injection	60	50	20	5	0	7	12	14	203
Alaska	none	0	0	0	0	0	0	0	0	0
Arizona	lethal injection	17	9	8	4	0	0	19	3	126
Arkansas	lethal injection	53	8	18	9	0	0	21	4	40
California	lethal injection or lethal gas	108	80	74	30	0	0	7	5	667
Colorado	lethal injection	25	13	3	6	0	0	1	0	2
Connecticut	lethal injection	5	10	5	1	0	0	0	0	9
Delaware	lethal injection	8	4	0	0	0	0	10	1	19
District of Columbia	none	20	16	4	0	0	0	0	0	0
Florida	electrocution or lethal injection	44	65	49	12	1	20	23	22	397
Georgia	lethal injection	137	130	85	14	0	14	9	15	107
Hawaii	none	0	0	0	0	0	0	0	0	0
Idaho	lethal injection	0	0	3	0	0	0	1	0	19
Illinois	lethal injection	61	18	9	2	0	0	12	0	13
Indiana	lethal injection	31	7	2	1	0	2	5	4	19
Iowa	none	8	7	1	2	0	0	0	0	0
Kansas	lethal injection	0	5	5	5	0	0	0	0	9[d]
Kentucky	lethal injection	52	34	16	1	0	0	2	1	39
Louisiana	lethal injection	58	47	27	1	0	18	7	2	88
Maine	none	0	0	0	0	0	0	0	0	0
Maryland	lethal injection	16	45	6	1	0	0	3	1	6
Massachusetts	none	18	9	0	0	0	0	0	0	0
Michigan	none	0	0	0	0	0	0	0	0	0
Minnesota	none	0	0	0	0	0	0	0	0	0
Mississippi	lethal injection	48	60	36	10	0	4	0	5	64

Missouri	lethal injection or lethal gas	36	15	7	4	0	1	40	15	48
Montana	lethal injection	5	1	0	0	0	0	2	1	2
Nebraska	electrocution	0	2	2	0	0	0	3	0	10[e]
Nevada	lethal injection	8	0	9	2	1	3	4	3	77
New Hampshire	lethal injection	1	0	0	0	0	0	0	0	0
New Jersey	lethal injection[f]	40	14	17	3	0	0	0	0	11[f]
New Mexico	none[g]	2	2	3	1	0	0	0	0	2[g]
New York	lethal injection	153	114	52	10	0	0	0	0	1[d]
North Carolina	lethal injection	131	12	19	1	0	3	12	19	173
North Dakota	none	0	0	0	0	0	0	0	0	0
Ohio	lethal injection	82	1	32	7	0	0	1	20	188
Oklahoma	lethal injection	34	13	7	6	0	0	19	56	84
Oregon	lethal injection	2	12	4	1	0	0	2	0	35
Pennsylvania	lethal injection	82	6	31	3	0	0	3	0	228
Rhode Island	none	0	0	0	0	0	0	0	0	0
South Carolina	electrocution or lethal injection	67	61	26	8	0	2	22	4	63
South Dakota	lethal injection	0	1	0	0	0	0	0	0	3
Tennessee	lethal injection	47	37	8	1	0	0	0	4	102
Texas	lethal injection	120	74	74	29	0	33	166	189	373
Utah	lethal injection	2	4	6	1	1	2	3	0	9
Vermont	none	1	1	2	0	0	0	0	0	0
Virginia	electrocution or lethal injection	28	35	23	6	0	8	65	29	21
Washington	lethal injection or hanging	23	16	6	2	0	0	3	0	9
West Virginia	none	20	11	9	0	0	0	0	0	0
Wisconsin	none	0	0	0	0	0	0	0	0	0
Wyoming	lethal injection	4	2	0	1	1	0	1	0	2
U.S. government	[h]	10	13	9	1	0	0	0	3	51
U.S. military	lethal injection	[i]	[i]	[i]	[i]	[i]	[i]	0	0	9
Total[j]		1,667	1,284	717	191	3	117	478	420	3,309[k]

(Table continues)

Table 10-18 *(Continued)*

a In some states, method depends on when sentenced. For details, see sources.

b Through March 11, 2009.

c As of January 1, 2008. On March 1, 2005, the U.S. Supreme Court ruled that it is unconstitutional to execute anyone who committed a crime while under the age of eighteen. Seventy-two death row inmates had been sentenced as juveniles (under eighteen at time of crime) as of December 31, 2004.

d In 2004 the death penalty statutes of Kansas (December 17) and New York (June 24) were declared unconstitutional.

e In 2008 electrocution in Nebraska (February) was ruled to be unconstitutional. Currently, no other method is in place.

f In December 2007, New Jersey replaced the state's death penalty with the sentence of life without parole.

g In March 2009, New Mexico repealed the death penalty.

h The method of execution depends on the state in which the crime was committed.

i One hundred and sixty executions have been carried out under military authority since 1930.

j The national total counts inmates receiving multiple death sentences once. However, they are included in the state total for each state in which they were sentenced to death.

k Number of inmates. Those sentenced in more than one state are listed in each state. Total as of January 1, 2008.

Sources: Number executed in 1930s–1970s: U.S. Department of Justice, Bureau of Justice Statistics, *Sourcebook of Criminal Justice Statistics—1989* (Washington, D.C.: Government Printing Office, 1990), 631; method, number executed in 1980–2008, number awaiting execution: Death Penalty Information Center (*www.deathpenaltyinfo.org*).

Table 10-19   Sentenced Federal and State Prisoners, 1925–2006, and Cost
per Prisoner per Year, 1980–2008

Year	Number of prisoners	Rate (per 100,000 population)[a]	Cost per prisoner per year
1925	91,669	79	—
1930	129,453	104	—
1935	144,180	113	—
1940	173,706	131	—
1945	133,649	98	—
1950	166,123	109	—
1955	185,780	112	—
1960	212,953	117	—
1965	210,895	108	—
1970	196,429	96	—
1975	240,593	111	—
1980	315,974	139	$10,350
1985	480,568	202	14,590
1986	522,084	217	15,220
1987	560,812	231	15,890
1988	603,732	247	16,320
1989	680,907	276	16,950
1990	739,980	297	17,550
1991	789,610	313	17,706
1992	846,277	332	18,330
1993	932,074	359	19,119
1994	1,016,691	389	19,433
1995	1,085,022	411	19,655
1996	1,137,722	427	19,801
1997	1,194,581	444	20,261
1998	1,245,402	461	20,608
1999	1,304,074	463	21,141
2000	1,331,278	478	22,280
2001	1,345,217	470	22,710
2002	1,380,516	476	—
2003	1,408,361	482	—
2004	1,433,728	486	—
2005	1,462,866	491	—
2006	1,502,179	501	b

Note: "—" indicates not available. Definition of prisoners has varied somewhat over the years. See sources for details. Costs, in current dollars, are the averages for federal and state agencies. Costs are approximate because of variations in reporting practices. Data for additional years can be found in earlier editions of *Vital Statistics on American Politics.*

[a] Prisoners with sentences of more than one year.

[b] The source stopped providing information on cost per prisoner per year. However, one estimate, for fiscal year 2008, is that the average cost across thirty-four states was about $29,000. "One in 31: The Long Reach of American Corrections," Pew Center on the States, March 2009 (*www.pewcenteronthestates.org*).

Sources: Number of prisoners and rate: U.S. Department of Justice, Bureau of Justice Statistics, "Sourcebook of Criminal Justice Statistics" (*www.albany.edu/sourcebook*); cost per prisoner: Criminal Justice Institute, *The Corrections Yearbook* (South Salem, N.Y.: Criminal Justice Institute, annual, 1981–2002).

11

Economic Policy

- **Gross Domestic Product (GDP)**
- **Consumer Price Index (CPI)**
- **Federal Budget**
- **National Debt**
- **Tax Breaks**
- **Labor Unions**
- **Minimum Wages**
- **Unemployment**

Economic policymakers labor under the burden of an overabundance of numbers. Statistics recording various aspects of the economy's performance appear regularly—often monthly. These statistics are important, not simply because of the conditions they report, but also because of the way in which they filter into economic calculations: expectations about and reactions to indicators of past performance are critical determinants of how the economy performs in the future. Moreover, there is a direct link to politics, because the public's perceptions of economic performance help to shape choices in the voting booth. Properly or not, presidents often are blamed when the economy turns down and (less often) are praised when it recovers. President Ronald Reagan's public approval ratings plummeted as an economic downturn continued through 1982, as did President George H. W. Bush's ratings during the run-up to the 1992 election as his opponent Bill Clinton stressed economic problems (see Figure 3-5 in *Vital Statistics on American Politics 2007-2008* and Figure 3-14 in this volume). Subsequent economic recoveries played a substantial role in shaping the mood of the voters to secure Reagan's 1984 reelection in a landslide and President Clinton's reelection in 1996, though good times were not enough to propel Al Gore into office in 2000 nor to keep President George W. Bush's ratings high in the face of growing criticism of the Iraq War (Figures 3-6, 3-14, and 3-18).

In even simple economic matters, fundamental issues and terms arise that distinguish the discourse from that in other areas of politics. One is the overall size of the economy, usually measured by the gross domestic product, or GDP (Table 11-1). Knowing what the GDP is and what it means is important even to a minimal understanding of economic statistics and policy. Without some sense of the size of the economy, one cannot make informed judgments about economic matters. For example, a trillion-dollar national debt is unquestionably large, but many argue that it needs to be assessed in terms of its relationship to the size of the total economy (Figure 11-2). Another case in point is the relative size of federal outlays, which almost always increase in total dollars (Table 11-3) but often not as a percentage of GDP (Figure 11-1).

A second key concept is that of constant dollars, which is explained in the introduction to Chapter 9 in connection with defense spending. Of importance here, the basis for many constant dollar calculations is the Consumer Price Index, or CPI (Table 11-2). This index reveals that a market basket of goods that cost $100 in 1982–1984 would have cost $29.60 in 1960. Unfortunately, although 1982–1984 is the base period in Table 11-2, other tabulations, such as those in Table 11-1, use a different base, making it more difficult to compare the data. However, the concept of a constant dollar is unchanged by which year is used as the base. (The CPI is not always used as the basis for such adjustments, and here it is not possible to move precisely from the figures in Table 11-2 to those in Table 11-1.)

During Reagan's and George H. W. Bush's presidencies, as well as during the first Clinton administration, economic news was dominated by the annual deficit and the accumulating national debt. It was also part of the many economic discussions in the early days of the Obama administration. By 2001 the annual deficit had been eliminated, and the accumulated debt (as a percentage of GDP) had decreased (Figure 11-2), but that happy situation turned around quickly in 2002 and beyond. By 2005, taxes had been cut again at the federal level. The growth in the federal debt (Table 11-6) helps to focus public attention on government spending and taxing, as politicians and economists alike try to assess ways of reducing the gap between income and expenditures. Economic growth in the late 1990s and into the new century provided the basis for greater tax revenues to balance the budget and reduce the deficit as well as to justify a massive tax cut under President George W. Bush. But the economic downturn in 2008 and 2009, as well as long-term concerns such as the growth of Social Security and health care expenditures as the population ages, place constraints on future government spending and on the size of any tax cuts or increases. If taxes must be raised in the future, one means of doing so is through ending selective tax breaks (Table 11-7), some of which were curtailed in previous tax reforms.

Cutting government spending is another means of reducing the deficit. Alternatively, cutting spending may allow the government to cut taxes without increasing the nation's debt. Although federal budget outlays (Tables 11-3 and 11-4) may give the impression of vast sums and a variety of programs suitable for cuts, Table 11-5 reveals that mandatory programs now account for about 60 percent of federal budget outlays. An increasing proportion of the federal budget has become relatively uncontrollable from the president's standpoint. Reducing spending in the mandatory category would require that Congress rewrite laws affecting payments to which beneficiaries are entitled on the basis of past commitments. Programs that fall under this heading, such as Social Security, are known as *entitlement programs.*

Labor union membership, the minimum wage, unemployment, and inflation are four other noteworthy features of the economic landscape that merit inclusion when considering politics. Testament to critical economic trends with political ramifications are the long slide in the percentage of the workforce belonging to unions (Table 11-8), the effects of inflation on the minimum wage (Figure 11-3), the large-scale entry of women into the labor force since World War II (Table 11-9), the fluctuations in the annual unemployment rate since 1929 (Table 11-10), and the relatively high unemployment rates among black teenagers (Table 11-11).

Because economic issues are an important aspect of political policy making and because economic conditions affect voter choices, economic data rank among the most vital of vital statistics on American politics.

Table 11-1   Gross Domestic Product, 1929–2008 (billions)

Year	Current dollars	Annual percentage change	Constant (2000) dollars	Annual percentage change
1929	$103.6		$865.2	
1930	91.2	−12.0	790.7	−8.6
1931	76.5	−16.1	739.9	−6.4
1932	58.7	−23.3	643.7	−13.0
1933	56.4	−3.9	635.5	−1.3
1934	66.0	17.0	704.2	10.8
1935	73.3	11.1	766.9	8.9
1936	83.8	14.3	866.6	13.0
1937	91.9	9.7	911.1	5.1
1938	86.1	−6.3	879.7	−3.4
1939	92.2	7.1	950.7	8.1
1940	101.4	10.0	1,034.1	8.8
1941	126.7	25.0	1,211.1	17.1
1942	161.9	27.8	1,435.4	18.5
1943	198.6	22.7	1,670.9	16.4
1944	219.8	10.7	1,806.5	8.1
1945	223.1	1.5	1,786.3	−1.1
1946	222.3	−0.4	1,589.4	−11.0
1947	244.2	9.9	1,574.5	−0.9
1948	269.2	10.2	1,643.2	4.4
1949	267.3	−0.7	1,634.6	−0.5
1950	293.8	9.9	1,777.3	8.7
1951	339.3	15.5	1,915.0	7.7
1952	358.3	5.6	1,988.3	3.8
1953	379.4	5.9	2,079.5	4.6
1954	380.4	0.3	2,065.4	−0.7
1955	414.8	9.0	2,212.8	7.1
1956	437.5	5.5	2,255.8	1.9
1957	461.1	5.4	2,301.1	2.0
1958	467.2	1.3	2,279.2	−1.0
1959	506.6	8.4	2,441.3	7.1
1960	526.4	3.9	2,501.8	2.5
1961	544.7	3.5	2,560.0	2.3
1962	585.6	7.5	2,715.2	6.1
1963	617.7	5.5	2,834.0	4.4
1964	663.6	7.4	2,998.6	5.8
1965	719.1	8.4	3,191.1	6.4
1966	787.8	9.6	3,399.1	6.5
1967	832.6	5.7	3,484.6	2.5
1968	910.0	9.3	3,652.7	4.8
1969	984.6	8.2	3,765.4	3.1
1970	1,038.5	5.5	3,771.9	0.2
1971	1,127.1	8.5	3,898.6	3.4
1972	1,238.3	9.9	4,105.0	5.3
1973	1,382.7	11.7	4,341.5	5.8

(Table continues)

Table 11-1   *(Continued)*

Year	Current dollars	*Annual percentage change*	*Constant (2000) dollars*	*Annual percentage change*
1974	1,500.0	8.5	4,319.6	−0.5
1975	1,638.3	9.2	4,311.2	−0.2
1976	1,825.3	11.4	4,540.9	5.3
1977	2,030.9	11.3	4,750.5	4.6
1978	2,294.7	13.0	5,015.0	5.6
1979	2,563.3	11.7	5,173.4	3.2
1980	2,789.5	8.8	5,161.7	−0.2
1981	3,128.4	12.1	5,291.7	2.5
1982	3,255.0	4.0	5,189.3	−1.9
1983	3,536.7	8.7	5,423.8	4.5
1984	3,933.2	11.2	5,813.6	7.2
1985	4,220.3	7.3	6,053.7	4.1
1986	4,462.8	5.7	6,263.6	3.5
1987	4,739.5	6.2	6,475.1	3.4
1988	5,103.8	7.7	6,742.7	4.1
1989	5,484.4	7.5	6,981.4	3.5
1990	5,803.1	5.8	7,112.5	1.9
1991	5,995.9	3.3	7,100.5	−0.2
1992	6,337.7	5.7	7,336.6	3.3
1993	6,657.4	5.0	7,532.7	2.7
1994	7,072.2	6.2	7,835.5	4.0
1995	7,397.7	4.6	8,031.7	2.5
1996	7,816.9	5.7	8,328.9	3.7
1997	8,304.3	6.2	8,703.5	4.5
1998	8,747.0	5.3	9,066.9	4.2
1999	9,268.4	6.0	9,470.3	4.4
2000	9,817.0	5.9	9,817.0	3.7
2001	10,128.0	3.2	9,890.7	0.8
2002	10,469.6	3.4	10,048.8	1.6
2003	10,960.8	4.7	10,301.0	2.5
2004	11,685.9	6.6	10,675.8	3.6
2005	12,421.9	6.3	10,989.5	2.9
2006	13,178.4	6.1	11,294.8	2.8
2007	13,087.5	−0.7	11,523.9	2.0
2008	14,264.6	9.0	11,652.7	1.1

Source: U.S. Department of Commerce, Bureau of Economic Analysis, "Gross Domestic Product" (*www.bea.gov*).

Table 11-2 Consumer Price Index, 1950–2008

| Year | All items | Food | Shelter | Fuel oil and other household fuel commodities | Gas and electricity | Apparel and upkeep | Transportation | | Medical care | All commodities | All services |
							Private[a]	Public			
1950	24.1	25.4	—	11.3	19.2	40.3	24.5	13.4	15.1	29.0	16.9
1955	26.8	27.8	22.7	12.7	20.7	42.9	26.7	18.5	18.2	31.3	20.4
1960	29.6	30.0	25.2	13.8	23.3	45.7	30.6	22.2	22.3	33.6	24.1
1965	31.5	32.2	27.0	14.6	23.5	47.8	32.5	25.2	25.2	35.2	26.6
1966	32.4	33.8	27.8	15.0	23.6	49.0	32.9	26.1	26.3	36.1	27.6
1967	33.4	34.1	28.8	15.5	23.7	51.0	33.8	27.4	28.2	36.8	28.8
1968	34.8	35.3	30.1	16.0	23.9	53.7	34.8	28.7	29.9	38.1	30.3
1969	36.7	37.1	32.6	16.3	24.3	56.8	36.0	30.9	31.9	39.9	32.4
1970	38.8	39.2	35.5	17.0	25.4	59.2	37.5	35.2	34.0	41.7	35.0
1971	40.5	40.4	37.0	18.2	27.1	61.1	39.4	37.8	36.1	43.2	37.0
1972	41.8	42.1	38.7	18.3	28.5	62.3	39.7	39.3	37.3	44.5	38.4
1973	44.4	48.2	40.5	21.1	29.9	64.6	41.0	39.7	38.8	47.8	40.1
1974	49.3	55.1	44.4	33.2	34.5	69.4	46.2	40.6	42.4	53.5	43.8
1975	53.8	59.8	48.8	36.4	40.1	72.5	50.6	43.5	47.5	58.2	48.0
1976	56.9	61.6	51.5	38.8	44.7	75.2	55.6	47.8	52.0	60.7	52.0
1977	60.6	65.5	54.9	43.9	50.5	78.6	59.7	50.0	57.0	64.2	56.0
1978	65.2	72.0	60.5	46.2	55.0	81.4	62.5	51.5	61.8	68.8	60.8
1979	72.6	79.9	68.9	62.4	61.0	84.9	71.7	54.9	67.5	76.6	67.5
1980	82.4	86.8	81.0	86.1	71.4	90.9	84.2	69.0	74.9	86.0	77.9
1981	90.9	93.6	90.5	104.6	81.9	95.3	93.8	85.6	82.9	93.2	88.1
1982	96.5	97.4	96.9	103.4	93.2	97.8	97.1	94.9	92.5	97.0	96.0
1983	99.6	99.4	99.1	97.2	101.5	100.2	99.3	99.5	100.6	99.8	99.4
1984	103.9	103.2	104.0	99.4	105.4	102.1	103.6	105.7	106.8	103.2	104.6
1985	107.6	105.6	109.8	95.9	107.1	105.0	106.2	110.5	113.5	105.4	109.9
1986	109.6	109.0	115.8	77.6	105.7	105.9	101.2	117.0	122.0	104.4	115.4
1987	113.6	113.5	121.3	77.9	103.8	110.6	104.2	121.1	130.1	107.7	120.2

(Table continues)

Table 11-2 *(Continued)*

| Year | All items | Food | Shelter | Fuel oil and other household fuel commodities | Gas and electricity | Apparel and upkeep | Transportation | | Medical care | All commodities | All services |
							Private[a]	Public			
1988	118.3	118.2	127.1	78.1	104.6	115.4	107.6	123.3	138.6	111.5	125.7
1989	124.0	125.1	132.8	81.7	107.5	118.6	112.9	129.5	149.3	116.7	131.9
1990	130.7	132.4	140.0	99.3	109.3	124.1	118.8	142.6	162.8	122.8	139.2
1991	136.2	136.3	146.3	94.6	112.8	128.7	121.9	148.9	177.0	126.6	146.3
1992	140.3	137.9	151.2	90.7	114.8	131.9	124.6	151.4	190.1	129.1	152.0
1993	144.5	140.9	155.7	90.3	118.5	133.7	127.5	167.0	201.4	131.5	157.9
1994	148.2	144.3	160.5	88.8	119.2	133.4	131.4	172.0	211.0	133.8	163.1
1995	152.4	148.4	165.7	88.1	119.2	132.0	136.3	175.9	220.5	136.4	168.7
1996	156.9	153.3	171.0	99.2	122.1	131.7	140.0	181.9	228.2	139.9	174.1
1997	160.5	157.3	176.3	99.8	125.1	132.9	141.0	186.7	234.6	141.8	179.4
1998	163.0	160.7	182.1	90.0	121.2	133.0	137.9	190.3	242.1	141.9	184.2
1999	166.6	164.1	187.3	91.4	120.9	131.3	140.5	197.7	250.6	144.4	188.8
2000	172.2	167.8	193.4	129.7	128.0	129.6	149.1	209.6	260.8	149.2	195.3
2001	177.1	173.1	200.6	129.3	142.4	127.3	150.0	210.6	272.8	150.7	203.4
2002	179.9	176.2	208.1	115.5	134.4	124.0	148.8	207.4	285.6	149.7	209.8
2003	184.0	180.0	213.1	139.5	145.0	120.9	153.6	209.3	297.1	151.2	216.5
2004	188.9	186.2	218.8	160.5	150.6	120.4	159.4	209.1	310.1	154.7	222.8
2005	195.3	190.7	224.4	208.6	166.5	119.5	170.2	217.3	323.2	160.2	230.1
2006	201.6	195.2	232.1	234.9	182.1	119.5	177.0	226.6	336.2	164.0	238.9
2007	207.3	202.9	240.6	251.5	186.3	119.0	180.8	230.0	351.1	167.5	246.8
2008	215.3	214.2	246.7	334.4	202.2	118.9	191.0	250.5	364.1	174.8	255.5

Note: "—" indicates not available. 1982–1984 equals 100. Data beginning in 1978 are for all urban consumers; earlier data are for urban wage earners and clerical workers. Data beginning in 1983 incorporate a rental equivalence measure for homeowners' costs and therefore are not strictly comparable with earlier figures. Data for additional years can be found in previous editions of *Vital Statistics on American Politics.*

[a] Includes direct pricing of new trucks and motorcycles beginning with September 1982.

Sources: 1950–1955: *Economic Report of the President* (Washington, D.C.: Government Printing Office, 1995), tables B-59, B-60, B-61; 1960–2007: (2009), tables B-60, B-61, B-62; 2008: U.S. Bureau of Labor Statistics, "2008 Consumer Price Index Detailed Reports" (*www.bls.gov*).

Table 11-3   Federal Budget: Total, Defense, and Nondefense Expenditures, 1940–2014 (billions)

Year	Current dollars			Constant (2000) dollars		
	National defense	Non-defense	Total	National defense	Non-defense	Total
1940	$1.7	$7.8	$9.5	$19.9	$88.9	$108.8
1941	6.4	7.2	13.7	64.7	82.4	147.1
1942	25.7	9.5	35.1	216.3	125.2	341.8
1943	66.7	11.9	78.6	526.0	173.8	700.1
1944	79.1	12.2	91.3	684.0	176.5	860.5
1945	83.0	9.7	92.7	774.6	115.6	890.6
1946	42.7	12.6	55.2	405.7	110.1	515.7
1947	12.8	21.7	34.5	112.6	184.3	296.9
1948	9.1	20.7	29.8	86.5	147.4	233.8
1949	13.2	25.7	38.8	123.8	187.9	311.7
1950	13.7	28.8	42.6	129.6	201.1	330.7
1951	23.6	21.9	45.5	211.7	144.1	355.9
1952	46.1	21.6	67.7	396.6	132.3	528.8
1953	52.8	23.3	76.1	416.1	140.3	556.3
1954	49.3	21.6	70.9	381.9	121.0	502.9
1955	42.7	25.7	68.4	320.1	150.5	470.4
1956	42.5	28.1	70.6	298.4	164.4	462.9
1957	45.4	31.1	76.6	303.5	175.0	478.3
1958	46.8	35.6	82.4	299.7	188.8	488.5
1959	49.0	43.1	92.1	297.6	229.8	527.5
1960	48.1	44.1	92.2	300.2	226.5	526.8
1961	49.6	48.1	97.7	301.5	242.9	544.4
1962	52.3	54.5	106.8	315.9	276.4	592.5
1963	53.4	57.9	111.3	309.4	284.7	594.3
1964	54.8	63.8	118.5	314.9	309.0	623.8
1965	50.6	67.6	118.2	291.8	321.6	613.2
1966	58.1	76.4	134.5	322.8	358.6	681.5
1967	71.4	86.0	157.5	383.3	393.8	777.2
1968	81.9	96.2	178.1	420.1	426.8	847.0
1969	82.5	101.1	183.6	400.1	423.2	823.5
1970	81.7	114.0	195.6	375.1	453.1	828.0
1971	78.9	131.3	210.2	340.8	493.4	834.3
1972	79.2	151.5	230.7	310.4	547.2	857.6
1973	76.7	169.0	245.7	278.6	588.5	867.3
1974	79.3	190.0	269.4	267.4	609.8	877.4
1975	86.5	245.8	332.3	262.7	719.2	982.1
1976	89.6	282.2	371.8	252.7	768.9	1,021.4
TQ[a]	22.3	73.7	96.0	61.0	194.7	255.8
1977	97.2	312.0	409.2	250.6	789.6	1,040.2
1978	104.5	354.3	458.7	251.1	842.7	1,093.8
1979	116.3	387.7	504.0	257.4	850.0	1,107.3
1980	134.0	456.9	590.9	267.1	907.9	1,175.1

(Table continues)

Table 11-3 *(Continued)*

Year	Current dollars			Constant (2000) dollars		
	National defense	Non-defense	Total	National defense	Non-defense	Total
1981	157.5	520.7	678.2	282.2	937.2	1,219.4
1982	185.3	560.4	745.7	307.0	944.8	1,251.7
1983	209.9	598.5	808.4	330.7	963.7	1,294.4
1984	227.4	624.4	851.9	334.0	965.6	1,299.5
1985	252.7	693.6	946.4	356.5	1,039.0	1,395.7
1986	273.4	717.1	990.4	380.7	1,045.1	1,425.7
1987	282.0	722.1	1,004.1	387.1	1,018.5	1,405.7
1988	290.4	774.1	1,064.5	393.1	1,053.4	1,446.5
1989	303.6	840.3	1,143.8	398.9	1,100.0	1,498.9
1990	299.3	953.8	1,253.1	382.7	1,207.0	1,589.9
1991	273.3	1,051.0	1,324.3	333.7	1,276.2	1,609.9
1992	298.4	1,083.3	1,381.6	354.3	1,269.8	1,623.9
1993	291.1	1,118.4	1,409.5	340.3	1,275.3	1,615.5
1994	281.6	1,180.3	1,461.9	322.8	1,319.3	1,642.2
1995	272.1	1,243.8	1,515.9	305.9	1,356.3	1,662.2
1996	265.8	1,294.9	1,560.6	289.2	1,384.0	1,673.0
1997	270.5	1,330.8	1,601.3	288.4	1,395.8	1,684.2
1998	268.2	1,384.5	1,652.7	282.4	1,438.7	1,721.0
1999	274.8	1,427.3	1,702.0	283.6	1,462.5	1,746.0
2000	294.4	1,494.8	1,789.2	294.4	1,494.8	1,789.2
2001	304.8	1,558.4	1,863.2	297.2	1,523.5	1,820.6
2002	348.5	1,662.7	2,011.2	329.3	1,599.8	1,929.2
2003	404.8	1,755.3	2,160.1	364.4	1,654.0	2,018.2
2004	455.8	1,837.2	2,293.0	394.3	1,687.8	2,081.9
2005	495.3	1,976.9	2,472.2	407.4	1,758.0	2,165.4
2006	521.8	2,133.6	2,655.4	411.9	1,836.8	2,248.7
2007	551.3	2,177.7	2,728.9	422.1	1,836.8	2,258.9
2008	616.1	2,366.8	2,982.9	461.3	1,909.0	2,370.4
2009 est.	690.3	3,307.5	3,997.8	511.9	2,615.1	3,127.0
2010 est.	712.9	2,878.2	3,591.1	522.2	2,281.8	2,804.0
2011 est.	658.7	2,956.1	3,614.8	476.0	2,310.0	2,786.0
2012 est.	634.1	2,998.7	3,632.7	450.7	2,302.4	2,753.1
2013 est.	635.8	3,181.7	3,817.5	443.9	2,395.8	2,839.7
2014 est.	644.8	3,371.2	4,016.0	442.3	2,488.0	2,930.3

[a] Transitional quarter when fiscal year start was shifted from July 1 to October 1.

Source: U.S. Office of Management and Budget, *Budget of the United States Government, Fiscal Year 2010, Historical Tables* (Washington, D.C.: Government Printing Office, 2009), 119–126.

Table 11-4 Federal Budget Outlays, by Function, 1980–2014 (billions)

Function	1980	1985	1990	1995	2000	2005	2009 est.	2011 est.	2014 est.
National defense	$134.0	$252.7	$299.3	$272.1	$294.4	$495.3	$690.3	$658.7	$644.8
Human resources	313.4	471.8	619.3	923.9	1,115.7	1,586.1	2,160.0	2,394.9	2,687.3
Education, training, employment, and social service	31.8	28.6	37.2	51.0	53.8	97.6	79.3	134.5	129.5
Health	23.2	33.5	57.7	115.4	154.5	250.6	353.4	372.4	426.9
Medicare[a]	32.1	65.8	98.1	159.9	197.1	298.6	430.8	502.0	635.9
Income security	86.6	129.0	148.7	223.8	253.7	345.8	519.3	539.5	516.6
Social Security[a]	118.5	188.6	248.6	335.8	409.4	523.3	680.5	728.3	845.5
Veterans' benefits and services	21.2	26.3	29.1	37.9	47.1	70.2	96.7	118.2	132.7
Physical resources	66.0	56.8	126.0	59.1	85.0	130.2	931.4	190.3	104.0
Energy	10.2	5.6	3.3	4.9	-0.8	0.4	8.8	12.8	19.8
Natural resources and environment	13.9	13.4	17.1	21.9	25.0	28.0	42.2	40.1	38.1
Commerce and housing credit[a]	9.4	4.3	67.6	-17.8	3.2	7.6	758.2	20.5	-53.1
Transportation	21.3	25.8	29.5	39.4	46.9	67.9	94.3	88.9	79.3
Community and regional development	11.3	7.7	8.5	10.7	10.6	26.3	28.0	27.9	19.8
Net interest[a]	52.5	129.5	184.3	232.1	222.9	184.0	142.7	254.5	460.1
Other functions[b]	45.0	68.2	60.7	73.1	113.8	141.8	165.0	204.0	219.7
International affairs	12.7	16.2	13.8	16.4	17.2	34.6	34.7	54.0	64.5
General science, space, and technology	5.8	8.6	14.4	16.7	18.6	23.6	31.2	32.0	34.6
Agriculture	8.8	25.5	11.8	9.7	36.5	26.6	20.4	23.8	19.7
Administration of justice	4.7	6.4	10.2	16.5	28.5	40.0	53.3	54.5	55.1
General government	13.0	11.5	10.5	13.8	13.0	17.0	21.9	24.6	25.0
Undistributed offsetting receipts	-19.9	-32.7	-36.6	-44.5	-42.6	-65.2	-91.7	-87.5	-99.8
Total outlays[a]	590.9	946.4	1,253.1	1,515.9	1,789.2	2,472.2	3,997.8	3,614.8	4,016.0

Note: Amounts in current dollars. Fiscal year ending September 30. Due to rounding, numbers for individual categories may not sum to the subtotals and totals. Data for additional years can be found in previous editions of *Vital Statistics on American Politics.*

[a] Includes both on- and off-budget amounts.
[b] Includes other outlays not shown separately.

Source: U.S. Office of Management and Budget, *Budget of the United States Government, Fiscal Year 2010, Historical Tables* (Washington, D.C.: Government Printing Office, 2009), 47–55.

Figure 11-1   Federal Outlays as a Percentage of GNP/GDP, 1869–2014

Percent of GNP/GDP

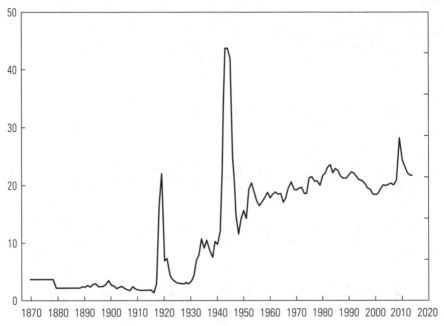

Note: Averaged by decade for 1869–1888. Percentage of gross national product (GNP) is shown through 1929, percentage of gross domestic product (GDP) thereafter. Figures for 2009 through 2014 are estimates.

Sources: 1869–1929: U.S. Bureau of the Census, *Historical Statistics of the United States* (Washington, D.C.: Government Printing Office, 1975), 224, 1,114; 1930–2014: U.S. Office of Management and Budget, *Budget of the United States Government, Fiscal Year 2010, Historical Tables* (Washington, D.C.: Government Printing Office, 2009), 24–25.

Table 11-5 Mandatory and Discretionary Federal Budget Outlays, 1970–2014 (billions)

Outlay	1970	1975	1980	1985	1990	1995	2000	2005	2007	2009 est.	2014 est.
Mandatory and related program outlays, total[a]	$75.4	$174.4	$314.6	$530.6	$752.6	$971.0	$1,174.4	$1,503.8	$1,688.1	$2,700.8	$2,720.7
Health	2.8	7.1	14.7	23.9	42.9	93.4	124.5	200.1	214.1	293.1	362.9
Income security	14.7	46.7	75.8	109.8	125.2	184.6	212.3	291.6	309.6	454.4	446.2
Medicare[b]	5.8	12.2	31.0	64.1	95.8	156.9	194.1	294.3	370.8	425.4	629.7
Social Security	29.6	63.6	117.1	186.4	246.5	333.3	406.0	518.7	581.4	675.0	837.9
Veterans' benefits and services	6.6	12.5	14.0	15.9	16.1	20.5	26.3	39.7	37.6	50.3	74.8
Undistributed offsetting receipts[c]	−8.6	−13.6	−19.9	−32.7	−36.6	−36.8	−42.4	−65.1	−68.5	−74.4	−99.0
Net interest[c]	14.4	23.2	52.5	129.5	184.3	232.1	222.9	184.0	237.1	142.7	460.1
Discretionary program outlays, total[a]	120.3	158.0	276.3	415.8	500.6	544.9	614.8	968.5	1,040.9	1,293.5	1,272.7
Domestic, total[a]	34.4	62.2	128.9	145.3	181.4	251.2	298.5	435.9	458.2	563.4	567.6
Education, training, employment, and social services	7.4	13.1	25.8	21.8	27.9	38.9	49.0	79.1	79.8	97.1	88.7
General science, space, and technology	4.5	4.0	5.8	8.6	14.4	16.7	18.6	23.6	25.5	30.9	34.5
Health	3.1	5.8	8.5	9.6	14.9	22.0	30.0	50.5	52.3	60.3	63.9
Income security	1.0	3.5	10.8	19.2	23.5	39.2	41.4	54.3	56.4	64.8	70.5
Natural resources and environment	3.5	8.1	15.5	15.1	17.8	21.9	25.0	30.3	30.9	42.0	36.8
Transportation	2.6	5.9	20.7	24.8	27.9	37.0	44.7	66.1	71.2	92.1	76.9
International affairs	4.0	8.2	12.8	17.4	19.1	20.1	21.3	39.0	34.8	43.6	66.3
National defense	81.9	87.6	134.6	253.1	300.1	273.6	295.0	493.6	547.9	686.5	638.9
Total outlays	195.6	332.3	590.9	946.4	1,253.1	1,515.9	1,789.2	2,472.2	2,728.9	3,997.8	4,016.0
Mandatory program outlays as a percentage of total outlays	38.5	52.5	53.2	56.1	60.1	64.1	65.6	60.8	61.9	67.6	67.7

Note: Amounts in current dollars. Due to rounding, numbers for individual categories may not sum to the subtotals and totals. Data for additional years can be found in previous editions of *Vital Statistics on American Politics.*

[a] Includes other outlays not shown separately.
[b] Medicare outlays began in fiscal year 1967.
[c] Includes both on- and off-budget amounts.

Source: U.S. Office of Management and Budget, *Budget of the United States Government, Fiscal Year 2010, Historical Tables* (Washington, D.C.: Government Printing Office, 2009), 134, 142–147, 154–159.

Table 11-6   The National Debt, 1940–2014

Year	Debt held by the public (millions)	As a percentage of GDP	Year	Debt held by the public (millions)	As a percentage of GDP
1940	$42,772	44.2	1977	549,104	27.8
1941	48,223	42.3	1978	607,126	27.4
1942	67,753	47.0	1979	640,306	25.6
1943	127,766	70.9	1980	711,923	26.1
1944	184,796	88.3	1981	789,410	25.8
1945	235,182	106.2	1982	924,575	28.7
1946	241,861	108.6	1983	1,137,268	33.0
1947	224,339	96.2	1984	1,306,975	34.0
1948	216,270	84.3	1985	1,507,260	36.3
1949	214,322	79.0	1986	1,740,623	39.5
1950	219,023	80.2	1987	1,889,753	40.6
1951	214,326	66.9	1988	2,051,616	40.9
1952	214,758	61.6	1989	2,190,716	40.6
1953	218,383	58.6	1990	2,411,558	42.0
1954	224,499	59.5	1991	2,688,999	45.3
1955	226,616	57.2	1992	2,999,737	48.1
1956	222,156	52.0	1993	3,248,396	49.4
1957	219,320	48.6	1994	3,433,065	49.3
1958	226,336	49.2	1995	3,604,378	49.2
1959	234,701	47.9	1996	3,734,073	48.5
1960	236,840	45.6	1997	3,772,344	46.1
1961	238,357	45.0	1998	3,721,099	43.1
1962	248,010	43.7	1999	3,632,363	39.8
1963	253,978	42.4	2000	3,409,804	35.1
1964	256,849	40.0	2001	3,319,615	33.0
1965	260,778	37.9	2002	3,540,427	34.1
1966	263,714	34.9	2003	3,913,443	36.2
1967	266,626	32.9	2004	4,295,544	37.3
1968	289,545	33.3	2005	4,592,212	37.5
1969	278,108	29.3	2006	4,828,972	37.1
1970	283,198	28.0	2007	5,035,129	36.9
1971	303,037	28.1	2008	5,802,725	40.8
1972	322,377	27.4	2009 est.	8,531,367	59.9
1973	340,910	26.0	2010 est.	9,881,895	67.1
1974	343,699	23.9	2011 est.	10,873,054	70.1
1975	394,700	25.3	2012 est.	11,468,384	69.6
1976	477,404	27.5	2013 est.	12,027,068	68.7
TQ[a]	495,509	27.0	2014 est.	12,594,847	68.5

Note: Amounts in current dollars. "GDP" is gross domestic product.

[a] Transitional quarter when fiscal year start was shifted from July 1 to October 1.

Source: U.S. Office of Management and Budget, *Budget of the United States Government, Fiscal Year 2010, Historical Tables* (Washington, D.C.: Government Printing Office, 2009), 127–128.

Figure 11-2 National Debt as a Percentage of GDP, 1940–2014

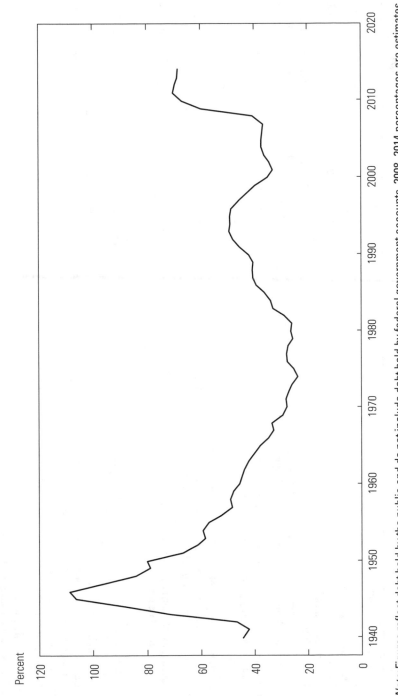

Note: Figures reflect debt held by the public and do not include debt held by federal government accounts. 2008–2014 percentages are estimates.

Source: U.S. Office of Management and Budget, *Budget of the United States Government, Fiscal Year 2010, Historical Tables* (Washington, D.C.: Government Printing Office, 2009), 127–128.

Table 11-7 Cost of Selected Tax Breaks: Revenue Loss Estimates for Selected Tax Expenditures, 1990–2014 (millions)

Type of tax expenditure	1990	1995	2000	2005	2006	2008	2010	2014
Commerce and housing								
Exclusion of interest on life insurance savings	$7,265	$10,075	$13,460	$17,440	$17,600	$18,530	$21,440	$30,980
Deductibility of interest on consumer credit	1,525	0	0	0	0	0	0	0
Deductibility of mortgage interest on owner-occupied homes	37,580	51,270	60,270	62,160	68,330	88,500	107,980	147,130
Deductibility of property tax on owner-occupied homes	9,520	14,845	22,140	19,110	21,260	29,130	14,980	32,540
Deferral/exclusion of capital gains on home sales[a]	15,865	21,960	18,540	35,990	35,270	30,090	30,460	60,440
Accelerated depreciation of machinery and equipment	4,665	3,820	2,640	4,370	12,740	16,800	4,350	8,200
Investment credit, other than ESOPs, rehabilitation of structures, energy property, and reforestation expenditures	0	0	0	0	0	0	0	0
Education, training, employment, and social services								
Deductibility of charitable contributions (education)	1,195	1,535	2,130	2,880	3,630	3,730	4,600	6,180
Credit for child and dependent care expenses	3,895	2,900	2,390	3,060	3,190	3,020	2,070	1,520
Deductibility of charitable contributions, other than education and health	10,870	14,015	19,400	28,440	35,820	36,830	45,470	61,000
Health								
Exclusion of employer contributions for medical insurance premiums and medical care	26,360	60,670	76,530	118,420	125,000	131,080	155,050	214,740
Deductibility of medical expenses	2,860	3,660	4,250	6,110	3,770	9,320	10,760	19,260
Exclusion of interest on state and local debt for private nonprofit health facilities (on hospital construction after 1997)	2,765	895	810	1,470	2,600	770	2,050	2,600
Deductibility of charitable contributions (health)	1,225	1,570	2,180	3,190	4,020	4,130	5,100	6,840
Social Security and Medicare								
Exclusion of Social Security benefits								
Disability insurance benefits	1,210	1,895	2,640	3,600	4,730	5,420	5,840	7,140

OASI benefits for retired workers	16,040	16,875	18,250	19,110	17,890	19,700	19,330	25,750
Benefits for dependents and survivors	2,995	3,610	3,910	3,940	3,360	3,570	3,280	3,800
Income security								
Exclusion of workmen's compensation benefits	2,735	4,475	5,120	5,770	5,660	5,830	6,010	6,400
Net exclusion of pension contributions and earnings								
Employer plans (includes 401k plans)	45,385	55,540	89,120	88,070	89,800	93,120	97,370	120,600
Individual Retirement Accounts	6,620	6,245	15,200	3,100	3,970	11,700	13,500	17,200
Keogh plans	1,460	4,435	5,500	9,400	10,130	12,000	14,000	21,000
Veterans' benefits and services								
Exclusion of veterans' death benefits and disability compensation[b]	1,580	1,985	3,090	3,320	3,580	3,870	4,140	5,690
General-purpose fiscal assistance								
Deductibility of nonbusiness state and local taxes other than on owner-occupied homes	18,875	27,250	42,650	36,460	43,120	49,140	30,290	65,390

Note: Amounts in current dollars. Fiscal year basis. ESOPs are Employee Stock Ownership Plans; OASI is Old Age and Survivors Insurance. Tax expenditures are defined as revenue losses attributable to provisions of the federal tax laws that allow a special exclusion, exemption, or deduction from gross income or that provide a special credit, a preferential rate of tax, or a deferral of liability. The Internal Revenue Service collected about $1.1 trillion in 2008 through individual income taxes. Losses shown are those for individuals. Data for additional years can be found in previous editions of *Vital Statistics on American Politics.*

[a] Prior to 1998, most capital gains on home sales were deferred, with an exclusion for those age fifty-five years and over. Beginning in 1998, most capital gains from home sales were excluded for those of all ages.
[b] Prior to 2000, veterans' disability compensation only.

Sources: 1990: U.S. Office of Management and Budget, *Budget of the United States Government* (Washington, D.C.: Government Printing Office, annual); 1995: U.S. Office of Management and Budget, *Budget of the United States Government, 1996, Analytical Perspectives* (Washington, D.C.: Government Printing Office, 1995), 43–46; 2000: *2002,* 66–70; 2005: *2007,* 291–295; 2006: *2008,* 239, 291–295; 2008–2014: *2010,* 241, 303–306.

Table 11-8 Membership in Labor Unions, 1900–2008

		Percentage in unions		
Year	Membership (in thousands)	Nonagricultural employment	Employed wage and salary workers	Labor force
1900	932.4	6.5		3.3
1905	1,947.1	10.8		6.0
1910	2,168.5	10.3		5.9
1915	2,597.6	11.5		6.6
1920	4,823.3	17.6		11.7
1925	3,685.1	12.8		8.2
1930	3,749.6	12.7		7.5
1935	3,649.6	13.5		6.9
1940	7,296.7	22.5		13.1
1945	12,254.2	30.4		22.8
1950	14,294.2	31.6		23.0
1955	16,126.9	31.8		24.8
1960	15,516.1	28.6		22.3
1965	18,268.9	30.1		24.5
1970	20,990.3	29.6		25.4
1975	22,207.0	28.9		23.7
1976	22,153.0	27.9		23.0
1977	21,632.1	26.2		21.8
1978	21,756.5	25.1		21.3
1979	22,025.4	24.5		21.0
1980	20,968.2	23.2		19.6
1981	20,646.8	22.6		19.0
1982	19,571.4	21.9		17.8
1983	18,633.6	20.7		16.6
1984	18,306.0	19.4		16.1
1985	16,996.0		18.0	14.7
1986	16,975.0		17.5	14.4
1987	16,913.0		17.0	14.1
1988	17,002.0		16.8	14.0
1989	16,960.0		16.4	13.7
1990	16,740.0		16.1	13.3
1991	16,568.0		16.1	13.1
1992	16,390.0		15.8	12.8
1993	16,389.0		15.8	12.7
1994	16,748.0		15.5	12.8
1995	16,360.0		14.9	12.4
1996	16,269.0		14.5	12.1
1997	16,110.0		14.1	11.8
1998	16,211.0		13.9	11.8
1999	16,477.0		13.9	11.8
2000	16,258.0		13.5	11.4
2001	16,387.0		13.4	11.4

Table 11-8   *(Continued)*

| Year | Membership (in thousands) | Percentage in unions | | |
		Nonagricultural employment	Employed wage and salary workers	Labor force
2002	16,107.0		13.2	11.1
2003	15,776.0		12.9	10.8
2004	15,472.0		12.5	10.5
2005	15,685.0		12.5	10.5
2006	15,359.0		12.0	10.1
2007	15,670.0		12.1	10.2
2008	16,098.0		12.4	10.4

Note: Comparisons of 1983–1984 show that the counts by Troy and Sheflin are about one million members higher per year than the counts based on the Current Population Surveys reported by the U.S. Bureau of Labor Statistics in *Employment and Earnings*. In 1985–1996, self-employed workers whose businesses are incorporated are excluded from the union member count. In 1997–2008, all self-employed workers are excluded. Wage and salary workers are workers who receive wages, salaries, commissions, tips, payment-in-kind, or piece rates in both the public and private sectors. Data for additional years can be found in previous editions of *Vital Statistics on American Politics*.

Sources: 1900–1984: Leo Troy and Neil Sheflin, *U.S. Union Sourcebook* (West Orange, N.J.: Industrial Relations Data and Information Services, 1985), 3–10, A-1, A-2; 1985–2000, membership and percentage of employed wage and salary workers: U.S. Department of Labor, Bureau of Labor Statistics, *Employment and Earnings*, January 1987 (Washington, D.C.: Government Printing Office, 1987), 219; (1988), 222; (1990), 232; (1992), 228; (1996), 214; (1997), 211; (1999), 219; (2001), 218; 2001–2008, membership and percentage of employed wage and salary workers: Bureau of Labor Statistics (*www.bls.gov*); 1985–2008, size of labor force: "Labor Force Statistics" (*www.bls.gov*).

Figure 11-3   Federal Minimum Wage Rates, 1950–2009

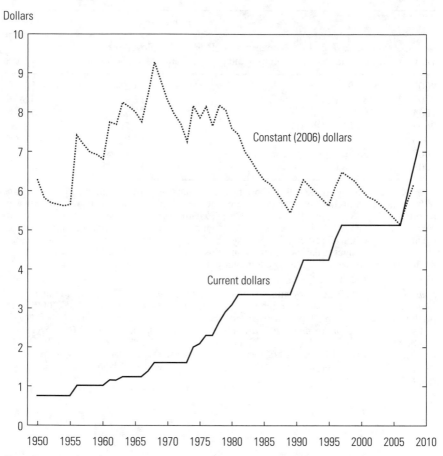

Dollars

Note: Constant (2006) dollars are derived using the CPI-U index (Consumer Price Index for all urban consumers). Originally, the minimum wage was applicable generally to employees engaged in interstate commerce or in the production of goods for interstate commerce. Coverage was expanded in 1961 and again in 1966. In 1996 a subminimum wage was established for employees under twenty years of age during their first ninety consecutive calendar days of employment with an employer. In 2007 a bill was signed into law increasing the minimum wage to $7.25 over a two-year period, with the first increase in the summer of 2007.

Sources: Minimum wage: U.S. Department of Labor, "Federal Minimum Wage Rates under the Fair Labor Standards Act" (*www.dol.gov*); consumer price index: Table 11-2, this volume.

Table 11-9   Civilian Labor Force Participation Rate, Overall and by Sex
and Race, 1948–2007 (percent)

Year	Total	Male	Female	White	Black and other nonwhite
1948	58.8	86.6	32.7	—	—
1950	59.2	86.4	33.9	—	—
1955	59.3	85.4	35.7	58.7	64.2
1960	59.4	83.3	37.7	58.8	64.5
1965	58.9	80.7	39.3	58.4	62.9
1970	60.4	79.7	43.3	60.2	61.8
1975	61.2	77.9	46.3	61.5	59.6
1976	61.6	77.5	47.3	61.8	59.8
1977	62.3	77.7	48.4	62.5	60.4
1978	63.2	77.9	50.0	63.3	62.2
1979	63.7	77.8	50.9	63.9	62.2
1980	63.8	77.4	51.5	64.1	61.7
1981	63.9	77.0	52.1	64.3	61.3
1982	64.0	76.6	52.6	64.3	61.6
1983	64.0	76.4	52.9	64.3	62.1
1984	64.4	76.4	53.6	64.6	62.6
1985	64.8	76.3	54.5	65.0	63.3
1986	65.3	76.3	55.3	65.5	63.7
1987	65.6	76.2	56.0	65.8	64.3
1988	65.9	76.2	56.6	66.2	64.0
1989	66.5	76.4	57.4	66.7	64.7
1990	66.5	76.4	57.5	66.9	64.4
1991	66.2	75.8	57.4	66.6	63.8
1992	66.4	75.8	57.8	66.8	64.6
1993	66.3	75.4	57.9	66.8	63.8
1994	66.6	75.1	58.8	67.1	63.9
1995	66.6	75.0	58.9	67.1	64.3
1996	66.8	74.9	59.3	67.2	64.6
1997	67.1	75.0	59.8	67.5	65.2
1998	67.1	74.9	59.8	67.3	66.0
1999	67.1	74.7	60.0	67.3	65.9
2000	67.1	74.8	59.9	67.3	—
2001	66.8	74.4	59.8	67.0	—
2002	66.6	74.1	59.6	66.8	—
2003	66.2	73.5	59.5	66.5	—
2004	66.0	73.3	59.2	66.3	—
2005	66.0	73.3	59.3	66.3	—
2006	66.2	73.5	59.4	66.5	—
2007	66.0	73.2	59.3	66.4	—

Note: "—" indicates not available. Figures are for persons sixteen years of age and over. The participation rate is the percentage of adults considered to be in the labor force. It is roughly those persons who are working, temporarily laid off, or looking for work. For details, see U.S. Bureau of the Census, *Statistical Abstract of the United States, 1992* (Washington, D.C.: Government Printing Office, 1992), 378. Data for additional years can be found in previous editions of *Vital Statistics on American Politics.*

Source: 1948: *Economic Report of the President* (Washington, D.C.: Government Printing Office, 1997), table B-37; 1950: (2001); 1955–1960: (2003); 1965–2007: (2009), table B-39.

Table 11-10   Unemployment Rate Overall, 1929–2007, and by Sex and Race, 1948–2007 (percent)

Year	Civilian workers	Male	Female	White	Nonwhite
1929	3.2	—	—	—	—
1933	24.9	—	—	—	—
1939	17.2	—	—	—	—
1940	14.6	—	—	—	—
1941	9.9	—	—	—	—
1942	4.7	—	—	—	—
1943	1.9	—	—	—	—
1944	1.2	—	—	—	—
1945	1.9	—	—	—	—
1946	3.9	—	—	—	—
1947	3.9	—	—	—	—
1948	3.8	3.6	4.1	3.5	5.9
1949	5.9	5.9	6.0	5.6	8.9
1950	5.3	5.1	5.7	4.9	9.0
1951	3.3	2.8	4.4	3.1	5.3
1952	3.0	2.8	3.6	2.8	5.4
1953	2.9	2.8	3.3	2.7	4.5
1954	5.5	5.3	6.0	5.0	9.9
1955	4.4	4.2	4.9	3.9	8.7
1956	4.1	3.8	4.8	3.6	8.3
1957	4.3	4.1	4.7	3.8	7.9
1958	6.8	6.8	6.8	6.1	12.6
1959	5.5	5.2	5.9	4.8	10.7
1960	5.5	5.4	5.9	5.0	10.2
1961	6.7	6.4	7.2	6.0	12.4
1962	5.5	5.2	6.2	4.9	10.9
1963	5.7	5.2	6.5	5.0	10.8
1964	5.2	4.6	6.2	4.6	9.6
1965	4.5	4.0	5.5	4.1	8.1
1966	3.8	3.2	4.8	3.4	7.3
1967	3.8	3.1	5.2	3.4	7.4
1968	3.6	2.9	4.8	3.2	6.7
1969	3.5	2.8	4.7	3.1	6.4
1970	4.9	4.4	5.9	4.5	8.2
1971	5.9	5.3	6.9	5.4	9.9
1972	5.6	5.0	6.6	5.1	10.0
1973	4.9	4.2	6.0	4.3	9.0
1974	5.6	4.9	6.7	5.0	9.9
1975	8.5	7.9	9.3	7.8	13.8
1976	7.7	7.1	8.6	7.0	13.1
1977	7.1	6.3	8.2	6.2	13.1
1978	6.1	5.3	7.2	5.2	11.9
1979	5.8	5.1	6.8	5.1	11.3
1980	7.1	6.9	7.4	6.3	13.1
1981	7.6	7.4	7.9	6.7	14.2

Table 11-10   *(Continued)*

Year	Civilian workers	Male	Female	White	Nonwhite
1982	9.7	9.9	9.4	8.6	17.3
1983	9.6	9.9	9.2	8.4	17.8
1984	7.5	7.4	7.6	6.5	14.4
1985	7.2	7.0	7.4	6.2	13.7
1986	7.0	6.9	7.1	6.0	13.1
1987	6.2	6.2	6.2	5.3	11.6
1988	5.5	5.5	5.6	4.7	10.4
1989	5.3	5.2	5.4	4.5	10.0
1990	5.6	5.7	5.5	4.8	10.1
1991	6.8	7.2	6.4	6.1	11.1
1992	7.5	7.9	7.0	6.6	12.7
1993	6.9	7.2	6.6	6.1	11.7
1994	6.1	6.2	6.0	5.3	10.5
1995	5.6	5.6	5.6	4.9	9.6
1996	5.4	5.4	5.4	4.7	9.3
1997	4.9	4.9	5.0	4.2	8.8
1998	4.5	4.4	4.6	3.9	7.8
1999	4.2	4.1	4.3	3.7	7.0
2000	4.0	3.9	4.1	3.5	—
2001	4.7	4.8	4.7	4.2	—
2002	5.8	5.9	5.6	5.1	—
2003	6.0	6.3	5.7	5.2	—
2004	5.5	5.6	5.4	4.8	—
2005	5.1	5.1	5.1	4.4	—
2006	4.6	4.6	4.6	4.0	—
2007	4.6	4.7	4.5	4.1	—

Note: "—" indicates not available. 1929–1947 figures are for persons fourteen years of age and over. 1948 and later figures are for persons sixteen years of age and over.

Source: 1929–1949: *Economic Report of the President* (Washington, D.C.: Government Printing Office, 1997), table B-33; 1950–1954: (2001); 1955–1958 (2003); 1959–2007: (2009), table B-42.

Table 11-11   Unemployment, by Race, Sex, and Age, 1955–2007 (percent)

	White				Black[a]			
	Male		Female		Male		Female	
Year	16–19	20 and over	16–19	20 and over	16–19	20 and over	16–19	20 and over
1955	11.3	3.3	9.1	3.9	13.4	8.4	19.2	7.7
1960	14.0	4.2	12.7	4.6	24.0	9.6	24.8	8.3
1965	12.9	2.9	14.0	4.0	23.3	6.0	31.7	7.5
1970	13.7	3.2	13.4	4.4	25.0	5.6	34.5	6.9
1975	18.3	6.2	17.4	7.5	38.1	12.5	41.0	12.2
1976	17.3	5.4	16.4	6.8	37.5	11.4	41.6	11.7
1977	15.0	4.7	15.9	6.2	39.2	10.7	43.4	12.3
1978	13.5	3.7	14.4	5.2	36.7	9.3	40.8	11.2
1979	13.9	3.6	14.0	5.0	34.2	9.3	39.1	10.9
1980	16.2	5.3	14.8	5.6	37.5	12.4	39.8	11.9
1981	17.9	5.6	16.6	5.9	40.7	13.5	42.2	13.4
1982	21.7	7.8	19.0	7.3	48.9	17.8	47.1	15.4
1983	20.2	7.9	18.3	6.9	48.8	18.1	48.2	16.5
1984	16.8	5.7	15.2	5.8	42.7	14.3	42.6	13.5
1985	16.5	5.4	14.8	5.7	41.0	13.2	39.2	13.1
1986	16.3	5.3	14.9	5.4	39.3	12.9	39.2	12.4
1987	15.5	4.8	13.4	4.6	34.4	11.1	34.9	11.6
1988	13.9	4.1	12.3	4.1	32.7	10.1	32.0	10.4
1989	13.7	3.9	11.5	4.0	31.9	10.0	33.0	9.8
1990	14.3	4.3	12.6	4.1	31.9	10.4	29.9	9.7
1991	17.6	5.8	15.2	5.0	36.3	11.5	36.0	10.6
1992	18.5	6.4	15.8	5.5	42.0	13.5	37.2	11.8
1993	17.7	5.7	14.7	5.2	40.1	12.1	37.4	10.7
1994	16.3	4.8	13.8	4.6	37.6	10.3	32.6	9.8
1995	15.6	4.3	13.4	4.3	37.1	8.8	34.3	8.6
1996	15.5	4.1	12.9	4.1	36.9	9.4	30.3	8.7
1997	14.3	3.6	12.8	3.7	36.5	8.5	28.7	8.8
1998	14.1	3.2	10.9	3.4	30.1	7.4	25.3	7.9
1999	12.6	3.0	11.3	3.3	30.9	6.7	25.1	6.8
2000	12.3	2.8	10.4	3.1	26.2	6.9	22.8	6.2
2001	13.9	3.7	11.4	3.6	30.4	8.0	27.5	7.0
2002	15.9	4.7	13.1	4.4	31.3	9.5	28.3	8.8
2003	17.1	5.0	13.3	4.4	36.0	10.3	30.3	9.2
2004	16.3	4.4	13.6	4.2	35.6	9.9	28.2	8.9
2005	16.1	3.8	12.3	3.9	36.3	9.2	30.3	8.5
2006	14.6	3.5	11.7	3.6	32.7	8.3	25.9	7.5
2007	15.7	3.7	12.1	3.6	33.8	7.9	25.3	6.7

Note: Data for additional years can be found in previous editions of *Vital Statistics on Americn Politics.*

[a] Black and other prior to 1972.

Source: 1955–1960: *Economic Report of the President* (Washington, D.C.: Government Printing Office, 2003), table B-43; 1965–2007: (2009), table B-43.

Appendix

Definitions of Regions

Analyses of U.S. politics often involve breaking the nation down into groups of states in order to highlight tendencies and trends in different regions. For ease of reference, four regional definitions, used in various tables in this book, are shown here. These four, while prominent, by no means exhaust the various definitions of regions that have been employed in the study of U.S. politics.

Table A-1   Regions as Defined by the U.S. Census Bureau and by Pew Research

Northeast	*Midwest*	*South*	*West*
New England	East north central	South Atlantic	Mountain
Connecticut	Illinois	Delaware	Arizona
Maine	Indiana	District of	Colorado
Massachusetts	Michigan	Columbia	Idaho
New Hampshire	Ohio	Florida	Montana
Rhode Island	Wisconsin	Georgia	Nevada
Vermont	West north central	Maryland	New Mexico
Middle Atlantic	Iowa	North Carolina	Utah
New Jersey	Kansas	South Carolina	Wyoming
New York	Minnesota	Virginia	Pacific
Pennsylvania	Missouri	West Virginia	Alaska
	Nebraska	East south central	California
	North Dakota	Alabama	Hawaii
	South Dakota	Kentucky	Oregon
		Mississippi	Washington
		Tennessee	
		West south central	
		Arkansas	
		Louisiana	
		Oklahoma	
		Texas	

Source: U.S. Census Bureau, "Census Regions and Divisions of the United States" (*www.census.gov*); and Pew Research, unpublished data.

Table A-2　Regions as Defined by Congressional Quarterly, *New York Times/ CBS News Poll*, and Voter Research and Surveys

East	*Midwest*	*South*	*West*
Connecticut	Illinois	Alabama	Alaska
Delaware	Indiana	Arkansas	Arizona
District of Columbia	Iowa	Florida	California
Maine	Kansas	Georgia	Colorado
Maryland	Michigan	Kentucky	Hawaii
Massachusetts	Minnesota	Louisiana	Idaho
New Hampshire	Missouri	Mississippi	Montana
New Jersey	Nebraska	North Carolina	Nevada
New York	North Dakota	Oklahoma	New Mexico
Pennsylvania	Ohio	South Carolina	Oregon
Rhode Island	South Dakota	Tennessee	Utah
Vermont	Wisconsin	Texas	Washington
West Virginia		Virginia	Wyoming

Table A-3　Regions for Party Competition Table (Table 1-4) and Apportionment Map (Figure 5-1)

New England	*Middle Atlantic*	*Midwest*	*Plains*
Connecticut	Delaware	Illinois	Iowa
Maine	New Jersey	Indiana	Kansas
Massachusetts	New York	Michigan	Minnesota
New Hampshire	Pennsylvania	Ohio	Nebraska
Rhode Island		Wisconsin	North Dakota
Vermont			South Dakota

South	*Border*	*Rocky Mountain*	*Pacific Coast*
Alabama	District of	Arizona	Alaska
Arkansas	Columbia	Colorado	California
Florida	Kentucky	Idaho	Hawaii
Georgia	Maryland	Montana	Oregon
Louisiana	Missouri	Nevada	Washington
Mississippi	Oklahoma	New Mexico	
North Carolina	West Virginia	Utah	
South Carolina		Wyoming	
Tennessee			
Texas			
Virginia			

Table A-4   Regions for School Desegregation Table (Table 10-13)

South	Border	Northeast	Midwest	West	Excluded
Alabama	Delaware	Connecticut	Illinois	Arizona	Alaska
Arkansas	District of	Maine	Indiana	California	Hawaii
Florida	Columbia	Massachusetts	Iowa	Colorado	
Georgia	Kentucky	New Hampshire	Kansas	Idaho	
Louisiana	Maryland	New Jersey	Michigan	Montana	
Mississippi	Missouri	New York	Minnesota	Nevada	
North Carolina	Oklahoma	Pennsylvania	Nebraska	New Mexico	
South Carolina	West Virginia	Rhode Island	North Dakota	Oregon	
Tennessee		Vermont	Ohio	Utah	
Texas			South Dakota	Washington	
Virginia			Wisconsin	Wyoming	

Source: Gary Orfield and Franklin Monfort, "Status of School Desegregation: The Next Generation" (Alexandria, Va.: National School Boards Association, 1992), 2.

Guide to References
for Political Statistics

General

Congressional Information Service. *American Statistics Index: A Compre-*
hensive Guide and Index to the Statistical Publications of the U.S.
Government. Washington, D.C.: Congressional Information Service, 1973–.
Annual, with monthly supplements. Available online at LexisNexis Statistical DataSets (*http://academic.lexisnexis.com*).
> Definitive guide, multiply indexed, to statistics "of probable research
> significance" in government publications; 1974 "Annual and Retrospective
> Edition" includes not only items in print but also significant items published
> over the preceding decade.

———. *Statistical Reference Index: A Selective Guide to American Statistical*
Publications from Sources Other Than the U.S. Government. Washington,
D.C.: Congressional Information Service, 1980–. Annual, with bimonthly
supplements. Available online at LexisNexis Statistical DataSets (*http://*
academic.lexisnexis.com).
> A complement to *American Statistics Index,* this resource indexes statistics from
> private and public sources other than the U.S. government.

Congressional Quarterly Weekly Report (*CQ Weekly* as of April 18, 1998).
Washington, D.C.: Congressional Quarterly, 1945–.
> Newsweekly covering political developments in Congress, the presidency, the
> Supreme Court, and national politics; individual voting records on all roll call
> votes in the House and Senate; texts of presidential press conferences and major
> statements. *CQ Weekly* is available online with an individual or library
> subscription (*www.cq.com*).

Congressional Research Service. *The Constitution of the United States: Analysis*
and Interpretation. Washington, D.C.: Government Printing Office, 2004.
108th Cong., 2nd sess., S. Doc. 108-17. Supplement, 108th Cong., 2nd
sess., S. Doc. 108-19.
> Not statistics-laden, but an essential document with commentary on and
> annotations of Supreme Court decisions and tables on proposed constitutional
> amendments pending and unratified, laws (congressional, state, and local) held
> unconstitutional by the Supreme Court, and Supreme Court decisions overruled
> by subsequent decisions. U.S. law requires a new edition every ten years with
> biennial supplements between editions to keep this work current.

Federal Statistics, *www.fedstats.gov*
> Gateway to statistics from over one hundred federal agencies.

Government Printing Office, *www.gpoaccess.gov/about/index.html*
Provides free electronic access to publications of the federal government.

Harvard Institute for Quantitative Social Science, *http://dvn.iq.harvard. edu/dvn*
Large collection of social science research data covering diverse topics.

Historical Statistics of the United States. Millennial ed. New York: Cambridge University Press, 2006.
Invaluable broad-ranging collection of more than twelve thousand time series covering the nation's history; often the series can be updated by the annual *Statistical Abstract of the United States* (see below).

LexisNexis Statistical, *http://web.lexis-nexis.com/statuniv/form/stat/s_power tabs.html*
Online statistics from U.S. and state governmental publications, among others, and international governmental organizations.

Library of Congress, *www.loc.gov*
The largest library in the world, it serves as the research arm of Congress.

Law Library of Congress, *www.loc.gov/law/index.php*
Established in 1832, has grown to become the world's largest law library with over 2.65 million volumes. Some resources available online.

Maier, Mark H. *The Data Game: Controversies in Social Science Statistics.* 3rd ed. Armonk, N.Y.: M. E. Sharpe, 1999.
Discussion of statistical source material, with an emphasis on inaccuracies, ambiguities, misinterpretations, and unavailability, as well as on the relationship between statistics and important social questions.

U.S. Census Bureau, *www.census.gov*
A primary source for population data, with links to federal government agencies and state data centers.

U.S. Census Bureau. *Statistical Abstract of the United States.* Washington, D.C.: Government Printing Office, 1879–. Annual.
Strong, indispensable collection of nationally significant statistics from public and private sources on economics, politics, and society; generally worth checking first (*www.census.gov/compendia/statab*). Also a useful guide to sources for additional statistics; indicates which time series update those in *Historical Statistics of the United States* (see above).

U.S. Congress. House. *Constitution, Jefferson's Manual, and Rules of the House of Representatives of the United States.* Washington, D.C.: Government Printing Office. Biennial.
Solid reference on the Constitution with full notes on all ratifications; indexed.

Elections

Archer, J. Clark, Stephen J. Lavin, Kenneth C. Martis, and Fred M. Shelley. *Historical Atlas of U.S. Presidential Elections, 1788–2004.* Washington, D.C.: CQ Press, 2006.
Maps showing regional voting patterns and context for U.S. presidential elections.

Bartley, Numan V., and Hugh D. Graham. *Southern Elections: County and Precinct Data, 1950–1972.* Baton Rouge: Louisiana State University Press, 1978.
A compilation of gubernatorial and senatorial contests, primaries, and referenda in southern states; some socioeconomic and geographic analysis of the elections.

Burnham, Walter Dean. 2007/2008. *Journal of the Historical Society.* Vols. 7–8.
Discussion of problems in estimating turnout, references to other efforts, and extensive data on turnout and election results for president, the U.S. House, and more.

Congressional Quarterly. *Guide to U.S. Elections.* 6th ed. Washington, D.C.: CQ Press, 2009.
Superb collection of vote returns for presidential, gubernatorial, and U.S. House elections since 1824, electoral college votes since 1789, U.S. Senate elections since 1913, presidential primaries since 1912, and primaries for governor and senator since 1956 (in southern states since 1919); general and candidate indexes; biographies of presidential and vice presidential candidates; lists of governors and senators since 1789; discussions of and data on political parties and presidential nominating conventions throughout the nation's history.

——. *Presidential Elections Since 1789.* 6th ed. Washington, D.C.: Congressional Quarterly, 1995.
Contains facts and figures on presidential elections, electoral college vote since 1789, primary returns since 1912, major-party candidate vote shares state by state, minor candidate vote totals, recent turnout and party support trends.

CQ Press Voting and Elections Collection, *www.cqpress.com/product/CQ-Voting-and-Elections-Collection.html*
Online searchable database with information about individual races as well as summary information related to open-seat races, party switches, race competitiveness, and so on.

DC's Political Report, *www.dcpoliticalreport.com*
Contain numerous links to candidates, political parties, election results, and governmental and political organizations.

Dubin, Michael J. *United States Congressional Elections, 1788–1997: The Official Results of the Elections of the 1st through the 105th Congresses.* Jefferson, N.C.: McFarland, 1998.
Complete, insofar as possible, returns for all U.S. House and Senate general elections; contains percentages for each Congress of representatives unopposed, seeking reelection, reelected, defeated, and first-termers.

——. *United States Gubernatorial Elections, 1776–1860: The Official Results by State and County.* Jefferson, N.C.: McFarland, 2003.
Detailed compilation of early gubernatorial elections.

——. *United States Presidential Elections, 1776–1860: The Official Results by State and County.* Jefferson, N.C.: McFarland, 2002.
Detailed compilation of early presidential elections.

Federal Election Commission, *www.fec.gov*
Official source for data on campaign contributions and expenditures in federal elections.

Glashan, Roy R. *American Governors and Gubernatorial Elections, 1775–1978*. Westport, Conn.: Meckler, 1979.
Details about state governors (such as birth dates, party affiliations, principal occupations, and terms of office) and election data. Continued in Mullaney (see below).

Kallenbach, Joseph E., and Jessamine S. Kallenbach. *American State Governors, 1776–1976*. Dobbs Ferry, N.Y.: Oceana Publications, 1977–1982.
Election results and biographical data on governors.

McDonald, Michael. "United States Elections Project." *http://elections. gmu.edu*
Turnout data for U.S. elections since 1948, with an emphasis on the "voter eligible population," correcting for numbers of noncitizens, certain ex-felons, and others in the voting-age population who are ineligible to vote. Also offers data and analyses of election administration and redistricting.

Mullaney, Marie. *American Governors and Gubernatorial Elections, 1979–1987*. Westport, Conn.: Meckler, 1988.
Continues the volume by Glashan (see above).

———. *Biographical Directory of the Governors of the United States, 1988–1994*. Westport, Conn.: Greenwood Press, 1994.
Details about state governors (such as birth dates, party affiliations, principal occupations, and terms of office). Continues earlier volume.

Nomination and Election of the President and Vice President of the United States. Washington, D.C.: Government Printing Office, 1960–. Quadrennial.
Compilation of federal and state laws and party rules governing nomination and election of the president.

Project Vote Smart, *www.votesmart.org*
Provides issue positions, biographical details, and campaign finance information on numerous candidates for president, Congress, and state legislatures, and information on statewide ballot measures.

Rusk, Jerrold. *A Statistical History of the American Electorate*. Washington, D.C.: CQ Press, 2001.
Includes lists and dates of election laws, initiative and referendum data, and measures of party competition, partisan swing, split-ticket voting, partisan strength.

Scammon, Richard M., Alice McGillivray, and Rhodes Cook, eds. *America at the Polls: A Handbook of Presidential Election Statistics*. Washington, D.C.: CQ Press, various years.
Two volumes that span 1920–2000, providing popular votes (state and county) for president as well as state presidential primary results.

———. *America Votes: A Handbook of Contemporary American Election Statistics*. Washington, D.C.: CQ Press, Elections Research Center, 1956–.
Convenient compilation of vote totals and statistics by state for general elections and primaries for president, governor, and senator, principally since 1945 (comparable district-level data for members of Congress); county-level totals and statistics for most recent general election for president, governor, and senator; state maps with county and congressional district boundaries.

U.S. Census Bureau, Current Population Reports, Population Characteristics, Series P-20. *Voting and Registration in the Election of November [Year]*. Washington, D.C.: Government Printing Office, 1964–. Biennial.
  Survey results on voter registration and turnout in presidential and midterm general elections for the nation and regions (and sometimes states and metropolitan areas) for various groups (*www.census.gov*).

Political Parties

Bain, Richard C., and Judith H. Parris. *Convention Decisions and Voting Records*. 2nd ed. Washington, D.C.: Brookings, 1973.
  Data on convention actions through 1972.

Congressional Quarterly. *National Party Conventions, 1831–2008*. 9th ed. Washington, D.C.: CQ Press, 2009.
  Summarizes conventions, with results of ballots, nominees, and party profiles.

David, Paul T. *Party Strength in the United States, 1872–1970*. Charlottesville, Va.: University Press of America, 1972. Updated for 1972 in *Journal of Politics* 36 (1972): 785–796; for 1974 in *Journal of Politics* 38 (1974): 416–425; for 1976 in *Journal of Politics* 40 (1976): 770–780.
  Measures of party competition in the states covering several offices and an admirably lengthy historical span.

Democratic National Committee, *www.democrats.org*
Republican National Committee, *www.rnc.org*
  The Democratic and Republican Parties' official Web sites containing news releases, transcripts, video, and related material.

Campaign Finance and Political Action Committees (PACs)

Campaign Finance Institute, *www.cfinst.org*
Center for Responsive Politics, *www.opensecrets.org*
CQ MoneyLine, *www.cqmoneyline.com*
National Institute on Money in State Politics, *www.followthemoney.org*
  Data on and analyses of campaign contributions and expenditures in federal and state elections.

Federal Election Commission. *Annual Report*. Washington, D.C.: Government Printing Office, 1976–.
  Cumulative figures since the mid-1970s on contributions and spending in federal election campaigns; also information on political action committee growth and activities (*www.fec.gov*).

Magleby, David B., Anthony Corrado, and Kelly D. Patterson, eds. *Financing the 2004 Election*. Washington, D.C.: Brookings, 2006.
  Coverage of fund raising and spending in all phases of the presidential campaign; continues work by Alexander Heard and by Herbert Alexander on financing presidential campaigns since 1960.

Public Opinion

Gallup Poll, *www.gallup.com*

Inter-university Consortium for Political and Social Research, *www.icpsr. umich.edu*

Pew Research Center for the People and the Press, *http://people-press.org*

Polling Report, *www.pollingreport.com*

Polling the Nations, *http://poll.orspub.com*
> Online access to current and historical collections of public opinion poll data.

American National Election Studies. "Guide to Public Opinion and Electoral Behavior." *www.electionstudies.org*
> Tables and graphs showing public opinion, political participation, and electoral choice in American politics since 1952; responses to questions asked in the American National Election Studies.

Astin, A. W., et al. *The American Freshman: Forty Year Trends.* Los Angeles: Higher Education Research Institute, University of California, Los Angeles, 2007. *National Norms for Fall,* 1998–. Annual.
> Reports of national surveys of college freshmen, including attitudes toward jobs, subject interests, and liberalism/conservatism.

Opinion Research Service. *American Public Opinion Index.* Louisville, Ky.: Opinion Research Service, 1981–2000. Annual.
> Indexes scientifically drawn samples of national, state, and local universes.

POLL (The Public Opinion Location Library). Storrs, Conn.: Roper Center for Public Opinion Research. *http://ropercenter.uconn.edu.* Also available at LexisNexis Academic (*www.lexisnexis.com/us/lnacademic*).
> A computer-based information retrieval system for public opinion survey data. Extensive coverage for 1955 to the present; some coverage of earlier years. Subscription service with limited free access.

Public Opinion Quarterly. Chicago: University of Chicago Press, 1937–. Quarterly.
> Analysis of the mechanics and findings of survey research; regular thematic presentation of poll results.

Media

ABC News, *http://abcnews.com*

CBS News, *www.cbs.com*

CNN, *www.cnn.com*

C-SPAN, *www.c-span.org*

Fox News, *www.foxnews.com*

MSNBC, *www.msnbc.com*

New York Times, www.nytimes.com

Time, www.time.com

USA Today, www.usatoday.com

Washington Post, www.washingtonpost.com

ADI Book. Beltsville, Md.: Arbitron Television. Annual.
> Reports of television usage, including demographic and market analyses.

Broadcasting Publications. *Broadcasting Cablecasting Yearbook.* Washington, D.C.: Broadcasting Publications, 1982–. Annual. Continues *Broadcasting Cable Yearbook,* which combined *Broadcasting Yearbook* (1968–1979) and *Broadcasting Cable Sourcebook* (1973–1979).
> International directory of radio, television, and cable industries as well as related fields. Presents some statistical overviews.

Cable and Station Coverage Atlas, 1986. Indianapolis, Ind.: Warren Publishing, 1986–. Annual.
> Data on television stations and the growing reach of cable systems.

C-SPAN Archives. West Lafayette, Ind.: C-SPAN, 1987–. *www.c-spanarchives. org/Info/collection.php*
> Records, indexes, and archives all C-SPAN programming; contains every program aired since 1987.

Dow Jones Factiva, *www.factiva.com*
> Online access to major U.S. newspapers, Dow Jones and Reuters's newswires, and business publications.

Editor & Publisher—The Fourth Estate. New York: Editor & Publisher, 1884–. Weekly.
> Weekly periodical covering the media.

LexisNexis, *www.lexisnexis.com*
> Wide-ranging material from journals, newspapers, reference books, and other sources. Includes databases, documents, maps, photographs, and more.

Media Tenor, *www.mediatenor.com*
> International organization monitoring and analyzing media content on topics that include U.S. electoral campaigns and government.

Newsbank, Inc., *www.newsbank.com*
> Online access to hundreds of U.S. and international newspapers and other sources.

Nielsen Television Index. Northbrook, Ill.: A. C. Nielsen, 1955. Annual.
> Overall and market section reports on television viewing and network program audiences.

Nielsen Wire, *http://blog.nielsen.com/nielsenwire/category/politics*
> Data on audience ratings for political events and topics.

Proquest, *www.proquest.com*
> Online access to major U.S. newspapers and magazines. Includes ProQuest Historical Newspapers—*New York Times* from 1851 and seven other major papers.

Television Digest. *Television and Cable Factbook.* Washington, D.C.: Television Digest, 1946–. Annual.
> Data on cable, television, and related industries; published in two volumes: "Stations" and "Cable and Services."

Vanderbilt Television News Archive. Nashville, Tenn.: Vanderbilt University. *http://tvnews.vanderbilt.edu.*
> Archives of nightly network news since 1968.

Congress

Library of Congress, Thomas: Legislative Information, *http://thomas.loc.gov*
U.S. House of Representatives, *www.house.gov*
U.S. Senate, *www.senate.gov*

Balinski, Michel, and H. Peyton Young. *Fair Representation: Meeting the Ideal of One Man, One Vote.* New Haven, Conn.: Yale University Press, 1982.
  Analysis of methods of apportionment of representatives among the states.

Barone, Michael, and Grant Ujifusa. *The Almanac of American Politics.* Washington, D.C.: National Journal, 1972–. Biennial.
  Data-rich political analyses of each state, congressional district, representative, senator, and governor; current composition of committees; state maps with congressional district and county boundaries.

Biographical Directory of Congress, *http://bioguide.congress.gov/biosearch/biosearch.asp*
  Biographical directory of the U.S. Congress, 1774–present.

Congressional Quarterly. *American Political Leaders, 1789–2005.* Washington, D.C.: CQ Press, 2005.
  Material on more than eleven thousand members of Congress: age, religion, occupation, women, blacks, turnover, and shifts between chambers; data on congressional sessions, party composition, and leadership. Also includes biographical summaries of presidents, vice presidents, Supreme Court justices, and governors.

——. *Congress A to Z.* 5th ed. Washington, D.C.: CQ Press, 2008.
  Mostly essays but contains useful listings of hard-to-find material such as treaties killed by the Senate, impeachment trials, and women members of Congress.

——. *Congress and the Nation.* Washington, D.C.: Congressional Quarterly/CQ Press, 1965–. Quadrennial. Years 1945–1964 contained in one volume.
  Akin to *Congressional Quarterly Almanac* (see below), but each volume now covers a presidential term.

——. *Congressional Districts in the 2000s.* Washington, D.C.: CQ Press, 2003.
  Profiles of each congressional district, with statistics on election returns, economic makeup, and demographics. Volume covering the 1990s published in 1993.

——. *Congressional Roll Call.* Washington, D.C.: Congressional Quarterly/CQ Press, 1974–. Annual.
  Compilation of every roll call vote by every member of Congress and summary voting measures (ideology, party unity, presidential support, and voting participation).

——. *[Year] Congressional Staff Directory.* Washington, D.C.: Congressional Quarterly/CQ Press, 1959–. Biennial.
  Names, addresses, phone numbers, and numerous biographies of senators' and representatives' personal staffs and the staffs of congressional committees and subcommittees.

———. *CQ Almanac*. Washington, D.C.: Congressional Quarterly/CQ Press, 1945–. Annual.
Each volume now covers legislation for a single session of Congress; appendixes contain particularly useful data on Congress and politics.

———. *Guide to Congress*. 6th ed. Washington, D.C.: CQ Press, 2007.
Massive, rich accounting of how Congress works and how it developed. Check here first for data covering all but the most recent years.

———. *Landmark Legislation, 1774–2002*. Washington, D.C.: CQ Press, 2003.
Summary and historical and political background of major legislation and treaties.

———. *Politics in America*. Washington, D.C.: CQ Press, 1981–. Biennial.
Data-rich political analyses of each state, congressional district, representative, and senator; current composition of committees; state maps with congressional district and county boundaries.

Congressional Research Service, *www.opencrs.com*
Many Congressional Research Service documents can be found here.

CQ Press Congress Collection, *http://library.cqpress.com/congress*
Online, searchable database with biographical and roll call voting information on individual members of Congress as well as summaries of interest group ratings, key vote analysis, policy analysis, and so on.

Dewhirst, Robert W., and John David Rausch Jr., eds. *Encyclopedia of the United States Congress*. New York: Facts on File, 2007.
Essays exploring the history, processes, and politics of Congress.

Freeman, Eric, and Stephan A. Jones. *African Americans in Congress*. Washington, D.C.: CQ Press, 2007.
Stories of and original documents about the history of African Americans in the U.S. House and Senate.

Martis, Kenneth C. *Historical Atlas of Political Parties in the United States Congress, 1789–1989*. New York: Macmillan, 1989.

———. *The Historical Atlas of the United States Congressional Districts, 1789–1983*. New York: Free Press, 1983.
Congressional-based perspective on the surge and decline of political parties.

Martis, Kenneth C., and Gregory A. Elmes. *The Historical Atlas of State Power in Congress, 1790–1990*. Washington, D.C.: Congressional Quarterly, 1993.
Maps, tables, and text describing changes in apportionment among the states.

Martis, Kenneth C., and Gyula Pauer. *The Historical Atlas of the Congresses of the Confederate States of America*. New York: Macmillan, 1994.
Maps, tables, and text describing Confederate districts, elections, and key votes.

Ornstein, Norman J., Thomas E. Mann, and Michael J. Malbin, eds. *Vital Statistics on Congress*. Washington, D.C.: Congressional Quarterly, 1980–1998. Washington, D.C.: AEI Press, 2000–. Frequency varies.
Data on characteristics of members, elections, campaign finance, committees, staff, expenses, workload, budgeting, and voting alignments. Most data series stretch back to World War II, some longer.

Parsons, Stanley B., Michael J. Dubin, and Karen Toombs Parsons. *United States Congressional Districts, 1883–1913*. New York: Greenwood Press, 1990.
Demographic and geographic data about American congressional districts between 1883 and 1913; continues coverage of volumes listed below.

Parsons, Stanley B., William W. Beach, and Michael J. Dubin. *United States Congressional Districts and Data*. 2 vols. Westport, Conn.: Greenwood Press, 1978, 1986.
These two volumes cover 1789–1883.

Sharp, Michael. *The Directory of Congressional Voting Scores and Interest Group Ratings*. 2 vols. 4th ed. Washington, D.C.: CQ Press, 2005.
Contains voting scores (for example, presidential support) and interest group ratings (eleven groups, as available) for all members of Congress from 1947 to 2004.

Silbey, Joel, ed. *Encyclopedia of the American Legislative System: Studies of the Principal Structures, Processes, and Policies of Congress and State Legislatures Since the Colonial Era*. 3 vols. New York: Scribner's, 1994–1996.
A thorough treatment of the national and state legislatures.

Stewart, Charles, III, David T. Canon, and Garrison Nelson, eds. *Committees in the U.S. Congress, 1789–1946*. 4 vols. Washington, D.C.: CQ Press, 2002.
A comprehensive history of congressional committee membership.

Treese, Joel, ed. *Biographical Directory of the American Congress, 1774–1996*. Washington, D.C.: CQ Press, 1997.
Biographies of U.S. senators and representatives to 1996.

U.S. Census Bureau. *Congressional District Atlas*. Washington, D.C.: Government Printing Office, 1960–. Frequency varies.
Detailed maps of congressional districts.

——. *Congressional District Data Book*. Washington, D.C.: Government Printing Office, 1961–. Frequency varies.
Census data by congressional district with maps.

U.S. Congress. Joint Committee on Printing. *Official Congressional Directory*. Washington, D.C.: Government Printing Office, 1809–. Biennial (in recent years).
Biographical data on current members and statistics on the sessions of Congress. Useful reference source on committees and subcommittees, foreign representatives and consular offices in the United States, press representatives, and state delegations.

Presidency and Executive Branch

Congressional Quarterly. *Federal Regulatory Directory*. Washington, D.C.: CQ Press, 1979–. Frequency varies.
Extensive profiles of the major and minor regulatory agencies—more than one hundred in all.

———. *[Year] Federal Staff Directory.* Washington, D.C.: CQ Press, 1982–. Biennial.
> Names, addresses, phone numbers, and numerous biographies of key executives and assistants in the executive branch of the federal government.

———. *Guide to the Presidency.* 4th ed. Edited by Michael Nelson. Washington, D.C.: CQ Press, 2007.
> Detailed coverage of numerous aspects of presidents and administrations. Focus on the institution complements CQ's volumes on Congress and elections.

———. *Washington Information Directory.* Washington, D.C.: CQ Press, 1975–. Annual.
> Names, addresses, phone numbers, and heads of thousands of federal government and private, nonprofit agencies in and about Washington, D.C.

DeGregorio, William A. *The Complete Book of U.S. Presidents.* 6th ed. New York: Gramercy Books, 2005.
> Biographies of presidents and cabinet members.

Kane, Joseph Nathan, and Janet Podell. *Facts about the Presidents: A Compilation of Biographical and Historical Information.* 8th ed. New York: H. W. Wilson, 2009.
> Chapter on each president and comparative statistics on all presidents.

Ragsdale, Lyn. *Vital Statistics on the Presidency: George Washington to George W. Bush.* 3rd ed. Washington, D.C.: CQ Press, 2009.
> Data largely on postwar presidents—their careers, elections, speeches and appearances, approval ratings, and congressional relationships—with some longer time series.

U.S. Government Organization Manual. Washington, D.C.: Government Printing Office, 1935–. Annual.
> Official federal government handbook detailing the organization, activities, and current officials in legislative, judicial, and executive governmental units.

Weekly Compilation of Presidential Documents. Washington, D.C.: Government Printing Office, 1965–.
> Collection of presidential activities. Includes texts of proclamations, executive orders, speeches, and other presidential communications; supplements include acts gaining presidential approval, nominations submitted for Senate confirmation, and a list of White House press releases (*www.access.gpo.gov/nara/nara003.html*). Indexed.

The White House, *www.whitehouse.gov*

The Judiciary

Federal Judicial Center, *www.fjc.gov/history/home.nsf*
U.S. Courts, The Federal Judiciary, *www.uscourts.gov*

U.S. Supreme Court, *www.supremecourtus.org*
Federal court personnel, administration, procedures, and opinions.

The American Bench. Sacramento, Calif.: Reginald Bishop Forster and Associates, 1977–. Biennial.
Comprehensive listing of all judges in the United States, along with brief biographies of about eighteen thousand judges.

Congressional Quarterly's Guide to the U.S. Supreme Court. 4th ed. Edited by David Savage. Washington, D.C.: CQ Press, 2004.
Solid, broad coverage of the Supreme Court and development of the law; an excellent source that also refers readers to additional references.

Congressional Quarterly. *[Year] Judicial Staff Directory.* Washington, D.C.: CQ Press, 1986–. Annual.
Personnel listings for federal courts, maps of court jurisdictions, biographies of judges and staffs.

The Corrections Yearbook. South Salem, N.Y.: Criminal Justice Institute, 1980–. Annual.
Inmate populations, budgets, facilities, staff, and other data for jails with average daily populations of two hundred or more.

Cushman, Clare, ed. *The Supreme Court Justices: Illustrated Biographies, 1789–1995.* 2nd ed. Washington, D.C.: Congressional Quarterly, 1995.
Biographies of justices, including backgrounds, careers, and issues and cases on which they passed judgment.

Director of the Administrative Office of the United States Courts. *Annual Report.* Washington, D.C.: Government Printing Office, 1940–. Annual.
Numerous statistics on the kind, timing, and disposition of cases in the federal courts and on numbers and workloads of federal judges.

Epstein, Lee, Jeffrey A. Segal, Harold J. Spaeth, and Thomas G. Walker. *Supreme Court Compendium.* 4th ed. Washington, D.C.: CQ Press, 2006.
Data on characteristics of justices, caseloads, voting alignments, public opinion, and legal developments.

Friedman, Leon, and Fred L. Israel, eds. *The Justices of the United States Supreme Court.* New York: Chelsea House, 1995.
Biography of each justice, including several typical opinions; tables showing acts of Congress held unconstitutional, decisions overruled by subsequent decisions, and summary biographical data.

Judges of the United States. 2nd ed. Washington, D.C.: Government Printing Office, 1983.
Biographies of all federal judges through 1983; see also *www.fjc.gov/public/home.nsf/hisj.*

State Court Caseload Statistics: Annual Report. Williamsburg, Va.: Conference of State Court Administrators and the National Center for State Courts, 1976–. Annual.
Data on judicial workloads in the state courts.

Federalism

Council of State Governments, *www.csg.org*
Library of Congress, State Government Information, *www.loc.gov/rr/news/ stategov/stategov.html*
The Pew Center on the States, *www.pewcenteronthestates.org*
National Governors Association, *www.nga.org*
> Information on the structure, personnel, and policies of individual states.

Alexander, Herbert E., and Mike Eberts. *Public Financing of State Elections: A Data Book and Election Guide to Public Funding of Political Parties and Candidates in Twenty States.* Los Angeles: Citizens' Research Foundation, 1986.
> Important compendium for understanding and comparing state regulation of campaign finances.

Almanac of the 50 States: Basic Data Profiles with Comparative Tables. Palo Alto, Calif.: Information Publications, 1985–. Annual.
> State-level summaries of data on government and elections, state expenditures, federal aid, population characteristics, crime, etc.

Beyle, Thad, ed. *State Government.* Washington, D.C.: CQ Press, 1985–. Annual.
> Analysis of recent developments in state governments; article reprints from a diverse set of state publications.

The Book of the States. Lexington, Ky.: Council of State Governments, 1935–. Biennial; annual since 2002.
> Definitive reference to the current data on state government activities across the board.

The County Year Book. Washington, D.C.: National Association of Counties and International City/County Management Association, 1975–. Annual.
> Surveys issues and trends in county government and administration; a reliable source of data on county government.

CSG State Directories. 3 vols. Lexington, Ky.: Council of State Governments, 1977–. Annual.
> Lists state elected officials; state legislative leadership, committees, and staff; state administrative officials by function. Originally issued as a supplement to *The Book of the States.* Previously biennial under various titles.

Dubin, Michael J. *Party Affiliations in the State Legislatures: A Year by Year Summary, 1796–2006.* Jefferson, N.C.: McFarland, 2007.
> Extensive data on states' electoral processes, term lengths, legislature size and membership by party, election dates, and more.

Federal Election Campaign Laws. Washington, D.C.: Federal Election Commission, 2008.
> Lengthy compilation of laws related to organization of campaigns, disclosure and reporting requirements, enforcement procedures, and so on.

Holli, Melvin G., and Peter Jones, eds. *Biographical Dictionary of American Mayors, 1820–1980.* Westport, Conn.: Greenwood Press, 1981.
> Covers 679 mayors in over a dozen cities; contains lists categorizing mayors by characteristics such as party, religion, and ethnicity.

Lilley, William III, Laurence J. DeFranco, Mark F. Bernstein, and Kari L. Ramsby. *The Almanac of State Legislative Elections.* 3rd ed. Washington, D.C.: CQ Press, 2007.
Maps and statistical profiles of the geographic, economic, and political composition of state legislative districts.

——. *The State Atlas of Political and Cultural Diversity.* Washington, D.C.: Congressional Quarterly, 1997.
Racial and ancestral makeup of top state legislative districts. Available diskette contains data on all state legislative districts.

Morgan, Scott, and Kathleen O'Leary Morgan, eds. *Crime State Rankings 2009.* Washington, D.C.: CQ Press, 2009.
Compilation of state rankings in numerous crime-related categories.

——. *Health Care State Rankings, 2009.* Washington, D.C.: CQ Press, 2009.
Compilation of state rankings in numerous areas of health.

The Municipal Year Book. New York: International City/County Management Association, 1934–. Annual.
Reliable source for urban data and developments.

National Conference of State Legislatures, *www.ncsl.org*
Compilations of laws and data on elections, redistricting, term limits, and other topics, as well as links to sites of individual state legislatures.

National Directory of State Agencies. Bethesda, Md.: National Standards Association, 1976–. Annual since 1986.
Heads, addresses, and phone numbers of state agencies.

State Legislative Sourcebook. Topeka, Kan.: Government Research Service, 1986–. Annual.
A guide to finding detailed information on state legislative material, including offices, addresses, phone numbers, and price lists. State statistical abstracts. A list of state statistical abstracts (or near equivalents) can be found in recent editions of the *Statistical Abstract of the United States.* They are of widely varying quality.

State Yellow Book. New York: Leadership Directories, Inc., 1973–. Quarterly.
Some statistics, but emphasizes contact information for executive and legislative branches, including departments, commissions, agencies, and legislative leadership and legislative committees. Continues *State Information Book* (*www.leadershipdirectories.com*).

Tax Foundation. *Facts and Figures on Government Finance.* Englewood Cliffs, N.J.: Prentice Hall, 1941–. Updated periodically.
Data on government revenues, spending, and debt at the federal, state, and local levels (*www.taxfoundation.org*).

U.S. Census Bureau. *Census of Governments.* Washington, D.C.: Government Printing Office, 1972–. Frequency varies.
Numbers and characteristics of governments, including special district governments dealing with subjects such as schools, parks and recreation, and sewage.

———. *City Government Finances; Government Finances; State Government Finances.* Washington, D.C.: Government Printing Office, 1909–; 1916–; 1965–. Annual.
>   These three series summarize government finances at the city and state levels; great detail for states and the larger cities.

———. *County and City Data Book.* Washington, D.C.: Government Printing Office, 1952–. Frequency varies.
>   Demographic, economic, health, agricultural, and other information about counties, cities, and towns. Presidential voting by county.

———. *State and Metropolitan Area Data Book.* Washington, D.C.: Government Printing Office, 1979–. Frequency varies.
>   Demographic, economic, health, education, and other data about states and metropolitan statistical areas.

Waters, M. Dane. *Initiative and Referendum Almanac.* Durham, N.C.: Carolina Academic Press, 2003.
>   History of, arguments about, and compendium of initiatives and referenda in American history.

Foreign and Military Policy

Cochran, Thomas B., et al. *Nuclear Weapons Databook.* Multiple vols. Cambridge, Mass.: Ballinger, 1984, 1987, 1989, 1994.
>   Comprehensive data on nuclear arsenals. Updated by the "Nuclear Notebook" section in each issue of the *Bulletin of the Atomic Scientists.*

Joint Chiefs of Staff. *Military Posture for Fiscal Year [Year].* Washington, D.C.: Government Printing Office. Annual.
>   Brief review of all aspects of military preparedness of the United States and of the world military environment.

The Military Balance. London: International Institute of Strategic Studies, 1959–. Annual.
>   Statistical analysis of military forces and defense spending; figures given for countries and regional organizations such as the North Atlantic Treaty Organization (NATO).

Patterns of Global Terrorism. Washington, D.C.: U.S. Department of State, 1983–2003. Annual.
>   Details on terrorist incidents around the world.

SIPRI (Stockholm International Peace Research Institute). *World Armaments and Disarmament: SIPRI Yearbook.* Stockholm: Almqvist and Wiksell; New York: Oxford University Press, 1970–. Annual.
>   Overview of the arms race and efforts to promote disarmament; detailed data on world military spending (*www.sipri.org*).

United Nations, *http://untreaty.un.org*
>   A large database of treaties and multilateral agreements. Requires subscription. Also contains references to hardcopy publications.

U.S. Arms Control and Disarmament Agency. *World Military Expenditures and Arms Transfers.* Washington, D.C.: Government Printing Office, 1965–2000. Annual (title varies).
A series of statistical accounts of military spending and the arms race.

Social Policy

Anderton, Douglas L., Richard E. Barrett, and Donald J. Bogue. *The Population of the United States.* 3rd ed. New York: Free Press, 1997.
Extensive description of the nation's population characteristics, focusing on the years since 1960; topics include poverty, income, housing, educational attainment, ethnicity, and migration.

Center for American Women and Politics, National Information Bank on Women in Public Office, Eagleton Institute of Politics, Rutgers University, *www.cawp.rutgers.edu*
Various reports provide data on women in public office, electoral turnout of women, and so forth. Both historical and contemporary information.

Heaton, Tim B., Bruce A. Chadwick, and Cardell K. Jacobson. *Statistical Handbook on Racial Groups in the United States.* Phoenix: Oryx, 2000.
Contains a broad range of more than four hundred charts and tables on non-Hispanic Whites, Native Americans, and African, Hispanic, and Asian Americans.

Joint Center for Political and Economic Studies, *www.jointcenter.org*
Lists black elected officials by office with summary tabulations on historical trends and comparative state figures.

National Center for Health Statistics. *National Vital Statistics Reports.* Previously titled *Monthly Vital Statistics Report.* Hyattsville, Md.: U.S. Department of Health and Human Services, 1952–. Varying numbers annually.
Statistical reports and analyses of various aspects of health.

National Roster of Hispanic Elected Officials, [Year]. Washington, D.C.: National Association of Latino Elected and Appointed Officials Education Fund. Annual.
Lists Hispanic elected officials by office and state (*www.naleo.org*).

Pew Hispanic Center, *http://pewhispanic.org*
Nonpartisan research organization conducting a broad range of demographic studies and opinion data on the Hispanic population in the United States.

The State of Black America. New York: National Urban League, 1976–. Annual.
Yearly review assessing the conditions of blacks in the nation.

U.S. Department of Education, National Center for Education Statistics. *Digest of Education Statistics.* Washington, D.C.: Government Printing Office, 1962–. Annual.
Current data on school enrollments, teachers, retention rates, educational attainment, finances, achievement, schools and school districts, federal education programs, and so forth (*http://nces.ed.gov*).

U.S. Department of Education, Office of Educational Research and Improvement. *The Condition of Education: A Statistical Report.* Washington, D.C.: Government Printing Office, 1975–. Annual.
>   Data survey of trends in elementary, secondary, and higher education. Data portray student characteristics and performance as well as fiscal, material, and human resources deployed in education (*http://nces.ed.gov*).

U.S. Department of Energy, Energy Information Administration. *Annual Energy Review.* Washington, D.C.: Government Printing Office, 1977–.
>   Data on energy supply and disposition, exploration, and reserves (*http://eia.doe. gov/emeu/aer/contents.html*).

U.S. Department of Justice, Bureau of Criminal Justice Statistics. *Sourcebook of Criminal Justice Statistics.* Washington, D.C.: Government Printing Office, 1974–. Annual.
>   Brings together nationwide statistical data on the criminal justice system, public opinion, illegal activities, persons arrested, judicial proceedings, and persons under correctional supervision (*www.albany.edu/sourcebook*).

U.S. Department of Justice, Federal Bureau of Investigation. *Uniform Crime Reports for the United States.* Washington, D.C.: Government Printing Office, 1930–. Annual.
>   Variety of charts and tables on types and frequencies of crimes, persons arrested, and law enforcement personnel; several forty-year trends (*www.fbi.gov/ ucr/ucr.htm*).

Economic Policy

The Economic Report of the President. Washington, D.C.: Government Printing Office, 1947–. Annual.
>   Reviews the national economic situation; presents a substantial appendix with long time series of critical economic data (*www.gpoaccess.gov/eop*).

The Economist. *Guide to Economic Indicators: Making Sense of Economics.* 5th ed. New York: Norton, 2003.
>   Explains some one hundred indicators, including information on their sources, reliability, and significance; provides guidelines for interpretation.

Frumkin, Norman. *Guide to Economic Indicators.* 3rd ed. Armonk, N.Y.: M. E. Sharpe, 2000.
>   Content, accuracy, relevance, and sources for fifty economic indicators.

[Year] Historical Chart Book. Washington, D.C.: Board of Governors of the Federal Reserve System, 1965–. Annual.
>   Long-range financial and business data, mostly from series maintained by the Federal Reserve Board.

Office of Management and Budget. *Budget of the United States Government.* Washington, D.C.: Government Printing Office. Annual.

Multivolume annual presentation of data on federal revenues and expenditures. Although the details of the federal budget documents may be numbing to the uninitiated, even the novice might find the *Historical Tables* useful (*www.gpoac cess.gov/usbudget*).

O'Hara, Frederick M. *Handbook of United States Economic and Financial Indicators.* 2nd ed. Westport, Conn.: Greenwood Press, 2000.
Defines several hundred economic indicators culled from over fifty sources; provides information on publication schedules and historical trends.

U.S. Bureau of Labor Statistics. *Employment and Earnings.* Washington, D.C.: Government Printing Office, 1961–. Annual.
Various statistics on the nation's nonfarm workforce, including lengthy time series with data beginning in 1909 (*www.bls.gov*).

——. *Handbook of Labor Statistics.* Washington, D.C.: Government Printing Office, 1927–. Frequency varies.
Collection of data on employment, unemployment, earnings, school enrollment and educational attainment, productivity, prices, strikes, and so forth (*www.bls.gov*).

——. *Monthly Labor Review.* Washington, D.C.: Government Printing Office, 1915–.
Covers most Bureau of Labor Statistics series, presenting data on employment, hours, pay, strikes, prices and inflation, and so forth (*www.bls.gov*).

U.S. Council of Economic Advisers. *Economic Indicators.* Washington, D.C.: Government Printing Office, 1948–. Monthly.
Data on total output, income, and spending; employment, unemployment, and wages; production and business activity; prices, currency, credit, and security markets; and federal finance.

U.S. Department of Agriculture. *Agricultural Statistics.* Washington, D.C.: Government Printing Office, 1937–. Annual.
Vast array of agricultural data, including politically relevant displays such as farm economic trends, price support programs, and agricultural imports and exports.

U.S. Department of Commerce. *Survey of Current Business.* Washington, D.C.: Government Printing Office, 1921–. Monthly.
Data on U.S. income and trade developments (*www.bea.gov/scb/index.htm*).

World Bank. *World Development Report.* New York: Oxford University Press, 1978–. Annual.
Analysis of and data on worldwide capital and economic indicators, with an emphasis on development (*http://econ.worldbank.org/wdr*).

Index